Marijuana
Debunked

A handbook for parents, pundits
and politicians who want to know
the case *against* legalization

Ed Gogek, M.D.

CHIRON PUBLICATIONS • ASHEVILLE, NORTH CAROLINA

www.innerQuestBooks.com

www.ChironPublicatons.com

innerQuest is a book imprint of Chiron Publications

Interior design by Cornelia G. Murariu

Printed primarily in the United States of America.

Library of Congress Cataloging-in-Publication Data Pending

This book is dedicated to the memory of my father,
Jack Gogek,
who taught by example that what matters in life is
doing a good job and helping others.

Permissions List

Figure 5-1 From <u>Andréasson S, Allebeck P, Engström A, Rydberg U</u>. Cannabis and schizophrenia. A longitudinal study of Swedish conscripts. *Lancet,* 1987. Dec 26;2(8574):1483-6. With modifications. Reprinted with permission.

Figure 6-1 From Substance Abuse and Mental Health Services Administration, *Results from the 2011 National Survey on Drug Use and Health: Summary of National Findings*, NSDUH Series H-44, HHS Publication No. (SMA) 12-4713. Rockville, MD: Substance Abuse and Mental Health Services Administration, 2012.

Figure 8-1 From Johnston, L. D., O'Malley, P. M., Bachman, J. G., Schulenberg, J. E. & Miech, R. A. (2012). *Monitoring the Future national survey results on drug use, 1975–2012: Volume I, Secondary school students*. Ann Arbor: Institute for Social Research, The University of Michigan. With modifications.

Figure 10-1 From "US Incarceration Timeline" Wikipedia: The Free Encyclopedia. Wikimedia Foundation, Inc. Jan. 24, 2012. Original by the November Coalition. http://november.org/graphs/ Modified by Sarefo July 28, 2009. <u>http://en.wikipedia.org/wiki/File:US_incarceration_timeline-clean.svg</u> Sources: Justice Policy Institute Report: The Punishing Decade & U.S. Bureau of Justice Statistics Bulletin NCJ 219416—Prisoners in 2006. Modified by changing from color to black & white. Original and modifications licensed under the Creative Commons Attribution-Share Alike 3.0 Unported license. <u>http://creativecommons.org/licenses/by-sa/3.0/legalcode</u>

Figure 12-1 From Bay Staters Fighting for Alcohol Industry Responsibility. <u>http://bfair-mass.org/1077-2/</u> Reprinted with permission.

Figure 18-1 From the Montana Department of Public Health and Human Services, Medical Marijuana Program Historical Data. Reprinted with permission.

Figure 18-5 From Jean-Francois Crépault *Cannabis Policy Framework* (Oct. 2014) Centre for Addiction and Mental Health. Reprinted with permission. Copyright 2014, Centre for Addiction and Mental Health

Figure 19-3 From Federal Bureau of Prisons, Inmate Statistics, Offenses.

Figure 24-3 From the National Institute on Drug Abuse. Monitoring the Future Survey, Overview of Findings 2013.

Acknowledgements

I would like to thank Bertha Madras, Edward Fenno, Carolyn Short, Christine Tatum and Allyson Essen for suggestions that improved the material, and Kevin Sabet for sharing data he obtained from the medical marijuana programs in Arizona and Rhode Island. Others I'm indebted to are: Jessica Dennis for her work on the graphs, Brian Gawley and Lesley Cameron for editing and for work on the footnotes, and Mark Herz for his tutorial on journalistic ethics and standards.

"Let me state this in the clearest terms possible: the problem of drug use is not solved with drugs!"[1]

Pope Francis

"These kinds of substances are generally considered poison...Our brain is something very special. So if that is damaged, that's awful."[2]

The 14th Dalai Lama,
when asked if he'd
ever smoked pot

"This is not a war on drugs; it is a defense of our brains."[3]

Bertha Madras, Ph.D.
Professor, Harvard Medical School

"How many people can get stoned and still have a great state or a great nation?"[4]

Jerry Brown,
Governor of California

"I think we were right about everything except the drugs."[5]

David Crosby, of Crosby, Stills, Nash & Young;
on civil rights, the peace movement and other
causes his generation espoused in the 1960s

Contents

Preface

Chapter 1	The One-Sided Debate	17
Chapter 2	What We've Heard So Often, We Often Believe	27
Chapter 3	What Research Tells Us About Teenage Use	31
Chapter 4	Marijuana And Driving	41
Chapter 5	Schizophrenia	47
Chapter 6	Is Marijuana Addictive—And Should We Care?	57
Chapter 7	Why Marijuana Gets Off Easy	71
Chapter 8	Teenagers Make Good Decisions About Drugs, If We Do	77
Chapter 9	Legalization increases use	83
Chapter 10	The Fictitious War On Marijuana	89
Chapter 11	"Medical" Marijuana Makes Liars Of Us All	111
Chapter 12	The Real Costs	131
Chapter 13	Alcohol Vs. Marijuana: A Meaningless Debate	141
Chapter 14	The Third Way: Recovery-Based Policies	149
Chapter 15	The Answer To Drug Cartels	167
Chapter 16	The Irrevocable Decision: Creating A Marijuana Industry	171
Chapter 17	The News Media's Love Affair With Marijuana	177
Chapter 18	Pro-Marijuana Experts Are Often Wrong	195
Chapter 19	Why Are Pro-Marijuana Editorials So Inaccurate?	213
Chapter 20	How The Entertainment Media Promotes Marijuana	233
Chapter 21	U.S. Political Parties and Marijuana	237
Chapter 22	How An Addiction Specialist Might See the Legalization Movement	249
Chapter 23	What Legalization Would Unleash	261
Chapter 24	The Fork In The Road	269
Endnotes		277

Two years later, however, when I quit smoking marijuana, I realized that of all the people who had talked to me about drugs, he had come closest to getting it right. And despite his anger—maybe even because of it—I remembered those few minutes with a warm feeling.

He wasn't judgmental about my drug use in any moral right or wrong sense, but he was adamant that it was bad for me and I shouldn't do it.

Drug users and their sympathizers might accuse me of being critical and judgmental, and not knowing what I'm talking about. That's exactly what I thought when my parents' lawyer-friend pulled me aside forty-three years ago. I didn't like what he said, but all he really wanted was for me to quit using. Likewise, the point of this book is not judgment; its only purpose is to get people to stop using—or to prevent them from starting in the first place.

Stories and language used in this book

Some of the stories used in this book are from patients, while many others are from interviews or other sources. In some cases, details have been altered to preserve confidentiality without compromising the essential nature of the story conveyed.

Certain terms used in this book deserve an explanation:

Marijuana lobby refers to the organizations that are specifically engaged in promoting the legalization of marijuana. Many of these groups also promote the legalization or decriminalization of other recreational drugs, so the book uses the terms *legalization lobby, pro-drug lobby,* and *marijuana lobby* interchangeably. The *marijuana movement* includes these lobbying groups plus everyone who speaks in favor of legalization, uses the drug in a public protest, writes a blog to promote legalization, or promotes marijuana in any other way.

Substance abuse means the continued and repeated use of an addictive drug in a way that is harmful to the person using it. Alcohol and tobacco are drugs, so while I usually refer to *alcohol and drug abuse* or *alcohol and other drugs,* there are times when for simplicity I only use the term *drug* to refer to alcohol and other drugs of abuse.

Substance abuse is any use that causes significant problems for the person. Since marijuana has permanent effects on the teenage brain even when used only a few times, all adolescent use is probably abuse.

Substance dependence, addiction, and *alcoholism* refer to substance abuse in people who find it hard to stop using and hard to stay clean. Withdrawal symptoms make it hard to stop, especially in people who have built up tolerance and require large amounts to get high. Cravings, urges, and euphoric recall (remembering drug use as wonderful when it was really awful) make it hard to stay clean.

Only one chapter in this book focuses exclusively on marijuana addiction. The rest of the book is about problems caused by both abuse and dependence. In these chapters, I sometimes refer to addicts and alcoholics while describing problems common to all substance abusers. At times, I also use the term *substance use disorder,* which is the new terminology used in the latest volume of the psychiatric *Diagnostic and Statistical Manual, DSM-5.* It was published just as I started work on this book.

Recreational use refers to any non-medical use of alcohol or any other drug—including substance abuse, addiction, and occasional use. All tobacco and alcohol use is recreational—there are no medical uses for these drugs. Most marijuana use is recreational, even when the marijuana is obtained for a supposedly medical reason.

Decriminalization means removing criminal penalties such as jail or prison while still keeping the action illegal. If marijuana possession is decriminalized, those caught possessing marijuana could still be fined.

Legalization refers to ending all legal prohibitions, making the manufacture and sale legal as well as possession.

Marijuana is what I call the drug throughout this book. The terms *pot* and *weed* are slang terms that have been around since I was a teenager, and I use them occasionally. However, I don't call it *cannabis.* That's a dressing-up word that makes marijuana sound acceptable.

In prisons, inmates often told me they were *self-medicating,* a term for abusing a drug for a medical reason, like alcoholics drinking to help their insomnia. The guys in prison usually had no medical excuse. So I'd smile and tell them, "You weren't self-medicating; you were slamming dope."

"Yeah," one person told me, "but 'self-medicating' sounds better."

"Exactly," I said, "but we don't want it to sound better. We want you to know how bad it is so you'll quit."

The marijuana industry wants to make marijuana mainstream and widely accepted. They want people to use the drug and feel good about it, so they might prefer a refined-sounding Latin name like *cannabis*. I think our society should try to prevent marijuana use and try to convince those who do use to quit. So I call it *marijuana*, a name more likely to remind us that it's a drug of abuse.

Ed Gogek, MD
Prescott, Arizona
April 21, 2015

Chapter 1

The One-sided Debate

Marijuana first became popular in the 1960s as the counterculture's drug of choice. It quickly spread to college campuses, but otherwise was not widely used. A 1969 Gallup poll found that only 4 percent of American adults had tried marijuana. By the early 1970s, the drug had made its way into high schools and even junior high schools. In 1973, another Gallup poll found that 12 percent of American adults had smoked marijuana, and by 1977, that number had doubled.[1] However, this dramatic growth wasn't a random phenomenon; the popular entertainment media promoted the drug.

A Child's Garden of Grass, the first how-to book for marijuana users, was published in 1970. Alternative newspapers wrote about drug use as a recreational activity and rock bands and folk singers glamorized its use. Marijuana humor went mainstream in 1971, when the first issue of *The Collected Adventures of the Fabulous Furry Freak Brothers* was published and the stoner comedy team Cheech & Chong released its debut album.[2]

No one glamorized heroin. There was no heroin addict comedy team, no popular book about how to shoot up dope. Even LSD, which had also just burst onto the scene, was treated mostly as a scary and dangerous drug. But marijuana showed up frequently in literature and movies, and almost always in a positive light. Popular culture consistently presented the drug as benign, fun, and hip.

The arguments for legalization used in the 1970s sound familiar: marijuana is harmless; alcohol is legal, so it's not fair to criminalize marijuana; it's wrong to put people in prison for using pot. Reporters rarely asked about the harm marijuana might cause teenagers, or how its widespread use might affect educational achievement or national economic competitiveness. It was a one-sided debate that led to one conclusion.

Between 1973 and 1977, eleven U.S. states decriminalized marijuana. In the 1976 presidential campaign, eight Democratic candidates, including Governor Jimmy Carter of Georgia and U.S. Rep. Morris Udall of Arizona, were in favor of decriminalization.[3] The words "legalization" and "decriminalization" were heard everywhere.

In one decade, the use and acceptance of marijuana had exploded. In the United States, more teenagers smoked marijuana in 1978 than at any other time in history. The belief that marijuana might be harmful was rejected more than ever.[4] It seemed we were on the road to legalization.

Instead, we reversed course. Since 1975, the University of Michigan has conducted a large ongoing study of young people's behavior and attitudes called Monitoring the Future. The study shows that teenage marijuana use peaked in 1978, and then declined steadily, reaching its lowest point in 1992.[5]

This dramatic change came about for one reason: Parents got organized.

In 1976, two parents in Atlanta realized their thirteen-year-old daughter, who had become withdrawn and cheerless, was smoking marijuana regularly. After they threw a party for their daughter, they realized her friends were also smoking marijuana. They shared their concern with friends and neighbors, and thus began the Parent Movement. In 1977, National Families in Action was formed, and in 1978, the Parents' Resource Institute for Drug Education (PRIDE) began. They wanted to use science-based information to fight back against the popular image of drug use as cool and harmless.[6]

These groups did not blame their children. They blamed the pro-marijuana news and entertainment media. Parent Movement groups called on journalists, writers, and television and movie producers to stop glamorizing drug culture and to start showing the downside of drugs.[7] The media took these complaints seriously, and for the next decade, television shows, movies, and print media shone a negative light on marijuana.

The Parent Movement insisted on asking direct questions about what marijuana was doing to kids who used it. According to a 1987 Monitoring the Future report, the eight years after 1978 were "a period in which a substantial amount of scientific and media attention was devoted to the potential dangers of heavy marijuana use."[8]

Over the fourteen years in which the Parent Movement was most active, the percentage of teenagers who believed marijuana was harmful doubled. In 1978, about 35 percent of teens thought regular use was harmful. By 1992, nearly 80 percent thought so.

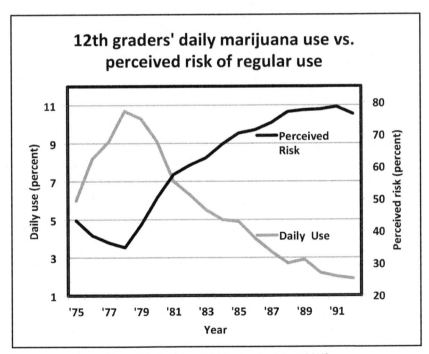

Figure 1-1. Data from Monitoring the Future 2013[9]

After 1978, marijuana use among teenagers steadily declined. By 1991, the number of high school seniors who had smoked marijuana at least once over the past month had dropped by two-thirds. Daily use dropped even more. In 1978, nearly 11 percent of high school seniors smoked marijuana every day. In 1992, fewer than 2 percent did.[10]

Here's the lesson: In the 1970s, by popularizing marijuana and presenting it as harmless, the news and entertainment media created an epidemic of teenage use. When parents pushed back, the epidemic abated.

Today, it's the 1970s all over again. The number of teens who believe marijuana is harmful is going down and adolescent use is going up. According to Monitoring the Future, between 2006 and 2013, daily marijuana use increased by 30 percent among high school seniors and 42 percent among 10th graders.[11]

Once again, the news media and popular entertainment industry are painting a positive picture of marijuana, and legalization is their preferred solution to every problem. Once again, we are barely discussing what marijuana does to kids or what it would do to our economy and educational attainment. Once again, it's a one-sided debate. But while today's discussion about marijuana is very similar to that of the 1970s, there are four important differences.

The marijuana lobby

The most notable difference is the marijuana movement. There are hundreds of pro-marijuana magazines, webzines, websites, and blogs. There's a multimillion-dollar marijuana industry, selling everything needed to grow, process, and use the drug, and selling the drug itself in states where recreational and so-called medical marijuana are legal.

Most importantly, several well-funded groups are using modern political techniques to promote legalization. In the United States, the big three in this marijuana lobby are the National Organization for the Reform of Marijuana Laws (NORML), started in 1970 and dedicated to changing public opinion; the Marijuana Policy Project (MPP), founded in 1995 to change state and federal laws through lobbying and ballot measures; and the Drug Policy Alliance (DPA), a group that aims to legalize or decriminalize all recreational drugs.[12]

The MPP received funding from pro-marijuana billionaire Peter Lewis, who died in 2013. Pro-legalization billionaire George Soros and his Open Society Foundations are linked to a plethora of groups worldwide, including the DPA, Canadian Drug Policy Coalition, Global Commission on Drug Policy, and the International Centre for Science in Drug Policy.[13]

The American Civil Liberties Union (ACLU), longtime defender of the first amendment, has also become part of the marijuana lobby. Its Washington affiliate donated to the state's legalization campaign and its Maine affiliate endorsed legalization. Its website called legalization in Colorado and Washington "sensible drug reform." In 2001, Peter Lewis donated $7 million to the group. And in 2014, the Soros-affiliated Open Society Foundations gave the ACLU $50 million, which will be used in efforts to de-felonize and decriminalize all recreational drugs.[14]

These organizations lobby politicians and court the news media, and they've been incredibly successful. They are the force behind nearly every medical marijuana law and legalization initiative. Their spokespeople feature regularly in newspapers and on TV and radio, and they're everywhere on the Internet and social media. It's unusual to read a news story or online post or watch a video about marijuana laws that doesn't quote someone from one of these groups.

However, the marijuana lobby's success has depended on a sympathetic news media that lets them dictate the terms of the public discussion. When the Parent Movement confronted the news media about one-sided coverage back in 1978, news content quickly changed. Today, much of the news media continue to paint marijuana in a positive light.

The science of marijuana

A critical factor that didn't exist in the 1970s is today's advanced research on marijuana. Over the past two decades, thousands of studies on substance abuse have been conducted. We now know far more about marijuana than we did thirty-five years ago.

That means we can confidently answer the following questions from a science-based perspective: Would legalization of marijuana increase use? Is marijuana addictive? Can it be harmful? Can the harm be permanent? And what is it doing to the still-developing brains of the 1.4 million American teenagers under age 18 who use it at least once a week?[15]

We have plenty of research on which to base our marijuana policy. Unfortunately, very little makes it into the news. Instead, journalists often use arguments that are almost identical to marijuana lobby talking points.

The marijuana lobby does cite research, but it picks and chooses studies to support its arguments. An honest scientific appraisal would examine the entire body of evidence and look at whether the research methods were credible or not. Special interest groups usually can't be trusted to provide honest appraisals of scientific evidence, yet the marijuana lobby currently enjoys the lion's share of the media's attention and focus.

There is probably no other issue on which journalists rely so heavily on the lobby of a special interest, and pay so little attention to scientists, policy experts and specialists in the field. So the research on marijuana is often ignored when it should be at the heart of the debate.

Divisive politics

The Parent Movement was started by Marsha Schuchard, a liberal Democrat who supported George McGovern, but the movement also attracted religious conservatives and Republicans.[16] And why not? Liberals and conservatives care equally about their children. So the issue was bipartisan.

Today, almost nothing is bipartisan. A 2014 Pew Research poll showed that one-third of Republicans and one-quarter of Democrats think the other party is destroying the country, and many liberals and conservatives don't want their leaders to compromise on anything.[17]

How can parents from different political parties work together when partisan news media encourage them to distrust each other? How can politicians reach across the aisle when Republicans who do get voted out by their own party?[18]

President Barack Obama was initially tough on marijuana. His Justice Department raided large-scale grow operations in medical marijuana states and warned that administering those programs was a violation of federal law. According to *Rolling Stone*, his crackdown went "far beyond anything undertaken by George W. Bush."[19] But the liberal wing of the Democratic Party apparently pressured the president to change his stance, and he relented. He might have stuck to his guns had he received support from Republicans, but he got next to none.

The other problem with divisive politics is that wedge issues become all-important. Most Republicans oppose legalization, but because many in their libertarian wing support it, they can't use the issue to unify the base or skewer Democrats. So no political leader or talk radio host stirs up the rank and file to fight against legalization.

With no leader saying this issue matters, even social conservatives stay away. Nothing destroys families like substance abuse, and social conservatives used to understand that better than anyone. Drug and alcohol abuse also contribute to teen pregnancy and the high abortion rate. Yet conservatives rarely donate to stop the legalization of drugs. They gave $39 million to fight gay marriage in California.[20] One-tenth of that could probably have defeated marijuana legalization in Colorado, Washington, Oregon, and Alaska.

This would be an easy fight to win. Successful political movements require two things: a band of activists and a majority who agree with them. There are activists who could easily reinvigorate the Parent Movement. The groups still exist, as do other anti-drug coalitions. And convincing a majority of the population to oppose legalization would be even simpler. Social conservatives innately understand why drugs are a problem, so they should almost all be on board. Moderate Democrats and independents could probably be won over. In 2010, when medical marijuana was on the Arizona ballot, I spoke to several Democratic groups, and the County Democratic Party where I live came out against the proposition. Many moderate Democrats were glad to vote against it once they had the facts. If anti-legalization groups had the means, they could reach political moderates and social conservatives—and that coalition would be an anti-drug powerhouse in every one of the fifty U.S. states.

A bipartisan coalition stopped legalization in 1978, and one could stop it now. But with today's divisive politics, we can't cooperate on anything, not even keeping the next generation off drugs.

This raises a question, especially for conservatives, who mostly oppose legalization yet bear much responsibility for the partisan divide. Can they work with people who only agree with them on this one issue, and can their elected leaders work across the aisle as well? If the answer is no, legalization will probably become the law of the land.

The addiction recovery movement

Alcoholics Anonymous (AA) was formed in 1935, and Narcotics Anonymous (NA) in 1953, so they certainly existed in the 1970s, but the widespread understanding of addiction treatment and recovery did not. Americans were shocked when their former First Lady Betty Ford entered treatment for alcoholism in 1978, but now celebrities enter treatment daily and shows about intervention and recovery are common.

In many ways, the addiction treatment field grew out of the recovery movement. Counselors who are in recovery understand the disease best and are in high demand. In 1986, I attended the Rutgers Summer School of Alcohol Studies, a program taught by many of the world's experts. Speaker after speaker told us that the best way to learn about addiction was to go to open AA and NA meetings. The understanding of addiction taken from the Twelve-Step movement is the ground on which modern addiction treatment stands.

One important lesson from AA is that addicts and alcoholics don't usually want treatment, and rarely seek help until life becomes unbearably painful. We can speed up the process and get them into treatment years earlier with a tool called intervention. And that's where drug laws help.

Drug courts for addicted criminals, DUI courts for drunk drivers, family dependency courts for addicted parents when Child Protective Services is involved, and treatment as part of probation and parole are all recovery-based programs that use the law, not as punishment, but as intervention to get addicts and alcoholics into recovery and keep them there.[21]

The marijuana lobby represents drug users, especially those who don't see drug use as a problem and just want to keep using. These people usually despise talk of recovery the way fire hates water.

They want us to think our only choices are either criminalization or legalization. But lessons learned from the Twelve-Step recovery movement underlie modern addiction treatment and offer an alternative solution to our drug problem—a third way that is neither legalization nor incarceration.

The takeaway

The marijuana lobby and divisive politics are active, powerful influences pushing us toward legalization. Meanwhile, the science of marijuana and knowledge amassed from the recovery movement are barely part of the public discussion.

The problem with the public debate about marijuana is that there is no debate. It's a one-sided conversation. We hear plenty about the pro-marijuana side, but most people, including most parents, have never heard the case against marijuana presented on an equal footing. It started to change after legalization took effect in Colorado, but not by much.

According to the polls, a majority of Americans and Canadians favor legalization, but those opinions are formed after hearing only one side of the story. Balanced news coverage, including an honest examination of the scientific evidence and the potential of recovery-based programs to solve our drug problems, could change public opinion dramatically.

Chapter 2

What We've Heard So Often, We Often Believe

Arguments in favor of legalization have been around since the early 1970s. But today, with the Internet, social media, and a sympathetic press and popular culture, there's a pro-marijuana echo chamber endlessly repeating pro-legalization arguments.

These claims have been repeated so often, and with such certainty and so little pushback, that many people believe they're true. Some journalists are resolutely pro-marijuana. Perhaps it's because they grew up hearing these arguments, and accepted them as true long before they were trained to be skeptical and to question everything.

Much of the support for legalization comes from assumptions people developed long ago. So with marijuana, we should question what we're told and we should question the beliefs we already hold. Here are twenty-four ideas that have been repeated and promoted over the years. See how you do on this quiz.

The Marijuana Beliefs Quiz

How many of these statements have you agreed with at one time or another in your life?

1. Marijuana is harmless.
2. Marijuana is safe for teenagers.
3. Teenagers are better off using marijuana than alcohol.
4. Marijuana users are safe drivers.
5. It never killed anyone.
6. It's not addictive.

7. People who are going to use marijuana will do so no matter what anyone else says or does.

8. Legalizing marijuana would not increase use, especially not teenage use.

9. With legalization, drug sellers would be regulated and would no longer be able to target youth.

10. Marijuana laws ruin the lives of millions of innocent people and fill our prisons with people who shouldn't be there.

11. Marijuana laws waste police time and money that could be spent pursuing violent criminals.

12. The best way to prevent cartel violence is by legalizing drugs.

13. The war on drugs is a police effort to find and prosecute individual drug users.

14. The police aggressively seek out marijuana users.

15. The war on drugs has failed to rein in substance abuse.

16. Prohibition of alcohol was a failure.

17. The only alternative to the war on drugs is legalization.

18. Taxing legal marijuana would be a windfall for states to fund education.

19. Medical marijuana laws are designed to provide compassionate care for the seriously ill.

20. Most medical marijuana users are seriously ill.

21. Medical marijuana users get recommendations from their own doctors, whom they've known for years.

22. Medical marijuana users must first try conventional medicines. They only get marijuana if other medicines don't work.

23. There are no medications that do what marijuana does.

24. The 1930s movie *Reefer Madness* was made by the government to scare people about marijuana.

None of these statements are accurate, as the following pages will show. We can dispense with one myth right away. *Reefer Madness* was filmed and financed privately by a church group that was concerned about youth marijuana use, but was quickly repurchased by Dwain Esper, a director who made "exploitation" films. In the 1930s, censorship rules were strict; sex, violence, and illegal drugs were not permitted in Hollywood movies, but were common topics in exploitation films.

These movies often presented themselves as warning against some danger to make them seem more exciting, but the movies were not meant to be educational. Some of Esper's other films were named *Sex Madness, Sinister Harvest* and *Forbidden Love*. Esper re-cut *Reefer Madness*, adding several "salacious insert shots," according to one film historian, and turned it into an exploitation film. The movie we see today never had any connection to the federal government, and was never meant to be taken seriously.[1]

The reason for listing these twenty-four untrue statements is that most of us have believed some of them at one time, and many of us still do. I scored 17 out of 24 on this quiz, which means that, in the past, I believed most of these statements.

However, just as the Parent Movement didn't blame kids for using drugs, I don't blame myself for having been fooled. All we know is what we're told, and although I'm an avid reader of the news, none of the news I read told me both sides.

Chapter 3

What Research Tells Us about Teenage Use

Brain development is a three-stage process. It begins in the womb, which is when most of our brain cells are created and begin to interconnect. Once we're born, our nerve cells respond to our life experiences by forming many more connections, called synapses, to other cells. Childhood is a time of learning, and the more we learn, the more connections our cells create.

By about age eleven we've formed trillions of synapses, but an eleven-year-old brain is like the rough draft of a novel. The content is there, but it's not organized. During adolescence (and until our mid-twenties), the brain reorganizes itself. Unused or rarely used connections are discarded. Synapses we use often are strengthened, refined, and expanded. At the end of this process, the brain has lost half of its connections between cells, but it's faster, more focused, and more efficient.

The developing adolescent brain chooses what to retain and what to discard based on what we're doing and which synapses are being used. If we spend our time studying math or playing hockey, the brain will shape itself to be expert at those things. The downside is that it lets go of what we're not using. Skills learned in childhood but not used in adolescence are lost, while skills practiced in the early to mid-teens remain. I quit piano at age ten and my ability to play is long gone. But the prologue to *The Canterbury Tales* I memorized in high school is still with me.

The whole process of pruning, shaping, and sculpting lasts until the mid-twenties, but most of it takes place in the early years of adolescence. To take advantage of this window of opportunity, Mother

Nature hardwired teenagers to take risks and to experience every-thing they can. The adolescent sense of invulnerability that causes parents such angst evolved for a reason. The more things they try, the greater their repertoire as adults.

That's fine if they're making friends or playing guitar, but not if they're experimenting with alcohol or other drugs. Teens see drugs and alcohol as just one more exciting experience, but addictive substances act directly on the brain and change it.

We all pursue happiness, usually through accomplishments, physical activity, close relationships, or distracting amusements. All these things stimulate the pleasure centers in our brains and make us feel good. However, addicts use drugs to directly stimulate their pleasure centers. It's a shortcut—and it can become a short circuit. People become addicted because the drug has changed how the brain works. As a result, addicts become focused on getting pleasure from the drug and lose interest in friends, family, work, and accomplishments. Instead of getting pleasure from a meaningful and productive life, they get it from a chemical.

Teenagers get addicted to drugs—including alcohol, marijuana, and tobacco—much more frequently than adults do because their brains are shaping themselves around their daily experiences and strength-ening the synapses of activities they're engaged in. If a teenager is using drugs, the parts of the brain that enjoy getting high will be strengthened—permanently.

That's why teenagers get addicted so easily. It also explains why anyone who starts using any drug at an early age finds it harder to quit. This includes tobacco.

Even worse, while the brain is shaping itself to get pleasure from substance abuse, it eliminates the underused pathways that would lead to seeking pleasure in healthy ways. And this also becomes permanent. Even if they later quit using, the brain's architecture is already set. People who use addictive substances in their teens subtly damage their ability to find healthy, meaningful happiness for the rest of their lives.

This doesn't mean they're dull and lethargic, in fact, just the opposite. They need extra stimulation just to feel normal. They don't understand people who are happy with their work and families and hobbies. Those people seem way too straight and boring. But the real problem is that teenage drug users have damaged their ability to get sufficient pleasure from activities most adults enjoy. So the excitement offered by drugs and alcohol is always tempting.

This gives a new twist to the gateway drug debate. What matters is not the choice of drug but the age at which it's first used. Any addictive drug used in adolescence will prime the brain for more drug abuse. Research shows that when teenage marijuana users grow up, they abuse alcohol and other drugs at higher rates than most other adults, while people who first smoke marijuana after their teens do not.[1]

Drugs also directly harm the adolescent brain in ways not seen in adults. Teens who drink heavily—defined as four or five drinks in one evening—cause lasting damage that shows up on brain scans—even if they only drink once or twice a month.[2]

Marijuana does even more damage, as several studies have shown. As adults, former teenage marijuana users have problems with executive function, the human ability to think, plan, solve problems, make decisions, and set priorities. Executive function resides in the brain's frontal lobes and makes us different from animals, who can't think beyond the moment. Without good executive function, we become like the caricature of the blissed-out stoner drifting through life.

Here are four scientific reports showing the long-term effects of teenage marijuana use:

- In a study published in the February 2000 issue of the *Journal of Addictive Diseases*, researchers from Duke University conducted MRI and PET scans on marijuana users. The ones who started smoking marijuana before age seventeen had smaller brains and less gray matter than those who started later. Gray matter includes the thinking part of the brain, which is in charge of decision-making and self-control.[3]

- A 2007 study from the University of California at San Diego compared teenaged heavy marijuana users who had been abstinent for one month to teens who had never used. Even after a month away from the drug, heavy users performed worse on several neurocognitive tests, including attention, memory, and the ability to plan.[4]

- A group of Harvard researchers found that heavy marijuana users performed worse on neurocognitive tests that assess executive function. These heavy users found it harder to solve problems, see patterns, and control their impulse to blurt out answers. The researchers wanted to see if all marijuana users had these problems, or if only the ones who started at an early age were affected. They separated out heavy users who had first smoked marijuana before age sixteen from the others, and found that those who started at age sixteen or later performed just as well on neurocognitive testing as those who had never used marijuana. However, those who started before age sixteen did significantly worse than both the control group and those who started using marijuana later.[5]

- A 2012 study by researchers from Duke University and the University of Otago in Dunedin, New Zealand, followed 1,000 people from birth until middle age, and compared IQ test scores at ages thirteen and thirty-eight. They found that IQ dropped among marijuana users as they grew older but not among nonusers. The marijuana users also had problems with reasoning and comprehension, but when they stopped using for a year, those who started as adults returned to normal brain function, while those who first used marijuana before age eighteen never did.[6]

This research shows that the age at which people start using matters. People who use marijuana before age seventeen or eighteen can inflict permanent damage. And most marijuana users start before age eighteen.[7]

In another 2012 study from Harvard, published in *Neuroscience Letters*, researchers conducted brain scans on marijuana users and nonusers while they completed a task requiring concentration and judgment. The marijuana users did nearly as well as the nonusers.

However, the brain scans showed that the marijuana users employed different parts of their brains and used more of their brains to accomplish the same task. This was especially true for those who first used marijuana in their early to mid-teens.[8] The best explanation is that part of the brain was disabled by marijuana use and so other parts compensated.

The body normally compensates for injuries. Limping after an injury is compensation; it's how the body manages to walk without using the injured part. When people are born deaf, the brain compensates by devoting more neurons to touch and vision.[9] It's not the same as being able to hear, but it helps.

Evidently, the brains of former teenage marijuana users compensate, but the users aren't aware of it, which is also normal. According to the *Traumatic Brain Injury Survival Guide* by Dr. Glen Johnson, people with brain injuries from a single trauma often have no idea they're disabled because it's hard to see.[10] An injury that comes on gradually, from years of smoking marijuana, is even harder to notice. So it simply becomes the new normal and the person forgets how they used to be.

In the IQ study done by Duke University and the University of Otago, the results showed that the heaviest marijuana users lost an average of eight IQ points.[11] That is a big enough difference to change their lives. Eight points could mean the difference between getting into a good or a mediocre university. It could mean not getting a promotion or not having the foresight to prevent a divorce.

Someone with a bad knee sees it next to the good one every day. But someone who misses a promotion at work probably sees no connection to their teenage drug use. It's quite a disability, but it goes unnoticed.

This is marijuana denial; users are subtly but globally affected, yet believe they're fine.

I first got stoned the night before my seventeenth birthday, and used regularly, sometimes daily, until quitting at age nineteen. After I quit, I knew my mind was fuzzier than it had been two years earlier. I still did well in school, but something was subtly different. I kept waiting for it to clear so I'd again have the sharp, incisive thinking I had in high school, but it never did, and I forgot about it. I realize now that I didn't simply cloud my brain with marijuana, I altered the microstructure of my brain cells. That crisp, clear thinking wasn't waiting to return once the drug got out of my system; it was gone forever. It was a very subtle change I barely noticed and soon forgot about, but it's probably still with me.

Public figures who admit to marijuana use often treat it like a benign rite of passage, but we shouldn't just accept their denial. Research tells us it's not benign. When they try to pass off their own teenage use as innocuous, we should ask at what age they first used and then remind them of what the science says. Adults who used marijuana in their teenage years are not quite the person they would have been otherwise, and we should all own up to it.

When teenage users grow up

There has been much research on the long-term implications of teenage marijuana use. For example:

- A review of the research published in the journal *Addiction* in 2000 found that students who started using marijuana in their early teens did worse in school and were more likely to drop out.[12]

- Another study done the same year at the Research Triangle Institute found that adolescents who started using marijuana before age sixteen were more than twice as likely as nonusers to drop out of high school.[13] And data from the National Survey on Drug Use and Health shows that one-quarter of all marijuana users started using by age fifteen.[14]

- A research project by the University of Maryland School of Public Health followed university freshmen for ten years. According to one of the authors, they found that substance abuse, "especially marijuana use," was linked to "college students skipping more classes, spending less time studying, earning lower grades, dropping out, and being unemployed after college."[15]

- On the more hopeful side is a 2006 study called "Reducing Substance Use Improves Adolescents' School Attendance." Substance-abusing teenagers who cut down their use of alcohol or other drugs went to school more often. This also held true for marijuana abusers, but only if they quit entirely. This study is evidence that drug abuse, including marijuana abuse, actually causes poor school performance and isn't just a statistical curiosity.[16] If it were simply a coincidental association, their school attendance wouldn't improve when they quit using.

The most dramatic study on what happens to adults who smoked marijuana in their teen years was published in 2008 in the journal *Addiction*. Two New Zealand researchers, David Fergusson and Joseph Boden, used data from approximately 1,000 people who were followed from ages fifteen to twenty-five. The researchers divided them into six groups based on how many times they had smoked marijuana by age twenty-one.[17]

The six groups were those who had:

- never used marijuana
- used 1–99 times
- used 100–199 times
- used 200–299 times
- used 300–399 times
- used 400 times or more

When the study participants were twenty-five, the researchers asked them three yes-or-no questions:

- Did you graduate from a four-year university?
- Have you ever been unemployed as an adult?
- Have you ever been on welfare as an adult?

The results were striking.

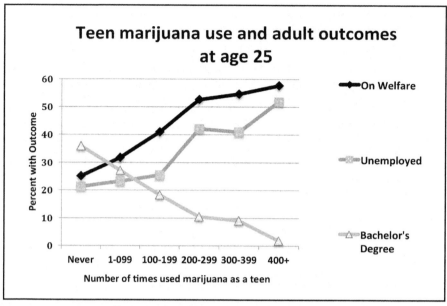

Figure 3-1. Data from Fergusson & Boden, 2008.[18]

Those who used marijuana were less likely to have earned a bachelor's degree by age twenty-five. One-third of nonusers and one-quarter of occasional users had four-year degrees. But those who used marijuana 200–399 times prior to age twenty-one had only a 10 percent graduation rate. Heavy users, who had used 400 times or more, had a 2 percent graduation rate. Marijuana users were also much more likely to have been unemployed or on welfare at some point between ages twenty-one and twenty-five.

The researchers also gave these twenty-five-year-olds two questionnaires. One asked about satisfaction with their intimate relationships. The other had them rate their level of dissatisfaction with their lives. Finally, the researchers asked them how much they earned each year. Those who had used marijuana more than 100 times by age twenty-one earned less as adults, were less satisfied with their intimate relationships, and were unhappier in general.

This makes sense given what we know. Drug use during adolescent brain development increases a person's ability to enjoy using drugs and decreases the ability to get pleasure from anything else. And that's exactly what the two questionnaires show.

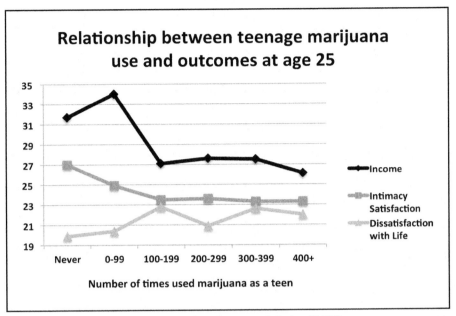

Figure 3-2. Data from Fergusson & Boden, 2008.[19]

Criticisms of such research usually come in two forms. One form comes from people who don't understand what probability means and who think one counterexample disproves everything. I've heard people say, "I know a physics professor who gets high every day." That may be. The study doesn't say teenage users never graduate from university, just that they're less likely to.

The second criticism is more substantial: just because two things are linked statistically doesn't mean one causes the other. Maybe marijuana users were doing worse in school before they even tried marijuana, and that's why fewer of them got university degrees. Maybe people who were abused as children use more marijuana, and that's why they have trouble with intimacy. Maybe marijuana users also abuse alcohol, and the alcohol abuse led to them losing their jobs and ending up on welfare.

The researchers made a list of sixteen other possible explanations for the findings and tested each one. And they came up with the same results. When they looked only at teenagers who grew up poor, the ones who used marijuana were more likely to have these six negative outcomes than those who never used the drug. When they looked only at teens who used alcohol, the ones who also used marijuana had more problems as adults than those who used alcohol alone. And teenage marijuana users who were abused as children had more negative adult outcomes than child abuse survivors who didn't use marijuana. This held true for each of the sixteen variables: adolescent marijuana users consistently performed worse as adults than nonusers.[20]

How much marijuana is safe?

This raises a question: How many times can adolescents use marijuana before suffering permanent damage?

In the study by Fergusson and Boden, the group that used 100 times or more—equivalent to using twice a month for almost five years—clearly had long-term problems. But the group who used marijuana no more than ninety-nine times as teenagers also had long-term problems. Most of this group had only tried it a few times. Twelve percent of them had only tried marijuana once, and half had tried it no more than ten times. Three-quarters of this group had tried it fewer than twenty-five times.[21] Yet even this group scored worse on most measures compared to those who had never used at all. This suggests that using the drug even a few times can have long-term consequences.

The research on heavy teenage use is overwhelmingly clear: heavy marijuana use in teenagers permanently alters the ability to think, remember, and process. More studies are needed on adolescents who use only a few times in their lives, but we can say this: If teenagers want to go to university or have successful careers or simply have all their wits about them for the rest of their lives, they should not use marijuana before age sixteen—and even afterwards, they should not use it more than a handful of times and, ideally, not at all. I can't speak with certainty for the adolescent I used to be, but if I'd known then what researchers are discovering about marijuana today, I might never have touched it.

Chapter 4

Marijuana and Driving

In a 2013 poll by the insurance company Liberty Mutual, 40 percent of teenage marijuana users said the drug had no effect on their ability to drive safely, and another 33 percent believed it helped them drive better. That means almost 75 percent of teenage marijuana users think they drive just as safely when they're high on marijuana as when they're not.[1]

This can't just be chalked up to the adolescent sense of invulnerability; in the same poll, nearly two-thirds said that alcohol had a negative effect on their driving.[2] However, teenagers hear a very different message about marijuana from the one they hear about alcohol.

- This is from theweedblog.com: "[C]onsuming marijuana doesn't make you a dangerous driver, and may in fact make some people safer drivers."[3]

- From cannabisculture.com's Marijuana Magazine: "All major studies show that marijuana consumption has little or no effect on driving ability, and may actually reduce accidents."[4]

- From the website of NORML: "Marijuana ... does not appear to play a significant role in vehicle crashes ..."[5]

- In 2014, the Drug Policy Alliance website read: "There is no compelling evidence that marijuana contributes substantially to traffic accidents and fatalities."[6]

The marijuana lobby and others in the pro-legalization movement have been saying that driving while stoned is safe. And teenagers have gotten that message.

Is it safe to drive high?

No. There's plenty of evidence that driving under the influence of marijuana is dangerous.

- In 2013, researchers from Dalhousie University in Nova Scotia looked at 860 drivers taken to the emergency room after car accidents. Marijuana use by itself, without alcohol or other drugs, was associated with a fourfold increase in the rate of collisions.[7]

- Researchers from Australia and New Zealand published a study in 2005 in the journal *Addiction* showing that, compared to nonusers, heavy marijuana users were nine times as likely to be injured in a car accident.[8]

- A study from France published in 2005 looked at over 6,000 drivers who were responsible for fatal accidents. They found that drivers with low concentrations of marijuana metabolites had double the chance of causing a fatal accident, and higher concentrations quadrupled the risk.[9]

- They're not even safe riding a bike. A study published in *Preventive Medicine* in 2014 found that 15 percent of bicycle crash victims had been using marijuana.[10]

So several good studies have found a clear association between marijuana use and car crashes. However, there's also research that doesn't find an association between marijuana use and auto accidents. These are called negative studies or negative findings, and they're often of little significance.

Why negative studies are often meaningless

Here's an example of a negative finding:

Spouse 1: Honey, can you look in the closet and see if my green sweater is there?

Spouse 2: (two seconds later) I don't see it.

Spouse 2 is not persistent, but at least he's honest. He carefully avoided jumping to the conclusion that the sweater wasn't there, and only said he didn't find it. That's a negative finding; he looked and didn't find it. When someone conducts a research project—in this case, seeing if the green sweater is in the closet—one negative finding doesn't prove anything. It doesn't prove the sweater isn't there. All it proves is the person didn't find it.

One negative study tells us very little. He didn't find the sweater. That might be because it's not in the closet, or because he didn't look carefully, or maybe because he's color-blind. We don't know. That's why negative findings shouldn't be overinterpreted.

Negative findings aren't proof, but several of them will lead us to suspect that what we're looking for doesn't exist. Suppose Spouse 1 asked Spouse 2 to look again and again.

> Spouse 1: Can you just look one more time? I'm sure it's there.
>
> Spouse 2: Honey, I've looked ninety-nine times and I haven't found it. I'm starting to think it's not there.

He still doesn't say it's not there, just that he thinks it's not there. That's because he knows it's impossible to prove a negative. Several negative studies lead us to believe we'll never find what we're looking for, but they never prove we can't find it. Negative findings can never be taken as proof because even if we repeat the experiment ninety-nine times, we still have the same two possibilities: maybe the sweater isn't in the closet and maybe we never looked for it correctly.

So Spouse 2 is careful not to say anything that might be untrue. Sure, he looked ninety-nine times and didn't find it. But those are negative findings, and he knows that one positive finding can render all those negative findings meaningless. For example:

> Spouse 1: Oh, good grief. I'll look. (stomps upstairs, goes to closet, pulls out sweater)
>
> Spouse 2: Oh, that green sweater!

Spouse 2 was right not to jump to conclusions. Those ninety-nine negative studies did not prove the sweater wasn't there. There was always the possibility that he wasn't looking for it correctly.

And once Spouse 1 finds the sweater, we know Spouse 2 had been searching for it incorrectly. In this case, one positive finding renders the ninety-nine negative ones meaningless. That's why scientists often don't bother to publish their negative findings. But they should because this analogy isn't perfect. There's no doubt that when Spouse 1 looked herself, she found the sweater. In scientific research, however, positive findings can be mistaken. That's why published research often ends with the caveat that the study should be repeated by different researchers in different labs to confirm the outcome. But the most important point here is that negative findings by themselves don't prove anything.

How negative findings are misused

Negative studies only tell us that either there's no link between marijuana and driving, or that the studies weren't designed carefully enough to find the link. But time after time, marijuana supporters take one negative study and call it proof.

For example, in 2010, a Hartford Hospital study using a driving simulator found little difference between drivers who had used marijuana and those who hadn't. In her press release, the researcher warned against overinterpreting the study: "The results do not imply that it is safe to drive under the influence of marijuana."[11]

But the pro-marijuana webzine International Cannagraphic wrote a story headlined "Study Proves Pot Has Little Effect on Driving," and led with "Research proves what we knew all along, pot users are overly-safe drivers ..."[12]

The *Hartford Courant* led with "Marijuana use had little effect on simulated driving skills, according to a Hartford Hospital study ..."[13] That's not what the study showed; all it showed is that this particular piece of research didn't find any effect. That's why it's important to understand negative findings.

Not finding any effect is like not finding the sweater; it doesn't mean it's not there. Maybe the study wasn't designed correctly to find it. We don't know. However, the *Courant*'s lead was the equivalent of "Sweater not in closet, according to spouse," and that's not what the spouse said.

Cherry-picking

Cherry-picking is another misuse of scientific findings to support a political belief. When advocates cherry-pick, they find the research they agree with and ignore the rest.

In 2015, the NORML website had a page called "Marijuana and Driving: A review of the scientific evidence" that was devoted to cherry-picking. It quoted from thirteen studies and government reports that concluded there was not yet evidence that driving while stoned is dangerous. But the studies and reports were all at least twelve years old. Research since 2002 showing that driving stoned can be dangerous and deadly was left out. That's cherry-picking; NORML picked out the research that supported its point of view.[14]

Of course, I could be accused of cherry-picking, too. So how do we settle arguments when both sides might be cherry-picking?

How scientists reach consensus

Some of the scientific evidence shows that marijuana makes driving more dangerous, and some finds no or very little increased risk. One way scientists resolve the dilemma of conflicting results is by using meta-analysis, combining several studies into one and looking at the overall result. Scientists have come up with rules about how to conduct meta-analyses, because such projects are only useful if the researchers are completely evenhanded.[15]

In 2012, researchers from Dalhousie University in Nova Scotia published a meta-analysis of marijuana and driving in the *British Medical Journal*. The authors of the meta-analysis, titled "Acute Cannabis Consumption and Motor Vehicle Collision Risk: Systematic review of observational studies and meta-analysis," combed through the scientific literature and tried to find every study ever conducted on marijuana use and car crashes. Then they eliminated the ones that did not match their quality standards. For example, a lot of studies included people who had also been drinking alcohol or using other drugs. Those were excluded because the researchers wanted studies of drivers who had only used marijuana.[16]

In any meta-analysis, the most important task is to eliminate studies impartially and without bias. Criteria must be set up ahead of time and adhered to strictly. Otherwise the whole analysis can be prejudiced.

The Dalhousie researchers ended up with nine studies they considered to be of high or medium quality. Two of them showed no link between marijuana use and auto accidents; the other seven did find a link. These nine studies were combined and analyzed, and the researchers concluded: "Acute cannabis consumption is associated with an increased risk of a motor vehicle crash, especially for fatal collisions." People who drove within a few hours of smoking marijuana were about twice as likely to be in a serious or fatal car wreck.

Three years later, in 2015, this was still the best estimate science had to offer. No one should write about marijuana's effect on driver safety without mentioning this particular meta-analysis. And no one should ever say, or even imply, that driving while stoned is safe. The most unbiased look at all the research tells us it's dangerous.

* * *

For the marijuana lobby, the debate over driving is just politics. To convince us to legalize the drug, they must first convince us that it's harmless. So they repeatedly claim that driving while stoned is safe, and ignore the most comprehensive study to date that says it can be deadly. This might help them win their political campaign, but it's terrible for the teenagers who believe them.

How to prevent stoned driving

Telling marijuana users about the increased risk of accidents doesn't dissuade them. A 2014 review of the research on marijuana and driving found that most users believe marijuana causes only minimal impairment. In fact, most users said they would continue to drive stoned despite the research showing it's dangerous. Being stopped and warned by police also failed to dissuade them. But knowing they would be punished worked. This review of the research concluded that "random roadside testing (with arrest of those found cannabis positive) would be a better deterrent."[17]

Chapter 5

Schizophrenia

Schizophrenia is an incurable psychiatric illness that strikes in the teens and early twenties. The most obvious symptoms are disordered thinking, making connections that make sense to the person with schizophrenia but to no one else. People with schizophrenia also have delusions, such as believing that other people control their thoughts or the television speaks directly to them. They may hear voices, but more significantly, they believe the voices are real. When people have such extreme beliefs that they're not in touch with reality, it's called psychosis.

People with schizophrenia also lose the ability to act or relate normally. They're missing part of what allows us to connect as people. They can seem uninterested in their own lives and incapable of having goals, as if they're not able to think or act on their own behalf. Family and friends describe losing the person they once knew.

People with this illness usually find it difficult to hold any but the most basic jobs, and even then they often need supervision. Many can't work at all and have a hard time living on their own without help from family members or mental health workers. Some can't function in the outside world and spend their lives in psychiatric hospitals.

Marijuana exacerbates psychosis by imitating it

During the teenage years, when the brain is deciding which nerve cell connections to keep and which ones to discard, the pruning back or strengthening of synaptic connections is mediated by neurotransmitters called endocannabinoids. These natural chemicals in the brain were given their name because they target the same receptors marijuana targets. This doesn't mean we're made to use marijuana. Quite the opposite, in fact.

Endocannabinoids play an important role in brain development, even before a child is born. They help to control how many and what type of brain cells are produced, how these cells migrate to their final positions in the brain, and how their wires (axons) find other cells to connect with.

Marijuana imitates our natural endocannabinoids and fools the developing adolescent brain. Natural endocannabinoids work with a purpose, shaping the brain in a focused and carefully controlled way, but marijuana works randomly. It disrupts synaptic pruning, leaving teenage users with more nerve endings leading nowhere, or nowhere useful. Natural endocannabinoids would never do that unless some disease process led them to.

One theory of schizophrenia is that an internal disruption of the endocannabinoid system causes synaptic pruning to go awry.[1] That would explain why the disease so often manifests in the late teens. If this theory is true, then marijuana imitates the abnormality that causes schizophrenia. So if someone already has schizophrenia, using marijuana could make their symptoms worse. And if they're predisposed to schizophrenia, using marijuana could precipitate the illness.

Research shows that marijuana can affect the course of schizophrenia in three ways. It makes the symptoms worse. It appears to cause schizophrenia to develop two to three years earlier than in nonusers. And it might even precipitate the illness in people who would not have developed it otherwise.

Marijuana users relapse more often

People with schizophrenia function at a lower level than those without the illness, but with support they often live stable lives. However, if they use marijuana, they're likely to suffer a worsening of symptoms.[2] After using the drug, they hallucinate more, they think less clearly, and their grip on reality slips. They're less able to maintain their already tenuous social relationships and are often hospitalized. I've seen patients with schizophrenia go downhill dramatically after using marijuana, and it then took weeks or months before they were stable enough to live outside of the hospital.

When I worked in outpatient mental health, I regularly told my patients with schizophrenia, "If you take your medicine and stay away from drugs and alcohol, you'll do okay. You'll keep that part-time or volunteer job, you won't lose your apartment, and you won't get hospitalized." I especially told them to stay away from marijuana.

A lot of research shows that patients with schizophrenia who use marijuana are less compliant about taking their medicine and are more likely to relapse, requiring a hospital stay.

- A study published in *Schizophrenia Research* in September 2009 found that patients with schizophrenia who used marijuana were twice as likely as nonusers to take medicine incorrectly or not at all, and six times as likely to drop out of treatment altogether.[3]

- A large-scale review of the research on schizophrenia published in 2008 in the *British Journal of Psychiatry* found that marijuana use was consistently associated with poor adherence to treatment, increased relapse, and frequent hospitalization. Some studies also showed lower rates of employment.[4]

- In 1994, researchers from the Academic Medical Center in Amsterdam published a study showing that people with schizophrenia who used marijuana were more likely than nonusers to relapse, and the heaviest users relapsed most often.[5]

- Another 1994 study, published in the *British Journal of Psychiatry,* followed patients with schizophrenia for twelve years and found that marijuana users had three times the relapse rate of nonusers.[6]

Marijuana-induced relapse is a widespread problem because people with schizophrenia smoke a lot of it. In 2005, only 6 percent of American teens and adults had used marijuana over the past month, an indicator of current use. In that same year, a review by three Australian researchers published in the *British Journal of Psychiatry* found 23 percent of people with schizophrenia were current users.[7] In a 2012 study by van Dijk and his co-researchers, nearly half of the males with schizophrenia used marijuana.[8]

Marijuana-induced relapse is also a costly problem. A study published in *Psychological Medicine* in 2014 found that schizophrenic patients who used marijuana had twice as many hospitalizations as nonusers and their hospitalizations also lasted longer. Over a thirty-year period, they required nearly three times as many hospital days as nonusers.[9]

If a quarter of people with schizophrenia use marijuana, as the Australian reviewers found, and people with schizophrenia who use marijuana account for three times as many hospital days as nonusers, that means marijuana users with schizophrenia account for half of all the hospital days used by people with schizophrenia. And hospitalization is expensive, something we should consider when estimating the cost of legalization.

Marijuana users function at a lower level

Research shows that people with schizophrenia who smoke marijuana have particularly disorganized thinking, are more paranoid, have more chronic symptoms that never let up, and are more often irritable and hostile.[10] In other words, they just don't do as well, and every psychiatrist who treats patients with schizophrenia knows this.

A typical story came from a woman who told me about her teenage son's first hospitalization for schizophrenia. He was confused, hearing voices, and feeling restless and despondent. After a week in the hospital, he was much better. He still had a blunted emotional response, but he was easier to talk to, he was no longer hallucinating, and his mood was calm and cheerful. So he was given a pass to go home for the day. He returned in terrible condition, as bad as when he first came in. But in a few days, he was better again. So he got another pass, and again he returned in full relapse. It turned out he was getting stoned with his friends; the whole hospitalization was caused by marijuana.

Another male in his late teens was also frequently in and out of the hospital, paranoid, hallucinating, and unable to cope even while living with his parents. He smoked marijuana several times a day and couldn't say "No." But then he got into a Twelve-Step program, surrounded himself with people who were clean and sober, and improved so remarkably that his doctor wondered if he even had schizophrenia. But he did.

Keeping schizophrenics away from marijuana is really difficult. Unlike drinkers who know exactly what causes hangovers, marijuana users tend not to connect their drug use to the problems that follow, and this is especially true for people with schizophrenia. For example, the patient who kept getting high when out of hospital on a pass would not believe that marijuana made his condition worse.

Also, even when they know marijuana is a problem, people with schizophrenia often lack the mental strength to make decisions and stick to them. They're often so easily influenced they can't say "No."

Marijuana appears to hasten the disease

Research shows that marijuana users with schizophrenia develop the illness at a younger age than nonusers. In one study, marijuana-using males with schizophrenia were first diagnosed seven years younger than nonusers.[11] However, a meta-analysis that combined the best studies showed marijuana users were first diagnosed two to three years younger than nonusers, and the difference showed up most in the heaviest users.[12]

Incidentally, alcohol abuse by itself does not cause schizophrenia to develop earlier.[13] So when people say marijuana isn't as bad as alcohol, they're not looking at this disease. For people with a predisposition to schizophrenia, marijuana is probably worse.

Can marijuana cause schizophrenia?

The most concerning research on marijuana is the evidence that it can precipitate schizophrenia in people who are genetically susceptible, pushing them over an edge they might not have crossed on their own. In 2006, Louisa Degenhardt and Wayne Hall published a review of the research. They found that teenage marijuana use is associated with higher rates of schizophrenia, and that the more often teenagers used marijuana the more likely they were to develop schizophrenia later in life.[14]

In one very large research project known as the Swedish Conscript Study, more than 50,000 people were interviewed about their marijuana use at age eighteen and then followed for the next fifteen years. Compared to people who had never used marijuana, those who had used the drug no more than ten times by age eighteen were 1.3 times more likely to develop schizophrenia as adults. Those who used marijuana fewer than fifty times were three times more likely. And those who smoked marijuana more than fifty times by age eighteen were six times as likely to develop schizophrenia.[15]

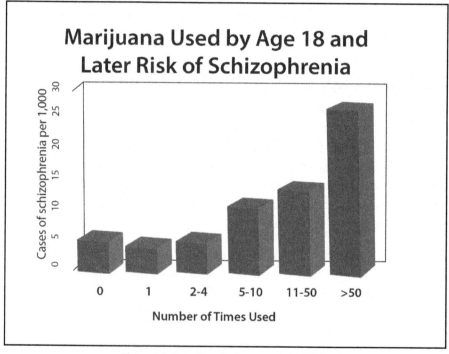

Figure 5-1. Data from Andreasson et al., 1987[16]

Other research found that not everyone carries an equal risk. Teenagers with a family history of psychotic disorders were far more likely to become schizophrenic after smoking marijuana than those with no such family history.[17] This is small comfort, though, as not many adolescents evaluate their family history before trying marijuana.

Teenage marijuana use is clearly associated with the development of schizophrenia, but that doesn't necessarily mean it causes the disease.

First, with all the marijuana teenagers are using, schizophrenia rates should be increasing—and they aren't. Second, research indicates that people who are genetically predisposed to schizophrenia might also be predisposed to using marijuana.[18] A study by researchers at Harvard Medical School, published in 2014 in *Schizophrenia Research*, found that all the increased risk of schizophrenia in marijuana-using patients could be explained by family history.[19]

However, there is also research supporting the idea that marijuana can cause schizophrenia. A study by McGrath found that marijuana users who started by age fifteen were more likely to develop a psychotic disorder than those who never used or started later. This study included several sibling pairs, and even with siblings the difference held.[20] So maybe marijuana use precipitates schizophrenia and maybe it doesn't. The science isn't conclusive.

Marijuana activists celebrate anyway

In response to the Harvard study, the magazine *High Times* ran an exceptionally irresponsible headline: "Smoke Weed and Don't Worry about Schizophrenia."[21] This is incredibly dangerous advice.

First of all, we don't know whether or not marijuana can cause schizophrenia; there's evidence to support both sides. Second, the Harvard researchers did not cast doubt on the finding that marijuana hastens the onset of schizophrenia.[22]

Third, the drug most definitely messes up the lives of people who already have schizophrenia. A study published in *Schizophrenia Research* in 2012 found that marijuana users did not have worse psychopathology than nonusers, but they still relapsed more often.[23] This tells us that marijuana itself is the problem in relapse, not some other predisposition. So people with schizophrenia should never be encouraged to smoke marijuana.

Another marijuana user with schizophrenia is a good example of how bad this drug can be. He did terribly for years. He was chronically unhappy, hallucinated, and his speech was confused, garrulous, and rambling. He didn't seem to respond to medicine and was frequently hospitalized. Then his family took complete control of his money, kept him away from drug-using friends, and kept him off marijuana. For several years, he stayed out of the hospital, was easy to talk to, and was happier. The hallucinations even went away. He did so well that he was eventually allowed to control his own money, which was his undoing. He started smoking marijuana again and all his problems returned.

A cautionary tale

On January 8, 2011, Tucson, Arizona, resident Jared Loughner woke up early, bought ammunition for the Glock pistol he'd purchased a month before, and took a taxi to a Safeway supermarket where U.S. Representative Gabrielle Giffords was meeting constituents. He opened fire, killing six people, including a federal judge and a nine-year-old girl. Congresswoman Gifford suffered a gunshot to the head.

In custody, Loughner was examined and diagnosed with schizophrenia. From interviews with those who knew him, we can piece together a picture of his deterioration.

Friends from his early teens described him as shy, but friendly and well liked. In high school he began using drugs and alcohol, and dropped out after his junior year. Marijuana was a particular problem. He was arrested for possessing paraphernalia, and the military rejected him when he told them how heavily he used the drug.

Sometime after he left school, friends and co-workers described a change in his personality. He started acting strangely, lost his ability to communicate normally, and was fired from jobs for bizarre behavior.

In the summer before the shooting, he enrolled in a community college class where other students noticed his "odd demeanor and incongruous comments." He disrupted the class with angry outbursts and classmates were afraid of him. The school eventually expelled him, telling him he could not return unless he sought psychiatric treatment. He never did.

Jared Loughner is just one example of someone who smoked marijuana heavily as a teenager and developed schizophrenia. James Holmes, who shot and killed twelve people at a movie theater in Aurora,

Colorado, is another. We don't know if marijuana causes people to develop the illness, and we don't know if Loughner or Holmes became schizophrenic years prematurely because of the drug. But we do know that marijuana makes the symptoms of schizophrenia worse.

Schizophrenia itself is only slightly associated with violence, but when substance abuse is combined with schizophrenia the risk of violence increases significantly.[24] We don't usually think of marijuana use as leading to hostility, but research shows that people with marijuana addiction are more prone to violence, and this tendency is independent of any other psychiatric or substance abuse problem.[25]

In the public debate after the Tucson shooting, the left said it was too easy to get guns, while the right said it was too easy for people with severe psychiatric illnesses to go untreated. Neither side offered a politically feasible solution that would have prevented the violence. No court had ever declared Loughner mentally unfit, so his gun purchase was legal. And psychiatric commitment laws much tougher than we already have would violate people's civil liberties.[26]

However, there's a good chance the Tucson shooting would not have happened had Jared Loughner never smoked marijuana, and teenage marijuana use is preventable. If we want to prevent similar tragedies in the future, the most effective approach would be to stop promoting marijuana as a harmless and supposedly safer drug. Instead, we should find ways to make the drug less attractive and less available so we can discourage all teenagers from using it.

Chapter 6

Is Marijuana Addictive—and Should We Care?

The legalization movement doesn't want to accept that marijuana is an addictive drug. In 2010, when legalization was on the ballot in California, they wrote this line into the initiative: "Cannabis is not physically addictive."[1] Had the measure passed, that statement would now be enshrined in state law, but that wouldn't make it true.

For years, advocates insisted that marijuana wasn't addictive, and the news and entertainment media repeated the line. For example, on June 10, 2013, the Canadian news magazine *Maclean's* told readers, "pot is not physically addictive."[2] On December 29, 2001, the *Doonesbury* cartoon character Zonker Harris called marijuana "a non-addictive drug that kills nobody."[3]

Recent research has made it so clear marijuana is addictive that even advocates rarely deny it. Instead, they make light of it. In June 2014, *High Times*, a magazine targeted to marijuana users, dismissed addiction as a political ploy. "What Is Marijuana Addiction?" the headline asked. The article answered: "Marijuana addiction is a scary talking point for the prohibitionists clinging to their jobs ..."[4]

The Indiana NORML website has a post titled "Marijuana Addiction is a Matter of Semantics."[5]

The DPA website says, "The risk of becoming physically and psychologically dependent on marijuana is mild compared to most other drugs."[6] The implication is that it's no big deal and people can handle it on their own.

Marijuana advocates only seem interested in protecting the drug's reputation. But if marijuana addiction is serious, and if some people need help to quit using, then telling them no such need exists is cruel. It's like telling someone with a broken leg he's fine and letting him hobble around in pain. So we should ask: Is marijuana addiction real and is it ever serious? And we should let the scientific evidence answer.

What is addiction?

Addiction is not just physical dependence. If it were, once people had quit for a few weeks they'd never go back to using again.

Addiction is a type of diseased thinking, a mental craving at times so intense that the addict is convinced he must have the drug. Ask any former cigarette smoker; years later most of them still have cravings. However, we can't see cravings, so addiction is recognized by multiple symptoms.

The current psychiatric *Diagnostic and Statistical Manual, DSM-5* describes substance use disorders with eleven symptoms that fall under four categories. Users who have only one or two symptoms have a mild disorder; with five or more symptoms, addiction is considered severe.[7]

We don't diagnose a substance use disorder based on a single event. It has to be a *persistent* pattern of loss of control causing *repeated* problems in the person's life. That's why the criteria include the words "often," "persistent," and "recurrent."

Here are the eleven criteria, grouped under their categories:

Social impairment

1. Recurrent substance use resulting in a failure to fulfill major role obligations at work, school, or home.

2. Continued substance use despite having persistent or recurrent social or interpersonal problems caused by, or exacerbated by, the effects of the substance.

3. Important social, occupational, or recreational activities are given up or reduced because of substance use.

Risky use

1. Recurrent substance use in situations in which it is physically hazardous.

2. The substance use is continued despite knowledge of having a persistent or recurrent physical or psychological problem that is likely to have been caused or exacerbated by the substance.

Impaired control

1. The substance is often taken in larger amounts or over a longer period than was intended.

2. There is a persistent desire or unsuccessful efforts to cut down or control substance use.

3. A great deal of time is spent in activities necessary to obtain the substance, use the substance, or recover from its effects.

4. Craving, or a strong desire or urge to use the substance.

Pharmacological criteria

1. Tolerance, as defined by either of the following:

   a. need for markedly increased amounts of the substance to achieve intoxication or desired effect

   b. markedly diminished effect with continued use of the same amount of the substance

2. Withdrawal, as manifested by either of the following:

   a. the characteristic withdrawal syndrome for the substance

   b. the same (or a closely related) substance is taken to relieve or avoid withdrawal symptoms

In previous editions of the *DSM*, the first two headings—social impairment and risky use—were labeled *substance abuse*. The others—impaired control, tolerance, and withdrawal—are the symptoms of addiction, which was called *substance dependence*.

People who are addicted to alcohol, heroin, or cocaine can show all of these symptoms. But do these symptoms show up in marijuana users as well?

Research on marijuana addiction

In 1998, Alan Budney and several other researchers published an article in *Experimental and Clinical Psychopharmacology* in which they described their research on marijuana users.[8] In the small city of Burlington, Vermont, they ran ads offering free treatment to people with marijuana problems. The researchers excluded anyone with a severe medical or psychiatric problem, and anyone who was also addicted to alcohol or another drug. They were left with 62 people. Here are nine of the symptoms of substance abuse and the percentage of marijuana users seeking help who reported having each one:

Continued use despite problems	97%
Repeated efforts to quit or cut down	86%
Used larger amounts or for longer periods	80%
Experienced withdrawal symptoms	75%
Excessive time spent using	73%
Needed to use to stop withdrawal symptoms	65%
Developed tolerance	63%
Used in hazardous situations or frequent use	53%
Important activities reduced or given up	41%

This study immediately showed two things. First, there are people who want help quitting marijuana. In fact, there are quite a few. One out of every 3,000 people in the Burlington metropolitan area asked for help with a marijuana problem.

Second, almost all the people who asked for help met strict criteria for addiction. Collectively, these addicted marijuana users showed every known symptom of substance use disorder, including withdrawal.

In another paper, published in 2004 in the *American Journal of Psychiatry*, Budney and associates reviewed all the research on symptoms people present when they stop smoking marijuana. Several symptoms showed up so regularly that Budney and his colleagues suggested diagnostic criteria for a marijuana withdrawal syndrome.[9]

Proposed Cannabis Withdrawal Syndrome

Common symptoms

- Anger or aggression
- Decreased appetite or weight loss
- Irritability
- Nervousness/anxiety
- Restlessness
- Sleep difficulties

Less common symptoms

- Chills
- Depressed mood
- Stomach pain
- Shakiness
- Sweating

Budney found at least half of all daily marijuana users experienced several of these withdrawal symptoms when they stopped using, which is more evidence that marijuana works like every other addictive drug.

So in answer to our questions, yes, there are people who get addicted to marijuana and for many of them it's a serious problem. If it were rare, mild, and didn't require treatment, as the Drug Policy Alliance implies, then Budney wouldn't have attracted so many volunteers just from running a few ads.

Needing help isn't the same as wanting it

The marijuana lobby uses another argument to convince us that pot addiction isn't a problem: they say marijuana users usually go into treatment because they're court-referred, not because they need it.[10]

The website DrugWarRant used the federal Substance Abuse and Mental Health Data Archive to compare primary drug of abuse to how they were referred to treatment, and found that 57 percent of marijuana abusers were referred by the criminal justice system. So they concluded that the large numbers of marijuana users in treatment are "more a function of referral than a reflection of actual problems with marijuana use."[11]

But just because someone is referred by the courts doesn't mean they don't need treatment. From my experience, the courts usually refer people who do need help. And court referral isn't just common for marijuana problems, it's common for all drug problems.

Criminal-justice referral is the most likely route into treatment for several commonly abused drugs. The DrugWarRant website found that court referral accounted for 59 percent of crystal meth users in treatment, 39 percent of alcohol abusers and 33 percent of cocaine users.[12] These are often people who needed help but would not have gotten it on their own.

Marijuana advocates apparently assume that if people don't want help, it means they don't need it. But that is not how substance abuse works.

Addiction is a unique illness. People suffering from most diseases want help. But people suffering from addiction usually insist they're fine and refuse treatment. "Leave me alone," they say. "I don't have a problem." The hallmark of the disease of addiction is that people with the illness insist they're not ill. That's why it's called the disease of denial.

The National Survey on Drug Use and Health asked how many people with drug or alcohol problems received any help. The survey estimated that, out of 23 million substance abusers in the United States in 2012, only 11 percent received treatment.[13]

In other words, nearly 90 percent of the people needing treatment got no help at all. With any other illness, that would be a national scandal.

But the problem here isn't that treatment is unavailable. Five percent of the people who needed treatment but didn't get it said they wanted it, but often they couldn't afford it or weren't quite ready to quit using. However, for 95 percent of the substance abusers who didn't get treatment it was because they didn't want it and didn't think they needed it.[14] The vast majority of substance abusers are convinced they don't have a problem even when they clearly do.

So when the marijuana lobby says very few people want help for their marijuana addiction, that doesn't mean their addiction isn't a serious problem. It's far more likely to mean that, like most other substance abusers, they're in denial.

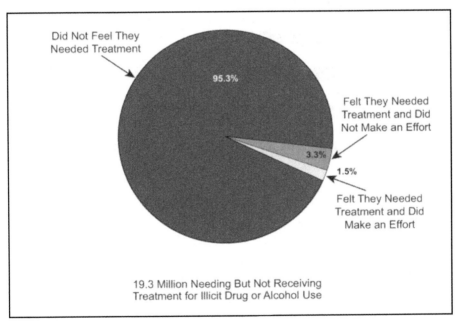

Figure 6-1. From Samhsa.gov, National Survey on Drug Use and Health, 2011[15]

Which addictive drugs cause the biggest problem?

Marijuana addiction is real and, for a lot of users, it's a serious problem. But how big a problem is it?

There are two ways to consider this question. One way is to ask how addictive the drug itself is: What percentage of people who try the drug get hooked? By this standard, heroin and tobacco are the most addictive drugs, and marijuana is one of the least. A 2002 review article by Budney and Moore showed that 23 percent of people who try heroin and 32 percent of people who try tobacco become addicted. With alcohol, the addiction rate is 15 percent, and with marijuana it's only 9 percent.[16]

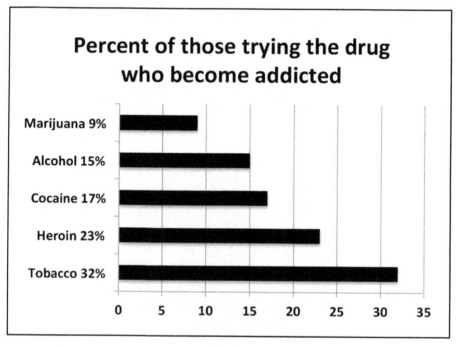

Figure 6-2. Data from Budney & Moore; 2002.[17]

However, addiction rates for marijuana go up significantly when people use it more often or start using regularly in their adolescent years. A study by Columbia University researchers published in 1997 followed more than 9,000 people, and found addiction rates among daily or near daily users were 18 percent for adults and 35 percent for teens. Other studies have obtained different numbers, sometimes higher, but this study was based on a large number of people, so the data are probably reliable.[18]

According to a 2012 survey done by the Partnership for Drug-Free Kids, nearly one in ten American teenagers use marijuana daily or almost daily.[19] For these kids, the addiction rate is going to be much higher than 9 percent. It will be closer to 35 percent. Once again, teenage use is the big problem with marijuana.

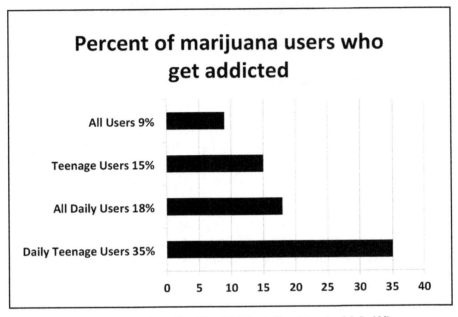

Figure 6-3. Data from Chen, Kandel & Davies[20] and Copeland & Swift[21]

While it's useful to know how addictive a drug is, what really matters is the addiction rate—the percentage of the population that is addicted. Heroin is very addictive, but few people try it, so nationwide addiction rates are comparatively low. Alcohol is far less addictive than heroin, but nearly half the population uses it, so the addiction rate is higher. The 2012 U.S. National Survey on Drug Use and Health provides a useful breakdown of the addiction numbers. Among all Americans, alcohol dependence is three times as common as marijuana dependence.[22]

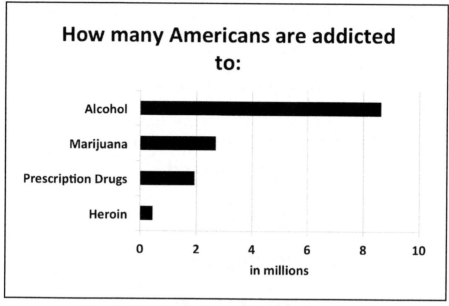

Figure 6-4. Data from Samhsa.gov, 2012, NSDUH Table 5.14a[23]

Among younger Americans—defined in this case as under the age of twenty-six—marijuana addiction closes in. But alcohol addiction still occurs more often.[24]

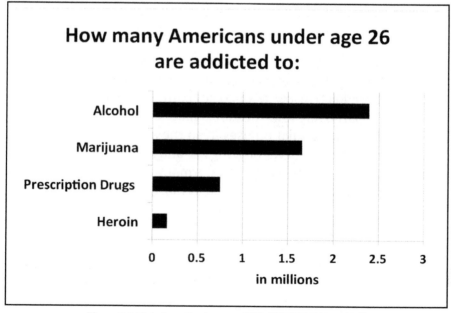

Figure 6-5. Data from Samhsa.gov, 2012, NSDUH Table 5.14a[25]

However, when we just look at Americans under the age of eighteen, marijuana addiction pulls ahead. More teenagers are addicted to marijuana than to alcohol.[26]

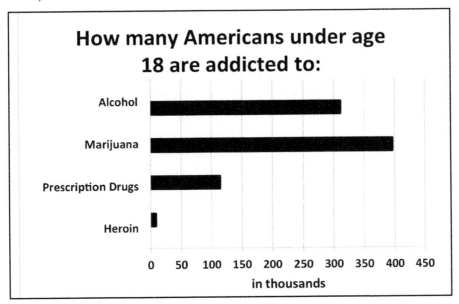

Figure 6-6. Data from Samhsa.gov, 2012, NSDUH Table 5.14a[27]

Why is marijuana addiction a problem?

For their 1998 study, Budney and his colleagues ran a few ads, and dozens of people contacted them for help quitting marijuana. What made them answer the ad? Why did these people want to quit?

Their biggest concerns were that smoking marijuana interfered with their jobs, their relationships, or their health. Three-quarters also said they spent too much time smoking marijuana and spent too much money on it.[28]

Another study, "Clinical Profile of Participants in a Brief Intervention Program for Cannabis Use Disorder," published in 2001, also recruited marijuana users who wanted to quit. Of the 229 participants, more than half gave each of these reasons for wanting to quit: lack of motivation, isolation, neglecting friends, lack of enjoyment, giving up hobbies, depression, going to work stoned, and spouses who wanted them to stop.[29]

A third study, also by Budney and colleagues and called "Marijuana Dependence and Its Treatment," reviewed the research on patients who seek treatment. According to the paper,

> "Adults seeking treatment for marijuana abuse or dependence average more than 10 years of near-daily use and more than six serious attempts at quitting. They continue to smoke the drug despite social, psychological, and physical impairments, commonly citing consequences such as relationship and family problems, guilt associated with use of the drug, financial difficulties, low energy and self-esteem, dissatisfaction with productivity levels, sleep and memory problems, and low life satisfaction. Most perceive themselves as unable to stop, and most experience a withdrawal syndrome upon cessation."[30]

These are the same symptoms we see with other addictive drugs. Marijuana dependence is as real as any other drug addiction. But to get a better feel for what it's like, it helps to hear some individual stories.

Kevin (not his real name) first got stoned at age twenty, but by age twenty-one was smoking up to eight times a day. During his second year of grad school, he began seeing his marijuana use as a problem. Money he had budgeted for food and entertainment was almost all going to marijuana. "I used to save money, but I burned through all my savings. My whole budget got converted to marijuana. I even stole from my grandfather to get money for weed."

His friends were mostly other grad students who didn't smoke marijuana and had no idea how much he used. "I lived a double life and had to hide everything. I was always making friends wait so I could get high before we went anywhere." The problems that got him to quit were depression and loss of interest in school. After several months drug-free, the depression resolved and he enjoyed his studies again.

A second story comes from Jenny Brundin, a reporter for Colorado Public Radio. It's about a seventeen-year-old high school senior named Jynessa, who first got high at age fourteen and really liked it. By her sophomore year, she was smoking marijuana daily. She'd been a straight-A student and catcher on the softball team, but she quit hanging out with goal-oriented friends and lost interest in sports. Then she started ditching school to get high and her grades got worse. She even failed a course. At age seventeen, a family intervention got her into treatment. Was she addicted? In her own words, "It's the same as if your body is telling you that you are hungry, how your stomach growls," Jaynessa says. "It just feels that I need to smoke weed. I'm craving it right now. I can feel it."[31]

In both stories, their lives did not completely fall apart. They were suffering, but to most people they seemed okay. And that's actually a problem.

Addicts and alcoholics usually live in denial until something jolts them awake. They get into an accident, their spouse leaves, they get fired, or they're forced to appear in court. This is called hitting bottom, and it's often a blessing because it gets them to quit. Addiction to marijuana is more subtle and insidious than addiction to other drugs, so it's easier to ignore.

As Robert DuPont, former Director of the National Institute of Drug Abuse and former White House drug czar, said, "Marijuana use, rather than creating deep, sharp and unmistakable bottoms—as most other drugs do—lets marijuana users slowly sink as their ambitions and their performances degrade in ways that are hard to distinguish from who they have become as people."[32] This doesn't make marijuana a kinder, gentler, or softer drug. It just means users can have serious problems without ever admitting they need help. But a damaged life is a damaged life. And with marijuana, the damage can go on for a long time.

Our responsibility to help

Despite what the marijuana lobby would have us believe, research shows that marijuana addiction is common and often severe. Four million Americans and Canadians are addicted to marijuana.[33] This is a public health issue with real-world consequences. Marijuana addiction takes a toll on people's relationships, ambitions, and finances. People who are addicted to alcohol, cocaine, and opiates learn—especially from the entertainment media—that addiction is a disease. Movies, television, and stories on the Internet send the message that treatment works and that people hooked on drugs or alcohol often need help to quit.

Marijuana addicts don't get that message. The marijuana lobby tells them it's not a real addiction, and that they can handle it on their own. The news and entertainment media rarely contradict this. Popular media act as if marijuana dependence doesn't exist. So marijuana addicts often feel embarrassed or guilty about not being able to quit, and many feel so foolish they get no help at all.

The marijuana lobby has a political agenda; that's why they downplay the seriousness of addiction. But just because the marijuana lobby acts as though addiction isn't serious doesn't mean the rest of us should. Marijuana addicts deserve the same acceptance and help society gives to alcoholics and those addicted to hard drugs. They need to know their addiction is real, that it afflicts millions, and that treatment works. Anything less is unfair to the 4 million Americans and Canadians suffering from this disease.

Chapter 7

Why Marijuana Gets Off Easy

Normally, a drug that damaged the teenage brain, caused fatal car wrecks, and got millions of people addicted would be condemned in the press. But marijuana is more often defended—even praised and celebrated.

We treat it differently than other drugs. In the 1970s, conservative William F. Buckley sailed out beyond the U.S. three-mile territorial limit, tried marijuana, and then wrote an editorial for the *National Review* saying it should be legal.[1] If he had said heroin should be legal after using it one time, he'd have been ridiculed or pilloried. Yet with marijuana, he was taken seriously.

This double standard exists because we think marijuana is benign— despite evidence to the contrary. This belief that marijuana is harmless persists for several reasons.

The harm goes unnoticed

When alcoholics get into fights or develop cirrhosis, they know what caused it. When I ask heroin addicts what brought them into treatment, they say things like, "I've lost everything," or "If I don't, I'll be dead or in prison."

But marijuana does damage quietly and insidiously. Marijuana users don't know they have subtle brain damage. They don't see a specific time when they became less interested in school or work. They might not even realize they're not as successful as their friends, and if they do, they don't see the cause. So users often believe it causes no harm at all.

For some people, marijuana can do no wrong

The marijuana lobby has done its job so well that many people can't even wrap their minds around the idea that marijuana is a harmful drug. They can't shake the belief that it's soft and safe. Even journalists, who are taught to question all their own assumptions, have a hard time rethinking marijuana. During the 2010 campaign against medical marijuana in Arizona, I talked to reporters who were surprised that anyone would be against the drug, and were certain that my criticisms of marijuana couldn't possibly be right.

My patients are drug addicts in voluntary treatment because they want to get clean and sober, yet they're often convinced marijuana doesn't count. They regularly tell me, "I don't believe it's addictive," or, "I don't consider marijuana a drug." They even say, "I believe in marijuana," which makes it sound like a religion. It's not a religion, but for some people it really is a firm, unshakable belief. No matter how much bad news comes out about the drug, they never waver in their certainty that marijuana is above reproach.

Popular culture isn't doing its job

However, one of the main reasons so many people assume marijuana is harmless is that's all they hear. For example, people are often surprised to learn marijuana is addictive. After all, they and their friends used it, and none of them got hooked, so how bad can it be?

But direct experience isn't how most people learn about addiction. Most of us don't know any heroin addicts, yet we all know heroin is addictive.

We learn about addiction not so much from friends and family, but from the news media, and from books, TV, the Internet, and movies. Alcoholics and drug addicts are part of popular culture. We might not know them in real life, but we see them on TV.

If people doubt the existence of marijuana addiction, it's because the press and popular media have all but ignored it. We rarely, if ever, see marijuana dependence on television or read about kids failing in school because they get high all day. People think marijuana is harmless because the news and entertainment media don't tell us otherwise.

We can't judge addiction by our own occasional use

Since movies and television don't show the negative effects of marijuana, all people have is their own experience. So they judge marijuana by their own occasional use. It's common for someone to say, "I tried marijuana once and I'm fine, so why is it illegal?" Substitute the word *heroin* or *meth* for *marijuana* and that sentence sounds ridiculous.

People who snorted cocaine a few times are also usually fine. Lots of teenagers try cigarettes a few times, don't get addicted, and suffer no harm. Millions of people use alcohol without ever driving drunk or assaulting anyone. The difference is that no one thinks occasional use of tobacco, cocaine, or alcohol proves those drugs are harmless.

Government surveys are partly to blame for this double standard. They used to focus on how many people had tried marijuana even once, and the press repeated it. Over the years, the *New York Times* has written, "About 24 million Americans have tried marijuana,"[2] "More than 43 million Americans have tried marijuana,"[3] and "About 53 million Americans have tried marijuana."[4] This is the wrong way to report on an addictive drug.

News stories about tobacco never tell us how many people ever smoked even one cigarette. They tell us how many are hooked on tobacco today. The same is true for stories about heroin, cocaine, or crystal meth.

When the press focuses on how many people are addicted to a drug, they're telling us about the misery it causes. When they report on how many people have tried it even once in their lives, the message is: "See? All these people used it and they're fine."

Lumping together everyone who has ever used a drug even once minimizes the problems it causes. If we look at cirrhosis rates for everyone who had even one drink of alcohol in their lives, the threat of liver disease appears small, but it's no small risk for hardcore drinkers. Cancer rates aren't high if we look at everyone who had even one cigarette as a teenager, but if we look at pack-a-day smokers, the rates are sky-high. That's why news reports on drugs of abuse focus on heavy use and addiction—except when the report is about marijuana.

Experimental or occasional use of any drug can't be compared to heavy or addicted use. The guy who snorts one line of coke at a party can't relate to the crackhead who sells his car to buy drugs. And after smoking marijuana only one time, William F. Buckley wouldn't understand the daily, around-the-clock pot smoker any more than someone who has a glass of wine with dinner understands the gutter drunk.

We don't see how long the effect lasts

When legalization was on the ballot in Portland, Maine, in 2013, supporters made an ad with an adult saying, "I prefer marijuana over alcohol because it's less toxic, so there's no hangover."[5]

Is this true? Do marijuana users really not get hangovers? Are people who smoke marijuana in the evening really better employees the next day than people who drank the night before? Probably not. While alcohol hangovers are obvious, marijuana users often have no idea how affected they are the next day, and tend to believe they're not affected at all.

A good description of marijuana's day-after effect comes from an Australian government report with the unsettling title *Cannabis and Its Effects on Pilot Performance and Flight Safety*. The report reviewed dozens of studies, including one that tested pilots, not just the next morning, but a full day after smoking marijuana. It read:

> "The results of this experiment indicated that there were significant effects on pilot performance 24 hours after smoking a single marijuana cigarette. Overall, the pilots demonstrated much more difficulty in aligning with and landing on the runway after delta-9-THC exposure. There were increases in the number and size of aileron changes, the size of elevator changes and the degree of vertical and

lateral deviation from the required flightpath during the approach to land. At 24 hours post-marijuana, the lateral deviation on approach to land was almost twice that of the pre-marijuana test. There was also a significant increase in the distance from the centre of the runway on touchdown. Indeed, one pilot 24 hours after smoking the marijuana landed off the runway entirely. More worrying, perhaps, was their finding that the pilots were not aware of any impairment of their flying performance at 24 hours after marijuana use."[6]

In layman's terms, a pilot making too many aileron and elevator changes is like a first-time driver who keeps jerking the wheel back and forth to stay on the road. A commercial pilot told me, "Doing that a little is sloppy and indicates poor pilot skill; doing it a lot is dangerous."

People think marijuana is harmless because, like these pilots, they don't see the harm it causes.

Marijuana denial

Marijuana causes problems, but users either dismiss those problems or don't even notice them. This belief among users that marijuana doesn't affect them at all when it clearly does is marijuana denial. We see it in adolescents who think they drive better stoned. We see it in adults who insist their teenage marijuana use didn't alter their lives. And we see it with airplane pilots who think they fly safely the day after getting high.

Marijuana denial is the certainty that marijuana can't possibly cause serious problems, even though research says it can and does. This pattern repeats itself with hangovers. When people drink too much, the next morning they know they're not firing on all cylinders. With marijuana, they think they're fine even though research says they're not.

So when marijuana advocates say it's harmless or run ads saying there's no hangover, that's denial. They really believe it, but it doesn't mean we should believe it, too.

It's only metabolites, officer

One of the arguments about drugged driving laws is that marijuana metabolites can be detected in the urine nearly for weeks after the drug is used, and it's not fair to prosecute someone for drugged driving after the drug has worn off.[7] But has it worn off? Marijuana users say it doesn't affect them the next day, and the press never seems to question this assumption, but it's not true. If marijuana is still affecting pilots after twenty-four hours, then it affects every user the next day, even if they don't know it.

And the subtle impairment might continue beyond twenty-four hours. Researchers from the RAND Corporation published a study in 2006 that looked at high school attendance. They found that when substance abusers cut down on their substance use, attendance improved. But with marijuana users, attendance didn't improve until they quit entirely and had abstained for three months.[8] A study that looked at university students found that infrequent users who smoked marijuana about twice a month were two-thirds more likely to drop out of school than nonusers.[9]

One possible explanation for both these findings is that marijuana stays in the body for so long that people only recover from its effects if they completely stop using for at least several weeks. This would mean the metabolites are an accurate gauge of subtle impairment and that marijuana affects users long after they think it has worn off.

Chapter 8

Teenagers Will Make Good Decisions about Drugs—If We Do

Economists use the term *inelastic demand* to describe consumption totally unaffected by outside forces. Price, legality, the opinion of others—none of those make any difference. When the demand for a product is inelastic, people will buy it and use it no matter what.

On January 24, 2014, an investigative journalist debating marijuana legalization on CNN said, "People are going to do this regardless."[1] This is an important pro-marijuana talking point. Parents won't support legalization if it means their kids are more likely to use the drug, so marijuana advocates have to convince us that legalization won't increase teenage use. They have to convince us that people who are going to use the drug will do so "regardless." In fact, all the pro-legalization arguments are based on the idea that we have to adapt our laws and our society to accommodate drug use because drug use will not change.

But is this true? Is the demand for drugs inelastic? In particular, are teenagers really going to use marijuana "regardless"? Is teenage drug use so preordained that nothing can prevent it?

Adolescents respond to information

One part of the Monitoring the Future survey asks teenagers how harmful they think drugs are. It asks what they think of individual drugs, including alcohol and tobacco, and how harmful it is to use the drug once, to use it occasionally, or to use it regularly.[2]

For most drugs, perception of harm remains fairly constant over the years. For example, the survey's data on attitudes toward alcohol use show very little change since 1975.[3] But sometimes opinions change dramatically.

In the 1970s and early 1980s, people thought cocaine was relatively safe. Even after the overdose death of John Belushi, star of the movie *Animal House* and founding cast member of the comedy show *Saturday Night Live*, cocaine was still mostly portrayed as a trendy club drug.[4] This changed overnight with the death of Len Bias, an All-American college basketball player who was the No. 2 pick in the 1986 National Basketball Association draft. Two days after the Boston Celtics picked him, he died of a cocaine overdose.[5]

In the news and entertainment media, cocaine quickly went from being seen as fun and glamorous to dangerous and deadly. As a result, over the next few years, the belief among high school seniors that using cocaine was risky nearly doubled, and their use of cocaine dropped by two-thirds.[6]

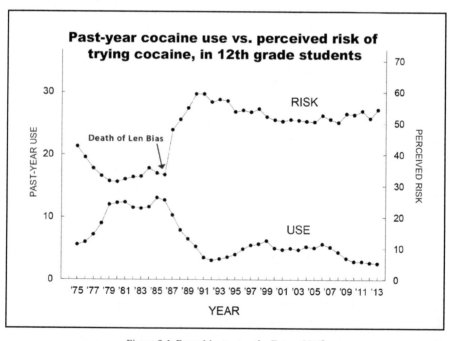

Figure 8-1. From *Monitoring the Future* 2011[7]

So adolescent drug use can change dramatically; they are not going to use "regardless." And we know what gets them to change. Teenagers pay attention to information about the dangers of drugs and adjust their use accordingly.

Note that this information did not come from school-based drug education programs, which have been shown not to work.[8] It came from popular culture and the news and entertainment media, which are very effective at influencing teens.

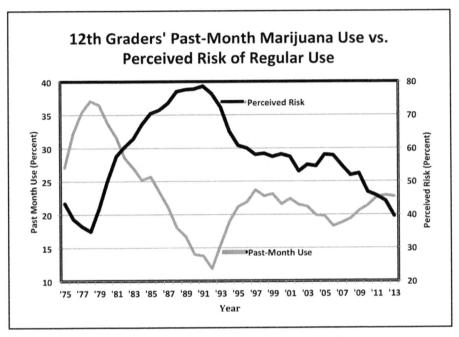

Figure 8-2. Data from *Monitoring the Future* 2013[9]

In the United States, adolescent marijuana use peaked in 1978, shortly after teens' belief that marijuana is harmful reached its lowest point ever. After 1978, when the Parent Movement became a real force, perceived risk went up and use went down. By 1992, the adolescent use of marijuana had reached its lowest point since the Monitoring the Future study began, and the belief among teens that using marijuana was harmful peaked.[10]

The change was huge. In 1978, the percentage of 12th grade students who had used marijuana during the past month was 37 percent. In 1992, it was 12 percent. It dropped by two-thirds.[11]

The change in perceived risk was equally dramatic. The percentage of 12th grade students who thought occasional marijuana use was harmful went from 12 percent in 1978 to 40 percent in 1991, and those who thought regular use was harmful went from 35 percent to 78 percent.[12]

Then, in the mid-1990s, the marijuana lobby went professional. The Marijuana Policy Project and the Lindesmith Center (which later became the Drug Policy Alliance) were founded.[13] Their promotional efforts really picked up steam a decade later when medical marijuana laws expanded, and this is reflected in teenage beliefs about marijuana. Between 2006 and 2013, the belief among teens that marijuana is harmful decreased steadily and the number trying it increased.[14]

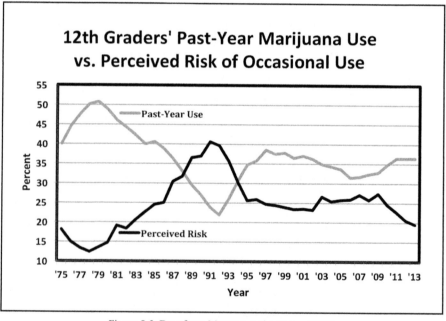

Figure 8-3. Data from *Monitoring the Future* 2013[15]

In sum, the argument that adolescents are going to use marijuana "no matter what" isn't reflected in the research. Teenage marijuana use is very elastic. Most adolescent use, including heavy use, is preventable.

When the media paints an idyllic picture of marijuana, as they did in the 1970s and have recently been doing again, the belief that marijuana is harmful goes down and use goes up. If we want to prevent teenage use, we have to get the news and entertainment media to show the negative side of the drug. The takeaway is that adolescent marijuana use is not written in stone. It can change dramatically, and the direction in which it changes is up to us.

Drug laws keep kids off drugs

The policies we choose have a big effect on whether kids use marijuana. If teenage use is increasing, it means we are choosing the wrong policies.

In a survey published in 2014 in the *International Journal of Drug Policy*, 10 percent of high school students said they did not use marijuana but would if it were legal.[16] This means marijuana laws are keeping many teens from trying the drug. This is an argument against legalization. In fact, it's the strongest argument. The way to prevent teenage use is to send clear, honest, factual, science-based messages that marijuana is harmful. Legalization would send the opposite message.

Keeping marijuana illegal also stops the marijuana industry from advertising and promoting it. Legalization would create an industry that would profit from increased adolescent use. Like the rest of us, adolescents are impressionable—they respond to cultural messages and try the drugs they see adults using. That's why cigarette smoking and underage drinking are such problems. Nothing tells kids "try this drug" like socially accepted adult use. There is no way to legalize marijuana for adults without also making it attractive to adolescents.

Fortunately, drug use is preventable. The lesson we should draw from the Monitoring the Future study is that teenagers mostly stay away from drugs they know are harmful. They will make good decisions if they have good information and good role models. It's the responsibility of adults to make sure they do.

Chapter 9

Legalization Increases Use

Shortly after the 2012 election, when Colorado and Washington voted to legalize marijuana, *Atlantic* magazine interviewed campaign directors to learn how they had won. They won by focusing on women, especially moms. Their advertising campaign promised women four things: "Fewer profits for the cartels. Increased funds for schools. More time for police to 'focus on violent crime.'" And "that their children would not be affected."[1]

To persuade moms that children would not be affected, the marijuana lobby had to convince them that legalization would make it harder for kids to get the drug.

That's a tough argument to make since it's not true. The law of supply and demand says that for any product, a lower price always equals increased use. A RAND Corporation report that studied California's 2010 legalization initiative concluded that, if it passed, marijuana prices would go down, and availability and consumption would both go up by 50–100 percent.[2]

So to convince voters that the law of supply and demand doesn't apply, the marijuana lobby came up with the idea of equating legalization with regulation.

Then, instead of saying we should *legalize* it like alcohol, they said we should *regulate* it like alcohol. And they ran ads reading: "Please, card my son. Regulate the sale of marijuana and help me keep it out of his hands."[3] By using the word *regulate* in this way, they made it sound like they were getting tougher on marijuana when they were actually loosening the laws.

The ploy worked with voters, but it's deceptive for three reasons. First, research on alcohol shows that making a drug more available for adults increases teen use. A study published in the journal *Addiction* found that when young people live in areas with higher concentrations of alcohol outlets, they're more likely to drink, even though it's illegal for them to do so.[4]

Second, the "regulate it like alcohol" argument is based on the belief that marijuana is easier to get than alcohol. Marijuana isn't easier to get than alcohol. The kids themselves say so.

When the Monitoring the Future study asked 8th, 10th, and 12th grade students which drugs were easy to obtain, at every grade level more students said alcohol and tobacco were easy to get. Among 8th graders, nearly 60 percent said alcohol was easy to buy while fewer than 40 percent said that about marijuana.[5] Legal drugs are always more readily available than illegal ones. Why? Because legal drugs are available at every corner market and in most homes.

Thirdly, there's something wrong with this whole comparison. If we want to know how hard it is for teenagers to buy illegal drugs, we shouldn't be using marijuana as our example. In Canada and the United States, marijuana is practically legal. With medical marijuana laws and decriminalization, marijuana is best described as quasi-legal.

If we want to see whether keeping a drug illegal makes it harder for teenagers to buy, we have to look at drugs that are truly illegal. And here the difference is striking. Students at all grade levels say alcohol and marijuana are relatively easy to obtain while prescription drugs and hard drugs are more difficult to get. Among high school seniors, about 20 percent say cocaine, meth, and heroin are easy to find. For alcohol and marijuana, it's more than 80 percent.

The difference is more extreme in 8th grade, which is when many kids start using. Only around 10 percent say illegal drugs are easy to buy, but nearly 60 percent say that about alcohol.[6]

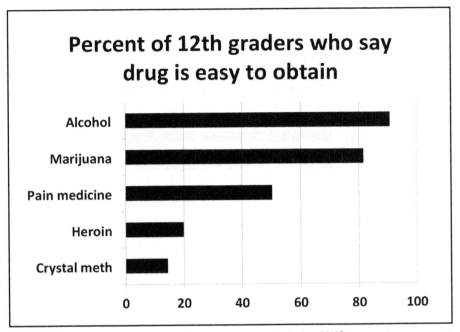

Figure 9-1. Data from Monitoring the Future 2012[7]

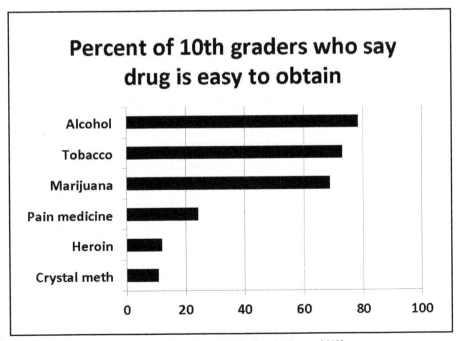

Figure 9-2. Data from Monitoring the Future 2012[8]

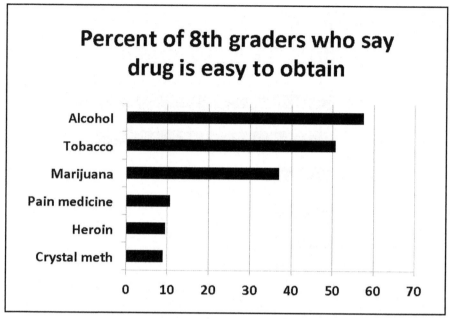

Figure 9-3. Data from Monitoring the Future 2012[9]

The marijuana lobby told voters that marijuana is easily obtained because it's illegal, but the opposite is more likely—kids find marijuana so accessible because it's already quasi-legal. This should come as no surprise. Teenagers always find legal drugs easier to obtain.

Despite what the marijuana lobby told voters in Colorado and Washington, legal drugs are always more widely used. History bears this out:

- In 2011 and 2012, the Florida legislature, along with several Florida cities and counties, banned the sale of synthetic drugs such as bath salts. Within a year, Florida emergency rooms reported a significant drop in the number of people coming in for treatment because of these drugs.[10]

- Prohibition of alcohol is routinely labeled a failure, but when the United States made alcohol illegal in the 1920s, use dropped by two-thirds. It increased again over time, but even at the end of Prohibition, alcohol use was still much lower than it had been before the law was passed. And it wasn't just social drinking that declined; hardcore alcoholism did, too. Deaths from cirrhosis dropped by nearly two-thirds, and drunk and disorderly arrests were cut in half.[11]

- One of the grimmest experiments in drug legalization occurred in 1858, when the British defeated China in the Second Opium War and forced the Chinese to legalize the drug. Their aim was to fund their other colonial adventures by selling opium to the Chinese people, and sadly, it was a great success. Kathleen Lodwick, a Penn State history professor who has written a book about the opium trade in China, said that after legalization, "use of the drug skyrocketed." Millions became addicted. At one point, 27 percent of China's adult male population used opium regularly.[12]

However, the best evidence that legalizing marijuana increases teenage use comes from the U.S. states that legalized medical marijuana. Research shows that adolescent marijuana use is higher in states with these laws.[13] But what's really significant is that teenage marijuana use is also increasing faster in these states. Between 2005 and 2011, teenage use in medical marijuana states went up by 33 percent. In states without these laws, it only increased 6 percent.[14]

There is no way to make marijuana legal for adults without also making it easily available to teenagers. That's what the research tells us, and it's what our experience with alcohol and tobacco should make obvious.

Yet the marijuana lobby told voters that legalizing pot would keep their kids from using it, and many voters apparently believed them.

The pot lobby's gall is remarkable. Teenagers use marijuana at such high rates today because of the marijuana lobby. The marijuana lobby runs ads saying it's medicine. They tell us not to worry about addiction or stoned driving. They've pushed through medical marijuana laws that effectively legalize the drug. They've done everything they can to weaken our laws and encourage use. And then, when teenage use does increase, instead of apologizing for a problem they created, they say it's our fault for making the drug illegal.

Chapter 10

The Fictitious War on Marijuana

In the lead-up to the 2003 U.S. invasion of Iraq, a University of Maryland study found many Americans held three incorrect beliefs that made them support the war. They believed that Iraq's leader was involved in the September 11, 2001, attacks, that Iraq had weapons of mass destruction, and that most of the world supported the war. And the press reinforced these beliefs. As a result, the United States started a war that most Americans later decided was a mistake.[1]

We're now repeating that error with drugs. The marijuana lobby has painted a picture of aggressive police and an out-of-control legal system bent on punishing harmless drug users. As a result, many people have three false beliefs:

1. They believe the War on Drugs is a war on otherwise innocent drug users.

2. They believe prisons are full of people whose only crime was to use marijuana.

3. They believe police zealously and intentionally pursue individuals who use drugs.

None of these beliefs are true.

1. The War on Drugs was never a war on drug users

In 1971, U.S. President Richard Nixon launched the War on Drugs with increased spending to enforce the law against distributors of illegal drugs, not against drug users. In fact, he got rid of mandatory minimum federal sentences for marijuana and other drugs, and called for treating substance abuse instead of simply criminalizing it.[2] At the time, the country's main drug problem was heroin addiction. In his message to Congress, Nixon said:

> "I am proposing the appropriation of additional funds to meet the cost of rehabilitating drug users, and I will ask for additional funds to increase our enforcement efforts to further tighten the noose around the necks of drug peddlers, and thereby loosen the noose around the necks of drug users. At the same time I am proposing additional steps to strike at the "supply" side of the drug equation— to halt the drug traffic by striking at the illegal producers of drugs, the growing of those plants from which drugs are derived, and trafficking in these drugs beyond our borders."[3]

Nixon's plan was to have tough law enforcement against major traffickers and more treatment for users. Of the $155 million he requested, two-thirds was to be spent on drug treatment. The man he put in charge of the drug war, a psychiatrist named Dr. Jerome Jaffe, was a pioneer in devising programs to help inner-city drug addicts. The main weapon in the war on drugs was treatment, not arrest or incarceration. To help addicts, the Nixon administration even gave financial support to the Haight-Ashbury Free Clinic, a symbol of the counterculture that was largely funded by the Grateful Dead.[4]

The legalization lobby says the drug war "failed," but under Nixon it was successful; deaths from drug overdose dropped significantly in most large cities, and so did crime. Drugs remained illegal, but the focus on treatment worked.[5]

So how did our image of the War on Drugs mutate into its exact opposite? Why do so many people believe Nixon used the police to target drug users? And how did the drug war get linked in the public mind to mass incarceration?

For the answer, we need to look at laws passed a decade later under President Ronald Reagan. These Reagan-era laws increased prison time for all types of crime. As a result, the incarceration rate increased, but most of this increased incarceration was for non-drug crimes.

However, the marijuana lobby conflated Nixon's drug war with the Reagan-era "lock-'em-up" policies and told everyone that drug laws caused prison overcrowding. And they repeated it so often that many people now believe it.

Here's what actually caused incarceration to skyrocket. In the 1980s and early 1990s, conservatives pushed through tougher penalties for all types of crime, not just drug crime. Lawmakers believed longer sentences would keep dangerous criminals off the streets. So nearly every state increased the length of prison terms for all types of crime. Some also passed persistent felony offender laws—a.k.a. three strikes laws, which locked people up for life after their third felony, no matter how minor.[6]

Several states and the federal government abolished parole, forcing inmates to serve entire sentences. And in the 1980s, Congress passed federal sentencing guidelines and established mandatory minimum sentences for several crimes. Many states also passed mandatory minimums.[7]

Crime prevention suffered. Nixon spent most of the drug war money on treatment because that was the best way to prevent crime.

Under Reagan, money for treatment was slashed and law enforcement increased. In inflation-adjusted dollars, the 1986 federal drug treatment budget was only one-fifth of what it had been in 1973.[8] Under President Reagan, the United States all but stopped trying to prevent crime and instead relied on locking up criminals for as long as possible. As a result, the U.S. prison population climbed by more than 400 percent.[9]

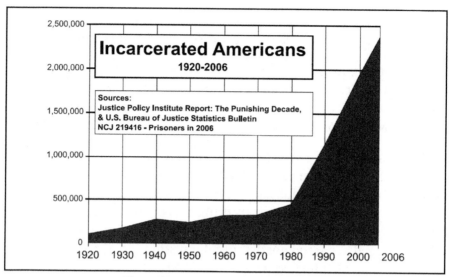

Figure 10-1. From the Wikimedia Commons[10]

Most of the mass incarceration had nothing to do with drug crime. According to the Pew Center on the States, between 1990 and 2009, the average length of time served increased by 37 percent for violent crimes, by 36 percent for drug crimes, and by 24 percent for property crimes.[11] All types of crime contributed to prison overcrowding.

In particular, neither Nixon's War on Drugs nor laws making drug possession illegal caused mass incarceration. In fact, Michael Massing, author of *The Fix*, said the United States could undo the damage by abandoning the Reagan-era laws and going back to Nixon's policies.[12]

One former White House policy advisor believed Nixon only used the draconian term "war on drugs" to appease his party's right wing.[13] Unfortunately, people remember the military-sounding language, but not the actual plan, which might have succeeded had it not been mostly jettisoned under Reagan. The sad story of the drug war is that it went from mostly treatment to mostly interdiction overseas, which is far less effective. However, it was never about criminalizing drug users. There was never a war on drug possession.

How the marijuana lobby redefined the drug war

Pro-legalization groups wanted to vilify drug laws, so they rewrote history; they used the term "drug war" to mean laws against possession. This allowed them to create a very compelling myth: The drug war, they said, is the intentional pursuit and mass incarceration of innocent people whose only crime was to use drugs, filling our prisons to unheard-of levels. They could then say the only solution to mass incarceration is to end the drug war by legalizing drugs.

It's a fiction that mischaracterizes the drug war and misstates the reason for prison overcrowding, but the marijuana lobby repeated its version over and over until nearly everyone believed it. And they're still trying to convince us.

- This is from the Drug Policy Alliance website: "The United States imprisons more people than any other nation in the world—largely due to the war on drugs."[14]

- On the ACLU website, one page had the sub-heading: "Campaign to End Mass Incarceration." Below that, the ACLU wrote, "Here's our list of what needs to be done," and first on the list was "End the War on Drugs."[15]

- Here's a quote about prison overcrowding from the Marijuana Policy Project: "We don't really need congressional hearings to determine where those millions of prisoners come from. Many are nonviolent drug offenders—disproportionately poor and African-American. Nixon declared war on them more than three decades ago, and we've been paying for it ever since. Nixon's favorite drug war target, of course, was the marijuana user."[16]

The implication in these statements is untrue. Most people in U.S. prisons were convicted of non-drug crimes, so even if we freed everyone imprisoned for a drug crime, we'd still have mass incarceration.[17] And vilifying Nixon for a time he was sensible and compassionate seems especially unfair.

However, Nixon's dishonesty is legendary, so there's poetic irony to the marijuana lobby twisting the public perception of his drug war into its exact opposite.[18] If anyone could appreciate how crafty the marijuana lobby has been, it would be Richard Nixon.

2. Incarceration solely for marijuana possession is incredibly rare

On its website, NORML has an article titled "Decriminalizing Pot Will Reduce Prison Population." The article said decriminalizing drugs, along with "modest reforms in sentencing and parole," could cut the prison population in half.[19] In a *Washington Post* op-ed, Katrina vanden Heuvel said that legalizing marijuana would "drastically decrease incarceration rates."[20]

Is this true? If we decriminalized marijuana and stopped prosecuting people whose only crime was simple possession, would it significantly decrease our prison population?

Two researchers set out to answer this question. In a paper published in *Contemporary Drug Problems*, Jonathan Caulkins and Eric Sevigny looked closely at Bureau of Justice Statistics reports for 1997. In that year, 274,324 state and federal inmates in the United States were in prison for drug crimes. That was 24 percent of all inmates. Most of these inmates were in prison for selling drugs, but 102,232 inmates— or 9 percent of all inmates—were convicted of drug possession.[21]

Normally that's all the information the Bureau of Justice Statistics provides, and pro-legalization groups use this data to claim that prisons are packed with people whose only crime was using drugs. However, in 1997, more than 18,000 inmates were interviewed as part of a state and federal multi-prison survey. Caulkins and Sevigny used the data to estimate how many inmates were truly guilty of nothing more than possessing drugs for personal use.

They made a serious effort to identify those inmates arrested for their role in drug trafficking or for a crime that had nothing to do with drugs. As they wrote in their article, the question they wanted to answer was, "How many people are imprisoned in the United States for drug-law violations simply because they used drugs, not because they played some role in drug distribution or other offenses?"

They found that many of the 9 percent of inmates in prison for possession were actually convicted of possession with intent to sell. Many others admitted in interviews that they'd been selling drugs. And many more were caught with such large amounts that it was clearly not for personal use. Police often claim that they use possession charges when they don't have enough evidence to make trafficking charges stick, and evidently this is true.

When the researchers excluded all the inmates who had clearly been selling drugs and not just using them personally, it left an estimated 41,047—3.6 percent of the nationwide prison population—who were incarcerated for simple possession and, according to the researchers, "not clearly involved in drug distribution."

When the researchers looked further, they found that half of that 3.6 percent had committed a non-drug crime along with drug possession and were in prison for both. For example, they were in prison for burglary and drug possession, or assault and drug possession. These people all had other reasons besides drugs for being in prison. So the researchers excluded all those people, which brought the estimated number of inmates convicted only of simple possession down to 20,479, or 1.8 percent of all inmates.

Then the researchers dug even deeper, looking at more data on these possession-only inmates. Half of them were convicted as part of a plea bargain. They pleaded down from a more serious crime or from multiple counts. So they pleaded guilty to possession, but they'd been arrested for something else, such as for selling drugs or for a violent or property crime.

Approximately one-quarter said the drug they were in prison for was one they themselves didn't use. That's a common story among drug dealers. A lot of people who sell meth and heroin know better than to use those drugs themselves.

The authors therefore excluded inmates convicted of possession as part of a plea bargain or who said they never used the drug they were convicted of possessing. That brought the estimated number of people in prison solely for possession of drugs down to 7,340, or 0.6 percent of all state and federal prison inmates.

Lastly, the authors excluded everyone who had been arrested for selling drugs in the past or who admitted to hanging out with friends while they were selling drugs. That brought the estimated number down to 5,380, or 0.5 percent of all prison inmates.

To sum it up:

- 274,324 are in prison for drug crimes. Of those in prison for drug crimes,
- 102,232 are in prison for possession with no trafficking charge. Of those,
- 41,047 are in prison for possession with no obvious evidence of drug sales. Of those,
- 20,479 are in prison for possession only, with no other crime and no evidence of drug sales. Of those,
- 7,340 are in prison for possession only with no plea bargain, no other crime and no evidence at all of drug sales. And, of those,
- 5,380 are in prison for possession only with no plea bargain, no other crime, and no current or past evidence of drug sales.

And that's possession of all drugs. Most people in prison for possession are there for heroin, cocaine, or crystal meth. In this study, the authors found only 5–7 percent of those people were in prison for possession of marijuana. Taking 7 percent of 5,380 gives approximately 377 inmates incarcerated solely for possession of marijuana.

So, in 1997, approximately 400 people, or 0.05 percent of all prison inmates, were in U.S. prisons solely for possession of marijuana. That's one-third of one-tenth of 1 percent of the prison population.

That's the lowest possible estimate based on their data. The researchers came up with a range rather than a single number, and estimated that 800–2,300 inmates were incarcerated for possession alone without any evidence of involvement in distribution. Even their highest estimate—2,300 individuals in prison just for marijuana use— would still only be two-tenths of 1 percent of the prison population.

These figures should surprise no one. Police tell us they actively pursue drug sellers, but not drug users, and that's what the prison statistics show. These numbers are so low the researchers concluded that "marijuana decriminalization would have almost no impact on prison populations..."[22]

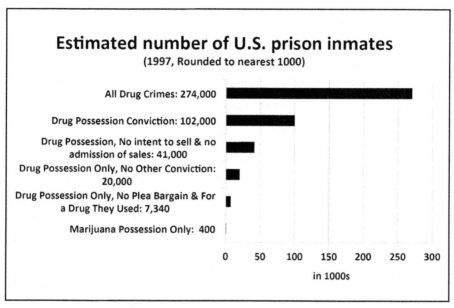

Figure 10-2. Data from Caulkins & Sevigny.[23]

It takes a special effort to get incarcerated for marijuana

Legalization advocates say that any marijuana user could be arrested and imprisoned. However, about 20 million Americans used marijuana in 1997[24] whereas only about 400 were in prison solely for possession. Were these 400 incarcerated at random, or did they do something unique?

Oklahoma has some of the toughest marijuana laws in the nation, yet defense attorneys interviewed for an article in *The Oklahoman* agreed that people arrested for marijuana possession mostly get treatment or probation. One prosecutor said, "You have to work very hard to go to prison on drug possession cases in Oklahoma.[25]

This is true everywhere, especially for marijuana. Police aren't out looking for marijuana users, so when anyone says they're incarcerated only for possession we should ask how they were caught. There's always more to the story. I've spoken with four inmates or former inmates who told me they were in prison only for marijuana possession. Here's what I learned about them:

- One was pulling a rental truck filled with the drug.

- The second was actually arrested for robbery, but was searched and marijuana was found. He said the store he robbed refused to press charges—they apparently didn't want the publicity—so the judge threw the book at him for the marijuana.

- The third was on probation when the police pulled him over and found marijuana in his glove box. I asked why they pulled him over, and he said he was driving without a license. So I asked how the police knew this, and it was because they had pulled him over the day before. In other words, he was on probation and had just been caught driving without a license, and then the next day he drove again anyway and carried an illegal drug. This is not just bad judgment, but a pattern of violating the law.

- The fourth really was in prison only for marijuana. He smoked marijuana outdoors, insisting it was his right. But his neighbors didn't want their children seeing drug use, so they called the police—repeatedly. After this man's ninth arrest, the judge made him serve some time. His story illustrates that it's not easy to get incarcerated just for marijuana. It takes real persistence.

Incarceration solely for possession is rare, but marijuana advocates want us to believe that it's common and could happen to anyone. In a 2015 effort to convince Congress to legalize medical marijuana nationally, Senator Rand Paul (R-Kentucky) stood with several medical marijuana users and said, "If one of these patients up here takes marijuana in the states where it's illegal, they will go to jail."[26] That is not true. But the campaign for legalization depends on convincing us that jails and prisons are filled with otherwise innocent marijuana users. So to sway public opinion, advocates like Senator Paul make claims that research long ago proved to be false.

In a September 2014 interview, pro-legalization billionaire Richard Branson said, "If my children had a drug problem, I'd want them to be helped, not sent to prison."[27] That's already what happens today.

Branson implied that anyone caught possessing drugs risks being sent to prison, but that's not the case. If his children were caught with drugs, they would probably get help. Judges want addicts in treatment, not jail. So the average person who uses marijuana or any other illegal drug is at virtually no risk of going to prison for possession.

3. Police do not pursue individual drug users

As people learned that prisons are not full of innocent drug users, the marijuana lobby changed tactics and started complaining about the number of people arrested. The DPA website says, "Marijuana arrests are the engine driving the U.S. war on drugs. Nearly half of all drug arrests each year are for marijuana-related offenses, the overwhelming majority of which are for personal possession."[28]

They are correct about one thing: the arrests are real. In 2009, the United States had more than 13 million arrests. Twelve percent, just over 1.5 million, were for drug crimes. And nearly 80 percent of those were for possession. Based on data from prior years, approximately 42 percent of the drug possession arrests were for marijuana.[29]

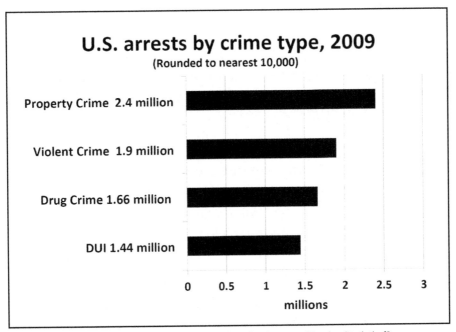

Figure 10-3. Data from U.S. Dept. of Justice Bureau of Justice Statistics[30]

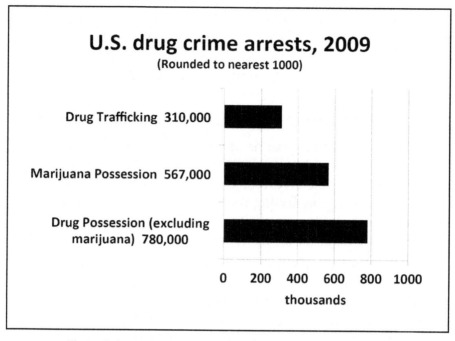

Figure 10-4. Data from U.S. Dept.of Justice Bureau of Justice Statistics[31]

The arrest picture is almost the opposite of the incarceration picture: 90 percent of those in prison for drug crimes are traffickers and barely anyone is there for possession; whereas 80 percent of drug arrests are for possession. And while the incarceration rate for marijuana possession is minuscule, arrests for marijuana possession make up nearly half of all drug crime arrests.

This raises two questions:

1. We apparently don't think drug possession is a crime deserving of incarceration, so why are so many people arrested for it?

2. Do all these arrests for possession represent drug policy gone mad, as the marijuana lobby claims, or is there another explanation?

There is a much more likely explanation: For the most part, police aren't looking for drug users; they find them unintentionally. Most arrests for possession probably happen incidentally when someone is searched after they're stopped or arrested for an entirely different reason. The real cause of the high arrest rate for possession is the high rate of drug abuse among criminals, and the tendency of drug abusers to always carry their drugs with them.

Who commits crime?

In the developed world, crime is mostly a symptom of substance abuse. According to *Behind Bars*, a report by the Center for Addiction and Substance Abuse, nearly two-thirds of all jail and prison inmates meet criteria for the diagnosis of substance abuse. This is seven times the rate of substance abuse found in the general population, which, according to the National Survey on Drug Use and Health, is 8.7 percent of everyone over age eleven.[32]

There's also research showing how many criminals used drugs shortly before being arrested. The Arrestee Drug Abuse Monitoring survey (ADAM) does annual drug screens on a sample of those arrested for all types of crime in five major cities. In 2012, the percentage testing positive for any illicit drug ranged from 62 percent in Atlanta to 86 percent in Chicago. The average across the five cities was 75 percent. The most commonly used drug was marijuana, ranging from 37 percent of those screened in Atlanta to 58 percent in Chicago. The average was 49 percent.[33]

I work with substance abusers. The patients I treat get high several times a day and carry their drugs everywhere. They never want to be far from their supply. They even carry drugs when committing a crime. First of all, most crime is spontaneous, not pre-meditated, and often committed by people who are under the influence. But even when it's planned out, getting caught is never part of their calculation, while getting high is.

According to the ADAM survey, at least three-quarters of all criminals use illegal drugs. If they carry their drugs at all times, they'll get arrested for drugs as well as for the crime they were caught committing.

This is the most likely explanation for the half million marijuana arrests every year. There are exceptions, of course. There are stories of police asking people if they're carrying marijuana, and then arresting them when they show it. But in most cases, police aren't out to find marijuana; it finds them.

Evidence that more criminals are carrying marijuana

On November 12, 2012, the *Vancouver Sun* ran an article with the headline, "Pot possession charges in B.C. up 88 per cent over last decade." According to the article, there were 3,774 marijuana possession charges in 2011. It also included quotes from three legalization advocates who painted a picture of police actively pursuing marijuana users.[34]

One quote was from a criminology professor who said, "It's a police-driven agenda..."[35]

Another quote was from the former editor of Cannabis Culture magazine, who said he was working on a referendum to prevent police from "searching, seizing or arresting anyone for simple cannabis possession."[36] That makes it sound like police are intentionally pursuing people whose only crime is marijuana possession.

The *Sun* also quoted the executive director of the pro-legalization Beyond Prohibition Foundation, who asked, "What are we doing continuing to waste very scarce and shrinking prosecutorial and judicial resources going after marijuana offenders?"[37] No one opposed to legalization was quoted, but there is another side to the story.

Kale Pauls, an officer with the Royal Canadian Mounted Police (RCMP), says they're misinterpreting the data. According to his master's thesis and a report he co-wrote for the Centre for Public Safety and Criminal Justice Research, barely anyone is charged for marijuana possession in British Columbia.[38] That would mean police are not actively pursuing marijuana offenders and the province is not wasting resources.

Here's how the data is misinterpreted: in British Columbia, each time someone is stopped or arrested for any crime, police are required to create a file for this one *incident*. The file includes every crime the person committed as part of this incident, whether they're charged for that crime or not. Police are also required to record how the file was disposed of, or *cleared*. If the person is charged with a crime, the case is recorded as "cleared by charge." If the person gets a warning but no charges, the file is recorded as "cleared by other means."

But there's a strange quirk in the rules. If the person is charged for one crime in an incident, the entire file and all of the offences contained in that file are listed as "cleared by charge." If someone is arrested and charged with a crime, and the police also confiscate marijuana but don't lay any charges for it, the marijuana possession would still be listed as part of the incident file that is "cleared by charge." So if the police arrest someone for burglary and find marijuana on the person when they are searched, the offender might only be charged with burglary. But because of the way in which police are required to report the data, Statistics Canada will also record the marijuana possession as "cleared by charge."

That's right: "marijuana possession, cleared by charge" doesn't mean the person was charged with marijuana possession. It's confusing, so it's hard to blame the *Vancouver Sun* for misreading the data. Still, their article, including the headline, got it wrong.

Here's the evidence: According to Pauls, in 94 percent of the cases recorded as marijuana possession cleared by charge, the person was also charged with another crime. When marijuana possession was the only crime, 96 percent of those cases were cleared "otherwise," which means the person was not charged with any offence. Those are often the cases that got only a warning.

In other words, when marijuana was the only crime, the individual was almost never charged with any offence. When someone was charged with an offence and marijuana was present, they were almost always charged for another crime, and not for marijuana possession. So almost no one was charged with marijuana possession.[39]

I say "almost no one" because in 249 of the cases in which marijuana possession was the only crime, the suspect was charged. But in the other 93 percent of cases that the *Vancouver Sun* called marijuana charges there were probably no marijuana charges at all.[40]

So why were 249 people charged with marijuana possession? According to retired RCMP officer Chuck Doucette, the most common reason for a stand-alone possession charge is that someone suspected of selling drugs was caught with drugs but without enough evidence to corroborate a charge of possession for the purpose of trafficking. Another common scenario is that someone on probation or parole is arrested for domestic violence but the spouse decides not to prosecute. Police often find drugs in these cases. But rarely is anyone charged with possession of marijuana unless they are also involved in other criminal behavior.

What happened to those 249 people charged with marijuana possession alone is also telling. Only forty-two were convicted, and of those, only seven served any time—four served one day in jail, two served one week, and one served two weeks.[41]

So the *Vancouver Sun* article was very misleading. It overstated the number of people charged with marijuana possession and then quoted three pro-marijuana activists who gave the impression that police are deliberately pursuing otherwise innocent marijuana users.

What the statistics actually show is that police almost never lay charges against otherwise innocent marijuana users. Those people almost always get warnings. (And we might not need the word "almost.")

The term for this type of restraint is *de facto decriminalization*; the laws are still on the books, but they're not enforced. And that means marijuana possession is already effectively decriminalized in British Columbia.

* * *

I speculated that the arrest rate for marijuana possession is sky-high in the United States because substance abusers, who make up the majority of all criminals, carry their drugs with them. In British Columbia, this is not speculation. The numbers reported in the *Vancouver Sun* show that B.C. police often find marijuana on people who get arrested for other reasons. In fact, the statistics show that over the ten years ending in 2012, the number of criminals carrying marijuana at the time of arrest increased by 88 percent.

The best explanation for the huge number of marijuana arrests throughout the rest of Canada and in the United States is the same: An increasing number of criminals use marijuana and carry it with them at all times, even when they commit crimes. The marijuana is found incidentally when people are stopped or arrested for different reasons. Police don't actively pursue the drug; it comes to them.

Legalization won't free up police time

There's a "War Against Marijuana Consumers," the NORML website says, that "places great emphasis on arresting people for smoking marijuana."[42] The ACLU says police nationwide have made the "War on Marijuana" a priority, and waste billions of taxpayer dollars on the "aggressive enforcement of marijuana possession laws."[43] It might sound like a dangerous time for drug users. However, there is no such war.

Police are not interested in marijuana. They don't dress in plain clothes at rock concerts to nab people who light up. They don't patrol university dorms with drug-sniffing dogs. There are no big sweeps to round up marijuana users. They don't even make arrests at some of the public marijuana protests.[44]

Big city police departments have special units to investigate homicide, fraud, child abuse, auto theft, stolen property, and many other major crimes, but there is no special unit to investigate marijuana possession. Police don't go undercover to flush it out and don't keep lists of suspects who might be using the drug.

They don't even pursue leads. Police never say, "We got word this person is smoking marijuana; let's stake the place out and see." Call them with a tip about stolen property, and they'll take you seriously. Call about your neighbor who gets high inside his own home, and they'll treat you like a crank.

The war on marijuana is a fiction, but a useful one. It was used to convince voters that legalization would free up police to pursue serious crimes. But police don't spend time or money looking for marijuana users, so there's nothing to free up.

Police departments don't want to say they're not enforcing the law, so they say marijuana possession is not a priority. It means they don't go looking for it, but they often find it while investigating other offences that are a priority.

The pot lobby wants the public to believe that marijuana arrests and the pursuit of serious crime are separate entities and that police can choose one or the other. Ironically, possession arrests only seem to happen when police *are* pursuing other crime.

Exploiting the oppressed

As part of its pro-legalization campaign, the marijuana lobby highlighted two groups of people who are seriously mistreated by the U.S. criminal justice system. One group is the million or so Americans in prison who probably would not have been incarcerated before the Reagan-era "tough on crime" legislation. The other is people of color.

The marijuana lobby has successfully drawn attention to the unequal treatment these two groups have received, and that's good. However, legalizing marijuana would not help either group. And focusing on legalization distracts attention from the real source of the injustices.

Legalizing drugs would free the wrong people from prison

I've worked in several jails and prisons and met many inmates. Some seemed like they shouldn't have been there at all, and many had sentences that seemed far too long for what they'd done. I've also met inmates with schizophrenia, locked up for obeying the voices they hear, who told me the only time they got medicine for their hallucinations was in prison. I've met inmates with severe head injuries, PTSD, and other psychiatric problems who never got treatment on the outside. Most of all, I've met men and women with drug and alcohol problems who had never received treatment and claimed it had never been offered or suggested.

The majority of people in prison have treatable problems, and treatment could keep them from coming back over and over. Many of them have received unfairly long sentences. Quite a few are veterans who fought for their country, yet never got the help that would have kept them out of trouble. But most of these people aren't in prison for drug crimes so legalizing drugs would not help them at all.

Legalization would not free any of the people whose sentences for violent and property crimes are too long, and it would not give people with psychiatric illness or substance abuse the treatment they need to avoid returning to prison.

Instead, legalizing drugs would free the inmates with whom I sympathized the least: dealers who sold drugs they didn't use themselves. These inmates knew how deadly crystal meth and heroin could be, and didn't care. It was just easy money. No untreated disease got them to commit crimes. They weren't drunk, high, or hearing voices. Drug dealers are in prison because their greed overrode their humanity.

Nearly 90 percent of people in state prison for drug crimes are in for trafficking. In federal prison, it's nearly 100 percent. Drug legalization advocates would come to the aid of these drug dealers while ignoring hundreds of thousands who, in my opinion, really are locked up unfairly.

By implying that high incarceration rates are mainly caused by drug arrests, the marijuana lobby is distracting attention from the real cause of prison overcrowding. And by claiming the solution is legalization, they're distracting us from the real cure.

Minorities and marijuana

In June 2013, the ACLU released a study showing black Americans are nearly four times as likely to be arrested for marijuana possession as whites, even though both races smoke marijuana at the same rate. The exact figure was 3.73 times more likely.[45]

According to the ACLU, America's police have carried out a "War on Marijuana" with "staggering racial bias."[46] From the news reports, it sounded like police were intentionally rounding up African-American marijuana users.

However, the most likely explanation for marijuana arrests is that police find the drug incidentally while searching someone who's been arrested or stopped for an entirely different reason. So, if blacks are arrested for marijuana possession at four times the rate of whites, it's probably because they are stopped, searched, and arrested for reasons unrelated to marijuana at four times the rate of whites. And they are.[47]

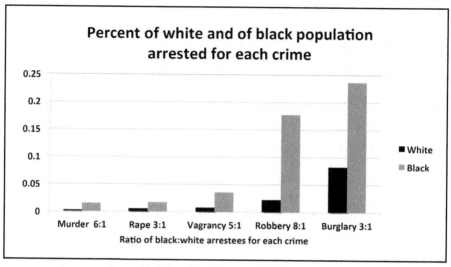

Figure 10-5. Data from Bureau of Justice Statistics[48]

African-Americans are arrested for almost all crimes at much higher rates than whites, and it has nothing to do with marijuana. African-Americans are arrested for violent crime at 3.9 times the rate of whites and for property crime at 2.6 times the rate. African-Americans are 2.8 times more likely than whites to be arrested for rape or burglary, 4.5 times more likely to be arrested for vagrancy, 5.9 times as likely to be arrested for murder, and 7.7 times more likely to be arrested for robbery. They're also stopped and searched much more frequently, even when there is no arrest.[49]

I'm not saying this is fair because it's definitely not. According to biological research, race is an imaginary distinction man made up based on a handful of superficial characteristics. From a scientific perspective, race is impossible to define and doesn't even exist.[50] We should probably use the terms "so-called white people" and "so-called black people" to free ourselves from this invalid notion of race.

So while the statistics tell us African-Americans commit proportionally more crime, this can't be attributed to racial differences because there are none. The high arrest rate for African-Americans for all crimes is due to something wrong with our criminal justice system or something wrong with our culture—or both. And we know it's both.

Racial profiling is real, and so is the United States' long history of discrimination. Many of the theories that seek to explain the higher crime rate among African-Americans point to persistent prejudice and mistreatment.[51] The legalization lobby wants to make marijuana laws the villain in this story, but the real culprit is racism.

However, that didn't stop newspapers across the United States from using the ACLU study as a slam on marijuana laws. It didn't stop the *New York Times* from writing a headline that started with "Blacks Are Singled Out for Marijuana Arrests," and then failing to mention the high black arrest rate for all crimes.[52] It didn't stop E.J. Dionne, of the *Washington Post*, from writing that marijuana should be legalized because it's unfair that blacks are arrested for possession at such high rates.[53] And it didn't stop the *New York Times* or *Washington Post* from using the articles to discuss legalization—even though no one suggests we legalize robbery or any other crime for which blacks are disproportionately arrested.[54] The ACLU and the press took a huge racial injustice and used it, not to aid those suffering from discrimination, but to promote legalization.

I am not defending the police. There is plenty of police harassment directed toward African-Americans. What I'm saying is that African-Americans are not singled out for marijuana; they're singled out for being black.[55] Drug laws are not the problem; the problem is racism.

Besides, legalizing marijuana would not help the African-American community. The drug is just as harmful for black teenagers as for whites, and it interferes with education and employment for African-Americans as much as for anyone else. The alcohol and tobacco industries already target black neighborhoods with advertising; a legal marijuana industry would only exploit them more. The marijuana lobby is using the plight of African-Americans to promote legalization, but legalization would make their plight worse.

Incidentally, what's not in the news coverage is the $7 million pro-marijuana billionaire Peter Lewis gave to the ACLU.[56] If a group took money from the oil or coal industry and came out with a study questioning global warming, that funding would be part of every news report and the research would be discredited. But for marijuana, the press apparently ignored this conflict of interest.

More evidence of media bias

The same week the ACLU released its report, the University of Maryland also released a study on marijuana. According to *USA Today*, this ten-year research project found that university students who used marijuana studied less, skipped more classes, earned lower grades, dropped out at higher rates, and were more likely to be unemployed later in life. "Even infrequent users—those who smoked about twice a month"—had more problems in school than nonusers.[57]

The quality of this research was very good, and the subject—the education of our youth—is certainly serious. But when I did a Google news search in June 2013, the ACLU story showed up in 193 news sources while the University of Maryland study showed up in one.[58]

Given a choice between a research study critical of marijuana and one that supports the drive for looser laws, the U.S. news media decided overwhelmingly to promote legalization.

Chapter 11

"Medical" Marijuana Makes Liars of Us All

When I first heard about medical marijuana, I took the idea seriously.[1] Most people do. But I didn't learn the real story until a patient excitedly told me how great medical marijuana was. Why, I wondered, was this twenty-year-old drug addict so revved up about treatment for elderly cancer patients?

I soon found out.

The idea of medical marijuana didn't come from doctors, or patient advocacy groups, or public health organizations, or the medical community. The ballot initiatives for medical marijuana laws were sponsored and promoted by pro-legalization groups.

That wouldn't be a problem if medical marijuana laws did what they promised. But calling something "medical" doesn't mean it is. Often when I criticize medical marijuana laws, someone argues back by pointing out that the drug is good for nausea, muscle spasms, pain, and other symptoms. That's true, but irrelevant.

Marijuana *the plant* contains chemicals with medical value; I don't dispute that. But this chapter is about the problem with medical marijuana *laws*, not a discussion of the plant's medically useful chemicals.

How medical marijuana laws work

Political campaigns sell marijuana laws to the voting public with ads that feature cancer patients using marijuana for nausea. But it's a bait and switch.

The patients using medical marijuana in real life are dispropor-tionately young and male, and few of them have serious illnesses. A 2007 study that looked at over 4,000 medical marijuana patients in California found their average age was thirty-two, three-quarters were male, and 90 percent had started smoking marijuana as teenagers.[2] That's not who we voted to help.

The pain loophole

Almost all of the marijuana patients get their marijuana for pain, which is allowed by most state medical marijuana laws. Data from 2012 show that in Arizona, 90 percent of the marijuana patients claimed pain while only 4 percent got the drug for cancer. In Colorado, 94 percent claimed pain; 3 percent claimed cancer. In Oregon, 94 percent also claimed pain.

A 2014 study that used data from seven states found that 91 percent of all the medical marijuana patients got their marijuana for pain while only 3 percent reported cancer. AIDS, glaucoma, Alzheimer's, Hepatitis C and ALS accounted for another 2 percent.[3]

There are several reasons to be suspicious of all these people claiming pain. First, pain is every drug addict's favorite complaint. There's no lab test for pain, so it's easy to fake and impossible to disprove. Doctors regularly see patients who exaggerate pain to get drugs.

Second, someone who uses marijuana as pain medicine has to be stoned nearly all the time. Most people don't want that. The marijuana lobby says patients prefer marijuana because they don't like the high from opiate pain medicines, but a pain specialist I spoke with said patients who don't want opiates don't want any psychoactive drug. They use ibuprofen.

However, the main reason for suspicion is that these cardholders claiming pain are disproportionately young and male, while pain patients are typically older and female.

Researchers know what percentage of pain patients should be male or female. A 2001 study at the University of Sydney Pain Management Research Centre found that 54 percent of people with chronic pain were women, and the most common ages were late sixties for men and early eighties for women.[4] Researchers in Ireland looked at who actually got help for chronic pain, and found twenty-three published studies answering this question. After reviewing this research, they concluded, "factors associated with help-seeking were increasing age, female gender, pain severity and disability."[5]

According to the book *Chronic Pain: A primary care guide to practical management* by Dawn Marcus, M.D., "Women are more likely than men to seek medical care for all medical problems, including chronic pain."[6] And according to the Centers for Disease Control and Prevention, "Women are more likely to have chronic pain."[7]

However, substance abusers are mostly young and male. To find out what percent of adult marijuana abusers are male, I turned to the National Survey on Drug Use and Health and looked at the people over age seventeen diagnosed with marijuana abuse or dependence between 2008 and 2012. When I averaged out the results, 69 percent were male (+/- 5 percent, for a 95 percent confidence level).

So, if the marijuana cardholders claiming pain are all genuine pain patients, fewer than 50 percent will be male. If they're all substance abusers faking pain, about 69 percent will be male.

Between 2011 and 2013, I contacted nearly every medical marijuana program in the United States to find out what percentage of their pain patients were male. Most did not keep track of gender and several refused to share their data, but here's what I found:

| Percent of Medical Marijuana Patients Claiming Pain Who Are Male ||
State	Male
Arizona	74%
Colorado	68%
Delaware	73%
Montana	64%
Oregon	61%
Rhode Island	74%
Vermont	67%

Table 11-1. Data Collected 2011-2013.

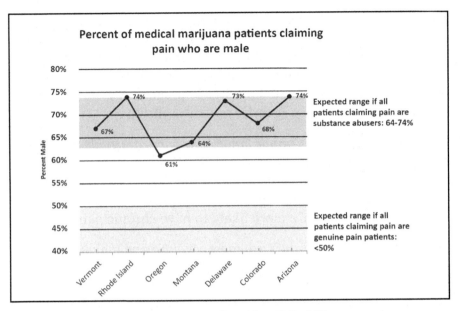

Figure 11-1. Data collected from 2011 – 2013.

Not one of these programs shows anywhere near the 50:50 male to female ratio we'd expect if they were all real pain patients. Instead, most of the numbers fall right in the range we'd expect if they were all substance abusers. So the best explanation is that nearly all of the marijuana patients are substance abusers who are either faking or exaggerating their pain. And since pain accounts for 90 percent of the medical marijuana patients, most of the medical marijuana is probably going to substance abuse, not to medical use.

The pot doc loophole

The way the laws are written, one would think people seeking medical marijuana would get recommendations from personal physicians they've known for years, and only after they've tried more standard treatments. That should screen out drug abusers and make sure only legitimate patients are prescribed marijuana. But it's another bait and switch.

Once these laws pass, most marijuana users tend to avoid their personal physicians. Instead, they get their marijuana cards from a handful of doctors who specialize in what are called "marijuana evaluations." These "pot doctors" often advertise, and even hire sign spinners to encourage walk-in traffic. While some are legitimate, many are almost certainly not. Their waiting rooms are usually full of guys in their twenties. Some pot docs see people one time only for as little as ten minutes, and rarely say "No" to anyone who pays their fee.[8] Every drug user in the state knows who they are.

The drug addicts I treat often have marijuana cards, all acquired in the same way: They made up a story about pain and saw a pot doctor who they knew wouldn't say "No." One person told me the secretary typed up the card before he even saw the doctor.

A study published in 2011 in the *Journal of Drug Policy Analysis* looked at 1,655 patients who applied for marijuana cards in California. Fewer than 2 percent were turned down, and they were turned down only because they made it impossible for the doctor to say, "Yes." They either refused to be under any medical care or would not even pretend to have an eligible medical condition.[9] Pot doctors make it easy, but "patients" still have to play the game.

The vast majority of doctors never recommend marijuana. Of the ones who do, most only recommend it for the few patients they believe would be helped. In Montana, two-thirds of the doctors who wrote recommendations had fewer than five marijuana patients. But it only takes a handful of pot doctors to turn medical marijuana into a conduit for drug abuse. In many states, a handful of doctors write most of the recommendations. In Montana, ten doctors wrote 90 percent of the state's marijuana recommendations, and one of those doctors wrote 40 percent by himself.[10]

Drug abusers rarely go to regular doctors who would act as honest gatekeepers. They go to someone who is guaranteed to say, "Yes." That's not a real doctor-patient relationship. It's drug dealing masquerading as medical care.

Laws vary

Not every state or national law is as easily abused some of the ones described here. In 2011, Montana tightened up its law, and the percent of patients claiming pain dropped significantly. New Mexico's law requires that patients claiming chronic pain obtain a second opinion from a pain specialist before marijuana can be approved.

We can often tell how strict a law is by how often marijuana users complain about it. For example, they fought against changes to the Montana law, which is probably evidence that lawmakers were trying to do the right thing.

Marketing marijuana

When pot doctors market aggressively, states see big increases in the number of patients. For example, in 2010, "cannabis caravans" started traveling around Montana to sign up new patients. One doctor saw 150 patients in one day. That's one every six minutes.[11]

That year, the number of people "needing" medical marijuana skyrocketed. In the first four years of Montana's program, only 2,000 people signed up. Between March 2009 and March 2011, the number of patients increased fourteen-fold to nearly 30,000.[12]

In 1996, the Reverend Scott Imler co-wrote California's Proposition 215, the nation's first medical marijuana law. He still believes the drug should be available to the genuinely ill. "But," he says, "today it is all about the money. Most of the dispensaries operating in California are little more than dope dealers with store fronts."[13]

The marijuana lobby maintains the pretense that these laws only give marijuana to people with a genuine medical need. But my drug-abusing patients usually laugh when they tell me they have marijuana cards; they think these laws are a joke. And they're not alone. In this excerpt of a *High Times* interview with Adam Devine and Kyle Newacheck, two of the stars of the stoner comedy show *Workaholics,* they also seem to think medical marijuana is a joke.[14]

High Times: What do you think of the pot scene in California?

ADAM: It's great.

KYLE: I just got my card, and I'm pretty amped about it. I feel like I just unlocked the treasures of Los Angeles.

ADAM: I need to get mine. I don't know why I haven't.

KYLE: It's just the most amazing thing in the world to go into a f---ing store and buy weed with your debit card.

These guys don't seem to even pretend it's medical. But why should they? It isn't.

The side effects of medical marijuana laws

A lot of people think drug abuse is a victimless crime, so it doesn't matter that most of the marijuana goes to recreational use. But medical marijuana laws cause three serious problems that outweigh the help they offer: traffic fatalities, teenage use, and cynicism.

Medical marijuana states have more traffic fatalities

In 2014, researchers from the University of Colorado published a study about car accidents and medical marijuana.[15] In 2009, the number of Colorado marijuana dispensaries, as well as the number of individual patients, began to increase. The state's medical marijuana registry went from just over 10,000 patients in July 2009 to more than 150,000 by the end of July 2011.[16] So the researchers examined traffic fatalities in Colorado and thirty-four non-medical-marijuana states for the two-year period beginning July 2009.

In the thirty-four non-medical-marijuana states, there was no increase in traffic fatalities caused by either alcohol- or marijuana-impaired drivers. In Colorado, there was no increase in fatal car accidents caused by alcohol-impaired drivers. However, in the two years from July 2009 to July 2011, Colorado traffic fatalities caused by marijuana-impaired drivers doubled.[17] This is strong evidence that loosening our marijuana laws makes our highways more dangerous.

Medical marijuana states have more teenage use

Canada has nationwide medical marijuana. It also has the highest rate of teenage use in the industrialized world. The U.S. states with medical marijuana laws have the highest rates of teen use in the country.[18]

But just because two things are linked doesn't mean one causes the other. Maybe states that passed these laws had higher teenage use to begin with. If we want to know how medical marijuana laws affect adolescent use, we have to look at changes in teen use after states passed these laws.

It turns out teenage marijuana use has increased faster in medical marijuana states. The National Survey on Drug Use and Health tracks past-month teenage marijuana use by state.[19] Between 2005 and 2011, teen use in non-medical-marijuana states increased by 6 percent. In states with medical marijuana laws, teen use increased by 33 percent.

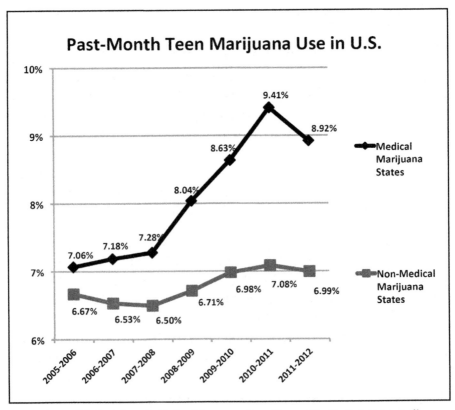

Figure 11-2. Data from the National Survey on Drug Use and Health, State Estimates[20]

This tells us that the higher rates of teenage use in medical marijuana states are not simply pre-existing. Something is happening in those states to accelerate adolescent marijuana use. There are two likely explanations.

First, these laws send the message that marijuana is safe. Adults use it openly, and there's an industry advertising and promoting the drug.

Second, marijuana is easier to get. According to a Monitoring the Future survey, in 2013, one-third of U.S. high school seniors who lived in medical marijuana states said they got the drug from someone with a medical card.[21]

In the U.S., teen use increased rapidly between 2006 and 2011, and most of that increase came from states with medical marijuana laws. In 2005, only ten states had medical marijuana laws, and those states contained only about 20 percent of the U.S. population. Yet they accounted for nearly 60 percent of the increase in adolescent marijuana use between 2005 and 2011. If it weren't for states with medical marijuana laws, teenage use in the United States would barely have increased at all.[22]

Medical marijuana teaches cynicism and dishonesty

Kids, especially adolescents, know marijuana is illegal, yet they see teachers and relatives they respect get the drug by lying. They know Daddy's medicine isn't really medicine, and that his back pain wasn't a problem before he got that marijuana card. When kids see adults gaming the system and getting away with it, they think that's what grown up people do. Medical marijuana teaches children that it's normal and acceptable for adults to lie to get what they want.

However, there is something even more corrosive about these laws. During the 2010 campaign, several people told me they knew medical marijuana was a subterfuge, but that was okay by them because they thought pot should be legal. So they knowingly voted for a system that lets people break federal law by lying.

Normally, when adults break the law, there is some higher authority saying it's wrong, and kids know that. With medical marijuana, adults are breaking the law and the state is in collusion. In fact, it's a state-run system.

There are always dishonest politicians, but now the wink-wink-nod-nod doesn't just come from corrupt people in government; it comes from government itself. The highest governmental authority is rewarding people for playing a dishonest game. There might be no better way to teach kids cynicism and mistrust.

How "medical" marijuana makes us all dishonest

Drug abusers faking illness to get marijuana aren't real patients, their fabricated stories aren't real medical needs, and pot doctors who pretend to believe them aren't practicing real medicine. Talking about this fake transaction as if it were real is dishonest.

For example, when speaking about medical marijuana laws, U.S. Rep. Dana Rohrabacher (R-Calif.) said, "A doctor has a right to treat his patient any way he sees fit ..."[23] First of all, that's not true; licensing boards spend most of their time telling doctors what they can and can't do. But more importantly, if my eighteen-year-old stoner patients know medical marijuana is a scam, so does Rep. Rohrabacher.

U.S. Sen. Barbara Boxer (D-Calif.) said, "If you have a doctor's note, you should be able to get whatever medicine you need."[24] She's talking about medical marijuana as if it were only used for genuinely medical purposes. In reality, the "need" she speaks of is usually fictitious, the "doctor's note" often goes to anyone with money, and the "medicine" is probably for getting wasted, not getting well.

W.C. Fields was doing comedy when he said, "Always carry a flagon of whiskey in case of snakebite, and furthermore, always carry a small snake." But his joke describes a common drug addict game. Addicts often call dope their medicine, especially around children. During Prohibition, pharmacies were allowed to sell alcohol with a doctor's prescription, and called it "medicinal" liquor. It's all a game.

A small amount of medical marijuana probably is used legitimately, but the evidence says most of it is not. So the term *medical* marijuana is just as dishonest as *medicinal* liquor or Daddy's *medicine*.

George Orwell, author of *1984*, coined the term *newspeak*, which has been defined as "deliberately ambiguous and contradictory language used to mislead and manipulate the public." He also came up with *doublethink,* which is "thought marked by the acceptance of gross contradictions and falsehoods, especially when used as a technique of self-indoctrination."[25]

The modern term doublespeak combines these two, and is defined as "language ... that is used to trick or deceive people."[26] More specifically, it is language designed so that simply using it causes us to think the opposite of what is true. *Medical marijuana* is classic doublespeak; just by using the term, we're saying something that isn't true. That's how it makes us all dishonest.

Yet we have to use the term to discuss these laws. So for the rest of this book, when you see the term *medical marijuana*, please remember that it doesn't mean that the marijuana is being used medically. It usually means just the opposite.

What we could do instead

There are two ways to benefit medically from marijuana without the current laws that promote drug abuse.

1. We could have real medical marijuana laws that provide marijuana only to the sick and suffering.

Before the implementation of Arizona's Medical Marijuana Act, the state's Department of Health Services asked for recommendations. Here are four recommendations I made that, had they been adopted, might have made sure most of the marijuana went to the genuinely ill. None of these recommendations would have broken new ground; they're all found elsewhere in the medical system.

1. Limit doctors to thirty active marijuana patients at one time. That's what we do with patients prescribed buprenorphine, an addictive drug used to treat opiate dependence. This one rule would put the pot doctors out of business.

2. Require patients to get recommendations from doctors they've known for a year who can document that they've tried two other treatments. Managed care already does something very similar. I'm regularly required to document that my patients have unsuccessfully tried two treatments

before the insurer will pay for a more expensive one. This rule would also eliminate pot doctors. We'd need an exception for cancer patients, who can't wait a year, but no other legitimate patient would be harmed by this requirement.

3. Anyone claiming pain, or any other condition that isn't diagnosed with a lab test, physical exam, or x-ray, must get a second opinion. And the health department—not the patient—chooses the second-opinion doctor. This would eliminate the pain loophole.

4. Limit marijuana recommendations to sixty days. That's what we do with Ritalin and other stimulants used for ADHD. No doctor hands out addictive drug prescriptions for a whole year.

Unfortunately, the Arizona Health Services Department rejected all these ideas.

2. Prescription cannabinoid medicines work just as well, and we don't need marijuana at all.

In 1979, the chairman of the board of NORML stated that the purpose of medical marijuana laws was to make marijuana look good and pave the way for legalization. He said NORML's plan was to get states to approve marijuana for chemotherapy and then use that "as a red herring to give marijuana a good name."[27] That's why we shouldn't let a pro-legalization lobby direct medical policy.

The Institute of Medicine (IOM), on the other hand, is a well-respected, nonprofit, nongovernmental group that evaluates medical issues. In 2003, the IOM released a report that said the components of marijuana have medical uses, and prescription cannabinoid medicines should be developed and made available: "If there is any future for marijuana as a medicine, it lies in its isolated components, the cannabinoids and their synthetic derivatives."[28]

That future has arrived. As of 2015, four cannabinoid medications have been developed. And these medicines work as well as or better than marijuana.

Dronabinol, a synthetic THC (tetrahydrocannabinol) marketed under the brand name Marinol, eases the nausea of chemotherapy and loss of appetite from AIDS, and works as an adjunctive treatment for pain. It decreases agitation in Alzheimer's patients. Research shows it's as effective as marijuana in managing these symptoms.[29]

Nabilone, another synthetic THC medication available in Canada and the United States, has been marketed under the brand name Cesamet since 2006. The drug's been approved for the nausea of chemotherapy and weight loss from AIDS. It's often used for chronic pain, and has been shown to help with multiple sclerosis.[30]

Nabiximols, trade name Sativex, is a cannabinoid mouth-spray containing both THC and cannabidiol (CBD) that's been shown to work for the muscle spasms of multiple sclerosis.[31] As of 2014, it's available by prescription in Canada and is moving toward approval in the United States.

Pure cannabidiol, with no THC, is in the research phase under the brand name Epidiolex. It's not yet available by prescription, but is available for children with treatment-resistant epilepsy through a special Food and Drug Administration (FDA) program that allows doctors to obtain investigational medications.[32]

Cannabidiol **(CBD)** was popularized by a Sanjay Gupta report on CNN. Gupta told his viewers about a Colorado marijuana dispensary that produces CBD, but not about the FDA program, which was running when he did his second show on medical marijuana.

Once Sativex is approved in the United States, all four medicines will be available—three as prescriptions and one as a special program for investigational drugs.

Sometimes natural isn't better

The pro-marijuana side says it's better to use the raw plant since it's natural, and normally I'd agree. I treat patients with both conventional pharmaceuticals and alternative medicine, and I prefer natural remedies.

However, marijuana is not "just a plant." It's an addictive drug that's abused in epidemic proportions. Even the most widely abused prescription drugs are much harder for teenagers to obtain than marijuana.[33] So when it comes to cannabinoids, prescription medicines are better because they're less likely to be abused.

One reason cannabinoid medications are abused less is that they're prescribed by doctors who try to prescribe appropriately rather than by pot docs. Another reason is that they don't get people nearly as high. In 2010, when "medical" marijuana was on the ballot in Arizona, the Marijuana Policy Project lobbyist said people didn't like using Marinol because, compared to marijuana, the high was too intense. The NORML website makes the same criticism: "Marinol is more psychoactive than marijuana."[34] They have to say this; otherwise, there's no justification for medical marijuana. However, the research says they're wrong.

A Columbia University study published in the journal *Neuropsychopharmacology* in 2013 compared the analgesic effects of marijuana and dronabinol. Both drugs worked equally well for pain, but dronabinol worked almost twice as long. And the participants said they didn't get as high from dronabinol as they did from marijuana.[35] The other synthetic THC medication, Cesamet, is reported to cause very little euphoria.[36]

Other research has found the high from Marinol to be similar to the high from marijuana,[37] but I've found no evidence that the high from Marinol or any other cannabinoid medicine is more intense. So there is no medical reason to use marijuana; cannabinoid medicines are just as effective and have fewer side effects.

Ignoring prescription medicines is a disservice to genuine patients

Rather than criticizing cannabinoid medicines, the marijuana lobby usually ignores them. NORML and MPP lobby state after state to pass "medical" marijuana laws, insisting there's a huge medical need. Yet they never seem to mention prescription cannabinoids that work just as well and are less likely to be abused.

News reports in states considering medical marijuana laws almost never mention how unnecessary the laws are. The news media has done story after story about sick people being helped by marijuana, but reports about Marinol, Cesamet, or Sativex are rare.

This is great for drug abusers, but bad for legitimate patients. Drug abusers like short-acting drugs that give them an intense high, so they'd rather smoke their marijuana. However, genuine medical patients don't want to be stoned all the time and don't want a medicine they have to take every few hours. They're better off with the longer-acting prescription cannabinoids that produce less of a high.[38]

So by promoting marijuana over prescription cannabinoids, the marijuana lobby is actually harming the legitimate patients they claim to help. The press should not follow this lead; genuine patients deserve to get news about the prescription medicines that would be better for them than marijuana.

Why aren't we using the protections we created?

In the United States, medications are approved if they're clearly useful and have few or minor side effects. Medications with more serious side effects can be approved if there is no better alternative. Marijuana fails that test. Even without the cannabinoid medications, there were usually safer alternatives. Now, with so many cannabinoid medications, there are always better alternatives.

Imagine the lawsuits that would fly if the FDA approved a drug that had no advantage over safer alternatives, went mostly to substance abuse, increased teenage drug use, and killed people on the highways. We should not be sidestepping the FDA approval process that was designed to protect us.

The news media's role

How reporters choose to cover medical marijuana can affect public opinion, and Dr. Sanjay Gupta's two-part series on CNN called *Weed*, which ran in 2013 and 2014, is a good example of this choice. The series largely stuck to the marijuana lobby line that these laws are legitimate, and ignored evidence that these laws are mostly deceptive.[39]

The series showed people who use marijuana under state medical marijuana laws, but it didn't show the young, male substance abusers with no serious problems. Instead, the audience saw only genuinely sick people. Anyone watching would come away thinking that medical marijuana goes only to people with serious illnesses.

The two-part series also never showed pot doctors who hand out recommendations to almost everyone who pays their fee. The audience saw only serious physicians whose patients were all legitimate and desperately ill.

Prescription cannabinoids were never mentioned in the first one-hour show. In the second show, Dr. Gupta introduced someone helped by the prescription drug Sativex, but said it was not available in the United States. Viewers did not hear that Sativex was in the late stages of the approval process; and did not hear about Marinol or Cesamet, which were available in the U.S. at the time.

As for the fourth prescription medicine that can replace marijuana, Epidiolex, Gupta said the British company GW Pharmaceuticals was working on it.[40] However, he was never shown naming the drug or telling his viewers the drug was available through an FDA program. Anyone who didn't know better would almost certainly come away from the two shows thinking no prescription cannabinoids were available in the United States.

During his second show in 2014, Gupta talked about families who moved to Colorado to get cannabidiol for their children. He stressed the disruption to families who couldn't get CBD in their home states, saying, "Each of these families wanted medical marijuana for their sick children. They also fought to get it in their home states, but lost. So they moved to Colorado where it's legal. Desperate and determined, they've become known as medical marijuana refugees." However, his audience was never told that the investigational drug Epidiolex, containing nearly pure CBD, was available through the FDA, and there was no need to move to Colorado.

Dr. Gupta changes his story

In 2009, Dr. Gupta wrote an article opposing medical marijuana laws. But he changed his mind, and in 2013 he wrote an article explaining why. He said that years earlier he had reviewed the scientific literature from the United States and found the evidence "unimpressive.

Reading these papers five years ago," he continued, "it was hard to make a case for medicinal marijuana. I even wrote about this in a *TIME* magazine article, back in 2009, titled 'Why I would Vote No on Pot.'"

"Well, I am here to apologize," Gupta wrote in 2013. And he apologized for not reading enough of the research and for not acknowledging that legitimate patients were helped by marijuana.[41]

But he apologized for a mistake he never made. In 2013 he apologized for not reading enough research to know that marijuana could help people and for being dismissive of legitimate patients who are helped by the drug. But, in 2009, he did not dismiss those patients and he had read enough research. If we look at his 2009 *TIME* magazine article, he quoted research that made the case for medicinal marijuana, and he acknowledged that legitimate patients are helped by the drug. Here's what he wrote:

> "[T]here are health benefits for some patients. Several recent studies ... show that THC ... can help slow the progress of Alzheimer's disease. (In fact, it seems to block the formation of disease-causing plaques better than several mainstream drugs.) Other studies have shown THC to be a very effective anti-nausea treatment for people—cancer patients undergoing chemotherapy, for example— for whom conventional medications aren't working. And medical cannabis has shown promise relieving pain in patients with multiple sclerosis and reducing intraocular pressure in glaucoma patients."[42]

However, he also explained why he did oppose medical marijuana laws:

> "I suspect that most of the people eager to vote yes on the new ballot measures aren't suffering from glaucoma, Alzheimer's or chemo-induced nausea. Many of them just want to get stoned legally. That's why I, like many other doctors, am unimpressed with the proposed legislation, which would legalize marijuana irrespective of any medical condition."[43]

He opposed the laws because they would allow people with no serious medical problem "to get stoned legally" under the protective cover of medical care. Despite his claim, what changed four years later was not his view on the effectiveness of marijuana as medicine. He thought it was effective in 2009 and he said so. What changed was his opinion on medical marijuana *laws*. He went from opposing the *laws* to supporting them.

But it wouldn't look good to say he no longer believed the laws "would legalize marijuana irrespective of any medical condition." First of all, the laws in 2013 were just as much a subterfuge as they were four years earlier. Secondly, he would have started a debate about whether medical marijuana laws are a sham, and that's the last thing anyone who is pro-legalization wants to do.

As I said in the beginning of the chapter, the laws themselves are hard to defend, so marijuana advocates often change the subject. Instead of talking about how the laws work, they prefer to debate whether *the plant* has medical benefits. Dr. Gupta changed the subject the same way.

In 2009, he opposed medical marijuana laws because he was "unimpressed with the proposed legislation..." But in 2013, he claimed the reason for his 2009 opposition was because he was unimpressed with the scientific literature.

In 2009, he said many supporters "just want to get stoned legally," but in 2013 he seemed to forget that was his reason for opposing these laws, and instead acted as if all the marijuana patients were legitimate.

Dr. Gupta retroactively changed his story, and misinformed readers about what he actually wrote back in 2009. However, his January 8, 2009 column is a matter of written record.

In early 2015, CNN anchorman Brian Williams was forced from his post after news broke that he'd changed his story and misrepresented his war reporting experience. The evidence was his own statement from years earlier. What Gupta did was similar, but, in a way, it was far worse. Williams changed his story and hurt only himself. Gupta was supporting medical marijuana laws that affect the lives of thousands of teens.

The takeaway

The marijuana lobby wants a debate centered solely on whether marijuana has medicinal properties because they could win that argument. But the debate we should have is whether medical marijuana goes primarily to medical use or to drug abuse, whether medical marijuana laws are harmful or beneficial, and whether we even need medical marijuana since cannabinoid medications work just as well.

Chapter 12

The Real Costs

One lesson everyone with a drug or alcohol problem eventually learns is that addictive substances never do what people think they will. Addicts start out believing the drug is their best friend, but end up trapped in a miserable relationship. The drug that promised happiness not only stops delivering, it also takes away any happiness the user once had.

The promise of riches from legalization is just as deceptive and will be just as disappointing. Legalization is far more likely to drain government coffers and cost society than it is to contribute.

What they promise

The campaigns in Colorado, Washington, Alaska, and Oregon promised that legalization would save money on law enforcement and bring in tax dollars to benefit public schools.[1] The Cato Institute, a libertarian think tank that supports legalization, estimates that legalizing marijuana would bring the United States $8.7 billion per year in tax revenue and save $8.7 billion per year in criminal justice costs.[2]

In 1994, NORML released a report titled *Economics of Cannabis Legalization: Detailed analysis of the benefits of ending cannabis prohibition.* It concluded that legalizing marijuana would save the United States between $8 billion and $16 billion each year. The savings, the report claimed, would come from taxing marijuana and from not having to enforce marijuana laws.[3] Politicians are often seduced by these promises, but there are several reasons these windfalls and savings will not materialize.

The estimates are too high

In a paper titled *Altered State,* the RAND Corporation criticized estimates that took law-enforcement budgets and pro-rated them equally among all types of arrests. Most marijuana arrests are for possession, which is rarely prosecuted and almost never leads to incarceration, so marijuana arrests cost far less than arrests for any other type of crime. Pro-rating law-enforcement costs equally will give overly optimistic estimates of savings, but that's how the researchers cited by the Cato Institute and NORML came up with their numbers.[4]

Regarding taxes, a much better projection came from economists at the nonpartisan Colorado Legislative Council. They estimated that Colorado would bring in $65 million per year in marijuana taxes.[5] Colorado has a population of 6 million; the entire U.S. population is 314 million. So if the whole country legalized and taxed marijuana, and brought in as much as Colorado was expected to, that would be around $3.4 billion per year. That's less than half of what Cato and NORML estimate.

But even that conservative estimate proved way too high. In the first six months, Colorado brought in $12 million, not the expected $33.5 million.[6] At that rate, the U.S. could only expect $1.3 billion annually in taxes if pot were legalized nationwide. And even that might be overly optimistic.

The realpolitik of marijuana taxes

Right now, the marijuana lobby says it supports taxes because it's trying to encourage legalization. That will change. No well-established industry ever supports high taxes on its products. The alcohol and tobacco industries lobby very effectively to keep their taxes low, and the marijuana industry will eventually do the same.

In 2011, the city of San Diego tried to regulate medical marijuana collectives that had sprung up unregulated. The rules the city tried to impose included requiring collectives and dispensaries to have permits, to locate at least 600 feet away from schools, and to close by 9:00 p.m.[7] These were not onerous requirements. And remember, the pro-legalization campaigns say marijuana should be regulated like alcohol.

Yet pro-marijuana forces rallied marijuana users to fight these regulations. They raised nearly $150,000, hired a signature-gathering firm, and got enough signatures to force a vote on the regulations. Such an election would have cost San Diego taxpayers as much as $3 million, so the city council capitulated and rescinded the law.[8] If the nascent marijuana industry will fight against regulation with such hardball tactics after promising states they could regulate the drug, it will most certainly fight against taxes—when the time is right.

The alcohol industry provides a good example of what to expect. Immediately after Prohibition was repealed, alcohol taxes were very high. But once the United States got used to legal alcohol again, the industry fought any and all increases. Since 1951, excise taxes on beer and wine have been increased only once and the tax on hard liquor has been increased twice. So alcohol taxes stayed flat while inflation steadily increased. Correcting for inflation, the tax on hard liquor is only 15 percent of what it was in 1951. The tax on beer is one-quarter its 1951 value.[9]

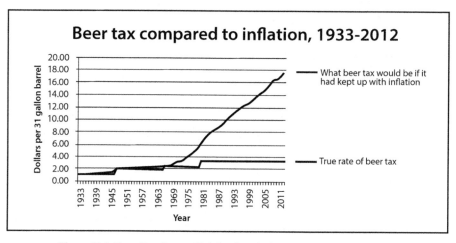

Figure 12-1. From Bay-Staters Fighting for Alcohol Industry Responsibility[10]

Shortly after Prohibition ended, taxes on alcohol provided nearly 10 percent of all federal tax revenue. Today, that figure is a fraction of 1 percent.[11] Increases in alcohol taxes are difficult to get through Congress and state legislatures because of alcohol industry muscle. The same is true for tobacco taxes and the tobacco industry.

The marijuana industry will probably go along with high taxes for as long as it needs the good public relations to convince us to legalize the drug. But once legal marijuana becomes established and impossible to dislodge, the marijuana industry will follow the example of the alcohol and tobacco industries.

The black market won't go away

When taxes are high, there's a strong incentive to evade them. We see this with tobacco. The Tax Foundation reported that in 2011, smuggling accounted for most of the cigarettes sold in New York, Arizona, and New Mexico. The Tax Foundation is conservative and anti-tax, but even Huffington Post and NPR have reported on the black market sale of cigarettes.[12]

Tax evasion became a problem in Colorado only a few months after legalizing marijuana. A July 30, 2014, story in the *Washington Post* showed drug dealers in Colorado selling black market marijuana at half the retail price. According to CNN, one reason tax revenues were so low was that about 40 percent of marijuana is sold through the black market to evade taxes.[13]

People will grow their own

Smokers can grow their own tobacco, and drinkers can brew their own beer, crush their own grapes, and distill their own spirits. However, not many do, because it's not simple to grow and cure tobacco or make alcohol, and it's even harder to turn out a quality product that's better and cheaper than you can buy at the corner market.

Marijuana is another story. It's a weed; anyone can grow it. We already have a decades-long history of people growing their own marijuana. If marijuana is legal, a significant number of people will grow their own—and pay no tax at all.

Hyping benefits and ignoring costs

However, there's a far bigger reason there will be no tax windfall or savings from legalization. The Cato Institute and NORML only gave us half the equation. They only looked at tax revenue and savings from fewer prosecutions and incarcerations. Those are the benefits, but we have to balance them against costs.

Costs matter. If a business brings in $1 million but has expenses totaling $2 million, it's a net loss. The pro-legalization reports never mention all the ways legalization would be a financial drain. They act as if that half of the equation didn't exist.

Research on alcohol shows how costs matter, and why the lure of a tax bonanza is a false promise. Taxes on alcohol come nowhere near the cost of paying for the problems it causes. One study, *Economic Costs of Excessive Alcohol Consumption in the U.S.*, found that in 2006, alcohol abuse costs local, state, and federal governments $94.2 billion, while local, state, and federal taxes on alcohol only brought in $14.6 billion.[14]

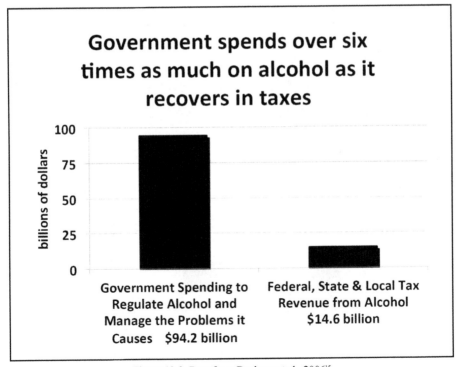

Figure 12-2. Data from Bochery et al., 2006[15]

Substance abuse costs us money in three main ways. First come criminal justice costs, which include police, courts, incarceration, and expenses incurred by crime victims. Healthcare costs are next, and include substance abuse treatment plus the cost of treating all the illnesses and injuries caused by drugs and alcohol.

The third set of costs is lost productivity. Many drug and alcohol abusers can't hold a job, or they frequently call in sick or show up too hungover to work. Some choose a life of crime over productive work. And some can't work due to imprisonment, hospitalization, or physical or mental incapacity.

A closer look at all three costs shows why legalizing marijuana would be a drag on the economy and state budgets.

Lost productivity: The price we all pay

A 1998 study by Henrick Harwood titled *Economic Costs of Alcohol and Drug Abuse in the United States* found lost productivity dwarfed healthcare and criminal justice costs. His estimate was that, in 1992, lost productivity due to substance abuse cost the U.S. $176 billion, criminal justice costs for substance-involved crime were $40 billion, and substance-related healthcare costs were $28 billion.[16]

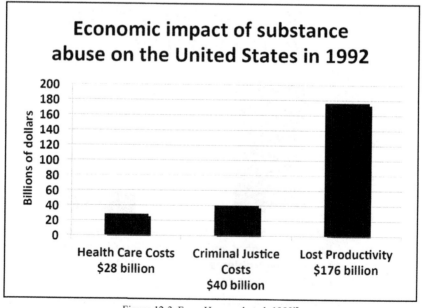

Figure 12-3. From Harwood et al, 1992[17]

People are often surprised that lost productivity is such a huge expense, but our whole economy is nothing more than everyone's productivity combined. Our combined productivity pays for health care and the criminal justice system as well as for food, housing, cars, entertainment, travel, and every other expense we have. The huge North American economy fuels the continent's high prosperity. Anything that takes a bite out of that economy hurts us all, and substance abuse takes a big bite.

The marijuana lobby doesn't want us to think about what widespread marijuana use would do to the North American economy. But lost productivity is the biggest expense every one of us would bear if marijuana were legal.

Here's a very rough estimate. A study by researchers Fergusson and Boden found that teens who used marijuana regularly earned 10 percent less as adults when compared to nonusers. According to the *Monitoring the Future* survey, 22 percent of high school seniors are past-month marijuana users. The median household income in the United States is just over $51,000, and in 2010 there were 115 million households.[18] If 22 percent of those households earn 10 percent less, the U.S. economy loses roughly $129 billion per year. That's 100 times as much as the $1.3 billion the U.S. could hope to earn annually in marijuana taxes.

Poor work habits and lost productivity caused by marijuana use were shown clearly in a study published in the *Journal of the American Medical Association* in 1990. The researchers looked at more than 2,500 postal employees and compared those whose pre-employment drug test was positive for marijuana against those who tested clean. The employees who tested positive for marijuana had more accidents and injuries, were more often disciplined, and were more likely to be late for work. They were 75 percent more likely to miss work altogether, and had a 55 percent higher turnover rate.[19]

Another large survey, from Norway, followed nearly 2,000 people for twenty-five years and found that those who used marijuana regularly were less committed to work, and their level of commitment grew worse over time. Neither of these studies were about marijuana use at work; they were about employees who used, even if just in their private lives.[20]

Lack of commitment plus absenteeism and disciplinary problems are a recipe for employees who under-produce. Pro-legalization groups ignore lost productivity, but it's the main way every drug of abuse—including marijuana—affects us financially.

Health care

Promises of an economic windfall also ignore increased healthcare costs. No economic analysis outlines all the medical expenses created by marijuana. But by looking at just one illness, schizophrenia, we can see how medical expenses caused by marijuana could outstrip all the money brought in through taxes.

Research published in 2002 in the *Journal of Clinical Psychiatry* estimated the cost of schizophrenia in the United States at $62 billion per year. Half of that is lost productivity, as people with schizophrenia are often unemployed. However, $22 billion is spent on direct healthcare costs, and since so many people with this illness are treated in public clinics, a lot of this money comes right out of tax revenue. The study also found that $9 billion was spent on law enforcement and homeless shelters. That money also comes right out of local, state, and federal budgets.[21]

According to the Rand Corporation report *Examining the Impact of Marijuana Legalization on Harms Associated with Marijuana Use*, in one year in California alone, the cost of hospitalizing marijuana-related cases of schizophrenia and other psychosis was $110 million.[22] California has a tenth of the U.S population, so that means marijuana-related cases of psychosis cost the United States roughly $1.1 billion each year.

Compare that to the $1.3 billion discussed earlier that the U.S. could reap annually in marijuana taxes. And remember, hospitalization for schizophrenia is just one of the healthcare costs created by marijuana. This doesn't include the cost of treating the anxiety disorders, depression, respiratory problems, and cancers that marijuana use can cause. It doesn't include the cost of treating injuries from automobile crashes caused by drugged driving. And it doesn't include the substance abuse treatment that addicted marijuana users would need. So healthcare costs could completely wipe out any tax benefit from legalizing marijuana.

For every dollar that local, state, and federal governments collect in alcohol and tobacco taxes, the same governments pay out almost nine dollars to clean up the problems substance abuse causes. According to the National Center on Addiction and Substance Abuse, "If substance abuse and addiction were its own [state] budget category, it would rank second behind elementary and secondary education."[23]

So despite the tax dollars they bring in, alcohol and tobacco are a net burden on state budgets. Marijuana would be no different. No one has yet calculated the precise healthcare costs or lost productivity associated with marijuana use, but we can already see why they would be far greater than any tax dollars marijuana would generate. When the press writes about Colorado's tax revenue without mentioning costs, they are telling only half the story.

Law enforcement

One of the talking points the marijuana lobby used to convince voters in Colorado and Washington to support legalization was that it would save the criminal justice system money.[24] But criminal justice costs don't vanish just because a drug is legal. We would still spend money enforcing marijuana laws, and law-enforcement costs in three areas would actually increase:

Consumption by minors. According to the RAND Corporation report *Altered State,* one-third of marijuana-related law-enforcement costs involve people under age twenty-one.[25] No one is proposing legalizing marijuana for minors, so this cost wouldn't go away, and as teens used more, it would probably increase.

Drugged driving and public intoxication. With increased use of marijuana, there would be more DUIs and more public use violations. It takes money to enforce these laws.

Tax evasion. Without law enforcement, taxed marijuana would never compete with the cheaper black market kind. States that want to collect tax dollars would have to spend money enforcing tax laws.

The marijuana lobby never seems to mention any of this. It simply assumes enforcement costs would disappear. However, with legalization, the cost of enforcing marijuana laws is likely to go up rather than down. After all, alcohol is legal, and in 2006, the United States spent nearly $5 billion tackling alcohol-specific crimes such as DUI and underage possession.[26]

* * *

The nature of all addictive drugs is to promise bliss but deliver woe. As the Reverend Billy Sunday said about alcohol a century ago: "It promises good cheer and sends sorrow. It promises health and causes disease. It promises prosperity and sends adversity. It promises happiness and sends misery."[27]

Addicts and alcoholics learn this lesson the hard way, but states and the federal government don't have to. Politicians who think marijuana taxes will be a financial boon should look carefully at what the marijuana lobby and pro-marijuana press are not telling us. Otherwise, what's been sold as a budgetary blessing could prove to be an economic curse.

Chapter 13

Alcohol vs. Marijuana: A Meaningless Debate

The strangest pro-marijuana argument is that alcohol is legal, so marijuana should be, too. It's strange because alcohol is a perfect example of why we shouldn't have another legal intoxicant. Alcohol is one of the most harmful drugs on the planet, responsible for more death, disease, and injury than all the illegal drugs put together. The reason it's so harmful is not because it does anything worse than black tar heroin or crystal meth, but because it's legal and anyone can buy it at the nearest corner market. This should warn us *against* legalizing another drug.

Also, we know what the legal alcohol and tobacco industries have done to sell their drugs. They've advertised to teens, made money off people who are addicted, and pretended what they sell is harmless. Then they've lobbied Congress and state legislatures for protection.[1] We've spent decades fighting with those industries. Why would we voluntarily create another such monster?

The fairness argument makes no sense

When advocates say it's not fair that alcohol is legal and marijuana isn't, we might ask: Unfair to whom? Unfair to marijuana? Does marijuana also deserve a chance to cause all sorts of health, safety, and economic problems?

Most likely they mean it's unfair to the 7 percent of the population who use marijuana. But the other 93 percent might want to raise drug-free kids and might not want our highways to become even more dangerous. Shouldn't we be fair to them? Isn't their need for a safe environment more important than someone's need to get high?

When people make the alcohol-is-legal-and-that's-not-fair argument, they make it sound as if we all sat down with a list of addictive drugs and decided which ones to ban and which ones to legalize. But alcohol is legal only because it's been around for thousands of years and is part of almost every culture. If it were invented today, we'd outlaw it as quickly as we ban spice, bath salts, and every new designer drug that comes along. Alcohol is legal by historical accident; marijuana is illegal because we realized it was a harmful drug before its use became widespread.

Also, if we were considering making alcohol illegal and replacing it with marijuana, then it would make sense to debate which one is less damaging to society. But we're not considering replacing alcohol with marijuana. We're only considering adding marijuana to the mix. So the debate should be whether legal alcohol by itself is better or worse than legal alcohol combined with legal marijuana.

There's one more reason the comparison to alcohol doesn't wash. The legalization lobby tries to make marijuana use seem normal by comparing it to alcohol use. But many people use alcohol socially, while there is no marijuana equivalent of a glass of wine with dinner. Normal alcohol use is one or two drinks that wear off quickly, whereas people who smoke marijuana are under the influence for the rest of the day, and subtly affected for days or weeks. Normal alcohol users do not drink to get drunk, whereas normal marijuana users smoke to get stoned. If everyone used alcohol the way people use marijuana—that is, drank only to get wasted—we'd probably still have Prohibition.

The way people use marijuana is never comparable to normal alcohol use, but it is comparable to binge drinking—using for the purpose of getting high. We're trying to discourage binge drinking by making it socially unacceptable, so why would we do anything different with marijuana?

Marijuana users don't just abuse weed

The real question we face is whether we'd be better off adding marijuana to the current mix of legal drugs. So the marijuana lobby came up with a new talking point: they promoted the idea that legalizing weed would cut down on alcohol problems.[2] They say marijuana is a substitute, and that allowing people to choose it instead of alcohol would make the world safer. The problem with this theory is that substance abuse doesn't work this way.

The guy who has an occasional glass of wine with dinner doesn't get into fights or drive drunk. So if he switches to marijuana it solves nothing, because he rarely causes trouble. Alcohol-related troubles come from the heavy drinkers, binge drinkers, and addicted drinkers. If they gave up alcohol and switched to marijuana, there might be some benefit. But that's exactly what doesn't happen. Problem drinkers don't switch; they just abuse marijuana along with alcohol.

Research proves this. If marijuana were a substitute and people chose one and avoided the other, then marijuana users would be less likely to abuse alcohol. Instead, research shows marijuana users are more likely to abuse alcohol.

In 2010, an article titled "Outcomes of Occasional Cannabis Use in Adolescence" was published in the *British Journal of Psychiatry*. The researchers followed almost 2,000 participants aged fifteen to twenty-four. Several times during that period, the participants were surveyed about their marijuana use and alcohol problems. And the study found that teenagers who smoked marijuana were more likely to abuse alcohol as adults.[3]

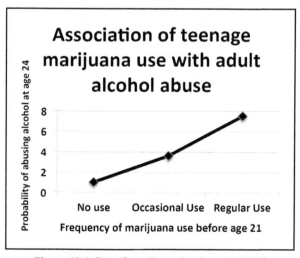

Figure 13-1. Data from Degenhardt et al., 2010[4]

This is the gateway effect. Teens who use marijuana are more likely to abuse other substances as adults. And the younger and more often they use marijuana, the more likely it is that they will have other substance problems later on.

Another study, this one from Australia's National Drug and Alcohol Research Centre, involved researchers who interviewed more than 10,000 people aged eighteen and older about their drug and alcohol use. Their use of each substance was classified according to the *DSM-IV.*[5]

For each substance, people were divided into four groups:

1. Those who never used the substance
2. Those who used it but did not meet criteria for a substance use disorder
3. Substance abusers whose use of the substance caused them problems
4. Those who were dependent—that is, had symptoms of addiction

The researchers looked at how likely the users, abusers, and addicts of one substance were to use, abuse, or be addicted to another. The results contradicted the substitution theory, which is based on the assumption that people who smoke marijuana are less likely to use and abuse alcohol. In this study, people who used marijuana were more likely to use and abuse alcohol. And the problematic marijuana users were most likely to also have an alcohol problem.

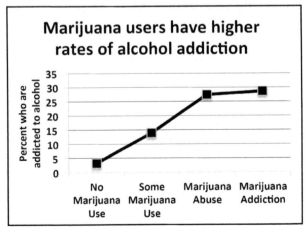

Figure 13-2. Data from Degenhardt, Hall, & Lynskey, 2001.[6]

The same study looked at other illegal drugs—sedatives, stimulants, and opiates—and found that heavy marijuana users were also more likely to abuse those drugs.

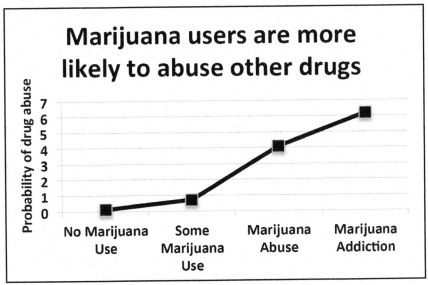

Figure 13-3. Data from Degenhardt, Hall, & Lynskey, 2001.[7]

And for completeness, the study also went on to show that people who abuse alcohol are more likely to also use marijuana and other drugs.[8] If the substitution theory were right and substance abusers gave up one drug when they used another, then these graphs would all slope downward to the right. Instead they slope upward, because the more someone abuses one addictive substance, the more likely they are to use and abuse them all.

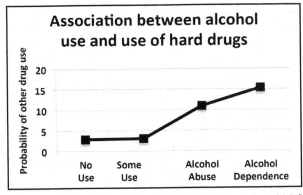

Figure 13-4. Data from Degenhardt, Hall, & Lynskey, 2001[9]

145

This is something addiction counselors have known for years: The disease isn't alcohol or heroin or marijuana. The disease is substance abuse, and abusing multiple substances is what people with this illness often do. For occasional alcohol users, the substitution theory might be true, but their use is not a problem. For substance abusers, the substitution theory is wrong. Legalizing marijuana won't cure alcohol abuse. It would just create more people who abuse alcohol and marijuana together.

Combined DUIs happen when we add marijuana

Not long ago, DUI meant driving under the influence of alcohol; now it includes driving high on drugs. Driving under the influence of more than one substance is both the fastest growing type of DUI and the most serious. It's happening more often because people who abuse one substance tend to abuse others, and we've added a new substance.

In May 2013, the *Phoenix New Times*, a very marijuana-friendly weekly, ran an article with the headline "Marijuana by Itself Not a Significant Factor in Fatal and Injury Crashes in 2012." The news story pointed out that only three serious car crashes involved marijuana alone.[10]

But the newspaper didn't count nineteen crashes caused by marijuana combined with either alcohol or another drug. Marijuana should get the blame for two-substance DUIs because, while drunk-driving figures are staying steady or going down, stoned driving and combined alcohol and marijuana DUI figures are both going up. And they're going up in tandem with increased marijuana use.

In Montana, for example, the medical marijuana law took off between 2007 and 2011. The state went from having fewer than 1,000 people with medical marijuana cards to more than 30,000. During those years, alcohol DUI convictions declined by 15 percent while the number of marijuana DUIs tripled. And most of that increase came from DUI cases involving both marijuana and alcohol, which quadrupled.[11]

The results were more striking when Montana analyzed fatal DUI cases. During one year, 2010–2011, the percentage of cases involving only alcohol decreased, as did the percentage of cases involving only drugs. But fatal accidents involving both alcohol and drugs went up.

And marijuana was the most commonly found drug.[12]

Marijuana advocates want us to believe that people will choose one drug over another and that adding marijuana to the mix will make the roads safer. Instead, the most rapidly increasing types of DUI are caused by alcohol and marijuana combined. The whole alcohol versus marijuana debate is useful for selling legalization to an unwary public, but real substance abusers use both.

Every drug is a problem

The false choice between alcohol and marijuana is especially unfair to parents. They don't breathe a sigh of relief because their kids are "only smoking weed" or "only drinking alcohol." They don't want their kids using either one.

In substance abuse treatment programs, we never tell anyone they're better off abusing one drug over another. No one says legalizing cocaine is the way to cure the heroin epidemic. We do use long-acting maintenance treatments, like methadone or buprenorphine, but maintenance medications aren't fun by themselves and are rarely anyone's drug of choice.

There are three reasons we don't recommend substituting one drug of abuse for another. First, addicts who switch usually get addicted to the new drug as well. Second, people who try switching drugs often find the new drug leads back to all the others. As one addict said, "I'm a cocaine addict, not an alcoholic, but every time I drink alcohol I end up using cocaine."

The third reason we don't recommend switching is that we can't do it in good conscience. There is no way to say one drug of abuse is safer than another. Each drug has at least one way in which it's worse than all the rest.

Alcohol: Hardest on the liver, kills most people in traffic crashes and violence.

Cocaine: Quickest to cause addiction.

Crystal meth: Causes the most physical deterioration.

Heroin: Hardest to quit. Most frequently leads to fatal overdose.

Marijuana: Causes the most permanent damage to the adolescent brain; causes the most students to drop out.

Tobacco: Kills the most people through cancer and heart disease.

If we tell teenagers marijuana is safer than alcohol, we're saying that dropping out of school is preferable to drinking and driving, and that it's better to risk schizophrenia than cirrhosis. That's terrible advice.

Put it this way: If you have a family history of schizophrenia, would you rather your teenage child used alcohol or marijuana? It's a terrible question because, for most parents, the answer is neither one. No one should be asked to choose.

Comparing one drug to another has just one purpose: to promote one of them. That's what the marijuana lobby is doing by comparing pot to alcohol. But drug abusers don't just use one or the other, so promoting one means promoting them all.

Instead of arguing about which drug of abuse is worse, we should be sending the message that all drug and alcohol abuse is harmful. And when anyone points out how much harm alcohol causes, instead of seeing it as evidence of discrimination against marijuana users, we should take it as a warning about the trouble legalizing another addictive drug could cause.

Chapter 14

The Third Way: Recovery-based Policies

The marijuana movement says our only options are legalizing pot or criminalizing it. Both have serious drawbacks. If we legalize marijuana, use will increase, more people will drive high, and a legal marijuana industry will target teenagers. On the other hand, marijuana criminalization can mean arrest records that follow people for the rest of their lives.

Fortunately, those are not our only two choices; there is a third way and it has big advantages. The third way would reduce drug abuse, reduce crime, and reduce the other problems drug abuse causes. It does this by reducing the demand for drugs.

Demand-side solutions

Making drugs less available—decreasing the supply—is one way to decrease drug use. Criminalization is a supply-side approach to our drug problem. When possession and sale are illegal, drugs are less available. When we interrupt drug distribution overseas, we also make drugs less available.

Demand-side programs get people to stop wanting drugs. Nixon's program that provided treatment for heroin addicts was a demand-side solution. And it was successful at reducing both drug abuse and crime.

Conservatives tend to favor supply-side solutions and liberals prefer the demand-side approach. However, neither works well by itself. The drug war under Reagan was almost all supply-side, and did nothing to help addicts. Free treatment is a great demand-side solution, but most active substance abusers don't want help and won't get treatment even if it's free. So both approaches are incomplete by themselves.

Recently, the U.S. Democratic Party and the Canadian Liberals have largely aligned with the marijuana movement and many of their elected officials are pro-legalization. But they weren't always this way. In the 1990s, the Democrats came up with what is arguably the best program for reducing substance abuse ever invented. It's both demand-sided and supply-sided, and it's an important part of the third way.

Drug courts: the Democratic answer to substance abuse

In 1989, in Miami-Dade County, Florida, a team including two judges, a public defender, and Democratic State Attorney Janet Reno used modern knowledge of addiction treatment to give substance-abusing criminals an alternative to prison. They called it drug court, and it worked so well that funding to expand the program nationwide was included in the 1994 Violent Crime Control and Law Enforcement Act—which written by Democratic Senate Judiciary Chairman Joe Biden and signed into law by Democratic President Bill Clinton.

Although initially promoted primarily by Democrats, support for drug courts has since become bipartisan. By the end of 2013, the U.S. had 2,907 drug courts, and most were established under President Bush.[1]

Drug courts are outpatient treatment programs supervised by a judge who has the power to impose consequences when patients don't cooperate.[2] Drug court participants are rewarded with compliments, certificates, hugs, and positive feedback. Negative consequences are increased supervision, criticism in front of the group, more frequent court appointments or drug screens, or an overnight or weekend in jail. As a last resort, the judge can send offenders back to jail or prison, but the best punishments are brief and immediate.

The purpose of drug courts is to get drug users to stay clean and sober, whether for the length of the program or for years afterward. Drug courts don't affect the supply of drugs; they affect the demand. But they also depend on firm laws, especially drug laws. The threat of punishment is what gets people into drug court and keeps them there.

Why drug courts work

In the 2012 ADAM survey, three-quarters of criminals tested positive for drugs, but only one-quarter had ever had treatment.[3] When substance abusers don't get treatment, according to the NSDUH, it's almost always because they don't want it.[4]

Drug courts are a type of intervention for these substance-abusing criminals who might never accept help otherwise. Jails and prisons are full of revolving door inmates whose untreated drug and alcohol problems get them into trouble over and over again. By coercing addicted criminals into treatment, drug courts can break that cycle.

There's a myth that substance abuse treatment only works if people go into it voluntarily, but no one really goes voluntarily. Addicts often say they did, but on closer examination, they went "willingly" only after their spouse threatened to leave, the boss threatened their job, the judge said they were facing prison, or they got beat up and slept in the bushes more times than they could count. That is the natural course of addiction. Addicts and alcoholics get clean and sober only when all other options become too painful.

Instead of waiting for life to get painful enough, treatment professionals have learned how to orchestrate the consequences of addiction to make treatment the least painful option now. This approach is called intervention and it works really well. Doctors and airline pilots have excellent recovery rates, 90 percent in some studies, because they're given a choice: either go to treatment and stay clean and sober, or give up a six-figure income and prestigious career. Intervention works because it imitates the natural process that gets addicts and alcoholics into recovery.[5]

Judges like drug courts because, instead of punishing people, they're helping them change their lives for the better. Patients often like drug courts, too, although usually not at first.

Years ago I spoke with a drug user who had been treated for years with antidepressant medicine. At each visit, his doctor reminded him he might get better if he quit getting high, but he wasn't interested. Then he got arrested yet again and was given the choice of jail or a year in drug court. At his drug court interview, he said he would stay away from drugs for a year but planned to go back to using afterward. He had no interest in getting better and said so. But six months into the program, he decided he liked being clean and sober and got involved in his own recovery. When I spoke to him three years after his drug court experience, he was still clean and sober, happy, and no longer needed to take medicine or see a psychiatrist.

Another drug user was in dependency court, a similar program for addicts and alcoholics whose children have been taken by Child Protective Services (CPS). Two years after the experience, she told me, "I hate to admit it, but the best thing that ever happened to me was CPS taking my daughter away." It was the only thing that got her off crystal meth long enough to see how she was hurting herself.

Before addicts get clean and sober, their mantra is "Leave me alone. I don't have a problem."

Afterwards, they're often thankful. As a patient of mine once said, "I didn't get arrested; I got rescued."

We can learn several lessons from drug courts. Substance abusers will fight against treatment tooth and nail and insist they don't have a problem, but when they do get clean and sober, they're usually glad they did. Punishment is not treatment, but the threat of punishment is often the only way to keep someone in treatment. And punishment works best if it is brief, immediate, and clearly being used to guide and help.

The third way keeps the focus on recovery

However, the most important lesson is that we're not limited to two choices. This third way comes from treatment professionals who see drug abuse as an illness. When treating an illness, the aim should always be recovery, so the third way is *recovery-focused* or *recovery-based*. And this recovery-based approach is as different from law enforcement and legalization as those two are from each other. Here are some ways the three approaches differ:

- Recovery-based programs decrease the demand for drugs. Interdiction overseas and at the border only decreases the supply. Legalization would increase both the supply and the demand.

- Recovery-based programs are managed by addiction profes-sionals. Prohibition and interdiction are run by law enforcement. Legalization would leave drug users and sellers in charge.

- Recovery-based programs see drug abusers as sick people who can get well. Law enforcement tends to see them as bad people who don't change. Legalization would just let them stay sick; it sees drug abuse as inevitable.

Recovery-based programs find value in the criminal justice system—not as punishment, but as a tool to get addicted criminals into treatment and to help them stay clean and sober. These programs keep the focus on recovery. Since so many substance abusers resist getting help despite having terrible problems, recovery-based programs are uniquely designed to get them the help they need at a much younger age than they might otherwise get it.

The third way also solves problems the other two ways cannot, partic-ularly the increased drug use that would come with legalization and the lifelong stigma of drug arrests that comes with criminalization. Here are five examples of recovery-based programs.

1. The Swedish plan

The legalization lobby often brings up the Netherlands and Portugal, countries that have decriminalized personal use. But Sweden is a better model to follow when it comes to drugs. Three facts explain why:

1. A UNICEF study that examined marijuana use at ages eleven, thirteen, and fifteen found that in Canada, 28 percent of kids at these ages had smoked marijuana during the past year; and in the United States, it was 22 percent. However, Sweden's rate was 5.5 percent, the second-lowest in Europe.[6]

2. Of the thirty-four countries in the Organization for Economic Cooperation and Development (OECD), Sweden has the second-lowest rate of traffic fatalities.[7]

3. Since 2004, the Swedish prison population has dropped by 1 percent each year, and Sweden has closed four of its prisons.[8]

This country must be doing something right.

However, Sweden was one of the first countries to decriminalize drugs, and initially it made all the mistakes we're making now. In the early 1970s, Swedish police were told to focus on more serious crimes, such as smuggling and large-scale trafficking, and to ignore possession and small-scale drug sales. As a result, drug use escalated. So after a public debate, the country reversed course and began prosecuting every drug law violation.[9]

Sweden is still a famously liberal country with a commitment to social welfare. What might seem like un-liberal drug laws are actually part of a public health approach. Sweden budgets more per capita to address drug abuse than any other European country except the Netherlands, spending generously on drug prevention in its schools and on treatment for those who need it. Strict drug laws are used not so much for punishment, but to send a strong anti-drug message and to get substance abusers into recovery. The criminal justice system relies heavily on probation and referrals for treatment.[10]

The Swedish plan is a three-pronged approach: lots of prevention, strict drug laws, and a focus on rehabilitation. There are five building blocks in any complete third way program, and Sweden uses them all: education and prevention, intervention, treatment and recovery.

A country that uses third way programs will develop a culture of recovery as opposed to a culture of moral judgment and punishment. Addicted criminals are seen as sick people, but like people with any other illness, they are expected to seek help and get better. There is no tolerance for drug abusers who choose to stay sick.

What stands out most about this model is that a country can keep marijuana strictly illegal without making it a moral issue. Sweden has the toughest marijuana laws in Europe, but treats substance abuse like the disease it is. Sweden's solution relies on neither legal-ization nor punishment. It's recovery-based.

One of the reasons Prohibition did not work well in the United States a century ago was that it relied entirely on criminalization. The lesson we should learn from Sweden is that strict drug laws work, but only if they are part of a comprehensive public health approach.

2. Prevention pays

Early intervention can prevent the development of severe substance abuse. Research from the 1980s showed that when smokers and heavy drinkers received repeated encouragement from their doctors to quit or cut down, they often did. This encouragement can take less than a minute, but it's effective. Gradually, programs called SBIRT (Screening, Brief Intervention, and Referral to Treatment) were developed. In doctor's offices, public clinics, emergency rooms, and university health centers that use SBIRT, everyone is asked about substance use. Most people have no problem. Those with mild problems get a brief intervention of about five minutes. Those with moderate or severe problems are referred to treatment. It's clearly effective at preventing serious alcohol problems, and appears to be equally effective with drug abuse.[11]

The federal SBIRT grantee program was set up in 2003 under President George W. Bush and continued under President Obama. It's another program with bipartisan support. By 2012, the program was sponsoring programs in half the U.S. states. But we can and should do more. This is a very simple, brief intervention that costs little and saves a lot by preventing medical problems and run-ins with the law. If any other illness were this common and caused such trouble, we'd be screening everyone. Expanding SBIRT to every physician and every clinic would allow us to do just that. If we screened everyone, we would prevent a lot of substance abuse. Preventing an illness is always better than treating it.

3. Destigmatization

On one point, I agree with the marijuana lobby. No one should be stigmatized for the rest of their life just because they were caught with drugs. However, just because we agree on the problem doesn't mean we agree on the solution. The marijuana lobby's solution to every problem is legalization. But if the problem is stigma, then let's get rid of the stigma, not the entire law.

There are three models for destigmatization. The National Association of Criminal Defense Lawyers has suggested *forgiveness*, removing laws that make life difficult for former criminals. Such laws deny public housing, a barber's license, voter registration, and dozens of other rights and privileges to people with criminal records. These laws keep them from living and working like the rest of us. Once someone has completed probation or parole, *forgiveness* allows them to re-enter society on an equal footing.[12]

Another model for destigmatization comes from the way the criminal justice system treats adolescents. If teenagers are convicted of a crime, we eventually erase their records. We could do the same for drug users once they've shown they can stay clean and sober. If someone arrested for possession stays clean and sober and out of trouble, after a certain number of years it no longer benefits society to maintain their criminal record.

New Jersey has such an expungement law. Except for certain very serious crimes, a person who has had only one conviction may apply to have their record expunged ten years after they've paid their fines, served their time, and finished probation or parole. Drug possession qualifies for expungement, but not drug sales. Once the conviction is expunged, the person can say "No" when asked about a criminal record on an application for employment, an apartment, or professional licensure. Eighteen other states have some form of "set aside," sealing, or expungement law, but not all apply to drug possession.[13]

A third model for destigmatization comes from laws around job interviews. We limit what prospective employers can ask job applicants—we don't let them ask about age or religion, for example. But employers can ask if applicants have ever been arrested or ever used drugs. Certain state and federal jobs even require an interview about illegal drug use, and people get turned down because of drugs they used decades earlier.

Do employers really need to know about drug use or a substance-related arrest that occurred more than a decade earlier? At some point, isn't the person with a distant criminal or drug-using past no different from any other job applicant? Sure, they could lie about their past use, but if someone has to lie to make it in this world, then he's a second-class citizen. We want people who have worked at long-term recovery to be first-class citizens. So after a certain number of years, we should stop asking.

These are only three models; there are probably other ways to destigmatize a criminal past. I'm not proposing specific changes, just a general concept. When people get help and turn their lives around, we should recognize how responsible they've been. At some point, they should be able to feel like full citizens again.

The stigma of an old arrest

Four days before the 2000 U.S. election, it was revealed that presidential candidate George W. Bush had been arrested for DUI twenty-four years earlier. According to his campaign manager, Karl Rove, many "voters—especially evangelicals and social conservatives—decided not to vote, taking votes away from Bush." Were it not for that 24-year old DUI, Bush probably would have won without controversy. Instead, he lost the popular vote and nearly lost the election. In fact, had there been a full recount of all disputed Florida ballots, research shows he would have lost the election.[14]

Bush stopped drinking in 1986, so in 2000, he had fourteen years clean and sober. In a culture that valued recovery, those fourteen years would tell us more about Bush, the person, than a DUI from a quarter century earlier.

It was a controversial election, and Bush was a controversial president, but when someone has done the right thing and gotten clean and sober, a substance-related arrest in their distant past should not cost them a job—whether it's the presidency or a license to cut hair.

The marijuana lobby uses any problem as an excuse to promote legalization. But we don't have to legalize drugs to solve this problem. The simplest and most specific response to the long-term stigma of a drug-using past or a drug-related arrest is to get rid of the stigma, not the whole law.

4. *De facto* decriminalization

Since legalization and criminalization both have such serious drawbacks, decriminalization, which falls in between, makes sense. Under decriminalization, it would still be against the law to grow, sell, or otherwise traffic in marijuana, so there wouldn't be a legal marijuana industry targeting teenagers. And with decriminalization, the other extreme would be avoided as well; no one would face jail or prison time for possession.

There's just one problem: marijuana laws serve a purpose. Strict laws send the message that it's a harmful drug, and that keeps many people from using it. Many others stay away simply because it's illegal. Ten percent of non-using teens said they would try marijuana if it were legal.[15] So drug laws are good prevention.

They also get people into treatment. Drug courts depend on these laws to help people. Even outside of drug court, the threat of jail keeps a lot of people in treatment and recovery. The patients I see aren't court-ordered, but a lot of them decided they needed help after an arrest. Even when they're not prosecuted, it still reminds them what could happen if they don't get help.

Drug laws also keep certain criminals off the streets. Most criminals, including most violent criminals, are substance abusers, and the most common reason substance abusers commit crimes is that they're under the influence.[16] A violent felon who is clean and sober on probation or parole usually does well, but if he relapses back to drugs, he's likely to commit another violent crime. So it's better to order him back to jail or treatment based on the drug violation than to wait until he commits a more serious crime. If drug possession is decriminalized, ordering him back into treatment becomes more difficult. If drugs are legal, it's impossible.

Tough drug laws, even if they're barely enforced, are really helpful. Addiction is a miserable illness. After working with addicts and alcoholics for years, I can say with certainty that every one of them is happier clean and sober. But for many it takes outside pressure to get them there; they won't do it on their own. That's why, for lots of substance abusers, the threat of jail is the best thing that ever happened to them. The threat of punishment is actually more useful than punishment itself.

So strict drug laws that are almost never enforced are the most helpful approach. And that's what we're already doing. Throughout much of Canada and the United States, we've already decriminalized marijuana in all but name. Almost no one goes to prison and the vast majority of those arrested for possession are never prosecuted.

The term for doing something in all but name is *de facto*. The laws are on the books, but we barely use them.

Decriminalization would prevent the development of the powerful marijuana industry we'd see with legalization. But there would still be widespread use and we wouldn't have the threat of punishment that convinces some people never to try the drug and convinces others it's time to get treatment. So while decriminalization is a good idea, *de facto* decriminalization is even better. And it has one more advantage: we're already doing it.

5. Community corrections

From a law-enforcement perspective, prisons are full of criminals. But from a public health perspective, prisons are full of untreated substance abusers who commit crimes because of their illness.

According to the Center on Addiction and Substance Abuse (CASA), two-thirds of U.S. state prison inmates have a substance abuse problem, and another 20 percent are locked up for some crime related to drugs or alcohol. So 85 percent of all crime is substance-involved.[17]

If an infectious disease caused 85 percent of all crime, everyone who broke even the most minor law would get a course of antibiotics. But substance abuse goes mostly untreated.

Three-quarters of arrestees test positive for drugs at the time of arrest.[18] If we want to solve our drug and crime problems, these are the people we have to treat.

Years ago, I visited California's 1,500-bed Substance Abuse Treatment Facility at the Corcoran State Prison. It was very impressive, but the program was eventually declared a failure. It had several problems, but one was glaring. After a year of treatment in prison, inmates were released with almost no support or follow-up.[19]

My inmate patients often told me they had stayed clean and sober for years during a prior jail or prison term, despite the availability of drugs, and so they thought they were cured. But they relapsed within days or weeks of getting out, and were arrested and locked up again within months. Substance abuse treatment as part of probation or parole could stop this revolving door. We need to treat criminals in the community so they learn how to stay clean and sober in real life.

Community corrections that incorporate substance abuse treatment are the most important of all recovery-based programs. For many, it will stop the revolving door of relapse and incarceration. But it can do far more. If we get them into recovery after their first arrests as teenagers, we can prevent entire lifetimes of crime and prison.

The marijuana lobby's war on drug courts

Recovery-based programs and policies offer the best of both worlds. The Swedish plan, community corrections, and prevention programs like SBIRT can decrease drug use and all the problems it causes. With destigmatization and *de facto* decriminalization, drug laws would no longer be punitive but they would still be persuasive. The recovery-based approach treats substance abuse like a disease—not a moral issue—but it does not let the disease go unchecked.

The marijuana lobby doesn't like any of this. They want Canada and the United States to legalize marijuana, so they have to convince us that legalization is the only alternative to arrest and incarceration.[20] A third way to handle our drug problem that won't increase drug use and actually decreases crime and incarceration ruins their whole argument. So the marijuana lobby finds fault with recovery-based programs—and they particularly despise drug courts.

The Drug Policy Alliance is the best-funded pro-legalization organization in the U.S., and its opposition to drug courts is obvious. On its website, the DPA has posted a press release with the headline "New Report Finds 'Drug Courts Are Not the Answer.'" This "new report" is the DPA's own report apparently done by its own people.[21]

Furthermore, according to Eli Sanders, associate editor for the Seattle weekly *The Stranger*, "Dan Abrahamson, director of legal affairs for the Drug Policy Alliance, admits that his group's report wasn't based on new research findings or even on a 'meta-analysis' of current findings. 'We never claimed to undertake any research on drug courts,' he says."[22]

This is a common tactic of pro-legalization groups. They publish their own professional-looking reports that come to the conclusions they wanted to come to anyway. These reports look impressive, but as Abramson admitted, the DPA report contains no new information or research; it's just their interpretation of old data.

And their interpretation is wrong.

Based on its own report, DPA writes, "drug courts have not demonstrated cost savings, reduced incarceration, or improved public safety."[23] None of this is true.

The National Center on Addiction and Substance Abuse at Columbia University reviewed all the research on drug courts, and concluded: "average per-client drug court costs are lower than standard processing, primarily due to reduced incarceration."[24] A report by the General Accounting Office (GAO) found that drug courts reduced recidivism. The report says, "drug-court program participants were generally less likely to be re-arrested."[25] In other words, drug courts *have* demonstrated cost savings, reduced incarceration, and a decrease in actual crime. The DPA told its readers exactly the opposite of what the research shows.

The Drug Policy Alliance also claims to support addiction treatment but opposes what addiction treatment professionals recommend. In a letter to the *New York Times*, a senior DPA attorney wrote, "Drug addiction is best treated by health professionals, separate and apart from the criminal justice system."[26] But the health professionals the DPA claims to support disagree.

The American Society of Addiction Medicine has a policy paper about the importance of treating addicted criminals both inside and outside of prison: "Treatment for substance use disorders should begin during incarceration in prison (pre-release treatment) and should always be followed up by a post-release residential treatment/work-release program and then by community-based outpatient treatment of appropriate duration ..."[27]

This is not voluntary treatment separate from their sentence; it's done in prison and on parole. And if they don't take recovery seriously and don't stay clean and sober, they can be sent back to prison. It's that threat that makes these programs work. The DPA says separating treatment from the criminal justice system is the best way to treat addiction, but the foremost society of addiction medicine physicians recommends exactly the opposite.

After all, it would be a wasted opportunity not to treat substance abusers when they're in the criminal justice system. There's no better way to get addicts and alcoholics to cooperate with treatment than to make it part of prison, probation, and parole. Addiction medicine experts know this, but the DPA is against it anyway.

The Marijuana Policy Project, the second biggest fund-raiser in the U.S. marijuana lobby, also opposes most recovery-based programs. It says in its mission statement that it supports "non-coercive policies."[28] In other words, no one should have to stay clean and sober as part of probation, parole, or drug court. Just like the DPA, they want to separate substance abuse treatment from the criminal justice system.

This would keep us from using drug courts, which are the most successful recent innovation for dealing with crime. And it would undermine community corrections and condemn prison inmates to the revolving door that keeps many of them behind bars for life.

The drive for legalization undermines drug courts

In 2000, California passed Proposition 36, an initiative that allowed first- and second-time drug possession offenders to receive treatment rather than jail. Prop 36 was financed by George Soros, Peter Lewis, and John Sperling—the three billionaires who have contributed heavily to the pro-legalization movement.[29] So this law was a good test of their philosophy.

Proposition 36 was written to specifically forbid any jail or prison time. Drug court, on the other hand, allows for flash incarceration—a night or weekend in jail ordered by the judge when an addict is not cooperating with treatment. Both programs provide treatment for substance abusers caught with drugs. The difference is that drug court uses coercion to keep them in treatment while Prop 36 did not. And the lack of coercion made a big difference.

An assessment of Prop 36 done by UCLA in 2007 found that a quarter of the offenders never even showed up for treatment, and half of the rest showed up but dropped out. So only 33 percent completed treatment. On the other hand, the UCLA report looked at several studies of drug courts and found they averaged a 50 percent graduation rate.[30] However, this comparison understates the advantages of drug court because those programs are often longer, so graduates get far more treatment.

Proposition 36 is, in effect, voluntary; there is no coercion. And it's been found to work about as well as other voluntary programs, whether they're within the criminal justice system or outside of it.[31] So the best way to understand the difference between Prop 36 and drug court is to compare voluntary programs to coercive ones.

A study published in 2002 in the *Journal of Drug Issues* compared two groups of substance abusers referred by the courts to the same treatment program. One group was referred by the Drug Treatment Alternative to Prison (DATP) program. They were told repeatedly that failure to complete treatment would mean incarceration, and they even signed a statement acknowledging this. The other group was simply referred by probation or parole. Consequences for failure were not made clear, and there was no certainty they'd face any consequences if they dropped out of treatment. After six months, the group with unclear and uncertain consequences had twice as many dropouts as the group referred by DATP.[32]

That's a comparison of different degrees of coercion. Voluntary programs, with no court mandate and no legal consequences at all, perform even worse. Research quoted in a report by the Center for Court Innovation found that voluntary programs lose half their patients in three months, and one study found that only 10–30 percent remained in long-term residential treatment after a year. On the other hand, the same report cited a review of drug courts that found 60 percent were still involved one year later.[33] In other words, drug courts have about three times the success rate of voluntary programs like Prop 36.

So in 2006, a task force that included public defenders and treatment professionals recommended changing the Proposition 36 program to allow sanctions, and in response, the state legislature changed the law to let judges briefly incarcerate non-compliant participants—two days for first-time violators, five days for second-time, and thirty days or dismissal from the program for those who didn't cooperate at all. The bill passed both houses of the Democratic-controlled California legislature with the two-thirds majority required to amend the initiative, and the governor signed it into law. This would have made the Prop 36 program more like drug courts and far more effective.

However, the marijuana lobby's goal is legalization, not effective treatment. They want to eliminate consequences, not use them to help people. So the Drug Policy Alliance went to court and won an injunction against this law, because Prop 36 had been written to say these drug offenders should not be jailed at all.[34] In response, the legislature stopped funding the Proposition 36 programs; they got more bang for their buck from drug courts, so they put the state's money there.

Proposition 36 not only performed poorly, it actually undermined drug courts. People convicted of possession could choose treatment but not go and face no consequences. Many addicts saw the law as a "free pass." However, it was only a free pass for the first two convictions. After that, the only way to avoid serving time was to enroll in drug court.

Then, in 2014, California further undermined drug courts by passing Proposition 47, another initiative supported by groups affiliated with George Soros. This ballot measure reduced drug possession to a misdemeanor.[35] For a misdemeanor, the longest possible jail time is six months, but effective drug court programs usually run a year or more. So there's now little incentive for anyone to choose drug court.

The trouble with both these propositions is that sidelining drug courts increases crime, or slows any decrease. One of the authors of the UCLA study said some of the Prop 36 participants with long rap sheets didn't belong in the program because they were too dangerous not to incarcerate.

The marijuana lobby won partly by outspending opponents fifteen to one, but they've also encouraged the belief that drug possession is victimless and unrelated to other crime.[36] It's not. Most inmates incarcerated for possession also committed other crimes, and most of those who commit other crimes also have substance abuse problems. With few exceptions, those facing time for possession are the people who commit other crimes. Drug users who don't are rarely arrested and almost never imprisoned.

Drug possession charges are used to lock up dealers when there's not enough evidence to prosecute them for trafficking, to let a criminal plead down when it would be difficult or expensive to prosecute the more serious crime, to violate probation or parole when an addicted criminal has clearly relapsed to drugs and is likely to commit other crimes, and to convince addicted criminals to get treatment and break the whole cycle of crime. These are all ways drug laws are used to prevent more serious crime. Weakening these laws sets criminals free. Here's an example from the *Los Angeles Times*:

> Santillan, 24, was convicted in three drug possession cases and remained free under Proposition 36. He said he treated jail after each new arrest as a chance to recuperate before hitting the streets again.
>
> "When I got out, I just didn't want to do nothing but get loaded," he said.
>
> Santillan ran out of chances last year and was sentenced to a year behind bars. He was released early because of jail overcrowding and returned weeks later, accused of car theft.[37]

Like Santillan, drug abusers are often the people who commit more serious crimes. Drug abuse plays such a big role in most violent and property crime that it makes no sense to call it victimless. As one researcher warned about some of the people Prop 36 set free, we're "putting our community in jeopardy by having them on the streets."[38]

Drug courts have been shown to reduce drug trafficking and property crime.[39] Violent crime is harder to assess because very few drug courts admit people with a history of violent offences. However, substance abuse treatment has been shown to decrease violence.[40]

So drug courts prevent all types of crime. By undermining drug courts with Prop 36 and Prop 47, California has undermined crime prevention, which will probably increase all types of crime.

Why the marijuana lobby says "No, no, no"

There are two possible reasons why the marijuana lobby would dislike recovery-based programs. First, their main argument only works if people believe there are just two options, legalization or mass incarceration. Recovery-based programs destroy that argument.

Second, NORML, MPP, and DPA all have the goal of gaining more legal rights for drug users. This would include drug abusers, who often want a society that accepts their drug abuse, doesn't see it as a problem, and allows them to use until they decide to get help.

Drug courts work from a belief that addicts—including those who don't want help—are happier clean and sober, and that society is better off when addicted criminals are clean and sober. Besides, waiting until an addict is ready is like waiting for a sinking ship to right itself.

The recovery-based approach would create a society that is the opposite of what drug abusers want. It would create a society that finds drug use unacceptable, that expects drug abusers to get help, and that uses the criminal justice system to encourage recovery.

Recovery-based programs include interventions that motivate substance-abusing criminals into treatment. Most active substance abusers loathe the idea of treatment, so the lobby representing them will do everything it can to derail the recovery-based approach.

When Amy Winehouse sang, "They tried to make me go to rehab, but I said no, no, no," she spoke for addicts everywhere. Rehab might have been the best thing for her, but addicts and alcoholics are driven by this disease to reject what is best for them—and to embrace the very worst. So when the marijuana lobby fights tooth and claw to discredit the best criminal justice innovation of the past century, they're doing exactly what their most self-destructive members are driven to do themselves.

Chapter 15

Responsibility for Cartels Lies with Drug Users

On September 10, 2014, the *Atlantic* ran an article by Conor Friedersdorf titled "Elder Statesmen Declare a War on the 'War on Drugs.'" The article was about a report from the Global Commission on Drug Policy calling for the decriminalization, not just of marijuana, but of nearly all illegal drugs.[1] However, his article contained a common error.

Friedersdorf blames the drug war for violent drug cartels. He writes, "But for America's decades-long War on Drugs, the drug cartels would not exist." But he is confusing the drug war with laws that make possession illegal, and they're not the same. The War on Drugs initially directed most of its funding toward treatment, and later it focused on pursuing major international traffickers. Neither of those helps the cartels.

Friedersdorf says he blames the drug war, but he is really blaming drug *laws* for violent cartels. He seems to be saying that if drugs were sold legally, the illegal drug cartels would be out of business. That's true, but he goes too far when he implies that the cartels are a result of making drugs illegal, because drugs were illegal decades before cartels became major players.

In the U.S., opiates and cocaine were limited by law to prescription only in 1914. Heroin was completely banned in 1924. Most U.S. states had banned marijuana by 1931, and it was banned nationally in 1937. Mandatory minimum sentences for possession of cocaine, heroin, and marijuana were passed in 1951, and increased in 1956.[2] None of those coincided with the creation of drug cartels.

Nixon got Congress to eliminate mandatory minimum sentences for drug possession in 1970 with the Controlled Substance Act. They were reinstated in 1986 under Reagan, but by then the cartels were already thriving.

The growth of cartels came shortly after American drug use exploded in the late 1960s and 1970s. Colombian drug cartels started in the 1970s and Mexican cartels in the 1980s. They started and grew in response to drug use in the United States.[3] So it's a mistake to blame either the drug war or drug laws. Drug use is responsible for cartels.

The money behind legalization

A bigger problem with the article is what Friedersdorf doesn't tell us. The Global Commission on Drug Policy is one of several groups promoting the decriminalization or legalization of all drugs. The U.S.-based Drug Policy Alliance and the Canadian Drug Policy Coalition are two more. These groups are not really independent organizations. They're all linked to hedge fund billionaire George Soros or his Open Society Foundations. Soros has helped to create a plethora of pro-legalization organizations much the same way Charles and David Koch helped to create several anti-environmental groups.[4]

However, it wouldn't be much of a news story to write, "George Soros says we should legalize all drugs." That's about as convincing as "Charles and David Koch say we should ignore climate change." So instead, Friedersdorf refers to the Global Commission as "elder statesmen." But when a little-known organization with a generic-sounding name makes a radical recommendation, the first thing everyone should want to know is who's behind it. Friedersdorf doesn't tell us.

Taking responsibility

However, the biggest problem with the article is that legalization advocates like Friedersdorf often see the world through the eyes of actively using drug addicts. And the argument that legalization is the cure for drug cartels is a good example of this type of thinking.

When substance abusers are still using, their denial usually shows itself in two ways. First, they deny responsibility; it's always someone else's fault. One man with a DUI said he knew he was too drunk to drive, so he was taking side streets. "That cop shouldn't have been stopping people on side streets," he said. To him, it was the cop's fault, not his.

Second, untreated addicts and alcoholics usually think it's impossible to quit using. One might as well try to quit breathing; it feels that unattainable. So when the disease causes trouble, they come up with every imaginable solution except quitting. Many years ago, a young alcoholic proudly told me she had sold her car so she wouldn't drive drunk. She expected a pat on the back. When I frowned instead, she asked what I thought she should do. "You should stop drinking," I said. She'd never considered that.

Most actively drinking alcoholics never do. They truly believe that everyone around them has to change because, in their deluded thinking, it's impossible for an addict or alcoholic to quit. They don't even consider it an option.

In treatment, we make them responsible. We tell them it's not the cop's fault for stopping people on side streets; it's their fault for driving drunk. We teach them that quitting is not impossible; in fact, it's the answer to all the problems substance abuse causes. And we teach them to stop demanding that the rest of the world rearrange itself around their illness.

That is also what we should do when legalization advocates try to blame drug laws for cartels. We should say the obvious: Marijuana and other drugs were just as illegal in the 1940s and 1950s as they are today, and there were no big cartels back then.

Ninety-two percent of the U.S. population doesn't use marijuana, and the percentage of nonusers is even higher for other drugs. So instead of demanding that we rewrite our drug laws to accommodate their drug use, the way to eliminate cartels is for drug users to stop using. No one has to use drugs, and if far fewer people did, the cartels would be out of business.

This is not overly idealistic thinking. Teenage marijuana and cocaine use both dropped by two-thirds when the news and entertainment media gave their audiences good anti-drug information. If we did that before, we can do it again.

The legalization lobby is like an addict who refuses to take responsibility for the problems his drug use causes. For such people, quitting is inconceivable, so they try to convince the rest of us to accommodate their drug use. And if we don't, they blame us and say we're responsible for all the problems they cause. But no one should fall for this story. Responsibility for cartels lies with drug users, not drug laws. So the best way to rein in cartels is not to legalize drugs; it's to stop using them.

Chapter 16

The Irrevocable Decision: Creating a Marijuana Industry

Medical marijuana laws almost certainly contributed to the recent surge in adolescent use. But the marijuana lobby doesn't accept that. According to Rob Kampia, executive director of the Marijuana Policy Project, teenage use is increasing because of prohibition. He says that, since it's illegal, marijuana is sold by "drug dealers who aren't required to check customer ID and have no qualms about selling marijuana to young people."[1]

This is an easy argument to disprove. Alcohol salespeople are required to check ID, and teenagers consistently say they can get alcohol more readily than marijuana.[2] But while this argument is wrong factually, it's great politically.

It lets advocates blame drug laws and drug dealers for growing teenage use. The obvious implication is that, with legalization, local drug dealers will no longer target our kids. What the marijuana lobby never seems to mention is that someone else will target our children, and they will do it far more effectively.

The world's most sophisticated drug dealers

Tobacco is legal, and no industry has done a better job of enticing teenagers to use an addictive drug. They've advertised in youth-oriented magazines and in convenience stores that teens frequent. They've reached out on the Internet and in social media, where teens get most of their information. They've designed fake prevention campaigns that actually encourage adolescents to smoke. They've even paid for product placement in movies teenagers watch.[3] What small-time drug dealer could do any of those things?

Tobacco companies are the world's experts at marketing an addictive drug, and the marijuana industry is following their example. An article called "Big Marijuana—Lessons from Big Tobacco," published in the July 31, 2014, *New England Journal of Medicine*, noted:

> "The tobacco industry has provided a detailed road map for marijuana: deny addiction potential, downplay known adverse health effects, create as large a market as possible as quickly as possible, and protect that market through lobbying, campaign contributions, and other advocacy efforts."[4]

The marijuana lobby has already done all that. This chapter is called The Irrevocable Decision because, with today's money-driven politics, once a powerful industry is allowed to develop, we never get rid of it. Powerful industries have the money to influence politicians and elections. As the *New England Journal of Medicine* article went on to say:

> "The tobacco industry, bolstered by enormous profits, successfully lobbied to be exempted from every major piece of consumer protection legislation even after the deadly consequences of tobacco were established. With nothing to sell or profit from, health advocates had difficulty fighting a battle that was clearly in the best interest of the public. The marijuana industry has already formed its own advocacy organization—the National Cannabis Industry Association—to protect and advance its corporate interests."[5]

Money buys influence

During the Obama administration, medical marijuana sales increased, enriching the industry, which in turn donates to politicians. The marijuana industry has influence with both U.S. political parties and with the Liberals in Canada.

We can see its power. After Colorado and Washington voted for legalization, President Obama could have enforced the federal law against selling marijuana—but he chose not to. Republicans who controlled the House of Representatives could have voted on a resolution demanding the President enforce marijuana laws—but they chose not to. Neither political party wants to take on this industry.

The danger of legalization is that a powerful industry can target teenagers with billions of dollars and state-of-the-art advertising, and then pay off politicians to let them do it. Former White House policy adviser Kevin Sabet wrote a book called *Reefer Sanity*, in which he described the threat of corporate marijuana extensively.[6]

Advocates defend the industry

Sabet is president of Project SAM (Smart Approaches to Marijuana), which he founded with former Congressman Patrick Kennedy. They also launched a project called Grass Is Not Greener, which has this warning on its website: "If we're not careful, the marijuana industry could quickly become the next Big Tobacco."[7]

In response to this warning, on August 8, 2014, the *Washington Post* ran an article by Christopher Ingraham called "Why Marijuana Won't Become Another Big Tobacco."[8] The marijuana lobby probably loved that headline, but the article contained no facts to back it up.

On its website, Grass Is Not Greener explains what it means by marijuana becoming another Big Tobacco: Financiers are turning marijuana into a major industry that will be corporate and profit-centered. And "marijuana food and candy, with names such as 'Ring Pots' and 'Pot Tarts' are being marketed to children."[9]

Ingraham's article doesn't give us one reason to think that the marijuana industry won't be run by profit-oriented businessmen and controlled by corporations, or that it won't use the same unscrupulous tactics the tobacco industry uses to target children. The only differences he presents have nothing to do with the industry; he simply points out that marijuana is less addictive and less deadly than tobacco. That's true, but it doesn't make the industry any less sinister.

Ingraham quotes Mark Kleiman, a pro-marijuana policy expert from UCLA, but even Kleiman says the marijuana industry would be just as "insidious" as the tobacco industry. Kleiman says the marijuana industry would be smaller and more like the alcohol industry, but that's not a difference because the alcohol industry also targets adolescents.[10]

This was a pro-legalization article quoting one of the most well informed legalization advocates. If the people who support legalization can't come up with one reason to believe the marijuana industry won't be as evil as Big Tobacco, then we can be certain Big Marijuana will target teenagers.

The marijuana industry would have to target kids to survive

Anyone selling an addictive drug depends on teenage users. In a March 9, 2014, Doonesbury cartoon, the character Mr. Butts explained why. Talking about tobacco, he said, "Studies show that almost 90% of all smokers start before they turn 18!"[11]

This is true. Almost all the adults addicted to tobacco started as teenagers. But if the comic strip replaced Mr. Butts with its marijuana salesman, Zonker Harris, it would be equally true. A survey of people in substance abuse treatment found that, among those with a marijuana problem, 87 percent had started by age seventeen.[12]

For both tobacco and marijuana, addiction starts primarily in adolescence, and and addiction is where the money is. As the Doonesbury cartoon character Mr. Brewski boasted: "The top 10% of drinkers consume 50% of all alcohol sold! In other words, fully half our sales are to alcoholics. How's that for a business model?"[13] That is quite a business model, but tobacco has Mr. Brewski beat: almost all regular cigarette smokers are addicted.[14]

Marijuana would fall in between, but much closer to tobacco. According to the Colorado Department of Revenue, the majority of marijuana smokers are occasional users, but they only account for 4 percent of all the marijuana consumed. Conversely, less than one-third of users smoke most days or every day, but they use 87 percent of the marijuana.[15]

Daily and near daily users would be the industry's bread and butter. The adult who gets high occasionally with friends will never spend much on marijuana, but round-the-clock, wake-and-bake users will. And the way to create money machines like that is to get them started as adolescents. It's already happening in Colorado with sweetened edibles and marijuana-infused soft drinks. Marijuana cookies, candy, lollipops, and soda appeal to kids, and the industry must surely know it.

There's another reason a marijuana industry would encourage teenage use. Researchers from Harvard found that regular adult users who started in their early to mid-teens smoke three times as much marijuana per week as those who started later.[16] Once again, almost all the money to be made in this business depends on getting teenagers started.

Just like the tobacco lobby, the marijuana lobby says adults should be free to choose. But if those industries depended only on people who started as adults, they'd both be out of business and I wouldn't be writing this book.

Any corporation selling marijuana would need to target adolescents with every trick the advertising industry can use. If they didn't, the competition would eat them alive.

Who wins in the end

Those who doubt that Big Tobacco will eventually be marketing marijuana and targeting teens should listen to professional stock market analysts. These are people who set aside all moral judgment and just look at the bottom line. Altria (formerly Phillip Morris), is America's largest tobacco company. It manufactures Marlboro and Virginia Slims, and also produces wine, cigars and smokeless tobacco.[17] In January 2015, the Value Line Investment Survey, one of the best stock assessments available, published this description:

> "[W]e expect Altria to be a key player in the growing U.S. marijuana market. The substance, like tobacco, can be very addicting, which fits in well with the other product lines. The primary reason that Altria has not moved into the marijuana market is because it is still illegal on a federal level, despite the fact

that four states have legalized it for recreational use. Should marijuana be approved in the coming years, the potential size and profits that come with the industry could have an extensive effect on the company's bottom line for years to come."[18]

That is one of the best arguments against legalization ever made.

Chapter 17

The News Media's Love Affair with Marijuana

Journalist organizations often make lists of underreported stories, important news that most of the press ignores. One story that should be on the list is the evidence that medical marijuana laws are mostly a sham, and are legalization disguised as medical care. If the press had reported on this after California passed the first medical marijuana law in 1996, it's unlikely another such law would ever have passed again.

Another news story receives almost no coverage: Canada and the United States are in the midst of a teenage marijuana epidemic that, in sheer numbers, dwarfs the cocaine, crystal meth, and opiate epidemics combined. Not only does the press not cover this epidemic, they helped create it.

And one story appears to go completely unreported: The slanted coverage that brought us to the brink of legalization. The media bias is so widespread it deserves to be covered as a news story itself.

Research shows slanted coverage

In *The High Road: A content analysis of newspaper articles concerning medical marijuana*, Samuel Vickovic described the results of a search of all U.S. newspaper articles from June 2008 until June 2009. During that year, two-thirds of the articles about medical marijuana laws were positive and one-third were negative. In positive stories, the author praised or supported medical marijuana laws; in negative stories, the writer criticized or argued against these laws.

Vickovic also looked specifically at stories about upcoming medical marijuana ballot measures or legislation. Those news articles matter particularly because they can shape public opinion and affect the outcome of elections. When he looked only at articles about states preparing to vote on medical marijuana laws, he found the news stories were 84 percent positive and only 13 percent negative. And the negative stories were mostly about confusion over the laws rather than reasons to vote against them.[1] In other words, the coverage was very one-sided.

Five types of bias

In 2010, Arizona voted on Proposition 203, a ballot measure to legalize medical marijuana. Opponents of the initiative predicted the marijuana would go mostly to drug abuse, and provided evidence for this from other states. Supporters insisted the law was only for people with serious illnesses such as cancer.

The public could be expected to vote for the proposition if they thought it was compassionate care, but against it if they thought it was mostly drug abuse. So how reporters framed their stories could decide the election. Reporters should have presented both sides equally, but coverage was biased in several ways.

Bias #1: Framing the discussion the way the marijuana lobby wanted it framed.

One Arizona TV station, ABC15, did a story about the drug abuse masquerading as medical care in California.[2] But it was virtually the only story framed that way. The rest of Arizona's news coverage was almost entirely stories that led with marijuana's role in treating serious illnesses, especially cancer.

For example, Cronkite News ran a story with the headline, "Supporters: Ailing Arizonans would benefit from medical marijuana." The bulk of the story was about marijuana's role in medical care.[3]

The TV station Phoenix Fox 10 ran a report that included interviews with two cancer survivors who spoke about treatment, one with marijuana and the other with the cannabinoid medicine Marinol. Although the report did a good job of showing that prescription Marinol could be used instead of marijuana, the story was entirely about cancer.[4] With so many news stories about the treatment of cancer, many voters may have thought that's all the proposition was about.

Bias #2: Lopsided reporting.

The Associated Press (AP) released a twenty-three-paragraph story on Prop 203.[5] It gave four paragraphs to the opposition, sandwiched between ten paragraphs for proponents and seven paragraphs describing the proposed law sympathetically.

Bias #3: Presenting pro-marijuana talking points as fact, even when the fact is wrong.

Advocates said the marijuana would only go to medical use. Opponents pointed to other states as evidence that this wasn't true. Here's what the Associated Press in Arizona wrote: "This proposal would allow the use of the drug only for serious diseases including cancer."[6]

The AP acted as if the pro-marijuana position had been proved true and the opposing position didn't even exist.

Bias #4: Accepting without question everything the marijuana lobby said.

The Marijuana Policy Project called its Arizona campaign Stop Arresting Patients. That slogan was on their signs and was the name of their website: www.stoparrestingpatients.org. They probably wanted us to picture grannies in prison, doing their knitting surrounded by tattooed gangbangers.

So in a live debate, I asked their lobbyist to name one genuine medical patient in jail or prison for marijuana. He couldn't. That's because few, if any, patients are being arrested. Law enforcement has already decided to leave patients alone. If their own lobbyist couldn't come up with one genuine patient who had been prosecuted for marijuana, that means the very name of their campaign was probably a hoax.

But why didn't reporters ask who had ever been arrested? Did they simply assume the slogan was true? The marijuana lobby was, in effect, screaming, "Stop arresting patients!" Yet to my knowledge, not one news outlet in the state asked who these patients were.

Reporters have no problem asking similar questions on other issues. In 2014, the Arizona legislature passed a bill that would let business owners turn away requests that violated their religious principles. Anderson Cooper interviewed a state legislator who, as Cooper put it, couldn't "cite one example where religious freedom is under attack in Arizona." *The Daily Show* ridiculed the legislator for protecting Arizona from a problem that only existed in his imagination.[7] But when the marijuana lobby runs a whole political campaign based on an imaginary problem, the press apparently takes them at their word.

Bias #5: Thou shalt not speak ill of marijuana.

In its September 2010 newsletter, the Glaucoma Foundation warned patients against using marijuana because it could decrease blood flow to the optic nerve and make their glaucoma worse.[8] That warning should have been newsworthy: Prop 203 listed glaucoma as a treatable condition. So Keep AZ Drug Free, the only registered opposition group, sent a press release to every media outlet in the state. To my knowledge, not one reported it.

The national media didn't pick up this story, either. Both the American and Canadian Glaucoma Societies have taken the position that they do not recommend marijuana for glaucoma.[9] Yet several medical marijuana laws include glaucoma as an indication. When there's misinformation about vaccines, the press jumps on it, but bad medical advice about marijuana they ignore.

Three months after Arizona's program kicked in, I wrote a guest op-ed for the *Arizona Republic* showing that opponents were probably right. Ninety percent of Arizona's marijuana patients got their marijuana for pain and pain patients are mostly female. So the marijuana patients should be mostly female. Instead, they were 75 percent male, which is approximately the percentage of adult marijuana abusers who are male. The numbers strongly suggest that Arizona's marijuana cardholders were almost all drug abusers pretending to need the drug for pain.[10]

Reporters should have been interested in evidence that medical marijuana was going almost entirely to substance abuse, but, to my knowledge, no one picked up on the story. However, two reporters who were doing sympathetic stories about marijuana did contact me. They wanted my comments to give the appearance of balance.

I asked if they would also do a story on people faking illness to get marijuana. After all, the evidence said that's what a majority of marijuana cardholders were doing. The *Arizona Republic* reporter said that was too difficult a story to do. The public radio reporter said they had no plans to do such a story. In other words, they would not do negative stories about marijuana.

Proposition 203 squeaked by in Arizona with 50.1 percent of the vote. Media bias almost certainly tipped the scales.

Doing the marijuana lobby's bidding

On June 29, 2012, the *Hartford Courant* ran a report about Connecticut's new medical marijuana law with the sub-headline "Tight restrictions assured."[11] However, in this article, the assurance came only from pro-marijuana sources who all repeated the same talking point: Unlike other state laws, they all said, Connecticut's would be tightly regulated.

The story started with unnamed "national experts" who said Connecticut's marijuana law would be "very tightly regulated—unlike in California and Colorado." Then came spokespeople from NORML, the Marijuana Policy Project, and, later in the article, the Drug Policy Alliance. The NORML director expressed hopes that it would be "the absolute model for the nation. I don't want it to be like in other states."[12]

The article even quoted a businessman who sold marijuana vending machines. "Connecticut really wants to make this the tightest, most regulated state possible," he declared, sticking to his talking point while hawking a device that could make marijuana available 24 hours a day.[13]

There's probably a reason for this talking point. People are starting to realize that medical marijuana laws are mostly conduits for drug abuse, and the marijuana lobby probably wants to calm their concerns. The *Courant*'s news report did what the marijuana lobby probably wanted, but it's one-sided journalism.

National media were no better. About Connecticut's law, Reuters wrote, "The new law puts in place restrictions to prevent the kind of abuse that has plagued some of the 16 other states and the District of Columbia where pot is legal for medical use."[14]

Reuters didn't attribute this to anyone; they took a pro-marijuana talking point and presented it as fact. Reuters did describe several restrictions in Connecticut's law, but most can be found in other state laws, and none of them prevent drug abuse. For example, other states require patients to register with the state and require patients to get a recommendation from a doctor, but those rules don't stop substance abusers from getting marijuana recommendations.

Neither the *Courant* nor Reuters quoted opponents of the law. In fact, they didn't even mention any opposition. Had they contacted opponents, they might have learned that marijuana advocates are like teenage Casanovas on the prowl; they tell every state their law is different from all the rest.

Politicians everywhere have been repeating this talking point, and the press never questions it. A news report from KOLD in Tucson quoted state legislator Matt Heinz: "This is not California's law. This is not Colorado's law, by a long shot," said Heinz. "Providers can't be just a 'doc in the box.'" Two years later, Arizona had pot docs who advertised, and just twenty-four of them had written three-quarters of all the recommendations.[15]

In Maryland, Delegate Dan Morhaim made the same promise, that their program would be the "tightest and most controlled" of any state's.[16]

In Illinois, Sen. Bill Haine of Alton, said, "It's the tightest, most controlled legislative initiative in the United State related to medical cannabis." According to the AP, their plan was "the strictest in the nation."[17]

In Massachusetts, proponents published a State Comparison Infographic showing how great the proposed Massachusetts law was compared to the terrible ones in California and Colorado.[18]

There's a problem here. These states can't all be the strictest; that's not how superlatives work.

Besides, these state laws all have loopholes that could allow recreational users to game the system. For example, Maryland's law allows severe pain as a condition and, although it requires a bona fide doctor-patient relationship, it doesn't define what that is.[19] So the strictness of these laws will depend on what regulations the states actually impose.

There's also one follow-up question reporters should have asked but apparently never did. NORML and the MPP are behind every medical marijuana law in the country, including the laws in California and Colorado they now criticize. Shouldn't reporters point this out? Shouldn't reporters remind NORML and MPP that they're responsible for those poorly written laws they're now criticizing?

The press should tell its audience who brought us the California and Colorado laws. When they don't, they're giving the marijuana lobby a free pass.

Letting the marijuana lobby write the story

On April 16, 2013, the *Vancouver Observer* ran an article with the headline, "Teen marijuana use common because of Canadian drug policy, says pot activist." Eight out of eleven paragraphs contained statements by the marijuana activist. No opposing viewpoint was presented.[20]

The article contained statement after statement claiming legalization would reduce teenage use. The first paragraph read, "The high rate of marijuana use among Canada's youth is a by-product of strict drug control, pot activist and BC Green Party candidate Jodie Emery said."

The next three paragraphs presented material to back up her claim. The article referenced the UNICEF report showing Canada had the developed world's highest rate of teenage use, and then quoted the pot activist saying, "In countries with more liberal drug laws, the use of marijuana and other drugs is lower." The *Observer* then called this quote, "A view that corresponds to the report's findings." But the *Observer* is wrong; what the pot activist said doesn't correspond to the report's findings.

The activist apparently came to her conclusion by comparing only two countries, Canada and the Netherlands. While Canada ranked first in teen use in the UNICEF report, the Netherlands ranked tenth out of 29. Both countries have medical marijuana laws, and both countries largely ignore possession; the Netherlands has decriminalized possession of small amounts, and enforcement in Canada is often very relaxed.[21] One visitor from California told this story:

> "[H]ave you ever had a cop catch you with bud before in Canada? Both times I've been caught they've just took my bud, laughed a bit that they found us toking, and told us to get on our way."[22]

So it's not fair to call Canada's laws strict, not even in comparison to Holland's. It's also unfair to only compare two countries. The UNICEF report compares 29 countries, and shows that those with liberal marijuana laws have some of the highest rates of teen use.

In the UNICEF report, there are six countries where more than 20 percent of fifteen-year-olds have used marijuana. Of those six countries, four have medical marijuana laws—Canada, the Czech Republic, Spain, and the United States. Switzerland, ranked #2, has legalized personal use in several cantons.[22] The UNICEF report also shows that Scandinavian countries, with some of the toughest drug laws, have the lowest rates.[23]

If we look at all 29 countries in the UNICEF report, we find that loose drug laws are associated with the highest rates of teenage use, and strict laws with the lowest rates. So both the pot activist and the the *Vancouver Observer* are wrong. Tight drug laws don't cause teen use; they probably prevent it.

The reporter who wrote the *Observer* article either didn't read the UNICEF report or didn't understand it, but he apparently believed what the marijuana activist told him the report said. As a result, his article read like it had been written by the marijuana lobby.

Marijuana gets special treatment in the press

During the crack cocaine and crystal meth epidemics, journalists did in-depth features about young lives torn apart by the drugs.

With marijuana, reporters do just the opposite. We see story after story about people who say marijuana helped them, but very few about kids whose grades plummet, who quit school, or who become psychotic because of marijuana.

Crystal meth works for attention-deficit disorder,[24] but no one writes sympathetic stories about kids who turned their lives and grades around with "medical meth." Suppose during the meth epidemic hardly anyone wrote stories about the drug's ravages, and instead we only read touching tales of people whom it helped: single moms who had the energy to work and raise three kids, truck drivers who made it home early to spend weekends with their families, or people fighting morbid obesity who were at last able to lose weight. That would have been outrageous, but it's what the news media has done for marijuana.

Hardly any news stories are written about the people faking pain to get medical marijuana. Yet there's evidence that most marijuana patients are doing just that. If any other government-sanctioned program were this fraudulent, reporters would be all over it. In fact, when there is just one episode of corruption in an otherwise well-run program, it's often big news. Yet here's a program that is almost entirely fraudulent, and instead of making that the focus of their reports, the press seems determined to maintain the myth that these laws are only used for legitimate medical needs.

There's clearly a double standard. The press doesn't cover marijuana the same way they cover any other addictive drug, and it doesn't cover medical marijuana the way it would cover any other deceptive operation.

Why won't the press call teenage marijuana use an epidemic?

According to the National Survey on Drug Use and Health, past-month crystal meth use peaked at 726,000 users in 2003, Oxycontin peaked in 2010 with 566,000 past-month users, and heroin use in 2012 reached 335,000 past-month users.[25] The Substance Abuse and Mental Health Services Administration (SAMHSA) reports that crack cocaine use peaked in 1996 with 668,000 current users.[26] And all four—crack cocaine, crystal meth, Oxycontin, and heroin—were referred to as epidemics by the press.[27]

How do these numbers compare to teenage marijuana use?

In 2011, the NSDUH showed that nearly 2 million teens under age eighteen had smoked marijuana during the past month.[28] That's more than the peak use of OxyContin, crack, and crystal meth combined. And those numbers for hard drug users included everyone; the numbers for marijuana only include teenagers.[29] Yet the press almost never calls teenage marijuana use an epidemic.

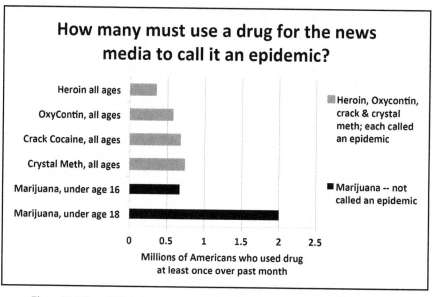

Figure 17-1. From SAMHSA National Survey Drug Use & Health 1996, 2012& 2013.[30]

Maybe it's because members of the press aren't concerned with past-month marijuana use and only consider daily marijuana use a problem. In 2012, the NSDUH reported that 425,000 teenagers under age eighteen used marijuana at least twenty times per month.[31] This falls right in the range of the other epidemics. So even if we only look at daily or near daily teenage marijuana use, it should still be called an epidemic.

Maybe journalists want more evidence of harm before calling it an epidemic. If so, the research on use before age sixteen unequivo-cally shows evidence of harm; before that age, it causes permanent changes in the brain and doubles the dropout rate. In 2011, in the United States, 674,000 adolescents under age sixteen were past-month marijuana users.[32] That number is virtually identical to the numbers that got the news media to declare a crack epidemic, a crystal meth epidemic, and an Oxycontin epidemic.[33] But the press doesn't call early teenage marijuana use an epidemic.

Maybe journalists won't use the term epidemic unless there are significant fatalities. In 2010, the *Wall Street Journal* reported the number of deaths from heroin overdose at 3,094.[34] In 2012, the Centers for Disease Control reported 3,635 heroin overdose deaths in twenty-eight states representing 56 percent of the country.[35] That works out to an estimated 6,500 per year for the entire United States.

Marijuana does not kill by overdose, but it is deadly behind the wheel. In 2012, according to research from Columbia University, 12 percent of all fatal traffic accidents involved drivers who tested positive for marijuana.[36] That same year, there were 33,561 traffic fatalities in the United States, according to the National Highway Traffic Safety Administration.[37] Twelve percent of that figure gives us just over 4,000 deadly accidents involving marijuana.

So marijuana is involved in nearly two-thirds as many fatalities each year as heroin. There are fewer marijuana deaths than heroin deaths, but it's in the same range, and the news media seem to all agree that the U.S. has a heroin epidemic.[38]

By any standard—the number of people abusing the drug, the number of adolescent users under age sixteen, the number of daily adolescent users, or the number of fatalities—American marijuana use in the 2010s is an epidemic.

In the summer of 2013, I did an online news search through Google for "marijuana epidemic" and found no matches. But we do have a marijuana epidemic, and especially a teenage marijuana epidemic; the press just isn't covering it that way.

Presenting legalization as inevitable

Two more stories are rarely presented as national news. One is the backlash against medical marijuana laws in some very liberal states. In 2012, five California cities had ballot measures to allow dispensaries. In one city, Imperial Beach, dispensary supporters raised twenty times as much money as opponents. Yet all five cities voted "No."[39] Dissatisfaction with medical marijuana in the state where it was born should be a national story, but it's not.

The other underreported story is how vastly the pro-marijuana forces outspend their opponents. There were twelve statewide ballot initiatives on marijuana from 2010 to 2014.

Because of funding from a few very wealthy individuals, the campaigns for legalization and for medical marijuana were able to outspend the opposition in every contest. Here's some data taken from followthemoney.org.[40] It shows how much each side raised and the ratio by which the pro-marijuana forces were able to outspend their opponents.

Legalization Initiatives: Money raised for and against				
State & Year	Money For	Against	Ratio	Outcome
Oregon 2014	$4,630,795	$255,869	18:1	Passed
Alaska 2014	$895,002	$155,590	6:1	Passed
Colorado 2012	$2,286,660	$706,826	3:1	Passed
Washington 2012	$5,027,430	$15,995	314:1	Passed
Oregon 2012	$446,886	$49,975	9:1	Defeated
California 2010	$3,293,723	$364,835	9:1	Defeated

Table 17-1. Data from National Institute on Money in State Politics.[41]

Legalization Initiatives: Money raised for and against				
State & Year	Money For	Against	Ratio	Outcome
Florida 2014	$6,149,531	$3,223,872	2:1	Defeated
Arkansas 2012	$1,446,629	$53,171	27:1	Defeated
Massachusetts 2012	$792,296	$16,344	48:1	Passed
South Dakota 2010	$78,715	$28,379	3:1	Defeated
Arizona 2010	$290,449	$26,492	11:1	Passed
Oregon 2010	$147,552	$12,148	12:1	Defeated

Table 17-2. Data from National Institute on Money in State Politics.[42]

In the six campaigns from 2010 to 2014 that the pro-legalization forces won, they outspent their opponents by an average of twelve to one. In the six campaigns they lost, the legalization lobby was only able to outspend the other side by three to one. Here's a cause that presents itself as inevitable, yet for the most part, it only wins when it has a huge spending advantage. That should be newsworthy, but the press rarely covers it.

That doesn't happen with non-marijuana stories. In early 2012, Newt Gingrich won the Republican South Carolina primary with $5 million from billionaire Sheldon Adelson, and numerous news stories described Adelson's donation and how vital that money was for Gingrich's campaign. The *New York Times* wrote that "the cavalry arrived."[43] Adelson's donation was important news that deserved coverage; the public should know that Gingrich's financial support was not broad-based but came from just one person.

So what about Peter Lewis, the former chairman of Progressive Insurance who died in 2013? In 2012, Lewis gave $2 million to the legalization effort in Washington state—one-third of their campaign budget. And that same year in Massachusetts, where pro-marijuana forces outspent opponents by nearly fifty to one, 94 percent of their money came from Peter Lewis.[44]

Lewis's role in the Massachusetts contest was just as significant as Adelson's in South Carolina. In both cases, one billionaire effectively bought the election. But few people have heard of Lewis, while Adelson got so much coverage he was practically a household name.

The press should give equal coverage to the role of billionaires in funding the pro-marijuana campaign. Otherwise, people might get the false impression that it's a grassroots movement with widespread support. And the public deserves to know that's not true.

Cheerleaders in the Newsroom

On January 3, 2014, Huffington Post ran this headline: "Here's an Updated Tally of All the People Who Have Ever Died from a Marijuana Overdose." The article showed an image of pandas frolicking with the caption, "Yeah, not a single person has ever died from a weed overdose."[45]

That's not a news story; it's a free infomercial for the marijuana lobby. Huffington Post could just as accurately show those pandas with the headline "All the People Who Became Schizophrenic from Using Heroin." But there is no heroin lobby.

However, hidden inside this infomercial is a real news story, and that story deserves to be told: For years, advocates claimed marijuana never killed anyone.[46] Then facts about stoned drivers causing fatal car wrecks came out, so many advocates switched to claiming pot never killed anyone—by overdose. What would have been a real news story was that pro-marijuana forces changed their claim, and pro-marijuana media outlets like Huffington Post played up the new claim without ever reporting that the old one was false.

Huffington Post also played up the new claim without reminding readers that death by overdose is not the only way drugs kill people. After all, nicotine overdose is extremely rare, but cigarettes are still deadly.

Huffington Post gets special mention because Arianna Huffington is an honorary board member of the Drug Policy Alliance. So the marijuana lobby and Huffington Post have a relationship that's even more explicit than the one the Republican Party has with Fox News. In fairness, Huffington Post deserves credit for also running articles and opinions that are anti-legalization. But when they run stories like this one, the pro-legalization bias is obvious.

Marijuana makes reporters lose their skepticism

Lots of news stories have told about veterans using marijuana for PTSD, and many have the same flaw: reporters ignore the possibility of substance abuse. On December 24, 2013, NPR ran a story about a man suffering from PTSD who said marijuana really helped his symptoms whereas the conventional medicines had made him worse.[47]

According to NPR, in 2009, he "crashed his truck while drunk and high on narcotic painkillers." This is a sign of a possible substance abuse disorder, and any doctor treating this man should want to know more before prescribing. Listening to the news report, that was my biggest question.

NPR doesn't make clear whether or not he had a substance abuse problem. This is an important issue because doctors are usually cautious about prescribing addictive drugs, especially to someone who has a substance abuse problem. It can cause more harm than help,[48] but the NPR report ignored this issue.

Most doctors know that any time a substance abuser says an addictive drug is the only thing that works, that's a red flag. I've spent a lot of time listening to addicts convincingly tell me that Xanax, Vyvanse, or Percocet were the only medicines that helped them. And it can be hard to tell what's true and what's not. Part of me is always a little suspicious anytime a patient says an addictive drug is the only thing that helps. So I'm amazed when tough, skeptical reporters are so credulous about people who claim that marijuana is the only drug that works for them.

And it's not just because drug addicts regularly lie to get drugs. Often, substance-abusing patients genuinely believe that an addictive medicine makes them better when it actually makes them worse. I've seen patients on opiates, anti-anxiety medicine, and marijuana who were certain the drug relieved a very real problem, yet when they stopped using it, the problem they thought it was for went away. This is especially true when the patient has a history of substance abuse. Such patients sincerely believe they need a medicine when it's really just their disease that wants it.

So when an addictive drug is prescribed for a patient with a substance problem, the doctor has to ask: "Is it really helping? Is it just the disease of addiction that makes him think so? Or is he out-and-out lying to get high?" Doctors deal with this question every day; NPR ignored it. We don't know whether the patient featured in the news story has a substance abuse problem, and it matters because prescribing an addictive drug to a substance abuser is usually harmful. And marijuana is an addictive drug.

The NPR story had two other faults. First, the report included two medical experts saying this was good treatment, but no one to present the opposite view. Did the reporter contact the American Society of Addiction Medicine? They would know why using an addictive drug to treat someone who had a drunk driving accident might not be a good idea.

Or he could have contacted the American Academy of Addiction Psychiatry. At their 2014 annual meeting, a researcher presented preliminary evidence that marijuana use by PTSD patients is associated with more severe symptoms and violence. In his study, those who never used marijuana or who quit using did the best. He also noted that, despite state laws approving its use, there is very little evidence to support using marijuana to treat PTSD.[49]

Secondly, the reporter acted as if medical marijuana laws were always legitimate and the patients were always genuine. Regarding this particular patient, the reporter actually said, "He qualified for medicinal marijuana ..."

Qualified! That sounds like an arduous process only a select few make it through. In reality, most people get marijuana cards from pot docs who say "Yes" to nearly every stranger who pays their fee. You *qualify* for medicinal marijuana the same way you *qualify* to spend a night with a hooker.

What's especially troubling is that this story came out at the same time as other news about veterans with PTSD using marijuana, and it seemed coordinated. It seemed as if the marijuana lobby was pressuring the Veterans Administration to let doctors recommend marijuana, and they enlisted the news media's help.

Patients at VA hospitals have high rates of substance abuse, and it's particularly high in patients with PTSD. A report from the National Center for Post-Traumatic Stress Disorder and Yale University School of Medicine listed several studies showing frequent drug or alcohol problems in patients with PTSD. In some studies, more than 50 percent were substance abusers.[50]

Doctors should always be cautious when prescribing addictive drugs. They should take a good substance abuse history, and they shouldn't be too quick to believe patients who say nothing else helps. Even when a patient sincerely believes that an addictive medicine is the only treatment that works, doctors should remain a little bit skeptical. Journalists reporting on people who say they're helped by marijuana should remain a little bit skeptical as well.

Another double standard

In 2013, the Texas state legislature passed an abortion law that opponents said was designed to ban abortion under the guise of providing better medical care. The law requires abortion clinics to meet the standards of ambulatory surgical centers and requires the doctors to have admitting privileges at a local hospital. In an NPR story about the law, the reporter pointed out that, "Both the American Congress of Obstetricians and Gynecologists and the American Medical Association say these two requirements are medically unnecessary."[51]

Was it important to point that out? Absolutely. Backers of this law probably didn't pass this law out of concern for the health and well-being of abortion patients. It was a pretense to let them accomplish their real purpose. So NPR's coverage was correct; it told us what we needed to know.

Compare this with how the press covers medical marijuana laws. The marijuana lobby is probably not fighting for these laws out of concern for the health and well-being of patients. Medical marijuana laws are also a front for another purpose.

And the positions taken by major physician organizations are just as strong. While it supports research on marijuana, the AMA has made clear that it does not support either medical marijuana laws or the medical use of marijuana. That's the same position the AMA took on the Texas abortion law. The American Society of Addiction Medicine and American Academy of Pediatrics take an even stronger stance, and oppose state medical marijuana laws.[52]

Yet, how often do reporters mention the AMA, ASAM or Academy of Pediatrics positions when doing a medical marijuana story? I've never heard it, but it should be part of the story every time.

The most important fact for news consumers to know about the Texas abortion law is that it uses the pretense of medical concern to effectively ban abortion. And the most important fact about medical marijuana laws is that they use the pretense of medical care to effectively legalize marijuana. An unbiased press would cover them both the same way.

Sounding a warning

On April 14, 1998, Abe Rosenthal, the former executive editor of the *New York Times*, wrote an opinion piece about the legalization lobby and its plans for the United States. He drew attention to the billionaires who created the movement, and quoted one of its leaders who made it clear back in 1993 that their aim was to legalize all drugs. Rosenthal also expressed disgust, asking if people were "sick to the gorge of the press and TV accepting the flood of false compassion that reformers used to attain the ... 'medicalization' of marijuana..."[53]

So in 1998, one of the best-known journalists in the United States warned, in the paper of record, that the press was swallowing pro-marijuana arguments whole. It's still a warning worth heeding. It's not too late for the press to start covering both sides of this story equally.

Chapter 18

Pro-marijuana Experts Are Often Wrong

Journalists should be cautious when using pro-marijuana sources. Anything that does not make intuitive sense should be carefully checked out—even if it comes from scientific experts. And journalists who lean in a pro-marijuana direction themselves should be especially careful about stories they would really like to believe.

A few pro-marijuana scientists and experts are cited regularly in news reports and editorials, and it's remarkable how often their information is either inaccurate or incorrectly interpreted by the press. Here are some examples of the press presenting inaccurate information from highly credentialed sources.

A negative finding treated as proof

In June 2012, three news outlets ran stories on some new research:

CBS: "Medical marijuana legalization won't boost teen pot use, study finds"[1]

Huffington Post: "Medical Marijuana Does Not Increase Teen Drug Use, Study Shows"[2]

MSNBC: "Study: Legalizing medical pot doesn't boost teen drug use"[3]

Not only are all three headlines very similar, they're also wrong. The study did not prove what the three news outlets said it proved. The research report—*Medical Marijuana Laws and Teen Marijuana Use* by Mark Anderson, Benjamin Hansen, and Daniel Rees—did not show that medical marijuana laws do not increase teenage marijuana use.[4] That would be a hard thing to prove.

In states with these laws, the researchers looked at data from seven years: the year the law was implemented, the three years before, and the three years after. And they found no increase in teen use. This is a negative finding. These were described in chapter 4, and as we saw, negative findings by themselves are not proof. The research project looked for evidence that medical marijuana laws increase teenage use and didn't find it. So it's possible these laws don't cause increased teen use, but it's also possible the research study was flawed.

CBS, MSNBC, and Huffington Post didn't tell their readers about the second possibility. They presented the first possibility as fact; but, as we shall see, the second possibility is much more likely. These are major media outlets. They deal with research all the time, and yet all three made the same mistake. How did MSNBC, CBS, and Huffington Post misinterpret the research the exact same way and then run nearly identical inaccurate headlines? One possible explanation is that they were given the same bad information and were all just too willing to believe it.

Poorly designed research

There's also a problem with the study itself. The researchers only looked at teenage marijuana use for three years after each state's law went into effect, but most state programs took off slowly.

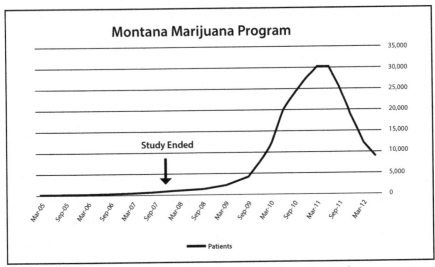

Figure 18-1. From Montana Dept. of Health Human Services[6]

Montana's program began in November 2004. By December 2007, they had only 572 medical marijuana patients, so not a lot of marijuana was passed on to the state's teenagers. After that, the program took off. In June 2011, when the legislature decided to rein it in, the program had more than 30,000 medical marijuana patients.[5]

By only looking at the law's effect on teenage use through 2007, these researchers missed 98 percent of the marijuana use. No wonder they didn't find any link between medical marijuana laws and teenage use.

They did the same thing with Colorado. Their study looked at teenage marijuana use in Colorado through 2004, by which time only 512 medical marijuana patients had signed up in the entire state. In 2010, however, there were more than 100,000 marijuana cardholders.[7] By stopping after 2004, these researchers missed 99 percent of the marijuana users.

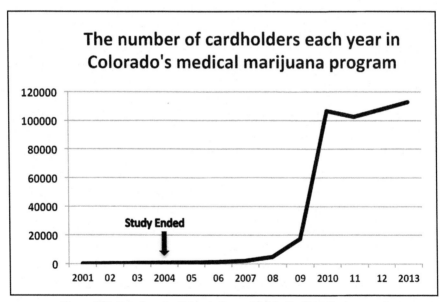

Figure 18-2. Data from the Colorado Dept. of Public Health & Environment[8]

ResearchGate, a networking website for researchers, displays a post warning against giving negative studies too much significance: "A negative finding ... can just as easily arise because the experiment was not done correctly, because it was poorly designed, because it was simply a bad idea in the first place.[9]

That's the most likely explanation here: Rees, Hansen, and Anderson found no evidence that medical marijuana laws increase teenage use because their study was poorly designed.

Implying causation

On November 30, 2011, the *Denver Post* ran a news story headlined "Report shows fewer traffic fatalities after states pass medical pot laws." It was based on another study by Rees and Anderson, this one called *Medical Marijuana Laws, Traffic Fatalities, and Alcohol Consumption*.[10] There are two problems with this news report.

First, the *Post* says, "The study stops short of saying the medical-marijuana laws cause the drop in traffic deaths," but the study doesn't stop short. The authors imply that causation has been proved.

For example, the authors report that "traffic fatalities fall by nearly 9 percent after the legalization of medical marijuana," and the next paragraph begins with, "Why does legalizing medical marijuana reduce traffic fatalities?" They don't write, "Why would ..." or "Why might ..." The way their question is worded, it implies they've already shown that it *does*.

Second, the *Post* quoted Rees and the head of a pro-legalization group, but not anyone who criticized the research. The Post quoted Rees saying, "The result that comes through again and again and again is (that) young adults...drink less when marijuana is legalized and traffic fatalities go down." This probably left many readers thinking medical marijuana laws are the cause of lower traffic fatalities and decreased alcohol use. Had the *Post* quoted a critic of the research, readers might have learned a far more likely explanation: binge drinking and drunk driving were going down before medical marijuana laws were passed, and continued to go down afterwards.[11] Medical marijuana laws probably had nothing to do with it.

This time, however, the news media didn't all play along. The ABC News website ran an article headlined "Driving Stoned: Safer than driving drunk?" The ABC article described the study and the authors' claims, and then came back with:

"Could other factors be at work? For example, some states like Tennessee and Virginia, have seen declines in traffic fatalities since 1994 even without medical marijuana laws. And in Colorado—where medical marijuana is legal—police have seen increasing numbers of stoned drivers. In 2010, 32 people involved in fatal crashes had ingested marijuana, according to the Colorado Department of Transportation."[13]

The ABC report is correct; other factors probably are at work. Between 2000 and 2012, fatal accidents caused by alcohol decreased by about 50 percent in both Colorado that had medical marijuana and Tennessee that did not. When Rees and Anderson implied that medical marijuana laws caused the decrease, it was a conclusion the data does not support.

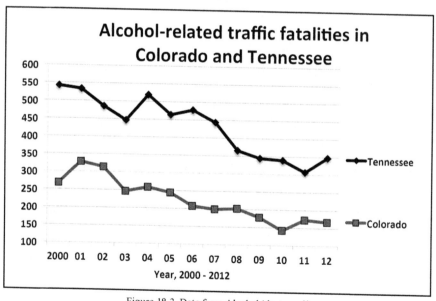

Figure 18-3. Data from AlcoholAlert.com[14]

Rees's implication that medical marijuana laws cause decreased alcohol use is also almost certainly wrong. Between 1980 and 1996, when the first "medical" marijuana law was passed, binge drinking by high school seniors decreased across the U.S. by 25 percent. And it continued to decline at about the same rate afterwards.

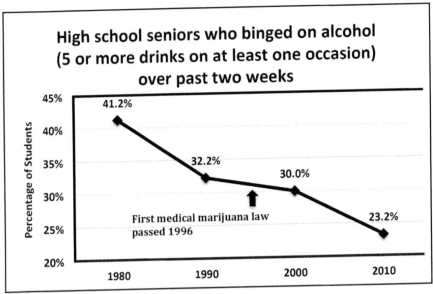

Figure 18-4. Data from Monitoring the Future 1980, 1990, 2000, 2010[12]

Rees and Anderson implied that medical marijuana laws save lives and decrease drinking, but they're almost certainly wrong. There is a much better explanation for the decrease in traffic fatalities and alcohol use, an explanation news consumers deserve to know. ABC News gave its readers this vital information, while the *Denver Post* did not.

Combining two flawed studies into a third

On November 3, 2013, the *New York Times* printed an editorial about a third scientific paper by Rees and Anderson.[15] This scientific report was mostly a review of several other studies, including their own two studies we just saw. The conclusion of this third paper comes right out of those other two papers and repeats the same errors. Here's the first two sentences of their concluding paragraph:

> "Based on existing empirical evidence, we expect that the legalization of recreational marijuana in Colorado and Washington will lead to increased marijuana consumption coupled with decreased alcohol consumption. As a consequence, these states will experience a reduction in the social harms resulting from alcohol use."

This "existing empirical evidence" includes their own flawed research that credited medical marijuana with decreasing drunk driving, even though drunk driving had already been declining for decades. So their conclusion that marijuana use decreases "social harms resulting from alcohol abuse" is unproven and probably untrue.

The rest of their concluding paragraph reads:

> "While it is more than likely that marijuana produced by state-sanctioned growers will end up in the hands of minors, we predict that overall youth consumption will remain stable. On net, we predict the public health benefits of legalization to be positive."

Their prediction that "youth consumption will remain stable" was at least partly based on their own study that looked at teen use when states had only a few hundred medical marijuana patients but not when they had more than 100,000. And their prediction of positive public health benefits is based on both of their flawed studies, so there's good reason to doubt it. Why did the *New York Times* base an entire editorial on this seriously flawed research?

Statements not supported by research

Regarding the first research paper, the three news outlets in question—CBS, NBC, and Huffington Post—were responsible for over-interpreting the data. But in the other two papers, Rees and Anderson made statements not supported by their own research.

They also make themselves available to the press, and news outlets with a pro-marijuana slant quote them frequently. That would be no problem if there was always research to support their claims, but they have said things that are either not supported by research or are beyond their expertise.

For example, this is from the *Hartford Courant*: "Daniel Rees ... said Connecticut's tight regulations will significantly curtail the number of patients who opt for the treatment—leaving only those who are 'genuinely sick' and most in need to use it. 'For them, they are going to have to get past clearly a bunch of regulatory hurdles,' Rees said, 'but if you're sick enough, you're going to do that.'"[16]

He's saying only truly ill people will try to get tightly restricted medical marijuana, and he's implying that substance abusers will not make the effort. Rees is an economist, not a substance abuse counselor, so this is beyond his expertise. It's also incorrect. Experts in addiction know that drug addicts will do anything to get their drugs. They trade stories and tell each other what works with different doctors. They memorize symptoms to fake diseases. They get phony medical reports to prove they need pain meds. Addicts will scale mountains to get drugs, so no law can ever be so tightly regulated that only the "genuinely sick" will get through.

Mark Anderson, the other outspoken author, is quoted by NBC as saying: "We are confident that marijuana use by teenagers does not increase when a state legalizes medical marijuana."[17] First of all, his study didn't prove that; it was a negative finding, and negative findings by themselves are not proof.

Secondly, he used the word "confident," implying that he is totally certain, and none of the research supports such confidence. Most researchers are very careful not to make statements the research does not support.

For example, in 2011, Magdalena Cerda published a study that looked at people of all ages, and found that states with medical marijuana laws have higher rates of marijuana use, abuse, and addiction. Melanie Wall also published a study showing teenage marijuana use is higher in these states.[18] Neither Cerda nor Wall claimed this proved medical marijuana laws caused the increased marijuana use; they stuck to what the research actually said.

Cerda and Wall also participated in a study published in 2015 that found no link between medical marijuana laws and increased teenage use. But they did not say they were confident no link exists. The strongest statement in the study was that their findings "suggest that passage of state medical marijuana laws does not increase adolescent use of marijuana."[19] Again, they're careful not to say more than the research actually supports.

And they should be careful. There is also research suggesting that medical marijuana laws do lead to teenage use. In the 2013

Monitoring the Future study, 40 percent of 12th grade students who lived in states with medical marijuana laws said they got marijuana through their own or someone else's marijuana card.[20] A study published in 2012 found that, in Colorado, 74 percent of teenagers in substance abuse treatment had used medical marijuana.[21] And, as we saw in Chapter 11, between 2006 and 2011, teenage marijuana use increased 33 percent in medical marijuana states, while only increasing 6 percent in states without those laws.[22]

Rees and Anderson make strong pro-marijuana statements and some journalists probably like that. But when researchers make statements that are beyond their expertise or beyond what the research actually supports, journalists should be wary of using them as the only source for a story.

Having it both ways

There's another problem with the first two Rees and Anderson papers: they contradict each other. In the traffic fatality study, the authors say medical marijuana laws increase use. The *Denver Post* put it simply: "Rees said the main reason for the drop [in alcohol fatalities] appears to be that medical-marijuana laws mean young people spend less time drinking and more time smoking cannabis."[23]

However, in the previous research study, *Medical Marijuana Laws and Teen Marijuana Use*, the whole point was that medical marijuana laws did not increase teenage use.

These authors seem to be saying that medical marijuana laws increase marijuana use among young people but not among teenagers. How could that be?

Alcohol and marijuana are both illegal for teens, and we know that when alcohol is more available, teen use goes up.[24] So why would increased availability of marijuana have no effect on teen use?

Also, their third study was described by the New York Times as saying that "the increase in the legal drinking age from 18 to 21 seems to encourage greater marijuana use among people under 21..."[25] That means making alcohol less available increases teenage marijuana use. So why would making marijuana more available not increase teen use, too?

It seems that when Rees and Anderson wanted to prove that medical marijuana laws don't increase teen use, they said these laws have no effect on teenage use. When they wanted to prove that "medical" marijuana decreases alcohol use, they said young people smoke more marijuana because of these laws. It's hard to see how those can both be right.

Pro-marijuana journalists really like pro-marijuana research

When journalists want to make a pro-marijuana argument, they often rely on the work of Rees and Anderson. On July 29, 2014, a *Washington Post* column by Christopher Ingraham stated in the headline that there was "a mountain of research" to disprove the claim that medical marijuana laws increase teenage use.[26]

But he didn't show us a mountain of research. His column was almost entirely about one scientific paper, the Rees and Anderson study on teenage marijuana use described above. Ingraham wrote, "A new study by economists Daniel Rees, Benjamin Hansen and D. Mark Anderson is the latest in a growing body of research showing no connection—none, zero, zilch—between the enactment of medical marijuana laws and underage use of the drug."[27]

However, his column contained very little evidence of a "growing body of research." Besides this one study, Ingraham provided a link to a *Forbes* magazine column by Jacob Sullum, but that was about the third Rees and Anderson study just described, the one that was based on their teen use study, so it's not really additional research.[28]

Ingraham also linked to a *Washington Post* column by Gail Sullivan about a study from Brown University,[29] but this was another study with serious flaws. The Brown University study relies on the Youth Risk Behavior Survey (YRBS), which contains no marijuana data from California, Colorado, Oregon, or Washington, four of the oldest and largest medical marijuana states.[30] So it's not a good survey for assessing these laws.

Also, instead of comparing all the medical marijuana states to all the states without these laws, the Brown University researchers picked five of each. This is a non-random selection that allows for lots of experimenter bias. Even worse, they chose neighboring states, which are the least likely to show any difference as pot-smokers can simply drive to the neighboring state to buy weed. In three of their non-medical marijuana states—Idaho, Massachusetts, and New Hampshire—the largest cities are an hour's drive from a state that sells medical marijuana. Despite these flaws, Sullivan declared, "the results of the study show medical marijuana laws didn't increase pot use by teens in any state."[31]

Sullivan was factually wrong. Ingraham was more careful, but still misleading. He wrote that the Rees and Anderson study, "provides straightforward evidence that there is no link between medical marijuana laws and teen marijuana use." But negative findings from a flawed study aren't "straightforward evidence." And negative findings from two flawed studies aren't "a mountain of research."

He also wrote, "The notion that medical marijuana leads to increased use among teenagers is flat-out wrong." This notion he calls "flat-out wrong" is probably right. But by cherry-picking the research and then misinterpreting it, Ingraham was able to tell his readers otherwise.

A questionable interpretation of the law

One of the news media's favorite pro-legalization experts is Mark Kleiman, a professor of public policy who has written several important books on drug policy. On February 16, 2014, the *Oregonian* ran an opinion by Kleiman arguing that states have the right to legalize marijuana even though it violates federal law.

That's a red flag right there: U.S. states are not allowed to violate federal law. What's going on in the states that have legalized recreational or medical marijuana is illegal, but both political parties have decided to ignore the law.

In support of the notion that states can violate federal law, Kleiman wrote:

"As a matter of law, Section 873 of the Controlled Substances Act orders the attorney general to "cooperate with local, State, tribal and Federal agencies concerning traffic in controlled substances and in suppressing the abuse of controlled substances." ... A straightforward reading of the law would therefore seem to require the attorney general to cooperate with those state efforts rather than trying to disrupt them."[33]

This pro-legalization argument depends on an extremely unusual description of the Attorney General's job. The word "cooperate" has two meanings. It can mean working together or it can mean complying with a request or obeying an order.[34] Kleiman is not an attorney and neither am I, but I doubt the federal Controlled Substances Act orders the U.S. Attorney General to obey states, especially when the states are violating federal law.

It's more likely the law meant they should work together. And since the section of the law Kleiman quotes is under the enforcement provisions, it means they should work together to enforce the law. Despite the wishes of legalization advocates like Kleiman, if a renegade state decides to break the law, the U.S. Attorney General is not required to help them break it.

A good research institute adopts bad science

According to watchdog groups, Canadian scientists who work for the government are under pressure to support government policies.[35] A survey found that almost all government scientists felt they would be censured or punished if they spoke out, even against harmful governmental decisions. Two-thirds of government researchers "believe political interference has compromised Canada's ability to develop policy, law and programs based on scientific evidence." The survey found that "nearly half (48%) are aware of actual cases in which their department or agency suppressed information," and 24 percent "had been directly asked to exclude or alter information" in government documents.[36]

In particular, critics have accused "the Harper government of 'muzzling' its scientists in an attempt to keep the scientific message on climate change and environmental issues in line with the government's."[37]

Is similar pressure shaping marijuana policy?

In October 2014, the Toronto-based Centre for Addiction and Mental Health (CAMH)—a world-renowned research institution—released a policy paper recommending the legalization of marijuana.[38] But the report is remarkably unscientific.

The policy paper's conclusions were covered widely by the press, but its flaws were not. For example, the *Toronto Star* ran a news article describing the recommendations. The *Star* quoted a CAMH director and two other experts who were also in favor of legalization—but no one who opposed or criticized the report.[39]

This one-sided coverage was a disservice to the *Star*'s readers. The CAMH *Cannabis Policy Framework* contains statements that are provably false, deceptive, or based on no evidence at all—which is shocking coming from such a reputable research center.

First, the provably false: The CAMH report says, "Cannabis use alone does not increase the likelihood that a person will progress to using other illegal substances."[40] Not so. A study published in the *British Journal of Psychiatry* found that teens who use marijuana regularly are seven times as likely to use other illicit drugs later in life.[41]

The CAMH report also says, "Removing criminal and civil penalties for possession of cannabis would eliminate the more than $1 billion Canada spends annually to enforce cannabis possession laws."[42] However, California has a population slighter larger than Canada's, and the Rand Corporation report *Altered State* estimates California only spends between $245 million and $330 million per year, and that's to enforce all marijuana-related crime, including trafficking, which causes most of the enforcement expenses.[43] CAMH's estimate is for possession alone.

The RAND Corporation report further contradicts CAMH by pointing out that these costs would not all be eliminated. One-third of enforcement costs are for underage possession, which wouldn't be eliminated. And Canada would still have to fight the black market, or no one would go to the higher-priced state-run marijuana stores. So CAMH's $1 billion savings estimate is not credible.

Also, by CAMH's own admission, the $1 billion number refers to a very different cost and should never have been used to describe the cost of enforcing marijuana possession laws. I asked about it on their blog. Here's my question:

> "…the CAMH Framework says Canada spends over $1 billion per year enforcing marijuana possession laws, but there's no footnote. Can you tell us how you came up with that amount? It seems awfully high."

And here is CAMH's response:

> "This figure was derived from a report called The Costs of Substance Abuse in Canada 2002. This study found that the costs of law enforcement for illegal drugs in Canada was $2.335 billion in 2002. Law enforcement costs specific to cannabis were estimated by assigning half of total enforcement costs – $1.167 billion – to cannabis."[44]

The report *The Costs of Substance Abuse in Canada 2002* did find that "the costs of law enforcement for illegal drugs … was $2.335 billion." However, that was not just the cost of enforcing laws against possession. That was the cost of enforcing laws against possession, sales and cultivation plus the cost of enforcing laws for violent and property offences committed by drug users who were under the influence or stealing to get money for drugs.[45] So marijuana possession laws cost Canada a tiny fraction of that $1.167 billion—not the entire amount as the *Cannabis Policy Framework* claimed.

Next, the deceptive: The CAMH report says, "The prohibition of cannabis and criminalization of its users does not deter people from consuming it. The evidence on this point is clear: tougher penalties do not lead to lower rates of cannabis use."[46] Notice the sleight of hand. The first sentence says prohibition doesn't deter use, but the evidence offered in the second sentence is not about the effect of prohibition. It's about severity of the penalties. While CAMH is right that tough penalties are no more persuasive than mild ones, CAMH is not recommending milder penalties. CAMH is recommending eliminating prohibition, which means no penalties at all.

Here's an analogy. Reducing the fine for speeding from $500 to $100 probably wouldn't change many driving habits, but eliminating speed limits altogether certainly would. CAMH used an irrelevant set of facts to argue against criminalization. These are world-class scientists; they must know when facts are irrelevant.

Also, their claim that prohibition does not deter use is wrong. A recent University of Michigan survey interviewed teens who never tried marijuana, and 10 percent said if it were legal, they'd try it.[47] Clearly, prohibition deters them.

Lastly, conclusions with no scientific basis: CAMH uses a U-shaped graph to show that the extremes of complete prohibition and complete legalization cause the most harm while regulated legalization causes the least. The CAMH report calls itself evidence-based, but this graph isn't based on research. It appears in other pro-legalization reports and documents, but as far as I can tell, it's just one man's theory that has never been proved scientifically.[48]

It was proposed by John Marks, a pro-legalization physician, and is derived mainly from his observations and from his experience with opiate and cocaine addicts.[49] It's also apparently based on his belief that treatment doesn't work and addicts will continue to use no matter how we intervene. Describing his clinic that gave addicts heroin and cocaine, Marks wrote, "The choice is: drugs from the clinic or drugs from the Mafia. They will get their drugs, one way or the other."[50]

Also, Marks's theory is about opiates and for at least two reasons it doesn't apply to marijuana. First, opiate addiction is hard to treat, and research supports maintenance programs such as methadone as a good option. However, addiction to marijuana, alcohol, and most other drugs responds to drug-free treatment. Secondly, methadone programs do not lead to drug use among the general population while marijuana legalization would. So that U-shaped graph is a theoretical argument for methadone maintenance and maybe even for heroin or opium maintenance, but it is not an argument for the legalization of marijuana.

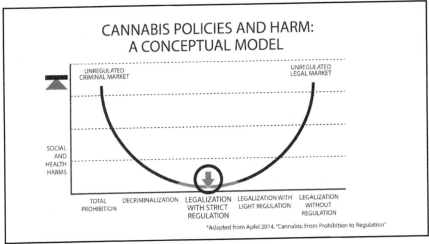

Figure 18-5. From CAMH *Cannabis Policy Framework.* [51]

Regarding this U-shaped graph, CAMH footnotes a report put out by the European Commission, which in turn footnotes a book called *How to Regulate Cannabis*, published by Transform, a pro-legalization group funded by George Soros's Open Society Foundations. This graph also shows up in a report by the Canadian Drug Policy Coalition, which is another group connected to George Soros and his Open Society Foundations.[52] CAMH's recommendations should be based on science, not an unproved theory from a partisan political group.

The graph also included the term "unregulated criminal market,"[53] which is part of a marijuana lobby talking point. The marijuana lobby wants us to believe legalization would mean tighter control, so instead of asking voters to *legalize* marijuana they say we should *regulate* it. This sounds tough, but only if we equate *illegal* with *unregulated*.

Merriam-Webster gives this definition for the word *regulate*: "To make rules or laws that control (something)." This means laws making marijuana illegal are regulations. In fact, they're the tightest possible regulations; no one is allowed to sell it or use it at all. The marijuana lobby wants us to believe legalization would mean tighter regulations, but it would actually mean going to much looser ones. So when CAMH calls the criminal market "unregulated" while saying legalization would include "strict regulation," they're using a dishonest argument that comes from the marijuana lobby.

The takeaway

News outlets often print statements from scientific experts, and it's understandable that journalists assume the scientists are accurate. However, they can't always make that assumption, and this is especially true when the experts are supporting the legalization of marijuana. Journalists should always check with neutral or anti-legalization experts before running with a story from a pro-legalization source— no matter how reputable they may be.

Like one negative finding, bad information from one scientist has no wider implications. However, repeated inaccurate arguments coming from experts in support of legalization should eventually lead to one conclusion: if even scientific experts can't make a valid case for legalization, there probably isn't a case to be made.

Chapter 19

The Inaccuracies In Pro-marijuana Editorials

Columnists and editorial writers are different from reporters. Their job is to argue one point of view, not present both sides. However, they still have to base their arguments on real and verifiable facts, and if the marijuana lobby can't come up with straightforward, factually correct arguments in favor of legalization, how can anyone else?

Editorial writers and columnists who want to take up the pro-legalization cause have no choice but to use the same arguments as the marijuana lobby, and it shows. What's telling about pro-marijuana editorials and opinions is how often they're inaccurate or misleading, despite coming from some of the most respected sources.

The *New York Times*

On May 19, 2013, the *New York Times* printed a column by Bill Keller titled "How to Legalize Pot." In it, Keller said there's "evidence indicating that states with medical marijuana programs have not, as opponents feared, experienced an increase in use by teenagers." Keller provided a link to the evidence: the study by Rees, Hansen, and Anderson that missed 98 percent of the marijuana use in some states.[1]

Technically, Keller is right; there is evidence. But it's highly questionable evidence from poorly designed research—and his readers wouldn't know that. They'd assume when Keller said "evidence" that he meant the preponderance of scientific evidence, not one flawed study. Keller's readers would come away believing that teen use hasn't increased in medical marijuana states. But not only has teenage use increased in those states, it has increased faster there than anywhere else.[2]

On November 3, 2013, the editorial board of the *New York Times* printed a pro-legalization editorial in which they quoted one study— by Rees and Anderson.[3] The editorial stated that Rees and Anderson "report that legalization of marijuana for medical purposes has been associated with reductions in heavy drinking ..." We looked at this study in chapter 18.

The editorial did not tell readers that heavy drinking was decreasing long before medical marijuana laws were passed and was also decreasing in states without such laws. Medical marijuana probably had nothing to do with the decline in alcohol abuse, but the *New York Times* led readers to believe it did.

The editorial writers used conditional words to imply things most research says are not true. For example, they never said legalizing marijuana *would* make our roads safer, they just said that it "could."

They also implied that driving stoned is safe, by writing, "marijuana-intoxicated drivers show only modest impairments on road tests. They slow down and increase their following distance."

That's true, but the same scientific review article that found they slow down also found that, during complicated driving situations, their control deteriorates and impairment becomes obvious. The article concluded, "Consuming cannabis before driving ... produces substantial morbidity and mortality on the roadway."[4] The *Times* only told half the story, the half that made driving stoned sound safe.

Also, road tests are not real life, because the driver knows he's being observed, and researchers are careful not to try anything too risky on an actual road test. So there are better ways to research impaired driving. The most rigorous, all-inclusive study on marijuana and driving is the meta-analysis, discussed earlier, from Dalhousie University in Nova Scotia. Those researchers found that people who drive stoned have twice the rate of serious and fatal accidents.[5] A review by Columbia University researchers of more than 20,000 fatal accidents found that the percentage caused by marijuana tripled in the first decade of this century. In 2010, marijuana was found in 12 percent of all fatally injured drivers.[6]

Yet this editorial downplayed any serious danger from driving stoned. By only citing road tests and ignoring this other research, the *Times* misled its readers. And this was dangerous misinformation because stoned driving can be deadly.

In July 2014, the *New York Times* editorial page ran a series of editorials calling for legalization that made questionable arguments. In the first editorial, the *Times* wrote: "Claims that marijuana is a gateway to more dangerous drugs are … fanciful."[7]

Research published in 2010 in the *British Journal of Psychiatry* showed that teenagers who use marijuana are twice as likely to use other illegal drugs as adults, and teens who use marijuana at least once a week are between seven and twelve times as likely to go on to other drugs. That is evidence for the gateway effect. Maybe it's still being debated, but it's not "fanciful."[8]

In the July 28, 2014, editorial, "The Injustice of Marijuana Arrests," the *Times* reported on two men in prison—one for thirteen years and the other for life—as an argument against marijuana laws.[9] However, the main reason these men got long sentences was not because of marijuana laws but because of repeat offender laws that tie judges' hands. The first man described could just as easily have gotten his "three strikes" for shoplifting or petty theft, but the *New York Times* does not suggest legalizing those crimes.[10] The other man was sentenced under a Missouri law that mandates life in prison for three drug felonies. So while there is certainly an injustice here, it's not due to marijuana laws but to mandatory sentencing and habitual offender laws. And this is a problem for all crimes, not just drug crimes. In order to support legalization, the *Times* misused these facts.

Huffington Post and *Time* Magazine

It's easy to show that drug convictions are not the main cause of prison overcrowding. The United States has two types of prisons, federal and state. State prisons hold 87 percent of prison inmates and federal prisons hold the other 13 percent. In 2011, according to the Bureau of Justice Statistics, 53 percent of all state prison inmates were incarcerated for violent crimes, 18 percent for property crimes, and 17 percent for drug crimes.[11]

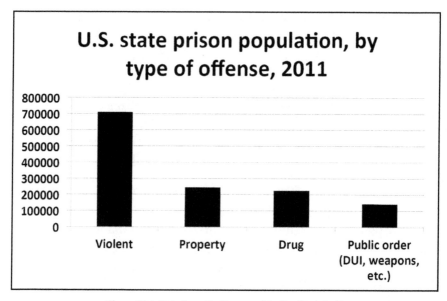

Figure 19-1. Data from the Bureau of Justice Statistics[12]

The data for federal prisoners in 2011 was very different: drug crimes accounted for 56 percent of those inmates. But the state prison system dwarfs the federal system, so when data for both are combined, the results are not too different from the state system alone.

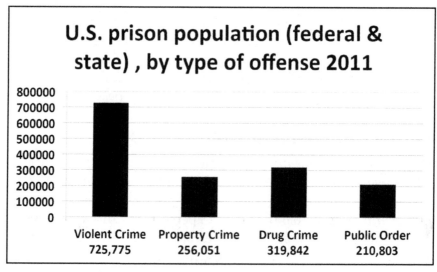

Figure 19-2. Data from Bureau of Justice Statistics[13]

Of the combined U.S. state and federal prison population, 79 percent of inmates are incarcerated for non-drug crimes. So drug crimes can't be blamed for the majority of prison overcrowding.

However, on March 10, 2014, Huffington Post ran a news story with the headline "Just How Much the War on Drugs Impacts Our Overcrowded Prisons, in One Chart." The article's first two sentences were: "America's prisons are dangerously overcrowded, and the war on drugs is mainly to blame. Over 50 percent of inmates currently in federal prison are there for drug offenses ..."[14]

That makes it sound like the majority of inmates are in prison for drug crimes, which isn't true. Here's how the article misled readers. The first sentence claimed that the drug war is the main cause of overcrowding. However, as we just saw, only 21 percent of U.S. prison inmates are incarcerated for drug crimes. The main cause of prison overcrowding is Reagan-era tough-on-crime legislation.

But Huffington Post gave readers the impression that most inmates are in prison for drug crimes with the second sentence, which read, "over 50 percent" are incarcerated "for drug offenses." But notice what they did; the first sentence made a claim about all prison inmates, but the second sentence was only about federal prison inmates. Readers who didn't catch the switch would think a majority of all inmates are in prison for drug crimes.

Then the website made another provably untrue statement: "The second-largest category, immigration-related crimes, accounts for 10.6 percent of inmates. This means that people convicted of two broad categories of nonviolent crimes—drugs and immigration— make up over 60 percent of the U.S. prison population."[15] That's wrong. Had the Huffington Post written "60 percent of the U.S. *federal* prison population," that would be true. But when all U.S. prison inmates are included, only about 23 percent are incarcerated for drug and immigration crimes. Once again, they're misleading readers into thinking most people in prison are there for drugs.

The website then showed the one chart the headline promised, but it was mislabeled. It was a graph copied from the Federal Bureau of Prisons website, but the title Huffington Post put on the graph reads,

"U.S. Prison Population As Of Jan. 25, 2014."[16] This tells readers it's a graph of all inmates, both federal and state, when it's actually only federal. The mislabeled graphs also tells readers that half of all U.S. prison inmates are drug offenders, and that is not true.

Figure 19-2 shows the actual U.S. prison population. Figure 19-3 is what Huffington Post claimed it to be. Since the whole point of the article was this one chart, it's hard to imagine that they mislabeled it by mistake.

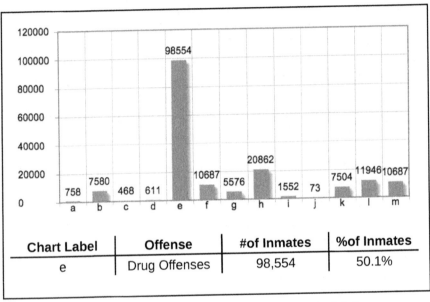

Chart Label	Offense	#of Inmates	%of Inmates
e	Drug Offenses	98,554	50.1%

Figure 19-3. From the Federal Bureau of Prisons Inmate Statistics[17]

Huffington Post then used misleading language to give the impression that all these drug offenders were in prison for possession. Right after the graph, the article went on to say: "And what was the drug of choice for those convicted of drug offenses? Marijuana ... 27.6 percent of drug offenders were locked up for crimes related to marijuana."

"Drug of choice" is a term that describes a drug that addicts like to use, not one they sell.[18] By using this term, Huffington Post is implying these inmates are in prison for using drugs, and nowhere does the story say otherwise. But the article quotes only federal prison data—and 99.8 percent of drug offenders in federal prison are there for trafficking, a word the article never mentions.[19]

The same misleading argument was used on April 2, 2012, in a *Time* magazine column by Fareed Zakaria titled "Incarceration Nation." In it, he wrote:

> "In 1980 the U.S.'s prison population was about 150 per 100,000 adults. It has more than quadrupled since then. So something has happened in the past 30 years to push millions of Americans into prison. That something, of course, is the war on drugs. Drug convictions went from 15 inmates per 100,000 adults in 1980 to 148 in 1996, an almost tenfold increase. More than half of America's federal inmates today are in prison on drug convictions. In 2009 alone, 1.66 million Americans were arrested on drug charges, more than were arrested on assault or larceny charges. And 4 of 5 of those arrests were simply for possession."[20]

In those few sentences, Zakaria misleads his readers in three ways:

1. He uses the term "war on drugs" to include arresting people for possession, but the drug war is the pursuit of major traffickers.

2. He implies that drug arrests are solely responsible for the skyrocketing U.S. prison population and never mentions Reagan-era legislation that increased penalties and incarceration rates for all crimes.

3. He uses federal prison data to support the notion that prisons are filled with drug criminals and ignores the state prison data that would prove him wrong.

Zakaria and Huffington Post both used federal prison data to support a claim about both state and federal inmates. How do two journalists writing independently come up with the same faulty argument?

The Legalization Three-Step

There's one more way Zakaria and Huffington Post misled their readers. They both put three unrelated statements together to give the impression that prisons are filled with people whose only crime was to use drugs.

They went from writing about,

1. *mass incarceration*, to writing about

2. *drug crimes,* implying that most people are in prison for drugs. And then wrote about

3. *drug users* or *possession,* as if that's all they were imprisoned for.

Here's Huffington Post's three-step:

1. "America's prisons are dangerously overcrowded ..."

2. "Over 50 percent of inmates ... in federal prison are there for drug offenses ..."

3. "And what was the drug of choice for those convicted of drug offenses?"

Here's Fareed Zakaria:

1. "something has happened ... to push millions of Americans into prison."

2. "More than half of ... federal inmates ... are in prison on drug convictions."

3. "4 of 5 ... arrests were simply for possession."

Neither writer said the three different facts were related, but they strung them together as if they were. This leads people to believe that *prisons are filled* with *drug offenders* whose only crime is *possession,* which isn't true.

Only 21 percent of all U.S. inmates are incarcerated for drug crimes, and almost all of them were involved in drug trafficking, but neither article tells us that. Instead, they imply that prison overcrowding is mainly the result of people locked up for drug crimes, and that all these inmates locked up for drug crimes are there for possession.

In fact, possession offenders are almost never incarcerated, so they're irrelevant to an article about prison overcrowding.

The three-step is a misleading argument that non-journalists use, too. Billionaire entrepreneur Richard Branson has called for the worldwide legalization of marijuana and possibly all other drugs as part of the Global Commission on Drug Policy, a group linked to George Soros's Open Society Foundations.[21] On September 23, 2014, Branson was on WAMU's Diane Rehm Show and explained: "Languishing in American prisons is something like 1.7 million people, or 1.8 million, many of them for drug-related issues. It's much cheaper to help those people and put them through drug clinics."[22]

That's the same three-step. He goes right from 1.8 million "languishing in prison" to "drug-related issues," letting people picture that all these inmates are in prison for drugs. Then he implies that they are all just drug users by describing them as people who need treatment.

He doesn't say they're just in prison for using drugs, but he implies it by saying it would be cheaper to "put them through drug clinics." He's implying they are all just drug users in need of help.

However, 90 percent of the drug criminals in prison are in for trafficking, and most of the rest are in for a non-drug crime along with possession. The drug dealers I met when I worked in prisons usually didn't even use the drugs they sold, so treatment in a drug clinic isn't appropriate. But Branson never mentioned drug dealers or trafficking. Instead, he painted a picture of prisons full of innocent drug users who just need treatment—and that's not who's in prison.

The *Washington Post*

On June 7, 2013, the *Washington Post* ran a pro-marijuana op-ed by Doug Fine titled "Five Myths about Legalized Marijuana." It contained so many factual errors that Kevin Sabet, in a response published by Huffington Post, limited himself to the five most serious ones.[23]

Some of the errors were just facts Fine got wrong. For example, he says Portugal legalized drugs, but Portugal only decriminalized possession for personal use. Decriminalization only means those arrested are fined but not jailed, while legalization means large corporations can manufacture and sell drugs, and even advertise and lobby legislators.[24]

But he also says it's a myth that legalization increases use. His entire evidence is Portugal, which never did legalize marijuana, and a study showing teen use didn't increase after Rhode Island passed a medical marijuana law. That study only looked at teen use for the three years after the law was passed, when Rhode Island had only 1,500 medical marijuana patients. We've seen studies like this before.[25]

Two weeks after the 2012 election, the *Washington Post* ran a column by Katrina vanden Heuvel titled "Time to End the War on Drugs." She starts by saying there's a war on drug users: "Since its launch in 1971, when President Nixon successfully branded drug addicts as criminals, the war on drugs has resulted in 45 million arrests and destroyed countless families." [26] Reading that, I figured she was just repeating the marijuana lobby line and didn't know better.

However, she provided a link to a timeline by PBS that included this statement: "During the Nixon era, for the only time in the history of the war on drugs, the majority of funding goes towards treatment, rather than law enforcement."[27] Apparently, she didn't read her own link, which would have told her that Nixon did not brand drug addicts as criminals; he branded them as sick people needing help. In fact, Nixon's first drug czar convinced the Pentagon to change its policy so addicted servicemen who asked for treatment would not be prosecuted.[28]

Vanden Heuvel then blames the drug war for filling prisons: "The result of this trillion dollar crusade? Americans aren't drug free—we're just the world's most incarcerated population." She fails to say that incarceration rates stayed low during Nixon's presidency and for the rest of the decade. And she never mentions the Reagan-era "tough on crime" measures that did fill America's prisons—mostly with people locked up for non-drug crimes.

Vanden Heuvel also does the three-step. She writes: "Marijuana is not the sole drug behind our astounding incarceration rate for nonviolent drug-related crimes. We're a long way from a just system that addresses drug use with treatment rather than punishment."[29]

Look closely at those two sentences. She starts with "astounding incarceration rate," and says it's for "drug-related crimes"—ignoring the 79 percent of inmates in prison for non-drug-related crimes. Then she goes immediately to people who need "treatment" for "drug use," as if that described the people in prison for drug crimes. She makes no mention of drug traffickers. Instead, she leaves readers with the impression that prisons are filled with innocent drug users.

So Branson, vanden Heuvel, the Huffington Post and Zakaria all used the same misleading argument. If a teacher had four students who did this on an essay test or in a paper, he'd start asking questions, and we should, too.

Lastly, vanden Heuvel says legalizing marijuana could "drastically decrease incarceration rates."[30] However, legalizing marijuana would probably free less than 1 percent of the prison population—most of them drug traffickers. That is not, by any definition of the word, a *drastic* decrease.

On August 5, 2014, the *Washington Post* ran a column by Radley Balko titled "Since marijuana legalization, highway fatalities in Colorado are at near-historic lows."[31] It's an attempt to convince readers that legalizing marijuana won't make our highways more dangerous, but Balko gets several things wrong:

- He acknowledges that the percent of fatal wrecks caused by drivers testing positive for marijuana have tripled, but he says marijuana is probably innocent, and that it's only there more often because more people are using it. "You'd also expect to find that a higher percentage of churchgoers, good Samaritans and soup kitchen volunteers would have pot in their system," he writes. However, marijuana use has not tripled, while the percent of traffic fatalities involving marijuana has, so the marijuana is not incidental.

- Balko tells us to credit this decline in highway fatalities to legalization. He writes, "The best way to gauge the effect legalization has had on the roadways is to look at what has happened on the roads since legalization took effect." But as we saw before, traffic fatalities were declining before Colorado changed its marijuana laws and continued to decline afterwards. And the same decline can be found in states without medical marijuana or legalization laws.

- Balko also assumes that marijuana wears off quickly and that drug screens are meaningless. He writes, "Metabolites can linger in the body for days after the drug's effects wear off." But no one knows when the effect wears off. As we saw with airplane pilots, they all thought they were fine a day later, but many of them couldn't land a plane safely.[32]

Maclean's

On June 10, 2013, the Toronto-based news magazine *Maclean's* ran an editorial titled "Why It's Time to Legalize Marijuana."[33] Most editorials use independent data or experts to back up their claims, but often *Maclean's* didn't even do that. Instead, the magazine quoted pro-legalization groups or individuals who agreed with the magazine's editorial bias and then treated that as evidence.

Referring to Marijuana Policy Project spokesperson Mason Tvert, *Maclean's* wrote: "As Tvert claims, backed by ample scientific data, pot is not physically addictive ..." However, that claim is not backed by scientific data. In fact, research shows just the opposite: marijuana withdrawal exhibits all the symptoms of physical dependence seen in other drugs.[34] *Maclean's* offered no actual evidence. It simply quoted a pro-marijuana partisan and then told us what he said was true.

In one case, Maclean's attributed a statement to a group that probably never said it. The editorial claimed drug laws cause Canada's high rate of teenage use, but the only evidence offered was a report by the Canadian Drug Policy Coalition, a pro-legalization group funded by George Soros's Open Society Institute.[35] However, I read the CDPC report and never found it saying teenage use is a consequence of drug laws. The CDPC report implied it, but the authors apparently knew better than to actually say so.

Maclean's also blames the police for a war on marijuana users, and backs up this claim by writing, "Since the Tories came to power in 2006 ... arrests for pot possession have jumped 41 per cent. In those six years, police reported more than 405,000 marijuana-related arrests."[36]

Liberal Party leader Justin Trudeau used similar numbers. According to the conservative *Toronto Sun*, Trudeau said there were 475,000 "convictions because of marijuana," but then changed it to "arrests."[37]

Trudeau and *Maclean's* were both wrong; those were incidents, not arrests. An incident is any encounter with the police.

As the *Edmonton Sun* states, "A reported incident does not mean an arrest has been made, a charge laid or a conviction earned."[38] As we saw in British Columbia, "incident" often means only that police found marijuana and let the person go with a warning.[39] But in order to support legalization, Trudeau and *Maclean's* took what were probably relatively benign encounters and turned them into something more serious.

Slate magazine

In May 2013, Gil Kerlikowske, the head of the U.S. Office of National Drug Control Policy, a.k.a. the drug czar, released the annual results of the Arrestee Drug Abuse Monitoring survey (ADAM).[40] That year the media picked up on three points.

1. Between 62 percent (Atlanta) and 86 percent (Chicago) of all adult male criminals tested positive for illegal drugs at the time of arrest.

2. The most commonly found illegal drug was marijuana. In three cities—Chicago, New York, and Sacramento—marijuana metabolites were found in the urine of more than 50 percent of adult male arrestees.

3. Very few of these drug-using criminals had received treatment at any time in their lives.

The ADAM survey reminds us that crime is basically a substance abuse problem and the way to reduce crime is to get people into treatment. But the marijuana lobby took offense. When McClatchyDC, the newspaper chain's Web-based news service, wrote about the ADAM report, they quoted a pro-marijuana spokesperson:

> "The drug czar should be ashamed of himself for attempting to deceive the American people in this manner," said Steve Fox, the national political director for the Marijuana Policy Project, a pro-legalization group in Washington. "We could release a study

tomorrow showing that 98 percent of arrestees in the United States drank water in the 48 hours before they engaged in criminal behavior. Does that mean that water causes crime?"[41]

There are two things wrong here. First, why did McClatchy's reporter contact a pro-marijuana group for comments about substance-abusing criminals? If it were a report about infectious disease, he wouldn't contact an anti-vaccine group. Second, MPP's Fox accused the drug czar of saying something he never said. In the McClatchy report, Kerlikowske never said marijuana caused crime. He said it is linked to crime, which it is.

The day after Kerlikowske spoke, *Slate* published an article by its crime reporter, Justin Peters, in which he practically channeled the MPP lobbyist. He even used the same offended, accusatory tone. He started with an incorrect headline: "New Study Tries, Fails to Show Marijuana Use Is Linked to Crime."[42] It didn't fail; the study showed the two are linked. Linked doesn't mean one causes the other, just that they occurred together.

Peters then imitated Fox's false analogy, writing, "Here are other things that over half of the adult male arrestees probably had in common: pants, food in their stomachs, a mother who loves them, an impoverished background, an affinity for one or more of the local sports teams." It's a false analogy because, except for the impoverished background, Peters named things that apply to everybody, whereas no other group besides criminals has a 50 percent rate of recent marijuana use.

Peters also put words in the drug czar's mouth the same way Fox did by saying, "Correlation is not causation. Just because a high percentage of arrestees tested positive for marijuana does not mean that smoking marijuana made them commit crimes." Again, no one claimed that marijuana caused crime, but Peters pretended the drug czar did and then argued against it.

Then, in the last paragraph, he admitted, "Kerlikowske only said that drug use and crime were *linked*, not that drug use *causes* crime." In other words, Peters admitted that his headline was factually wrong, and that his entire rant against the drug czar was undeserved. Yet *Slate* ran the article anyway.

The *Vancouver Sun*

On September 12, 2013, the *Vancouver Sun* ran an editorial endorsing the effort to officially decriminalize marijuana in British Columbia and legalize it throughout Canada.[43] It included a list of politicians who have smoked marijuana, and references to Colorado and neighboring Washington. But then it made an untrue claim.

It claimed, "There is no definitive evidence to show that pot smoking is any more harmful to people's health than alcohol use." However, marijuana causes psychosis to develop earlier while alcohol doesn't.[44] And the permanent structural changes marijuana use causes in the teenage brain show up on MRI scans.[45] That's as definitive as medical science gets.

The editorial also said, "Many have argued, logically, that banning it only encourages an underground, illicit distribution and sales network." The word "only" makes this statement misleading, and possibly untrue. Banning marijuana does encourage illegal sales, but it also discourages teenage use, which is much more important. The *Vancouver Sun* didn't acknowledge this.

In addition, the editorial wedged readers into a false choice: "Decades of criminalizing pot use has failed to result in its elimination. Which strongly suggests that a new approach may well be worth trying." This is coded language for legalization, but it's also a silly argument; decades of criminalization have also failed to eliminate armed robbery and murder, but the *Vancouver Sun* doesn't suggest legalizing them.

The point of criticizing these editorials isn't to play "Gotcha!" We're on the verge of legalizing marijuana and we should be discussing its pros and cons. Editorial and opinion pages are some of the best places for that discussion. But if editorial writers print falsehoods, mislead us, and make silly arguments, and if the opinion sections present only one side, then there is no exchange of ideas. They are taking a forum created for public conversation and using it to force an issue rather than debate it.

The *Economist*

On March 7, 2009, the *Economist* ran an editorial supporting legalization of all drugs of abuse.[46] But even the English-speaking world's foremost news weekly was not able to write a pro-legalization opinion without misleading its readers.

First, it would not admit that legalization increases drug use. One might think a magazine called the *Economist* would recognize the universal role of supply and demand. Instead, it stated, "It is not clear that drug demand drops when prices rise."

Actually, it's very clear. Every time cigarette prices go up, more people quit.[47] According to a study by the RAND Corporation, legalizing marijuana would cut the price and increase consumption.[48]

Second, the magazine dismissed parents' fears, stating, "That fear is based in large part on the presumption that more people would take drugs under a legal regime. That presumption may be wrong."

It's not wrong. Alcohol use in the United States fell by at least half during Prohibition, and doubled in the ten years after the 18th Amendment was repealed.[49] So parents are right to fear that drug use would go up under legalization and the *Economist* is wrong to tell them otherwise.

The two lines just quoted also used language dishonestly. Qualifiers such as "may be" and "it is not clear" should be used only when we're not certain of the truth. The *Economist* used them to sow doubt about things that are certain. It's the same way the tobacco industry and global warming deniers deal with science they dislike.[50]

The editorial further claimed: "There is no correlation between the harshness of drug laws and the incidence of drug-taking; citizens living under tough regimes (notably America but also Britain) take more drugs, not fewer. ... harsh Sweden and more liberal Norway have precisely the same addiction rates."

This argument is irrelevant. Legalization isn't about making punishments less harsh, it's about having no punishments at all. Even if making drug laws less harsh doesn't increase use, allowing corporations to manufacture and advertise those drugs certainly would. Besides, the magazine's examples are wrong. Sweden does have the toughest drug laws in Europe, but Norway's are only slightly more liberal. And America's is not a tough regime. Half the U.S. states have either decriminalized marijuana or passed medical laws that are so loose any adult can smoke it without fear of the law.[51]

Lastly, the *Economist* made this unrealistic pro-legalization argument: "By providing honest information about the health risks of different drugs and pricing them accordingly, governments could steer consumers toward the least harmful ones."

Here's the reality: Tobacco and alcohol companies lobby politicians to keep taxes low and to keep warnings away. A marijuana lobby or heroin lobby would do the same. Once an industry is created, it will influence politicians far more than politicians will influence it. Besides, New York City was ridiculed for banning Big Gulps, so it's hard to imagine Americans letting the government tell them which addictive drugs to abuse.[52]

Even the *Economist* can't write a pro-legalization opinion without saying things that are untrue, misleading, and unrealistic. If legalization were a good idea, opinion writers wouldn't have to use bad arguments to support it.

Bias this pervasive should be a news story itself

E.J. Dionne, *Washington Post* columnist and Senior Fellow at the Brookings Institution, wrote a column in 2013 titled "The Dramatically Changing Politics of Marijuana."[53]

He noted that, "Sentiment in favor of legalization has increased by 20 points in just over a decade," but "attitudes toward legalization are marked by ambivalence. Many of those who favor legalization do so despite believing that marijuana is harmful."

Dionne never asked why attitudes changed so fast or why so many supporters were ambivalent, but here's a good guess: the ambivalence means support for legalization isn't firm support.

Uncertainty might be a better word than *ambivalence*. And part of the uncertainty comes from not hearing the whole story.

As for quickly changing attitudes, that only occurs when something dramatic happens or when there's a huge public relations campaign. In this case, it was a campaign run by the marijuana lobby and supported by a very compliant news media. Dionne is silent about his own profession's role in promoting marijuana, but it's a role that deserves scrutiny. Biased coverage has played such a major part in the marijuana lobby's success that it should be a news story itself.

Journalists who use marijuana shouldn't write about it

In a blog post, Christine Tatum, former national president of the Society of Professional Journalists, tells of turning down a request to write a story on Colorado's new marijuana stores. Her husband is an expert on marijuana addiction, and she and her husband have both gone on record as opposing legalization. With this in mind, she didn't think she could write an unbiased story, and the editor who contacted her agreed.[54]

A conflict of interest can be defined as a "situation that has the potential to undermine the impartiality of a person because of the possibility of a clash between the person's self-interest and professional interest or public interest."[55]

It's not just financial. Usually, reporters are not allowed to cover stories they're too emotionally connected to. For example, no reporter could objectively cover his or her spouse, or anyone with whom they're in a close relationship. As the former *New York Times* executive editor A.M. Rosenthal once told a reporter, "You can [make love to] an elephant if you want to, but if you do you can't cover the circus."[56]

Substance abuse is a love affair; it's an intense relationship. Users tolerate no criticism of their beloved, and often put it on the highest pedestal.

Marijuana users can be extremely partisan and absolutely convinced of their arguments. They're usually very convinced the law is wrong.

As Tatum points out, marijuana users feel so strongly, they willingly violate the law. It's hard for people to be unprejudiced about a law they've been breaking, so how could they cover this debate impartially?

Drug-using reporters will empathize with people whose main goal in life is to get high. They'll probably agree with the argument that people are going to use drugs no matter what, and they're more likely to think programs designed to get people to quit using are unfair and unrealistic. And their beliefs will seep into their writing.

In addition, it's a disease of denial; users hold a lot of beliefs that don't go away until they've spent enough time substance-free. So a reporter who uses drugs regularly might not just sympathize with pro-drug arguments, he'd be certain of them and unable to see his own bias.

In her blog post, Christine Tatum says we have the right to know if journalists covering the marijuana issue use the drug, but transparency is not enough. Marijuana-using reporters should not cover this issue; it's impossible for them to do it fairly. A lot of the misleading journalism described in the past three chapters might actually be the result of letting marijuana users cover this issue.

With that in mind, here's a question for every journalist in Canada and the United States who reports on, writes or opines about, or otherwise covers the marijuana issue. Editors and anyone who supervises journalists or assigns stories should also answer this question:

> Have you or your significant other used marijuana during the past year?

No one who has recently used marijuana should be covering this issue. They might think they're objective, but there's a good chance they aren't, and the public deserves journalism that is fair and impartial.

Chapter 20

How the Entertainment Media Promote Marijuana

The entertainment media—TV, music, film and video—define popular culture and shape attitudes about what is normal. Creators of entertainment are expected to follow popular trends, and apparently substance use is trendy. A study published in the *Archives of Pediatrics and Adolescent Medicine* analyzed *Billboard* magazine's 279 most popular songs of 2005 and found references to alcohol and other drugs in one-third of them, mostly presenting substance use in a positive light. Fourteen percent of the songs mentioned marijuana. The report concluded, "The average adolescent is exposed to approximately 84 references to explicit substance use daily in popular songs."[1]

Why would creators of entertainment see drugs and alcohol as cool? There are only a few possibilities: they use the drugs themselves, they hear from users that drugs are cool, or they get that impression from the news media. However, it's also possible that they don't think substance use is trendy, but they're paid to include it anyway. This doesn't happen with illegal drugs, but product placement has definitely been an issue with alcohol and tobacco, and its effect on teen use has been studied.

Indirect advertising works

In 1998, several U.S. states settled a lawsuit with tobacco companies and the industry agreed to stop using product placement in films and on TV. Prior to that, research published in *JAMA-Pediatrics* found that among the top 100 box office hits each year, at least half showed a cigarette brand. In 1999, just as the settlement was taking effect, 98 out of 100 top films showed brand name cigarettes. Over the next decade, this dropped to 22 out of 100.[2]

The alcohol industry, however, had no such agreement. Alcohol producers could still pay filmmakers to include their brand. During the same decade that cigarette product placement plummeted, the number of brand name alcohol placements in youth-rated movies nearly doubled.[3]

All this product placement in youth-rated films matters. According to a 2012 report by the U.S. Surgeon General, "There is a causal relationship between depictions of smoking in the movies and the initiation of smoking among young people."[4] Another researcher said, seeing so many movies with adults using alcohol sends the message that alcohol use is everywhere.[5]

For the alcohol and tobacco industries, product placement was money well spent. As the *JAMA* research article noted, "Children's exposure to movie imagery of these substances has been associated with not only smoking but also early onset of drinking, heavier drinking, and abuse of alcohol."[6]

Product placement makes alcohol and tobacco use seem more widespread than they really are, and makes kids think that using these two drugs is normal. Although individual marijuana businesses aren't paying TV and movie producers to feature their products yet, entertainment featuring marijuana probably entices teens the same way that those images of alcohol and tobacco do.

There's a TV show called *Workaholics*, a Comedy Central sitcom about three marijuana-smoking twenty-somethings. In an episode that ran on March 26, 2014, the three decided that to maintain their reputations as serious marijuana users, they had to smoke an entire brick of weed in one sitting—which they did.

What stretched believability was how three guys with low-wage jobs and only one car between them could afford to smoke that much marijuana in one day. Addicted marijuana users often say lack of money is their biggest problem. Yet by having the main characters come right out and say real marijuana users smoke a whole lot at once, this TV show told its young viewers that it's cool to waste money on marijuana. Of course, the show's producers will say it's comedy and no one takes it seriously, but they're wrong. TV is one of the media that define normal. Some people who saw those three likable characters smoke a whole brick of weed at once probably decided they had to do it, too.

Workaholics is a light-hearted show about drug abuse; any entertainment that paints marijuana in a positive light encourages use. That's why we don't have light-hearted comedies about alcoholics or heroin addicts; it's behavior we don't want to encourage. And we shouldn't be encouraging marijuana use, either.

It's not just entertainment

Networks usually fall back on the defense that they're just giving people what they want, but that can't be the case here. Only 7 percent of people use marijuana.[7] The public is not screaming for shows about stoners. We're not demanding programs that make marijuana look safe and fun.

Even at the ages with the heaviest use—late teens to early twenties—at the most, 25 percent of people use marijuana.[8] Comedy Central is running entertainment that makes marijuana use look normal, but for at least 75 percent of their viewers, it's not normal. So the message they're sending teenagers—that marijuana is chic, fun, and harmless—probably isn't what the majority of Comedy Central's audience asked for.

When any form of entertainment is loaded up with positive images of drug use, it's promoting those beliefs. And that's true throughout the industry. Pro-drug messages in our favorite songs and shows don't reflect public opinion; they create it.

Chapter 21

U.S. Political Parties and Marijuana

1. Republicans Share Responsibility

When they want to, Republicans know how to create a national firestorm. Over Whitewater, Obamacare, and Benghazi, they held hearings and press conferences, shut down the government, and cranked up the entire right-wing echo chamber until it reverberated with their one issue. Yet they barely whisper about marijuana.

A 2013 Pew Research Center[1] poll showed that most Republicans oppose legalization, so the GOP should be leading the fight against it. But the leadership isn't interested.

In Arizona, several county attorneys are vocal about marijuana, but only one member of the Republican-dominated state legislature—Rep. John Kavanagh—really made it an issue. Arizona's medical marijuana law passed with 50.1 percent of the vote, so if it were on the ballot again, it could easily lose. Yet when this one anti-drug legislator tried to get his fellow Republicans to refer medical marijuana back to the voters, they refused.[2] This is the same Arizona legislature that regularly passes laws the whole country condemns, so it can't be fear of repercussions holding them back.

After the 2014 election, when Washington, D.C. voted to legalize marijuana, the Republican-controlled Congress blocked the law as part of the budgeting process, a move that apparently came from a few very conservative House members.[3] However, a few weeks earlier, Republican leaders in the Senate were uninterested. When asked if they planned to do anything about marijuana legalization, Senator Lindsey O. Graham (R-S.C.) said, "That's pretty far down my list of priorities," Senator John McCain (R-Ariz.) said, "Focused on other things," and Senator Rob Portman (R-Ohio) said, "I haven't given it one thought."[4]

The Republican Party leadership is just not concerned about marijuana—or the 3.5 million American teenagers who now use it regularly.[5] There are several reasons why they don't care.

It's not a good wedge issue

With modern partisan politics, elections are won by turning out the base, not by reaching out to the center. So politicians stick to issues the whole party agrees on, and the Republican Party is divided on marijuana. Social conservatives are usually anti-legalization, but many libertarians are not. So this is not a good issue for Republican politicians.

The libertarian influence is growing

Charles and David Koch donate heavily to Republican causes, but they're also staunch libertarians. They've played major roles in founding and running three libertarian think tanks: the Cato Institute, the Reason Foundation, and the Mercatus Center. All three of these institutions favor legalization.[6] The Reason Foundation also opposes drug courts. The Charles G. Koch Summer Fellow Program even pays for internships at the Drug Policy Alliance.[7]

Although substance abuse is responsible for most crime and most child abuse,[8] many libertarians see drug use as victimless and support legalization for ideological reasons. Charles Koch wrote an op-ed for the *Wall Street Journal* criticizing any attempt by government to help people decide what is best for them.[9] He did not mention drugs, but for many libertarians, freedom to choose extends to drug use. Even though almost all addiction starts in the teen years, some libertarians are so wedded to their ideology that they call it an adult choice. This libertarian influence makes it hard for Republicans to speak out against legalization.

Politicians no longer look beyond their base

Conservatives are so used to focusing on their base, they've apparently forgotten that some conservative positions could win widespread support. Two days after the Republican victories in the 2014 midterms, MSNBC's Rachel Maddow did a show on the election's few silver linings for Democrats, and she said one of them was marijuana legalization, which passed in two states and in Washington, DC.[10] Maddow apparently assumed her audience agreed that legalization was a good thing, and most probably did. If so, this means liberal Democrats support a policy that is probably increasing teenage drug abuse across the country.

Parents don't want their kids using drugs, and that's just as true for politically liberal and moderate parents as it is for conservatives. Republicans should be able to capitalize on that, but they'd have to look beyond their base.

Money in politics makes us socially liberal

Anyone who doubts that money can buy a political outcome should look at the legalization lobby's success. If not for a few very wealthy people, it's unlikely a single medical marijuana or legalization law would ever have passed in the United States. The ultra-rich are buying legalization, and they've been helped by Republican policies that allow unlimited spending.

In both political parties, these wealthy donors are usually less socially conservative than the rank and file, but more conservative on other issues. So a political system dominated by money makes both parties more socially liberal (or libertarian) and more economically conservative. And they're pulling the whole country in that direction. It's ironic that social conservative support for the Republican Party has actually made society more socially liberal, but that's what happens when we empower those with wealth. And the legalization movement thrives in this setting.

The partisan press is part of the problem

The left and right so distrust each other's news media that they mostly ignore each other's press. The left dismisses anything coming from Fox News, an attitude mirrored on the far right by bumper stickers that say, "Don't believe the liberal media." As a result, partisan news media can slant its coverage and the audience will never know.

For example, the conservative *Washington Times* ran an editorial blasting George Soros and Peter Lewis for spending over $100 million through groups like the ACLU and DPA to fund the legalization effort.[11] Meanwhile, the *Atlantic*—which is eclectic, but has many liberal readers—ran an article on mega-donors, naming the Koch brothers and Sheldon Adelson, but not Soros, Lewis, or marijuana.[12] Had the *Washington Times* reported on the Koch-supported American Legislative Exchange Council and had the *Atlantic* described the Soros legalization plan, readers on both sides of the political divide would have had new information. Instead, no one learned anything new; they just had their partisan beliefs reinforced.

We only know what our own side tells us. The other side can sound a warning, but it won't be heard. Conservatives might like having their own news media, and might take pride in ignoring what they call the "lamestream media," but they should look at what happens when the left adopts the same attitude. When Democrats and left-leaning independents stick to their own news sources and ignore right-wing media, it's impossible to alert them that they're being misled on marijuana.

Racial profiling hands the marijuana lobby a weapon

One of the pro-legalization movement's most effective tactics is to imply that marijuana laws are used to discriminate against minorities. In 2014, they campaigned in Washington, DC, with the slogan "Legalization Ends Discrimination," and won with 65 percent of the vote.[13] A DPA press release said, "The policies of prohibition in the District have been borne on the backs of people of color for decades."[14] The same year, the Canadian Centre for Addiction and Mental Health endorsed legalization, and one reason they gave was that "police often use the charge of cannabis possession as an easy way of harassing or making life difficult for marginalized populations."[15]

This argument isn't valid; legalization wouldn't change discrimination, much less end it. However, racial profiling and discrimination are real, and that makes this argument credible. A large numbers of blacks, Hispanics, and sympathetic whites distrust the police and see the criminal justice system as an adversary rather than a friend. And when they're told they can strike back at discrimination by voting for legalization, many do.

We can go a long way toward solving racial discrimination by simply acknowledging it. According to the FBI, of the fifteen teens shot and killed while fleeing from police between 2010 and 2012, fourteen were black.[16] All these kids were doing something wrong, but a black teenager is 80 times more likely to be shot and killed for it as a white teenage doing the exact same thing. Simply acknowledging that this is unfair would change the conversation. If we can't acknowledge that it's unfair, we will continue to create an issue the marijuana lobby can easily exploit.

2. What Democrats Stand To Lose

In the run-up to the votes on legalization in Colorado and Washington, the Democratic Party began shifting gears and supporting the marijuana lobby. In 2012, Colorado Democrats included legalization in their platform.[17] Since then, Democratic-controlled legislatures in Connecticut, Illinois, Maryland and Minnesota all passed medical marijuana laws, as did New York and New Hampshire where Republicans barely controlled the state senates but Democrats controlled the state houses. According to a 2014 posting on followthemoney.org, of the fifteen candidates who received more than $1,000 from the Marijuana Policy Project, thirteen were Democrats.[18] And Democrats in Congress voted overwhelmingly to strip the Justice Department of money used to prosecute the diversion of medical marijuana to recreational use.

But Democrats should think twice before becoming the party of pot. The party would lose far more than it would gain.

Legalization would undermine important Democratic programs

The Great Society. Under President Lyndon Johnson, the Democratic Party created a safety net for the working poor and unemployed. Food stamps, school lunches, Section 8 housing, and other welfare programs are all part of this safety net that has helped millions, especially children. Welfare works as a hand-up for people who are down and out, and most people use it that way—they want to go back to work. However, addicts and alcoholics generally find it hard to get off welfare and often take advantage of these programs. A 1995 report by the Legal Action Center noted that virtually all state and local welfare program directors said drug and alcohol treatment was vital for getting recipients off welfare.[19]

A 1997 report by the same agency summarized several surveys and found that 15 to 20 percent of welfare recipients had drug or alcohol problems—twice the rate of non-recipients, but still a small minority.[20] The vast majority of adults on welfare are not substance abusers. But conservatives who oppose welfare use the small number of substance abusers to discredit whole programs.

Conservatives also want to drug-test welfare recipients. It's a bad idea because it would punish children whose substance-abusing parents refused to quit drugs. But if Democrats support laws that increase the number of drug abusers, and then fight for their right to go on welfare without drug testing, that would make drug abusers—who are clearly a drain on society--a protected Democratic constituency. That is not a defensible position.

In addition, a study from the University of Michigan found that welfare recipients use marijuana at 1.5 times the rate of non-recipients. It's a drug that's been shown to decrease commitment to work, so it's not surprising to see users on welfare.[21] How can Democrats adopt policies that increase the number of marijuana users and then expect the public to pay to support them?

The only way to maintain the integrity of welfare programs is to fight against substance abuse, including marijuana abuse. We can't defend Great Society programs and at the same time create conditions for people to misuse them.

Drug courts. These are mostly a Democratic invention. Former U.S. Attorney General Janet Reno helped create drug courts and the 1994 crime bill written by then-Senator Joe Biden turned them into a national phenomenon. Court-monitored treatment programs are probably the best way to reduce both crime and substance abuse, but the marijuana lobby resists all forms of coerced treatment, especially drug courts. It's too early to tell if Democrats will bow to the legalization lobby and turn against the party's own invention, but it's looking that way.

In 2014, the National Association of Drug Court Professionals (NADCP) gave its Governor of the Year award to Texas Governor Rick Perry, a conservative Republican. "No Governor has done so much and for so long to expand the reach of Drug Courts," the NADCP declared.[22]

Republican-dominated Texas now the leads the U.S. in reducing crime.[23] And by passing Proposition 47 that de-felonized all drug possession, California leads the country in undermining drug courts, which will probably increase crime.*

Democrats criticize Republicans for inventing the Dream Act and the individual mandate for health insurance, and then turning against their own inventions. But that's what the marijuana lobby wants Democrats to do with drug courts.

Education is a centerpiece of the Democratic plan to keep the economy strong, yet teens who smoke marijuana regularly do worse in school and are twice as likely to drop out. Teenage marijuana use spiked upward between 2008 and 2012, and medical marijuana laws are probably mostly to blame.[24] How can the Democratic Party call education crucial for a competitive America and then support laws that will blunt the next generation's ability to learn and compete?

In short, Democrats have a choice: Maintain the social safety net, have a well-educated next generation, and use recovery-based programs like drug courts to reduce both crime and substance abuse; or legalize marijuana. Doing both is probably not an option.

Supporting legalization turns Democrats into hypocrites

Marijuana is creating the same traits in the political left that they criticize in the far right. They fumed when President Bush proposed gutting the Clean Air Act and called it the Clear Skies Initiative, and when President Reagan named a missile *Peacekeeper.* But was using

---

* California's Proposition 47 was described in Chapter 14.

those names any more dishonest than calling marijuana "medical" when it almost all goes to recreational use?

Marijuana activists cherry-pick data to convince us that driving high is safe when most research says it's dangerous. They rely on flawed scientific studies to prove medical marijuana laws don't increase teen use. How can liberals criticize Republicans for misusing science on climate change and then ignore what the marijuana movement does?

Democrats criticized President George W. Bush for withdrawing from the Anti-Ballistic Missile treaty with Russia, but say nothing when a Democratic Justice Department allows states to legalize marijuana in violation of international treaties that are still in force.[25]

On January 7, 2014, MSNBC's Rachel Maddow did a story about Republicans who do everything they can to sabotage the war on poverty and then have the gall to say it's not working. That's no different from the marijuana lobby's chutzpah; they promote "medical" laws that increase use, and then point to increased use and call it evidence that drug laws don't work.

Democrats support government regulation that protects us from dangerous products, but marijuana advocates want us to distrust the government. The whole purpose of medical marijuana laws is to evade the regulatory power of agencies like the DEA. Democrats fought for tighter government regulation of tobacco; how can the party now be against the regulation of marijuana? Democrats negotiated the Master Settlement Agreement[26] to rein in tobacco companies; why are they paving the way for businesses to targets teenagers with another addictive drug?

An electoral nightmare

Democrats are in a precarious position. Egged on by the press,[27] many Democratic leaders have allied themselves with a pro-drug lobby that is promoting falsehoods to the American people. Eventually the news media will tell the whole story and the dishonesty will be apparent to everyone. When that happens, drug users will laugh and the press will do some soul-searching. But it could be devastating for the Democratic Party, the causes it supports and the people who depend on it.

3. The Two Tea Parties

Since the right-wing Tea Party burst onto the U.S. political scene in 2009, pundits have been looking for a left-wing equivalent. The marijuana movement probably comes closest. On the left, they smoke their tea; on the right, they throw it in the Boston Harbor. But they have far more in common than just this one word.

Both tea parties distrust government. A poll by the Pew Research Center found 96 percent of Tea Party members trusted government "never" or "only some of the time." That was the highest rate of any group.[28] However, the marijuana lobby believes the DEA is intentionally thwarting them for corrupt purposes. The Marijuana Policy Project website says, "The DEA will employ any logic, however twisted, to quash efforts to make marijuana available as a medicine."[29] It's a paranoid view of a malevolent government, when the DEA is really just doing its job—there is no actual need to use marijuana as medicine.

Both tea parties disregard science. Scientists are nearly unanimous that global warming is real and man-made, and according to a 2013 Pew Research Center poll, 67 percent of all Americans and 61 percent of non-Tea Party Republicans say there is solid evidence of global warming. But among Tea Party Republicans, only 25 percent believe it's real.[30] The marijuana lobby also shuts its eyes to research with which it disagrees. For years they insisted marijuana wasn't addictive, and they still deny that driving stoned is dangerous.

Each tea party has taken over a major political party, turning them away from reasonable policies. In several elections, Republican U.S. Senators lost primaries to Tea Party challengers, and the party only stopped the losses by moving further to the right. As a result, policies most people support, like immigration reform, are stalemated.[31] Democrats have become so pro-marijuana that a large majority of House Democrats voted to take away money the Justice Department used to enforce the law against large-scale medical operations that were diverting the drug to recreational use.[32] And a Democratic Justice Department is letting states legalize marijuana in violation of federal law.

Both tea parties show the danger of money in politics. What the two tea parties have most in common is that they are not real grass roots movements. The people who go to their rallies are genuine supporters, but neither movement would have much political success without wealthy donors.

In the 1980s, the tobacco industry came up with the idea of creating smokers' rights groups to fight against anti-smoking laws. The field director of RJ Reynolds envisioned a movement that would demand freedom, choice, and less government, and in 1984, with tobacco industry help and David Koch as an official co-founder, Citizens for a Sound Economy (CSE) was formed. CSE criticized the FDA and supported the agendas of several industries that gave millions to the group. In 2002, Citizens for a Sound Economy started a project called U.S. Tea Party. In 2004, CSE split into Americans for Prosperity, a conservative group opposed to climate change legislation and health care reform, and FreedomWorks, a conservative libertarian group involved in political campaigns. Americans for Prosperity organized the protests against the Affordable Care Act that launched the Tea Party. FreedomWorks raised money for local Tea Party groups, trained activists, and instilled them with pro-business libertarian beliefs.[33]

The crusade to legalize drugs has a similar history. Although NORML had been around since 1970, its push to legalize marijuana during that decade crumbled at the first hint of opposition. However, starting in the 1990s, George Soros used his millions to support legalization, eventually creating the Drug Policy Alliance and several other pro-legalization groups. Peter Lewis put time and money into the Marijuana Policy Project. These are well-funded, professional lobbying organizations, and they created the pro-marijuana movement of the 21st century.

Pundits often ask why the Occupy Wall Street movement foundered while the Tea Party is going strong. The answer is money and professional organization. Big Tobacco created the tea party of the right, and pro-marijuana billionaires brought us the tea party of the left. Neither tea party would be successful without this support.

Both tea parties depend on partisan news media. Oil and coal interests, especially Koch Industries and Exxon-Mobil, have donated millions to groups that deny climate change science.[34] And climate denial groups have a disproportionate effect on the national discussion.

Surveys have shown that 97 percent of climate scientists believe global warming is real and is man-made. Only 3 percent are doubters. According to a PBS *Frontline* report called *Hot Politics,* "Many of the researchers expressing doubts about the science of global warming have financial ties to the oil, auto, electricity and coal industries. These experts appear regularly at Congressional hearings, on television, radio and in print ... in order to spread their message." [35]

In 2013, a U.N. report found the evidence for man-made climate change "extremely likely," yet the press gave deniers so much coverage that it probably left their audiences believing there's still doubt in the scientific community. The more conservative outlets were the worst offenders. Only 3 percent of climate scientists doubt man-made climate change, but in news about the U.N. climate report, doubters made up 17 percent of the quotes in the *Washington Post,* 20 percent on CBS, 29 percent in the *Los Angeles Times,* half the quotes in the *Wall Street Journal,* and 69 percent of the guests on Fox News. And while half of the believers quoted by the press as experts were actual climate scientists, only three of the doubters were. Most of the rest had no scientific credentials, and many were paid partisans.[36]

The reporting on marijuana is similar. The press covers medical marijuana almost entirely with stories about genuinely sick patients and legitimate doctors despite evidence that most users are recreational and a handful of pot doctors write most of the recommendations. That's no different from right wing media featuring mostly global warming deniers despite evidence that the vast majority of scientists think man-made climate change is a proven fact.

Reporters regularly quote spokespeople from the Drug Policy Alliance, NORML, and the Marijuana Policy Project. These spokespeople usually have no scientific credentials and are often paid partisans.

When the media want someone with academic credentials, they regularly turn to Daniel Rees, Mark Anderson, and Mark Kleiman. They seem to be the news media's three preferred experts. The press seems to favor scientists who support legalization, while medical experts who speak for the American Society of Addiction Medicine, American Academy of Pediatrics, or the AMA are apparently rarely contacted.

So like the right-wing media, the mainstream media give ink, bytes, and airtime to industry shills and well-credentialed partisans who support their preferred viewpoint even though most of the science doesn't. And then, when people start believing the only side they've ever heard, the press calls it a groundswell of support.

Chapter 22

How an Addiction Specialist Might See the Legalization Movement

As an addiction psychiatrist, I've noticed that individual addicts and the pro-legalization movement often behave the same way. This makes sense, as the legalization movement would naturally attract drug users. After all, who is most interested in having the right to use drugs? Looking at the similarities between individual substance abusers and the legalization movement might help us understand how this movement works and how to deal with it. Here are some of the characteristics of actively using substance abusers that can also be seen in the pro-legalization movement.

They will do anything to get drugs

In 2013, a twenty-one-year-old heroin addict in New York was arrested for scamming her family and several area businesses out of thousands of dollars by claiming to have cancer. She was so convincing that strangers held fund-raisers, her dad emptied his retirement fund, and her grandmother sold her house. And, according to the district attorney, the woman spent the money on drugs.[1]

Addicts read medical books and buy MRI scans with their names on them to confirm illnesses they don't have. They make phony drugs to sell on the street, to get money to buy real drugs for themselves. When police investigate identity theft, they regularly find crystal meth users.[2] One man told me he used his five-year-old son as collateral on dope deals. Instead of returning with the money, it was his child's job to escape and run home.

Not everyone in the marijuana movement is a drug user, and most are probably not addicts, but like many drug users, the legalization movement also engages in elaborate cons. Medical marijuana is the most obvious. One of my drug-addicted patients was amazed that people voted for these laws, saying, "I can't believe anyone falls for that. Don't they know what scammers we are?" But unless someone has worked with drug users, or has been one, it's hard to realize what con artists they can be.

They play on our sympathy

In December 2012, a tourist snapped a photo of a New York City police officer giving a pair of boots to a barefoot homeless panhandler. In the days that followed, the panhandler was spotted begging for money, still shoeless. Reporters discovered he had an apartment and a long arrest record, including arrests for drugs.[3]

Substance abusers manipulate us through our kindness. Even when we suspect we're being conned, it's hard to refuse a person who seems to be in need. After years of working with addicts, it would be nice to say I've become expert at not being conned, but that's not the case. So at the treatment programs where I work, we have a policy: Any time I'm convinced a patient needs an addictive medicine, the entire staff has to approve it. They usually say "No," and the patient usually does just fine without it. Drug addicts are the world's best con artists.

Addicts know how to tug at our heartstrings, and the marijuana movement knows how to tug on a national scale. They imply that prisons are full of marijuana users and that medical marijuana laws are just for serious illnesses like cancer, and of course we sympathize. But those stories are just as fictional as the stories of many panhandlers. What the marijuana lobby and drug users have in common is that they know how to exploit our compassion.

Dishonesty is not limited to heroin and meth addicts

An alcoholic told me about robbing his own kid's piggy bank to buy beer. An addicted pot smoker said he stole silver from his brother's coin collection to buy weed. A former cigarette smoker admitted he would manipulate his family into going to restaurants where he could smoke, even though his kids wanted to eat somewhere else. Drugs corrupt, as certainly as money and power. And the dishonesty is not limited to hard drug users.

The disease of denial

The biggest lies addicts and alcoholics tell are not to others but to themselves. It's an unconscious process called denial. A useful mnemonic is: **D**on't **E**ven k**N**ow **I A**m **L**ying. People in denial believe what they're saying. When a heroin addicts says he'll just use one more time and then quit, he believes it. When an alcoholic says, "I'm not an alcoholic," he thinks it's true.

As strange as this might sound, the focus of substance abuse treatment isn't the drugs and alcohol, it's the dishonesty—the lying and the denial. Anyone can be tapered off drugs in one or two weeks, but if they don't get honest, they probably won't stay clean and sober. This isn't a moral criticism. The problem for addicts is that they habitually lie to themselves to rationalize their drug and alcohol use, and if they don't unlearn this habit, they will talk themselves right back into using. Getting honest is a slow process. That's why treatment takes four to six months, and recovery is lifelong.

Somewhere deep inside, all addicts know they're out of control, but they block this thought and convince themselves otherwise. Their classic response to offers of help is: "Leave me alone, I don't have a problem." Now they have political organizations to back them up. With legalization, drug users will be *left alone*. That's the whole purpose. Despite the harm marijuana causes, pro-marijuana organizations insist marijuana users *don't have a problem*. They've turned a belief that grows out of denial into a political position.

Their one goal

The dishonesty of drug abuse has a distinguishing feature. Everything drug abusers say leads in one direction—drugs. They lie to doctors— to get drugs. They steal to get money—for drugs. They lie about where they're going—to drink or use drugs in peace. If a drug addict tells a story that makes it seem necessary for him to use an addictive drug, the story is usually not true. Doctors hear these stories all the time.

Substance abusers find hundreds of ways to rationalize their drug and alcohol use to themselves. In their minds, it becomes the only reasonable thing to do and the only solution to their problems. Whether they're out-and-out lying or in denial, dishonesty directed toward getting and using drugs is the central symptom of the disease—and the most important one to treat.

The marijuana movement is obsessed with legalization the same way addicts are obsessed with getting high. They will use anything— the plight of African-Americans, "three strikes" victims, or people having treatment for cancer—as an excuse to legalize marijuana.

Legalizing marijuana would make it more available and easier to use, which is probably why so many users want it legalized. For users whose main aim is to get high, dishonesty in support of legalization is dishonesty for the purpose of getting drugs.

Telling a whole country that legalization will keep teens from using drugs when it won't, and insisting that medical laws are just for the seriously ill when most of it goes to drug abuse, are just as much an expression of the disease as lying to a doctor to get Xanax.

They try to make their substance use seem normal

People in denial tell themselves the opposite of what's true. Substance abusers don't want to feel guilty or ashamed, and they don't want to be reminded, either by others or by their own consciences, that what they're doing is self-destructive. So they convince themselves that their substance use is normal, and that everybody else is just like them.

Part of treatment is reminding patients that drug use isn't normal, and it's often done with humor. A prison inmate from the East Coast told me he once had three years clean and sober and stayed out of trouble the whole time. But then something really good happened and, he said, "I decided to celebrate. So I got some heroin to shoot up ..."

"Hold on," I said in a light-hearted tone. "I've celebrated a few good things in my life, but it never occurred to me to shoot up heroin. Is that how they do it in Jersey?" He laughed, but he also got the point: Shooting up heroin is not normal.

To convince us that their drug use is normal, marijuana users often say things like, "Everyone likes to get high," or, "Everyone my age smokes weed." And they believe it. But let's look again at the numbers.

According to the 2012 National Survey of Drug Use and Health, 7 percent of the U.S. population over age 12 uses marijuana, which is defined as having used it at least once during the past month.[4]

Marijuana use peaks at age 20, yet three-quarters of twenty-year-olds do not use it. Half have tried it, but most don't continue. Most teenagers, even at age 19, have never tried it even once.[5] In any truly random group of teenagers, at least three out of four will not be marijuana users.

The Centers for Disease Control Youth Risk Behavior Survey for 2011 shows similar results. Forty percent of high school students have tried marijuana, and 23 percent have used it over the past month.[6] However, three-quarters of the students don't use it and most have never even tried it.

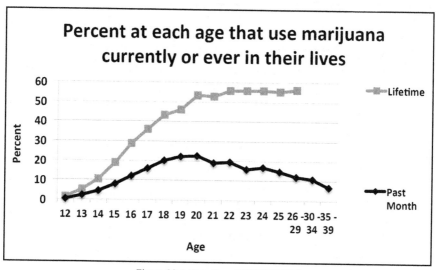

Figure 22-1. Data from NSDUH 2012[7]

Pot smokers usually find these numbers hard to believe, but that's their denial; they've convinced themselves everyone does it. There are only two groups of people who can accurately claim that most people like them smoke marijuana—drug abusers and criminals.[8]

For those two groups, marijuana use is normal; at least 50 percent are current users. For everyone else, at any age, marijuana users are a small minority. The marijuana lobby wants us to accept marijuana use as a normal part of life by telling us it already is. But despite what users think and what the marijuana lobby would like us to believe, what's normal for people of all ages is not to use it at all.

Denial isn't limited to drug and alcohol abusers

Anyone can pick up these beliefs. Family members often repeat an alcoholic's excuses: "He didn't mean it; he was just drunk." Or, "He just has a little bit too much at times," when it's not a little bit and it's all the time. Without ever taking a drink, these family members are in just as much denial as the alcoholic they live with. So when someone defends marijuana by saying, "It's just weed," "It never killed anyone," or, "It should be legal," they might not smoke pot, but if not, they've probably been listening to someone who does.

They train others to be enablers

The disease of addiction makes individuals center their lives around using. In turn, these addicts and alcoholics manipulate their families into arranging their lives around the illness. The family learns to accept the addict's excuses, and even to repeat the alibis to the outside world. One heroin addict told me he taught his four-year-old son to lie to police.

The family not only allows the addict to use, they protect him from the consequences of his illness. If he loses his license, they drive him. If he can't earn a living, they support him. They learn to never criticize the addict's substance use and to pretend all his problems really are caused by someone or something else. In effect, family members become co-conspirators. They are an extension of the addict's denial mechanism.

The technical term is "enablers." Without them, the addict probably couldn't continue using and certainly couldn't use in peace. No one would make excuses to his boss, or pay the rent when he spent the money on dope.

Again, addicts shape the world around them to support their substance abuse. It's a two-part process. First, the mind of the addict is manipulated by the disease into serving the addiction, not his real needs and wishes. And then the addict manipulates family and friends into serving the addiction instead of their own well-being.

Recovery goes in the opposite direction. Friends and family wake up to what is going on, stop believing the deception, and intervene to get the addict into treatment. That's why so many treatment programs include a family component. The best way to keep someone clean and sober is to get the family to expect and demand it. And this is just as true for society as a whole as it is for individual families.

The marijuana lobby is creating enablers on a national and international scale. They are creating a community of people who believe and even repeat their stories and excuses. They've convinced us to tolerate their drug use, never criticize it, and even make the drug easily available. They are transforming us from a society that serves what is best for everyone into one that serves the needs and desires of substance abusers. And so far, Canada and the United States have acted like enablers in serious need of family treatment.

The only way to help is to say "No"

Very few addicts or alcoholics are interested in quitting. They only get clean and sober when their family, their employer, or the legal system intervenes, or when life gets so painful they can no longer ignore the misery.

In other words, they only get help when their system of enablers breaks down and they have to experience the painful consequences of their illness. This means giving them what they want just helps them stay sick, and the only way to help them get better is for their enablers to say "No."

They won't like it, but they never like what helps. I see this at work. If I give an addict the medication he wants, he'll tell me I'm the best doctor in the world. If I say "No," suddenly I'm terrible.

That's also how the marijuana movement works. They want to make marijuana easily available and they want to use it without any interference. They want protection from drug laws. They've written medical marijuana laws with provisions to protect themselves from landlords who might evict them and from employers who might fire them.[9] They argue that marijuana metabolites in the bloodstream are no reason to be charged with driving under the influence. In other words, they want us to protect them from the trouble their drug use creates. They want society to take on the burden and responsibility of problems they've caused.

And the worst thing we can do is say "Yes." If we want to prevent the problems widespread marijuana use would cause, we have to start saying "No" to the marijuana lobby.

The unique features of marijuana users

Marijuana activism

While all substance abusers have certain features in common, each drug also affects users in unique ways. A special feature of marijuana users is that they're politically active. In the book *A Child's Garden of Grass,* the authors say pot-smokers are the world's greatest proselytizers, and they are. They think marijuana is great and they want everyone to know.

When I started smoking marijuana, I was a senior in high school and was taking a debate class. Protests were raging over the war in Vietnam and there was a brand new environmental movement, but the only cause I cared to debate was legalizing marijuana. It was partly adolescent enthusiasm, but it's also how marijuana users tend to think; nothing is more important.

The large protests, with hundreds of people publicly smoking marijuana, came after I quit using, but I had the same "let's do this in public" attitude. The last day of my freshman year in college, a friend and I smoked a joint in the back row of chemistry lecture—and we wanted it to be really obvious. Someone might sneak alcohol into class, but they'd keep it hidden; we wanted everyone to know.

It had the feeling of protest. We had a tell-the-world attitude like we were standing up for something that was treated unjustly. I felt marijuana deserved respect, and people had to know what a good thing it was.

In the ADAM study, criminals were asked if they used drugs and were then drug-tested. They lied about most drug use, but were much less likely to lie about marijuana.[10] I think this comes from the same feeling I had; it was important to tell people about the relationship I had with this drug—not for my sake, but for the drug's sake. Marijuana users have an allegiance to the drug.

People might feel this strongly about other drugs, but they don't become activists who have to promote it to the world. There are no outdoor cocaine protests, or underage drinking protests. Ecstasy is used at large concerts, but it's not political. Although a lot of people think they're using meth for concentration or low energy, there's no demand for medical meth. There's no huge movement to legalize LSD or bring back its medical use. But marijuana users are politically active and energized.

Almost as soon as I started using marijuana, I thought others should try it and I thought it should be legal. This was 1971; I didn't know there was a pro-legalization movement. I came to this on my own. Marijuana users really are great proselytizers; it's a unique feature of the drug.

And it seems to go away when people quit using. Three months after I stopped using, I no longer cared if marijuana was legal. I looked back on what I'd thought and said about it, and asked: What was that all about? Why did I talk about pot like it was manna from heaven?

I still supported legalization, but the passion was gone. And I've also seen the pro-legalization fervor ebb and vanish in my patients after they quit using. They might still support legalization, but once they quit using the drug, the zeal to promote it just isn't there. And that zeal is probably one of the factors that created and maintains the marijuana movement.

How marijuana denial helps spur a movement

Denial is a bit different for each drug. Cigarette smokers are killing themselves; they often die in their forties, fifties, and early sixties.

Most smokers know this and want to quit, but the ones who don't want to quit usually rationalize it. They say things like, "Everyone has to die from something," ignoring the fact that it's a lot nicer to die from old age in their nineties than from a heart attack in their forties. Cigarette smokers are rarely in denial about being addicted; their denial is about needlessly killing themselves at an early age.

What's unique about alcoholic denial is the insistence that they can't possibly be alcoholic. So they say things like, "I never drink before noon," "I still have my job," and "I can take it or leave it." They're trying to convince themselves that they're not addicted. This isn't exclusive to alcoholics. Smokers and heroin addicts sometimes say they're not addicted when they obviously are, but they don't do it nearly as consistently as alcoholics do. Alcoholic denial is about seeing themselves as still in control.

Heroin addicts usually know they're addicted, but they're in denial about how completely the drug controls them. They believe they can just use one more time and then quit. I've known heroin addicts who drove two hours to Phoenix every day for a year, and each day they bought just enough dope for that one day because they were certain it would be the last time. They say things like, "I'm done," "I've had enough," "I'm through with it." In fact, they're usually not done; heroin addicts have the highest relapse rate.

With heroin, alcohol, and tobacco, addicts are in denial about their addiction—how severe it is, whether they are addicted, or whether quitting matters—but they know the drug is harmful and that being addicted to it is a bad thing.

Marijuana denial is slightly different; marijuana users are in denial about the drug itself. Marijuana denial is the belief that the drug causes no harm and is even beneficial. As we saw with airline pilots and teenage drivers, there's a belief that it has no negative effects. Even when users hear the research on traffic fatalities and adolescent brain development, they often respond with, "But it's just weed." They dismiss the research and go on believing it's harmless and couldn't possibly hurt anyone. Marijuana denial is the belief that the drug is blameless.

But it's also the belief that the drug is valuable and important. When I smoked pot daily, I sometimes saw that I was wasting my time and not living the life I wanted, but I told myself marijuana was special and significant. Marijuana is the drug that lets you waste your life while thinking you're doing something wonderful.

Marijuana users seem to truly believe the drug is a boon to mankind. They tell us it's food, it's medicine, it's clothing, George Washington grew it, the Declaration of Independence was written on it ... they're relentless.

And that shows us the difference between alcoholic denial and marijuana denial. Alcoholics know that alcoholism is a bad thing, so they defend themselves by saying they can't possibly be alcoholic. Marijuana users in denial think no use of marijuana could possibly be bad, so they defend marijuana.

Here are some more ways of looking at the difference in denial with these two drugs.

- Alcoholics claim that *their own* drinking isn't a problem. Marijuana users claim that *marijuana* isn't a problem.

- Alcoholics insist *they personally* are not addicted. Marijuana users insist that *marijuana* is not addictive.

- Alcoholics minimize the harm caused by *their own* drinking. Marijuana users minimize the harm caused by *marijuana*.

- Alcoholic denial is that *they personally* have done nothing wrong. Marijuana denial is that *marijuana* can do no wrong.

- Alcoholics lament that the world treats *them* unfairly. Marijuana users maintain that the world treats *pot* unfairly.

These play out differently. Since alcoholics are only defending themselves, they only try to convince friends and family. Marijuana users are defending marijuana, and that works best on a wider scale— national or international.

Marijuana denial very naturally lends itself to political activity, and might be largely responsible for the pro-legalization movement. People who believe marijuana is wonderful and can do no wrong don't just tell their friends, they tell the world.

The takeaway

On July 4, 2013, marijuana activists arranged to have an American flag made of hemp flown over the U.S. Capitol.[11] That is a perfect image of how so many marijuana users think. They elevate it over everything. It is their one true allegiance. To them, marijuana is so important it deserves a position above our greatest institutions.

But it doesn't. It's nothing more than a drug of abuse. So what makes marijuana users exalt it and defend it against all criticism? What made them create this feverish legalization movement we don't see with any other drug?

Not everyone who is pro-legalization comes to it this way, but for many of the most passionately motivated, the intense belief that marijuana is treated unfairly seems to come from using the stuff, and seems to leave when they get clean and sober.

If so, the cure for their frustration with marijuana laws is not to legalize the drug; the cure is to stop using it.

Chapter 23

What Legalization Would Unleash

The drive to legalize marijuana should be seen in context—the marijuana lobby's overarching goal is to decriminalize or legalize all currently illegal drugs. The Global Commission on Drug Policy has already called for all countries to decriminalize all drug possession and to "regulate drug markets."[1] Remember, they believe that only a legal drug can be regulated, so when they use the term *regulate*, they mean *legalize*.

The Canadian Drug Policy Coalition issued a report calling for "the decriminalization of all drugs for personal use."[2] The Drug Policy Alliance's mission statement says it "envisions a ... society in which ... punitive prohibitions of today are no more."[3] That certainly sounds like legalizing all drugs.

The DPA's director of media relations made that explicit in a blog post by writing, "My colleagues and I at the Drug Policy Alliance are committed to ensuring the decriminalization of all drug use ..."[4] This movement believes people should have the legal right to obtain and use any drug.

The three groups just named are all funded by George Soros and his Open Society Foundations or Institute. Legalization or decriminalization of all drugs has apparently always been their aim; now they're saying it openly, and so are many opinion writers.

For example, Conor Friedersdorf of the *Atlantic* wrote an article titled "America Has a Black Market Problem, Not a Drug Problem." In it, he blames drug laws for gang violence and describes the benefits, as he sees them, of legalizing all drugs.[5]

The *Economist* has called for legalizing all drugs. Eugene Robinson of the *Washington Post* blamed the heroin overdose death of actor Phillip Seymour Hoffman on drug laws, saying that when drugs are black market commodities, it's impossible for addicts to know what they're injecting.[6] It's an erroneous argument, however, because the abuse of prescription opiates kills far more people than heroin, and addicts know exactly what manufactured pharmaceuticals contain.

Libertarians are also very open about their aim. Not all libertarians are pro-legalization, but many are. The libertarian Cato Institute and other strongly ideological libertarian organizations support the legalization of all drugs.[7]

So the legalization of marijuana should be seen in the context of what would certainly come next: a push to decriminalize or legalize all drugs of abuse. The movement is already laying the groundwork and painting a rosy picture of universal legalization.

But to paint this rosy picture, they ignore all the costs and all the problems legalizing drugs would cause. For example, the Cato Institute published a report estimating that the United States would reap $88 billion in savings and tax revenue from legalizing all drugs, but never mentioned a single cost.[8] That's like computing all the gas money you'd save by selling your car without ever considering what you'd spend to get around without one.

The social and economic cost of legalizing all drugs would be substantial. In fact, they'd be staggering. It's hard to grasp all the suffering this would unleash. Substance abuse plays a role in every social problem we have, and a major role in the most serious ones.

One of the most serious is child abuse, which has extra significance because it's also a cause of nearly every social problem. As we will see in the rest of this chapter, child abuse and substance abuse together cause much of the world's grief. However, adults with alcohol and other drug problems are responsible for most of the child abuse, so substance abuse is still the primary problem that leads to all the others. That should be our main consideration when we contemplate legalizing drugs.

Pandora's bag and bottle: Twenty-one ways legalization would harm us all

Here's a list of twenty-one problems that plague modern society. Substance abuse and child abuse are on the list, but they are also the causes of every problem on the list.

Only crime, domestic abuse, and child abuse involve violence, but all twenty-one problems drag us down economically and emotionally. This is what the legalization lobby doesn't tell us. These twenty-one problems affect us all, and they will grow in size and severity if we legalize all drugs. Here is some of the evidence the substance abuse and child abuse are, at least partially, causes of all twenty-one problems:

Crime

Two-thirds of prison inmates are substance abusers.[9] Three-quarters of arrestees test positive for drugs.[10] Most crime—including most property and violent crime—is a symptom of substance abuse.[11] Legalization would increase drug use, which would increase crime. Research also shows that people who were abused or neglected as children are nine times as likely to break the law as adults, and were more likely to be serving time for a violent crime than inmates who were not abuse victims.[12] So child abuse also increases crime. Two aspects of crime deserve special mention:

> *Prison overcrowding.* Nearly 80 percent of U.S. prison inmates are incarcerated for crimes that are not drug-related, but even these non-drug crimes are mostly caused by substance abuse. So these crimes would increase with drug legalization, and the net result would be more crime and more people in prison.

> *Gangs.* Gang members use drugs and alcohol at high rates, and are responsible for most crime in the U.S., including armed robbery, identity theft, and weapons trafficking.[13] Factors that predispose teenagers to join gangs include substance abuse, serious problems at home (often involving substance abuse), and neighborhoods with lots of drug use.[14] More drugs would mean more gang members.

Child abuse

According to CASA Columbia, "70% of abused and neglected children have alcohol or drug abusing parents."[15] Child abuse is primarily a symptom of substance abuse, so it would increase with legalization.

Domestic violence

Substance abuse precipitates violence in violence-prone people so regularly that it's an ingredient in the majority of domestic violence cases.[16] A 1995 study found that 92 percent of perpetrators had used drugs or alcohol the day of the assault.[17] Legalization of all drugs would mean more domestic violence.

Drug and alcohol abuse

Drug and alcohol abuse cost the United States over a $400 billion per year, most of it in lost productivity.[18] Substance abuse would certainly increase with legalization.

Drunk and drugged driving

Drunk driving fatalities have declined since Mothers Against Drunk Driving was founded in 1980. But drugged driving and combined drug- and alcohol-impaired driving have increased. The number of traffic fatalities caused by drugged driving has increased with greater availability of marijuana, and would increase even more with legalization.

Homelessness

According to research cited in *Treating the Homeless Mentally Ill*, about two-thirds of the chronically homeless are substance abusers.[19] However, substance abuse by itself does not lead to homelessness. A study of homeless adults found that nearly half had been so severely abused as children they were removed from their homes by CPS.[20] At Healthcare for the Homeless in central Phoenix, where I worked, severe childhood abuse was also a part of nearly every patient's story.

Welfare dependency

Only 15–20 percent of people on welfare have substance abuse disorders, but they stay on welfare the longest.[21]

High healthcare costs

Adults who were abused as children have more surgeries and more medical and psychiatric problems.[22] Substance abusers run up healthcare bills for a host of medical problems that often require hospital stays, emergency room visits and addiction treatment.

Teen pregnancy

Women who were sexually abused are three times as likely to get pregnant in their teens.[23] Abused boys are more likely to father a teen pregnancy.[24] And substance abusers are notorious for indulging in promiscuity and risky sexual behavior. According to Joseph Califano, former Health, Education, and Welfare secretary, "Most unplanned teenage pregnancy occurs when one or both parties are high at the time of conception."[25]

Abortion and unwanted pregnancy

Research shows that substance abusers have higher rates of abortion than nonusers.[26] One study showed 5 percent of abortions occurred because women were afraid they'd harmed the fetus with drugs or alcohol, or that substance use would make them or their partner an unfit parent.[27] A study done at California State University in 1993 found that childhood sexual abuse was related to an increased likelihood of a woman having an abortion.[28] So preventing substance abuse would lower the abortion rate whereas legalizing drugs would increase it.

AIDS

About 40 percent of new HIV cases involve intravenous drug users or their heterosexual partners. But even among gay men with HIV, most have used illegal drugs.[29] The reason is that substance abusers of all sexual orientations are more likely to have unprotected sex and multiple partners—and those behaviors put them at risk of AIDS.[30]

Prostitution

Street prostitutes almost always have a history of substance abuse.[31] The prostitutes we treated at Healthcare for the Homeless all used the money to pay for drugs. But childhood sexual abuse is also part of the story. In *The Sexualization of Childhood,* edited by Sharna Olfman, prostitution researcher Melissa Farley calls sexual abuse of children the "training ground for prostitution." She describes research showing that sexually abused girls are twenty-eight times as likely to engage in prostitution, and another study that found 82 percent of prostitutes in Vancouver, B.C., were sexually abused as children.[32]

Poverty

Substance abuse drags people into poverty three ways. Addicts and alcoholics find it much harder to hold onto a job. They spend their money on drugs and alcohol. And they develop health problems that drain their savings and make it harder to work.

Chronic unemployment

The unemployed have twice the rate of substance abuse as the general population.[33] And usually it's substance abuse that leads to poverty and unemployment, not the other way around. A review of the research published in 2011 showed that drug and alcohol abusers had more difficulty finding employment and were more likely to lose jobs they had.[34]

High school dropouts

Students who use marijuana regularly before age sixteen drop out twice as often as nonusers.[35] A study published in the *Lancet* found that even occasional marijuana users have an increased dropout rate.[36] And marijuana is not the only cause; teens who abuse alcohol or other illegal drugs also drop out at higher rates.[37]

Divorce

Research on divorce found substance abuse to be the third most common reason, after infidelity and incompatibility.[38]

Single moms

Families headed by a single mom are five times as likely to be poor as families headed by a married couple.[39] Two of the most common causes of single parenthood are divorce and unwanted pregnancy, both of which are often caused by substance abuse.

Deadbeat dads

Research shows that one-quarter of all parents who are owed child support receive nothing. And state programs that pursue parents who don't pay child support often find the problem is substance abuse.[40]

Grandparents raising grandkids

The 2000 U.S. census found that over 2.4 million grandparents were raising their grandchildren.[41] Families headed by a grandparent often have financial problems. According to the American Academy of Child and Adolescent Psychiatry, common reasons for biological parents leaving their kids with grandparents are substance abuse and several problems that are often caused by substance abuse: divorce, teenage pregnancy, and incarceration.[42]

* * *

The point of listing these twenty-one problems is to show that drug and alcohol abuse affect society far more than we realize. Substance abuse truly is the modern world's Pandora's box; every social problem is linked to this disease. Anyone who supports drug legalization should study this list and picture living in a world where all those problems are more common.

These twenty-one problems are why legalization is no small issue. I've seen victims of child abuse and domestic violence every day of my working life for thirty years. One of the main reasons for writing this book is that I can't just watch Canada and the United States adopt policies that would make those problems—and nearly two dozen other social ills—even more common.

The legalization lobby avoids this side of the story, but each of these twenty-one social problems will get worse if we legalize drugs. On the other hand, recovery-based policies would reduce substance abuse and curb every one of these problems.

Given that choice, it's hard to understand why there's even a debate.

Chapter 24

The Fork in the Road

We've tried the legalization experiment. As of July 2014, the United States had medical marijuana laws in twenty-three states. Those laws effectively legalize the drug, and in those states, teenage use was much higher and increasing much faster than in non–medical marijuana states.

Colorado has one of the most widely used (and abused) medical marijuana laws, so it's a good example of what legalizing the drug can do. In 2006, the state had about 1,000 medical marijuana cardholders. By 2012, there were over 100,000. During those six years, Colorado saw increases in several problems caused by marijuana.[1]

Marijuana-related Problems that Increased in Colorado with Expansion of Medical Marijuana between 2006 – 2012			
	2006	2012	Increase
Percent of all traffic fatalities in which drivers tested positive for marijuana	6.92%	16.53%	139%
Past-month marijuana use, ages 12-17	7.6%	10.47%	38%
Drug-related school suspensions (most were for marijuana use or possession)	3,988	5,279	32%
Marijuana-related hospitalizations	3,886	6,720	73%
Calls to Poison Center about children under age 6 ingesting marijuana. Eating brownies or cookies were the most common complaints.	4	15	275%

Table 24-1. Data from *The Legalization of Marijuana in Colorado: The Impact*, Volume 1, 2013.
The Rocky Mountain High Intensity Drug Trafficking Area Program.
White House Office of National Drug Control Policy.[2]

On January 1, 2014, Colorado began selling marijuana legally for recreational use. Nine months later, citations for public consumption had increased by nearly 500 percent, and Colorado's Democratic governor said the decision to legalize marijuana had been "reckless."[3] Most significantly, a 2014 study by the Colorado Department of Public Health found that Colorado's rate of adult marijuana use was nearly twice that of the rest of the country, and one-third of these adult users reported daily use and nearly one-fifth reported driving stoned.

So it's not very surprising that a September 17, 2014, poll showed a slight majority of Colorado voters were unhappy with the decision to legalize the drug.[4] The legalization experiment—whether under the guise of medical use or openly for recreational use—can't be called successful in Colorado.

When looking at the effects of legalization, we should consider both medical marijuana laws and legalization for recreational use. News reports claimed that young people's marijuana use didn't increase after legalization in 2014, but that was misleading because Colorado effectively legalized the drug years earlier with its medical marijuana law, and marijuana use in all age ranges went up.[5] Past-month teenage marijuana use increased by 47 percent from 2006 to 2013, and was already one of the highest in the nation before complete legalization kicked in.

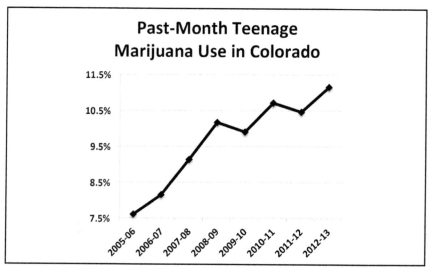

Figure 24-1. Data from National Survey on Drug Use and Health[6]

Journalists make this mistake on a national level, too. On December 16, 2014, Chris Ingraham wrote a column for the *Washington Post* with the headline, "Teen marijuana use falls as more states legalize."[7] According to the Monitoring the Future survey, several measures of teen use were effectively flat after 2011 and decreased in 2014. For past-month and past-year use, the decrease is only statistically significant for 10th grade students.[8] Ingraham took this as possible evidence that legalization does not increase teen use. He's right that teen use decreased in 2014, but there was a much larger jump in teen use from 2006 through 2011 when medical marijuana laws were being expanded. Even with the downtick in 2014, teen use is higher than it was in 2006 and much higher than it was in 1992.

Medical marijuana laws like the one in Colorado should be seen as legalization because that's what they do; they effectively legalize marijuana for any adult who wants it. By this standard, legalization has been accompanied by an overall increase in adolescent use.

The recovery-based experiment

Sweden went the opposite way of Colorado, using strict drug laws combined with prevention and recovery-based programs, and the results of those policies are also clear. Sweden has been closing prisons and has one of the lowest rates of adolescent marijuana use in the world.[9]

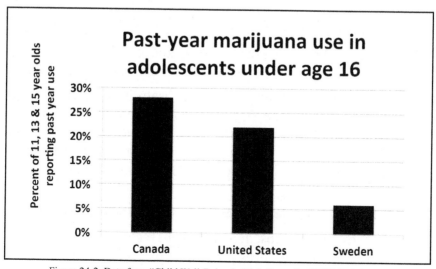

Figure 24-2. Data from "Child Well-Being in Rich Countries," UNICEF, 2013.[10]

Those are our choices: Colorado or Sweden, legalization or recovery-based policies.

Sweden initially tried the lax drug policies Canada and the United States are trying now, and had the same bad results, so it reversed course. If Canada and the United States decide to reverse course and follow Sweden's example, here's what the countries would have to do:

1. Overturn medical marijuana and legalization laws. They serve no useful purpose.

2. For the small number of marijuana patients who are genuine, educate physicians about the use of cannabinoid medications dronabinol, nabilone, nabiximols and CBD—medications that work as well as marijuana.

3. Change U.S. drug war spending from mostly interdiction overseas to mostly prevention and treatment at home.

4. Keep tough drug laws, but destigmatize them so they're not a lifelong curse. Eliminate mandatory sentencing and give judges more discretion. The aim should be to get substance abusers into treatment and recovery, and this often requires flexibility.

5. For the majority of criminals who have drug and alcohol disorders, use prison, jail, parole, and probation to treat their substance abuse, using the law and the possibility of punishment to keep them in recovery.

6. Repeal California's Proposition 47 and warn other states that de-felonizing drug possession will undermine drug courts.

7. In the U.S., declare a truce in the partisan divide and permanent campaign so that opposing politicians can work together on a bipartisan drug policy. In Canada, one of the political parties would have to run on a recovery-based approach and make clear how it differs from both legalization and criminalization.

Our decision today has far-reaching effects

If we take those seven steps, and implement recovery-based policies, we could start to solve our drug problem. A recovery-based approach would also reduce every one of the twenty-one social problems listed in the previous chapter. That would mean we'd have less crime, less child abuse, and less violence overall, and fewer people would be weighed down by terrible family and financial problems. Since every dollar spent on substance abuse treatment has been shown to save taxpayers at least $7, government would spend less and so would we.[11] We would be more productive and more competitive.

And the benefits would not stop there. The choice between legalization and the recovery-based approach is a choice about what type of society we want to live in. The two different approaches would create two very different cultures.

A culture of resignation vs. a culture of optimism

Most of the support for legalization is grudging support that comes from believing there's no alternative. It often comes with a sigh, a shrug of the shoulders, and a resigned acceptance. It's a powerless feeling that comes from believing drug use is inevitable and the best we can hope for is to decrease the harm it causes.

But drug use is not inevitable. We've seen teenage marijuana use rise and fall through the years depending on the information they receive.

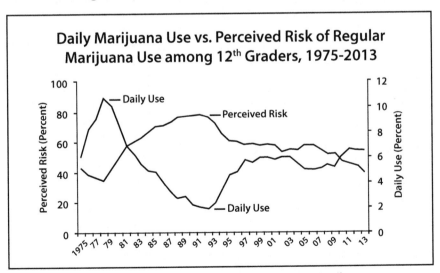

Figure 24-3. From the National Institute on Drug Abuse[12]

That's why people who work in the addiction recovery field are so upbeat. We don't buy into anyone's hopelessness; we know the disease is 100 percent treatable. A recovery-based culture would see each of those twenty-one social problems in the previous chapter as treatable and preventable. We might not coax them all back into Pandora's box, but we can go a long way in that direction. And knowing we have the power to fix our problems should make us genuinely optimistic.

A culture of drug abuse vs. a culture of recovery

Years ago, a patient told me about a heroin-addicted uncle who pointed a gun at him during an argument. My patient called the police, but his family begged him to drop the charges, which my patient finally did. One week later, the uncle overdosed and died. As my patient noted, dropping those charges was no favor; jail might have saved his uncle's life.

That is our situation. It's hard to say "No," and at times we are all enablers, but enabling is not the same as helping. We don't help substance abusers by giving them what they want. We have a choice between saying yes and letting people stay sick, or saying no and helping them get well.

In a culture of drug abuse, addicts would simply stay sick. We would see drug use as normal and put no pressure on substance abusers to get clean and sober. We'd tolerate the disease and we'd accept the twenty-one social problems it causes as inevitable.

In a culture of recovery, we would expect sick people to try to get well, and substance abusers would feel that expectation. In a recovery-based culture, we would see most crime, child abuse and all those twenty-one problems not as inevitable, but as preventable symptoms of a treatable disease.

A culture of selfishness vs. a culture of kindness

At the deepest level, the choice between legalization and recovery-based policies is a choice between a self-centered culture and a culture in which we're concerned about each other. The Big Book of Alcoholics Anonymous says, "Selfishness—self-centeredness! That, we think, is the root of our troubles ... Above everything, we alcoholics must be rid of this selfishness."[13]

Substance abuse is a selfish disease. Rather than seek happiness by living meaningful lives, substance abusers use chemicals to stimulate the pleasure centers of their brains. And often this becomes all they care about. What could be more self-centered?

Substance abuse plays a role in every social problem we can imagine; yet substance abusers push for legalization anyway. As one addict put it, "Drugs always come first." Addicts want their drugs easily available and don't care that this would harm millions. What could be more selfish?

Recovery, on the other hand, includes helping others. The A.A. book *Twelve Steps and Twelve Traditions* says, "Here we experience the kind of giving that asks no rewards."[14] Many addicts get clean and sober through churches and other religious groups that also put a premium on service to others. Even programs with no spiritual component, like Smart Recovery, support those who "give back by helping others."[15] Generosity and genuine concern are valued in a recovery-based culture.

If we enable substance abusers to keep using and we organize our world around the demands of their disease, we will create a more selfish society. If we support recovery, we will create a more compassionate world. At the deepest level, the choice we face is between a culture of "every man for himself" and a culture that believes "I am my brother's keeper."

* * *

Canada and the United States are on a path to legalizing marijuana and other drugs. It's a path that will lead to increased drug use, especially among the young.

Americans and Canadians care about their children and want them to live happy lives. They don't want their kids using drugs and they don't want a world filled with the problems drugs cause.

Drug use was minimal in the past and we can create a society with minimal drug use again. A look at the research, at Sweden, and at the Parent Movement from the late 1970s, tells us how it can be done.

Endnotes

Preliminaries

1. Arit John " Pope Francis Says Drug Legalization Is a Bad Idea" (June 20, 2014) *The Wire*.

2. Elizabeth Dias " Exclusive: The Dalai Lama Talks Pot, Facebook and the Pope With TIME" (Feb. 19, 2014) *Time*.

3. Bertha K. Madras "Office of National Drug Control Policy A scientist in drug policy in Washington, DC" (2010) *Annals Of The New York Academy Of Sciences*.

4. Jaime Fuller " Gov. Jerry Brown on legalized marijuana: 'How many people can get stoned and still have a great state?'" (Mar. 2, 2014) The *Washington Post*.

5. Larry Atkins " Hippies' proud legacy: peace, love, activism" (June 21, 2007) *Baltimore Sun*.

Chapter 1

1. Lydia Saad Aug. 2, 2013 "In U.S., 38% Have Tried Marijuana, Little Changed Since 80s" Gallup.

2. J. Margolis and R. Clorfene. (1971). *A Child's Garden of Grass: The Official Handbook for Marijuana Users* Pocket Books.

   "The Fabulous Furry Freak Brothers #1" Comics.org (January 1, 2015).

   "Cheech & Chong": Amazon.com

3. Johnston, L. D., O'Malley, P. M., Bachman, J. G., Schulenberg, J. E. & Miech, R. A. (2014). *Monitoring the Future national survey results on drug use,*

1975–2013: Volume I, Secondary school students. Ann Arbor: Institute for Social Research, The University of Michigan.

"Jimmy Carter on Drugs" *On The Issues* (Jan 1, 2015).

"CBS Evening News for Friday January 16, 1976" *Vanderbilt Television News Archive* (Jan 1, 2015).

Emilee Mooney Scott "Marijuana Decriminalization" *Connecticut General Assembly cga.ct.gov* (May 5, 2010).

4. See http://www.monitoringthefuture.org/pubs/monographs/mtf-vol1_2013.pdf (Table 5-3, p. 270)

5. See http://www.monitoringthefuture.org/pubs/monographs/mtf-vol1_2013.pdf (Table 8-1a, p. 418)

6. Hilary DeVries, "Parents Band Together to Push Back Drug Tide. Preventing Drug Abuse: What's New, What's Working." Second of a series. *The Christian Science Monitor,* May 4, 1982.

   Mark Kleiman et al. *Encyclopedia of Drug Policy* (Jan 2011) Sage Publications, page 47.

7. Emily Dufton "Parents, Peers and Pot: The Rise of the Drug Culture and the Birth of the Parent Movement: 1976-1980" (Mar. 15, 2013) *Trans-Scripts 3.*

8. Johnston, L. D., O'Malley, P. M., Bachman, J. G., Schulenberg, J. E. & Miech, R. A. (2014). *Monitoring the Future national survey results on drug use, 1975–2013: Volume I, Secondary school students.* Ann Arbor: Institute for Social Research, The University of Michigan. (p. 127)

9. Johnston, L. D., O'Malley, P. M., Bachman, J. G., Schulenberg, J. E. & Miech, R. A. (2014). (Table 8-1a, p. 418)

10. Johnston, L. D., O'Malley, P. M., Bachman, J. G., Schulenberg, J. E. & Miech, R. A. (2014). (Table 5-4, p. 229)

11. Johnston, L. D., O'Malley, P. M., Bachman, J. G., Schulenberg, J. E. & Miech, R. A. (2014). (Table 8, page 68).

12. NORML Dec. 31, 2014 "About NORML" Marijuana Policy Project Dec. 31, 2014 "Our Mission and Vision"

    Tony Newman "Beyond Marijuana: Gearing Up For the Battle to Decriminalize All Drugs" (June 20, 2013) Huffington Post.

13. David Bienenstock and Richard Cusick "Peter Lewis Resigns From The Marijuana Policy Project" (June 15, 2010) *High Times.*

Canadian Drug Policy Coalition Dec. 29, 2014 "About Us".

Open Society Foundations March 31, 2015 "About Us".

Open Society Foundations Dec. 29, 2014 "War on Drugs: Report of the Global Commission on Drug Policy".

Dan Werb et al. "The temporal relationship between drug supply indicators: an audit of international government surveillance systems" (Sept. 30, 2013) *BMJ Open*.

Open Society Foundations Nov. 7, 2014 "Voices: Ending Mass Incarceration".

Michaela Montaner & Dan Werb "Here's Why Drug Policy Reform Is Gaining Momentum" *Open Society Foundations.org* (October 29, 2013).

"George Soros Backs Marijuana Legalization, Donates $1 Million To Prop 19" Oct. 26, 2010 *Huffington Post*.

Colin R. Mangham "Mingling Activism with Policy Influence: Harm Reduction Ideology and the Politicisation of Canadian Drug Policy" *The Journal of Global Drug Policy and Practice* Volume 5, Issue 4 - Winter 2011.

14. American Civil Liberties Union (July 18, 2001) "Individual Donor Sets Record With $7 Million Donation, Largest-Ever Endowment Gift to ACLU" (Press release).

    National Institute on Money in State Politics "Initiative 502: Concerns Licensing and Regulating Marijuana was on the ballot in Washington, 2012; Top Supporting Donors" Dec 31, 2014.

    American Civil Liberties Union of Maine (Feb. 21, 2013) "Legalizing Marijuana".

    American Civil Liberties Union (Nov. 7, 2012) "Marijuana on the Ballot".

15. Substance Abuse and Mental Health Services Administration, *Results from the 2011 National Survey on Drug Use and Health: Summary of National Findings*, NSDUH Series H-44, HHS Publication No. (SMA) 12-4713. Rockville, MD: Substance Abuse and Mental Health Services Administration, 2012. Table 6.1a

16. Emily Dufton "Parents, Peers and Pot: The Rise of the Drug Culture and the Birth of the Parent Movement: 1976-1980" (Mar. 15, 2013) *Trans-Scripts 3*.

17. Pew Research Center for the People & the Press June 12, 2014 "Political Polarization in the American Public Section 2: Growing Partisan Antipathy".

Pew Research Center for the People & the Press June 12, 2014 "Political Polarization in the American Public Section 4: Political Compromise and Divisive Policy Debates".

18. Jonathan Weisman and Theodore Schleifer, "Mississippi Race Points to Appeal of Partisanship" *The New York Times* June 23, 2014.

19. Tim Dickinson, "Obama's War on Pot," *Rolling Stone,* Feb. 12, 2012.

20. "Proposition 8: Who gave in the gay marriage battle?" *Los Angeles Times*.

21. National Association of Drug Court Professionals (Dec. 29, 2014) "Types of Drug Courts".

Chapter 2

1. "Kevin Murphy and Dan Studney "Reefer Madness History" (2005).

Julian Grant " Strange! Daring! Shocking! True!: Propagative Strategies For Cult Cinema Engagement" (2015) *academia.ed.*

Chapter 3

1. Louisa Degenhardt, PhD et al. "Outcomes of occasional cannabis use in adolescence: 10-year follow-up study in Victoria, Australia" (Apr. 2010) *British Journal of Psychiatry.*

2. L.M. Squeglia et al. "Initiating Moderate to Heavy Alcohol Use Predicts Changes in Neuropsychological Functioning for Girls and Boys" (Dec. 2009) *Psychology of Addictive Behaviors.*

3. W. Wilson et al. "Brain morphological changes and early marijuana use: a magnetic resonance and positron emission tomography study" (Feb. 2000) *Journal of Addictive Diseases.*

4. Krista Lisdahl Medina et al. "Neuropsychological functioning in adolescent marijuana users: Subtle deficits detectable after a month of abstinence" (Sept. 2007) *Journal of the International Neuropsychological Society.*

5. Staci A. Gruber et al. "Age of Onset of Marijuana Use and Executive Function" (Sept. 2012) *Psychology of Addictive Behaviors.*

6. Madeline H. Meier et al. "Persistent cannabis users show neuropsychological decline from childhood to midlife" (Aug. 27, 2012) *Proceedings of the National Academy of Sciences.*

7. Substance Abuse and Mental Health Services Administration, *Results from the 2011 National Survey on Drug Use and Health: Summary of National Findings*, NSDUH Series H-44, HHS Publication No. (SMA) 12-4713. Rockville, MD: Substance Abuse and Mental Health Services Administration, 2012. (Table 4.2B)

8. Staci A. Gruber et al. "Age of Onset of Marijuana Use Impacts Inhibitory Processing" (Mar. 9, 2012) *Neuroscience Letters*.

9. Mary Bates "Super Powers for the Blind and Deaf" (Sept. 18, 2012) *Scientific American*.

10. Dr. Glen Johnson (2010) *Traumatic Brain Injury Survival Guide.*

   Dr. Glen Johnson (2010) *Denial After Brain Injury: There's Nothing Wrong With Me.*

11. Madeline H. Meier et al. "Persistent cannabis users show neuropsychological decline from childhood to midlife" (July 30, 2012) *Proceedings of the National Academy of Sciences*.

12. Madeline H. Meier et al. "Persistent cannabis users show neuropsychological decline from childhood to midlife" (Aug. 27, 2012) *Proceedings of the National Academy of Sciences*.

13. J.W. Bray et al. "The relationship between marijuana initiation and dropping out of high school" (Jan. 2000) *Health Economics*.

14. Substance Abuse and Mental Health Services Administration, *Results from the 2011 National Survey on Drug Use and Health: Summary of National Findings*, NSDUH Series H-44, HHS Publication No. (SMA) 12-4713. Rockville, MD: Substance Abuse and Mental Health Services Administration, 2012. (Table 4.2B)

15. Center on Young Adult Health and Development (May 2013) "The Academic Opportunity Costs of Substance Use During College".

16. J. Engberg and A.R. Morral "Reducing substance use improves adolescents' school attendance" (Dec. 2006) *Addiction*.

17. D.M. Fergusson and J.M. Boden "Cannabis use and later life outcomes" (June 2008) *Addiction*.

18. Ibid.

19. Ibid.

20. Ibid.

21. Personal communication from Joseph Boden.

Chapter 4

1. Larry Copeland "Survey: Nearly a quarter of teens drive while impaired" (Apr. 25, 2013) *USA Today*.

2. Ibid.

3. Johnny Green (May 22, 2013) "Studies show marijuana consumption not associated with dangerous driving" *The Weed Blog*.

4. Dana Larsen (Jan. 11, 2005) "Stoned drivers are safe drivers" *Cannabis Culture*.

5. NORML Library (Dec. 30, 2014) "Marijuana and Driving: A Review of the Scientific Evidence".

6. Drug Policy Alliance (Jan. 25, 2014) "Ten Facts About Marijuana" (Mar. 31, 2015 "Sources".

7. M. Asbridge et al. "Cannabis and traffic collision risk: findings from a case-crossover study of injured drivers presenting to emergency departments" (Apr. 2014) *International Journal of Public Health*.

8. S. Blows et al. "Marijuana use and car crash injury" (May 2005) *Addiction*.

9. B. Laumon et al. "Cannabis intoxication and fatal road crashes in France: population based case-control study" (Dec. 2005) *British Medical Journal*.

10. M. Asbridge et al. "Cycling-related crash risk and the role of cannabis and alcohol: a case-crossover study" (Sept. 2014) *Preventive Medicine*.

11. Hartford Hospital (June 7, 2010) "Marijuana Smoking Associated With Minimal Changes In Driving Performance, Study Finds" (Press release).

12. Festivus (June 8, 2010) "Study Proves Pot Has Little Effect On Driving" *International Cannagraphic Magazine*.

13. "Hartford hospital studies effects of marijuana use on driving skills" (Dec. 31, 2014) *Hartford Courant*.

14. NORML Library Dec. 30, 2014 "Marijuana and Driving: A Review of the Scientific Evidence".

15. MOOSE (2000) "MOOSE Guidelines for Meta-Analyses and Systematic Reviews of Observational Studies" *editorialmanager.com*.

16. Mark Asbridge, Jill A. Hayden, & Jennifer L. Cartwright. (Feb. 2012). Acute cannabis consumption and motor vehicle collision risk: systematic review of observational studies and meta-analysis. *BMJ, 344*. doi:

17. Rebecca L. Hartman and Marilyn A. Huestis "Cannabis Effects on Driving Skills" (Dec. 7.2012) *Clinical Chemistry*.

Chapter 5

1. Matthijs G. Bossong & Raymond J.M. Niesink. (Nov. 2010). "Adolescent brain maturation, the endogenous cannabinoid system and the neurobiology of cannabis-induced schizophrenia."

2. L. San et al. "Factors associated with relapse in patients with schizophrenia" (Feb. 2013) *International Journal of Psychiatry in Clinical Practice*.

3. R. Miller et al. "A prospective study of cannabis use as a risk factor for non-adherence and treatment dropout in first-episode schizophrenia" (Sept. 2009) *Schizophrenia Research*.

4. Stanley Zammit, Theresa H.M. Moore, Anne Lingford-Hughes, Thomas R.E. Barnes, Peter B. Jones, Margaret Burke, & Glyn Lewis. "Effects of cannabis use on outcomes of psychotic disorders: systematic review."

5. D.H. Linszen et al. "Cannabis use and the course of recent-onset schizophrenic disorders" (Apr. 1994) *Archives of General Psychiatry*.

6. M.J. Martinez-Arevalo et al. "Cannabis consumption as a prognostic factor in schizophrenia" (May 1994) *British Journal of Psychiatry*.

7. Bob Green, MSW et al. "Cannabis use and misuse prevalence among people with psychosis" (Oct. 2005) *British Journal of Psychiatry*.

8. Ibid.

9. E. Manrique-Garcia et al. "Prognosis of schizophrenia in persons with and without a history of cannabis use" (Sept. 2014) *Psychological Medicine*.

10. D. Caspari "Cannabis and schizophrenia: results of a follow-up study" (Feb. 1999) *European Archives of Psychiatry and Clinical Neuroscience*.

11. N.D. Veen et al. "Cannabis use and age at onset of schizophrenia" (Mar. 2004) *American Journal of Psychiatry*.

12. G. Sugranyes et al. "Cannabis use and age of diagnosis of schizophrenia" (June 2009) *European Psychiatry*.

13. M. Large et al. "Cannabis use and earlier onset of psychosis: a systematic meta-analysis" (June 2011) *Archives of General Psychiatry*.

14. Louisa Degenhardt & Wayne Hall. (Aug. 2006). "Is Cannabis Use a Contributory Cause of Psychosis?" *Canadian Journal of Psychiatry, 51*(9): 556.

15. Ibid.

16. Dec 26;2(8574):1483-6. Cannabis and schizophrenia. A longitudinal study of Swedish conscripts.

17. Rajiv Radhakrish et al. "Gone to Pot – A review of the association between cannabis and psychosis" (May 2014) *Frontiers in Psychiatry.*

18. R.A. Power et al. "Genetic predisposition to schizophrenia associated with increased use of cannabis" (Nov. 2014) *Molecular Psychiatry.*

19. A.C. Proal et al. "A controlled family study of cannabis users with and without psychosis" (Jan. 2014) *Schizophrenia Research.*

20. John McGrath, M.D., PhD, FRANZCP et al. "Association between cannabis use and psychosis-related outcomes using sibling pair analysis in a cohort of young adults" (May 2010) *Archives of General Psychiatry.*

21. David Bienenstock "The Clinic: Smoke weed and don't worry about schizophrenia" (Dec. 13, 2013) *High Times.*

22. John M. Grohol "Harvard: Marijuana doesn't cause schizophrenia" (Dec. 10, 2013) *PsychCentral* (By the way, his title is wrong. It was a negative finding.)

23. Daniel van Dijk et al. "Effect of cannabis use on the course of schizophrenia in male patients: a prospective cohort study" (May 2012) Schizophrenia Research.

24. Elizabeth Walsh, MRCPsych et al. "Violence and schizophrenia: Examining the evidence" (June 2002) *British Journal of Psychiatry.*

25. Todd M. Moore and Gregory L. Stuart "A review of the literature on marijuana and interpersonal violence" (Jan.-Feb. 2005) *Aggression and Violent Behavior.*

26. Linda Feldmann "Why Jared Loughner was allowed to buy a gun" (Jan. 10, 2011) *Christian Science Monitor.*

"Loughner's parents and friends watched a change they couldn't control" *Tucson Citizen* (May 6, 2013).

Mark Thompson "How Jared Loughner Changed: The View from His Schools" *Time* (Jan. 11, 2011).

Joshua Norman "Sheriff Releases Loughner's Arrest Records" *CBS* (Jan. 12, 2011).

Drew Griffin et al "Massacre suspect 'mentally disturbed,' former teacher says" *CNN* (Jan 10, 2011).

Dennis Wagner "Tucson shooting records shed light on January 2011 rampage" *Arizona Republic* (Mar 27, 2013).

Raquel Villanueva "Aurora theater shooting trial adjourns for day" 9News (*April 28, 2015).*

Nick Allen "Batman Colorado shooting: James Holmes fixated by altered states of mind" *The Telegraph* (Jul 23, 2012).

Chapter 6

1. Ballotpedia (Dec. 31, 2014) "Text of Proposition 19, "the Regulate, Control and Tax Cannabis Act of 2010" (California).

2. Ken MacQueen "Why it's time to legalize marijuana" (June 10, 2013) *Maclean's.*

3. Garry Trudeau "Doonesbury" (Dec. 29, 2001) *gocomics.com.*

4. Russ Belville "What is marijuana addiction?" (June 6, 2014) *High Times.*

5. Neal Smith "Exploding the myths: Marijuana addiction is a matter of semantics" (Mar. 27, 2011) *Indiana NORML.*

6. Drug Policy Alliance (Jan. 18, 2012) "Marijuana and Health".

7. American Psychiatric Association (Jan. 1, 2015) "DSM-5 Implementation and Support".

8. A.J. Budney et al. "Adults seeking treatment for marijuana dependence: a comparison with cocaine-dependent treatment seekers" (Nov. 1998) *Experimental and Clinical Psychopharmacology.*

9. A.J. Budney et al. "Review of the validity and significance of cannabis withdrawal syndrome" (Nov. 2004) *American Journal of Psychiatry.*

10. Drug Policy Alliance (Jan. 18, 2012) "Marijuana and Health".

    StoptheDrugWar.org (March 27, 2009) "Feature: More Than A Quarter Million Marijuana Smokers in Drug Treatment Each Year—Are We Wasting Valuable Treatment Resources?".

11. DrugWarRant.org (March 31, 2015) "Treatment Statistics...or, one more way they lie"

12. Ibid.

13. Substance Abuse and Mental Health Services Administration, *Results from the 2011 National Survey on Drug Use and Health: Summary of*

National Findings, NSDUH Series H-44, HHS Publication No. (SMA) 12-4713. Rockville, MD: Substance Abuse and Mental Health Services Administration, 2012.

14. Op. cit. Tables 5.53B & 5.56B

15. Op. cit. Figure 7-10

17. Ibid.

18. K. Chen et al. "Relationships between frequency and quantity of marijuana use and last year proxy dependence among adolescents and adults in the United States" (June 1997) *Drug and Alcohol Dependence.*

Wayne Hall and Rosalie Liccardo Pacula (2003) *Cannabis Use and Dependence: Public Health and Public Policy* Cambridge University Press.

19. Partnership for Drug-Free Kids (May 2, 2012) "Survey finds marijuana use on the rise among teens"

20. K. Chen et al. "Relationships between frequency and quantity of marijuana use and last year proxy dependence among adolescents and adults in the United States" (June 1997) *Drug and Alcohol Dependence*

21. Jan Copeland & Wendy Swift "Cannabis use disorder: epidemiology and management." (April 2009) *International Review of Psychiatry.*

22. Substance Abuse and Mental Health Services Administration, *Results from the 2011 National Survey on Drug Use and Health: Summary of National Findings*, NSDUH Series H-44, HHS Publication No. (SMA) 12-4713. Rockville, MD: Substance Abuse and Mental Health Services Administration, 2012.

23. Ibid.

24. Ibid.

25. Ibid.

26. Ibid.

27. Ibid.

28. A.J. Budney et al. "Adults seeking treatment for marijuana dependence: a comparison with cocaine-dependent treatment seekers" (Nov. 1998) *Experimental and Clinical Psychopharmacology.*

29. J. Copeland et al. "Clinical profile of participants in a brief intervention program for cannabis use disorder" (Jan. 2001) *Journal of Substance Abuse Treatment.*

30. Alan J. Budney, PhD et al. "Marijuana dependence and its treatment" (Dec. 2007) *Addiction Science and Clinical Practice.*

31. Jenny Brundin "Addicted teen struggles to break marijuana habit" (Mar. 20, 2014) *Colorado Public Radio.*

32. Personal communication.

33. Substance Abuse and Mental Health Services Administration, *Results from the 2013 National Survey on Drug Use and Health: Summary of National Findings*, NSDUH Series H-48, HHS Publication No. (SMA) 14-4863. Rockville, MD: Substance Abuse and Mental Health Services Administration, 2014. page 83.

Chapter 7

1. Patrick Anderson (Jan. 21, 2010) "High in America: The true story behind NORML and the politics of marijuana (Chapter 6)" *Schaffer Library of Drug Policy.*

2. United Press International. (Jan. 20, 1972). "U.S. survey reports 24 million have tried smoking marijuana."

3. Harold M. Schmeck. (Oct. 09, 1979). "Research on marijuana finds many risks, some benefits; Marijuana: Many risks, some benefits effects on immune system."

4. *New York Times* – Opinion. (June 18, 1982). "The spread of drugs, and indifference."

5. Randy Billings and Dennis Hoey "Portland buses to carry advertisements that back legalizing marijuana" (Oct. 1, 2013) *Portland Press Herald.*

6. Australian Transport Safety Bureau (Mar. 2004) "Cannabis and its Effects on Pilot Performance and Flight Safety: A Review" ISBN1 877071 57 9.

7. High Times (Dec. 11, 2013) "Remains of the jay: How long does pot stay in your system?" *hightimes.com.*

   Radley Balko "Since marijuana legalization, highway fatalities in Colorado are at near-historic lows" (Aug. 5, 2014) *The Washington Post.*

8. J. Engberg and A.R. Morral "Reducing substance use improves adolescents' school attendance" (Dec. 2006) *Addiction.*

9. David Schick "Study: Marijuana use increases risk of academic problems" (June 7, 2013) *USA Today.*

Chapter 8

1. Erin Burnett "Obama, Perry backpedal on marijuana" (Jan. 24, 2014) *cnn.com*.

2. Johnston, L. D., O'Malley, P. M., Bachman, J. G., Schulenberg, J. E. & Miech, R. A. (2014). *Monitoring the Future national survey results on drug use, 1975–2013: Volume I, Secondary school students*. Ann Arbor: Institute for Social Research, The University of Michigan.

3. Ibid.

4. Bob Woodward "Wired: The Short Life and Fast Times of John Belushi" (Nov. 1985) Simon & Schuster.

5. Michael Weinreb "the day innocence died" *ESPN* (June 19, 2008).

6. Johnston, L. D., O'Malley, P. M., Bachman, J. G., Schulenberg, J. E. & Miech, R. A. (2014). *Monitoring the Future national survey results on drug use, 1975–2013: Volume I, Secondary school students*. Ann Arbor: Institute for Social Research, The University of Michigan.

7. Op. cit. Figure 8-5.

8. Prof. David J. Hanson, Ph.D. (Nov. 4, 2014) "Alternatives to the failed DARE (Drug Abuse Resistance Education) program" *Potsdam.edu*.

9. Johnston, L. D., O'Malley, P. M., Bachman, J. G., Schulenberg, J. E. & Miech, R. A. (2013). *Monitoring the Future national survey results on drug use, 1975–2013: Volume I, Secondary school students*. Ann Arbor: Institute for Social Research, The University of Michigan. Figure 8.4.

10. Emily Dufton "Parents, Peers and Pot: The Rise of the Drug Culture and the Birth of the Parent Movement, 1976-1980" (Mar. 15, 2013) *Trans-Scripts 3 (2013)* Document19.

11. Johnston, L. D., O'Malley, P. M., Bachman, J. G., Schulenberg, J. E. & Miech, R. A. (2013). *Monitoring the Future national survey results on drug use, 1975–2013: Volume I, Secondary school students*. Ann Arbor: Institute for Social Research, The University of Michigan.

12. Ibid.

13. "Nation's Leading Drug Policy Reform Organization Now Called Drug Policy Alliance" drugpolicy.org (Jan. 28, 2002).

"Our history" Marijuana Policy Project mpp.org (Jan 1, 2015).

14. Johnston, L. D., O'Malley, P. M., Bachman, J. G., Schulenberg, J. E. & Miech, R. A. (2013). *Monitoring the Future national survey results on drug use, 1975–2013: Volume I, Secondary school students.* Ann Arbor: Institute for Social Research, The University of Michigan.

15. Op. cit. Table 5-2, 8-3

16. Michelle Castillo "Will legalization lead to more teens smoking pot?" (Feb. 26, 2014) *CBS News.*

Chapter 9

1. Casey Michel "The secret ingredients for marijuana legalization: Moms and Hispanics" (Nov. 19, 2012) *The Atlantic.*

2. Beau Kilmer "Insights on the Effects of Marijuana Legalization on Prices and Consumption" (Sept. 2010) *Rand.org.*

3. Campaign to Regulate Marijuana Like Alcohol (2012) 'Regulating Marijuana Works!" *regulatemarijuana.org.*

4. T. Huckle, J. Huakau, P. Sweetsur, et al. (2008). Density of alcohol outlets and teenage drinking: Living in an alcogenic environment is associated with higher consumption in a metropolitan setting. *Addiction, 103*:1614–1621. PMID: 18821871. T. Huckle, R.Q. You, & S. Casswell. (2010). Increases in quantities consumed in drinking occasions in New Zealand 1995–2004. *Drug and Alcohol Review, 30*:366–371. PMID: 21355906

5. Johnston, L. D., O'Malley, P. M., Bachman, J. G., Schulenberg, J. E. & Miech, R. A. (2014). *Monitoring the Future national survey results on drug use, 1975–2013: Volume I, Secondary school students.* Ann Arbor: Institute for Social Research, The University of Michigan.

6. Ibid.

7. Ibid.

8. Ibid.

9. Ibid.

10. Partnership for Drug-Free Kids (Aug. 7, 2013) "Experts say bans on synthetic drugs in Florida have reduced sales".

11. Daniel Okrent (Jan. 1, 2015) Last Call Quotes: *Last Call: The Rise and Fall of Prohibition.*

Mark H. Moore "Actually, Prohibition was a success" (Oct. 16, 1989) *The*

New York Times.

12. Penn State University Archives "Legalization of Hard Drugs Won't Work Says Professor of History at Penn State Allentown" (July 22, 1996) *psu.edu.*

   Carl E. Taylor "Crusaders Against Opium: Protestant Missionaires in China 1874-1917 (Review)" (Winter 1997) *Bulletin of the History of Medicine.*

13. Melanie M. Wall, PhD et al. "Adolescent marijuana use from 2002 to 2008: higher in states with medical marijuana laws, cause still unclear" (Sept. 2011) *Annals of Epidemiology.*

14. Ed Gogek, Marijuana Debunked, Chiron Publications, Asheville, (2015), Fig 11-2, pg 118.

Chapter 10

1. The PIPA/Knowledge Networks Poll (Oct. 2, 2003) "Misperceptions, The Media And The Iraq War" Principal Investigator Steven Krull.

   Gallup (2014) "Foreign Affairs: Iraq".

2. Tilem & Associates "The Richard Nixon Era – The Comprehensive Drug Abuse Prevention and Control Act of 1970 Eliminates Mandatory Minimums" (Jan. 19, 2009) *New York Criminal Attorney Blog.*

   Keith Humphreys "Who started the war on drugs?" (June 1, 2011) *The Reality-Based Community.*

3. Richard Nixon "Special message to Congress on drug abuse prevention and control" (June 17, 1971) *The American Presidency Project.*

4. Michael Massing "The Fix" University of California Press 2000.

5. Ibid.

6. The Pew Center on the States (June 2012) "Time Served: The High Cost, Low Returns of Longer Prison Terms".

   "Timeline: The Evolution Of California's Three Strikes Law" NPR (Oct 28, 2009) npr.org.

7. National Center for Policy Analysis (Jan. 13, 1999) "States Are Abolishing Parole".

   Families Against Mandatory Minimums (Sept. 21, 2013) "Frequently asked questions about the lack of parole for federal prisoners".

Families Against Mandatory Minimums (Feb. 25, 2013) "Federal Mandatory Minimums".

Families Against Mandatory Minimums (June 30, 2013) "Recent State-Level Reforms To Mandatory Minimum Laws".

"Excerpt from Introduction to Federal Sentencing Guidelines".

8. Michael Massing "The Fix" University of California Press 2000.

9. From "US Incarceration Timeline" Wikipedia: The Free Encyclopedia. Wikimedia Foundation, Inc. Jan. 24, 2012. Original by the November Coalition. Modified by Sarefo July 28, 2009. Sources: Justice Policy Institute Report: The Punishing Decade & U.S. Bureau of Justice Statistics Bulletin NCJ 219416 – Prisoners in 2006. Modified by changing from color to black & white. Original and modifications licensed under the Creative Commons Attribution-Share Alike 3.0 Unported license. The edited version here is available for use and licensed under the same Creative Commons Attribution-Share Alike 3.0 Unported license, available available through Creative Commons.

10. Ibid.

11. The Pew Center on the States (June 2012) "Time Served: The High Cost, Low Returns of Longer Prison Terms".

12. Michael Massing "The Fix" University of California Press 2000.

13. Keith Humphreys "Who started the war on drugs?" (June 1, 2011) *The Reality-Based Community.*

14. Drug Policy Alliance (July 21, 2014) "The Drug War, Mass Incarceration and Race".

15. American Civil Liberties Union (Jan. 1, 2015) "Smart Justice, Fair Justice".

16. Marijuana Policy Project (Jan. 1, 2015) "Like it or not, we can't afford marijuana prohibition".

17. Howard N. Snyder, PhD (Sept. 2011) "Arrest in the United States 1980-2009" *U.S. Department of Justice.*

18. Rick Perlstein *Nixonland: The Rise of a President and the Fracturing of America* (May 2008) Scribner.

19. NORML (Nov. 21, 2007) "Decriminalizing pot will reduce prison population, have no adverse impact on public safety, study says" (Press release).

20. Katrina vanden Heuvel "Time to end the war on drugs" (Nov. 20, 2012) *The Washington Post.*

21. Institute for Behavior and Health (July 31, 2009) "How Many People Does The U.S. Imprison For Drug Use And Who Are They?" Jonathan P. Caulkins and Eric L. Sevigny.

22. Ibid.

23. Ibid.

24. Substance Abuse and Mental Health Services Administration, *Results from the 2011 National Survey on Drug Use and Health: Summary of National Findings*, NSDUH Series H-44, HHS Publication No. (SMA) 12-4713. Rockville, MD: Substance Abuse and Mental Health Services Administration, 2012.

25. Juliana Keeping "Oklahoma's harsh marijuana possession law has its critics" (Feb. 2, 2014) *The Oklahoman*.

26. "Senate's old guard just says 'no' to pot overhaul" (March 24, 2015) *Politico*.

27. "Richard Branson: 'The Virgin Way'" (Sept. 23, 2014) *The Diane Rehm Show* WAMU.

28. Drug Policy Alliance (Dec. 30, 2014) "Reducing the Harms of Marijuana Prohibition".

29. Bureau of Justice Statistics (Sept. 2011) "Arrest in the United States, 1980-2009" Howard N. Snyder, PhD.

30. Bureau of Justice Statistics (Jan. 1, 2015) "Drug and Crime Facts".

31. Bureau of Justice Statistics (Sept. 2011) "Arrest in the United States, 1980-2009" Howard N. Snyder, PhD.

32. The National Center on Addiction and Substance Abuse at Columbia University (Feb. 2010) "Behind Bars II: Substance Abuse and America's Prison Population".

    Substance Abuse and Mental Health Services Administration, *Results from the 2011 National Survey on Drug Use and Health: Summary of National Findings*, NSDUH Series H-44, HHS Publication No. (SMA) 12-4713. Rockville, MD: Substance Abuse and Mental Health Services Administration, 2012.

33. Office of National Drug Control Policy Executive Office of the President (May 2013) "Arrestee Drug Abuse Monitoring II 2012 Annual Report".

34. Zoe McKnight "Pot possession charges in B.C. up 88 percent over last decade: Poll suggests three-quarters of population would rather tax and regulate marijuana" (Nov. 4, 2012) *The Vancouver Sun*.

35. Ibid.

36. Ibid.

37. Ibid.

38. Kale Pauls. "The nature and extent of marihuana possession in British Columbia; A report submitted in partial fulfillment of the requirements for the degree of master of arts in criminal justice in the school of criminology and criminal justice" (Spring 2013) University of the Fraser Valley.

Kale Pauls, Darryl Plecas, Irwin M. Cohen & Tara Haarhoff. "The nature and extent of marihuana possession in British Columbia" (Nov. 24, 2013) Centre for Public Safety and Criminal Justice Research.

39. Ibid.

40. Ibid.

41. Ibid.

42. NORML (Jan. 1, 2015) "War Against Marijuana Consumers" http://norml.org/legal/item/war-against-marijuana-consumers

43. American Civil Liberties Union (Jan. 1, 2015) "The War On Marijuana In Black And White: Billions of dollars wasted on racially biased arrests".

44. *Vancouver Sun* – Editorial. (Sept. 12, 2013).

45. American Civil Liberties Union (Jan. 1, 2015) "The War On Marijuana In Black And White: Billions of dollars wasted on racially biased arrests".

46. American Civil Liberties Union (Jan. 1, 2015) "The War On Marijuana In Black And White: Billions of dollars wasted on racially biased arrests".

47. Bureau of Justice Statistics (Sept. 2011) "Arrest in the United States, 1980-2009" Howard N. Snyder, PhD.

48. Ibid.

49. Ibid.

BlackDemographics.com (2012) "African Americans & Crime"

50. Alan R. Templeton (Sept. 1998) "Human Races: A Genetic and Evolutionary Perspective" *American Anthropologist.*

"Interview with Richard Lewontin" (2003) *PBS.*

Tony Fitzpatrick (Feb. 9, 2010) "Biological differences among races do not exist, WU research finds" Washington University in St. Louis.

51. Helen Taylor Greene & Shaun L. Gabbidon *Race and Crime* (2012) SAGE Publications.

52. Ian Urbina "Blacks are singled out for marijuana arrests, federal data suggests" (June 3, 2013) *The New York Times.*

53. E.J. Dionne, Jr. "Opinion: Marijuana Injustices" (Jan. 8, 2014) *The Washington Post.*

54. Annys Shin "D.C. Marijuana Study: Blacks far more likely to be arrested than whites, ACLU says" (June 4, 2013) *The Washington Post.*

55. "Cops see it differently, Part Two" (Feb 13, 2015) *This American Life,* WBEZ.

56. American Civil Liberties Union (July 18, 2001) "Individual donor sets record with $7 million donation, largest-ever endowment gift to ACLU" (New release).

57. Amelia Arria, PhD et al. "The Academic Opportunity Costs of Substance Abuse During College" (May 2013) Center on Young Adult Health and Development.

David Schick "Study: Marijuana use increases risk of academic problems" (June 7, 2013) *USA Today.*

58. June 2013 Google news search

Chapter 11

1. Edward Gogek, M.D. (Letter to the Editor) "Dangers of Marijuana" (Dec. 5, 2002) *The New York Times.*

2. Thomas J. O'Connell and Ché B Bou-Matar (Nov. 3, 2007) "Long term marijuana users seeking medical cannabis in California (2001-2007): demographics, social characteristics, patterns of cannabis and other drug use of 4117 applicants" *Harm Reduction Journal.*

3. Arizona Department of Health Services (Apr. 14, 2011-Nov. 7, 2012) *Arizona Medical Marijuana Act Monthly Report.*

Colorado Department of Public Health and Environment (Dec. 31, 2012) "Medical Marijuana Registry Program Update".

Oregon Health Authority (Oct. 1, 2014) "Oregon Medical Marijuana Program Statistics".

Kevin Sabet et al. "Why do people use medical marijuana? The medical conditions of users in seven U.S. states" *The Journal of Global Drug Policy and Practice* (Volume 8, Issue 2 Summer 2014).

4. Blyth et al. "Chronic Pain in Australia: A prevalence study" (Jan. 2001) *Pain.*

5. N. Cornally and G. McCarthy "Help-seeking behavior for the treatment of chronic pain" (Feb. 2011) *British Journal of Community Nursing.*

6. Dawn A Marcus, M.D. (2008) *Chronic Pain: A Primary Care Guide to Practical Management* Humana Press.

7. Centers for Disease Control and Prevention (July 2, 2013) "Deaths from prescription painkiller overdoses rise sharply among women" (Press release).

8. Morgan Loew "Medical marijuana going to young, healthy" (May 15, 2013 Updated May 14, 2014) CBS5 Phoenix.

   David Segal "When Capitalism Meets Cannabis" (June 26, 2010) *The New York Times*.

   Carey Goldberg "No 'Pot Doctors,' Neon, Candy: Mass. Medical Pot Rules Take Shape" (June 18, 2013) *WBUR*.

   Shelby Thom "BC College of Physicians looking to weed out 'pot doctors'" (May 6, 2015) *CKNW*.

   Helen Nunberg, M.D. et al. "An Analysis of Applicants Presenting to a Medical Marijuana Specialty Practice in California" (Feb. 2011) *Journal of Drug Policy Analysis*.

9. Ibid.

10. Montana Department of Public Health and Human Services (Oct. 1, 2014) "Montana Marijuana Program October 2014 Registry Information".

11. Sue O'Connell (for the Children, Families, Health and Human Services Interim Committee (Apr. 15, 2010) "Montana's Medical Marijuana Act: Emerging Issues".

    Montana Department of Public Health and Human Services (June 7, 2013) "SB 423: Montana Marijuana Act Registry Statistics".

    Sue O'Connell (June 12, 2013) "SB423 Monitoring: Montana's Medical Marijuana Act, Developments Through June 2013".

    Frequently Asked Questions: Medical Cannabis Provider and Practitioner Q and A New Mexico Department of Health Publications.

12. Matt Volz (Associated Press) "Cannabis caravans fuel medical pot boom" (June 3, 2010) *nbcnews.com*.

    Montana Department of Public Health and Human Services (Oct. 10, 2014) "History of Qualifying Patients, Providers and Doctors (Jan. 2005-June 2012)".

13. Jerry Wade "A Comparison of Medical Marijuana Programs in California and Oregon" (Fall '06 Issue 39) *Alternatives: Resources for Cultural Creativity*.

14. Mike Hughes "Weekday Warriors" (May 22, 2012) *High Times*.

15. American Association for the Advancement of Science (May 15, 2014) "Marijuana use involved in more fatal accidents in Colorado" (Press release) Eurekalert.org.

16. Colorado Department of Public Health and Environment (Jan. 13, 2015) "Medical marijuana statistics" Document19.

17. Salomonsen-Sautel et al. "Trends in fatal motor vehicle crashes before and after marijuana commercialization in Colorado" (July 2014) *Drug and Alcohol Dependence*.

18. UNICEF Innocenti Research Centre (2007) "Child Poverty in Perspective: An overview of child well-being in rich countries" (Figures 5.2c, p.30) *The United Nations Children's Fund* Peter Adamson (Figure 5.2c, p. 30).

 The Marijuana Policy Initiative (May 10, 2014) "Teen marijuana use highest in 'medical' marijuana states".

19. Substance Abuse and Mental Health Services Administration (2012) "National Survey on Drug Use and Health: State Estimates of Substance Use".

20. Ibid.

21. Michigan News (Dec. 18, 2013) "American teens more cautious about using synthetic drugs" (Press release Contacts: Jared Wadley and Susan Barnes).

22. Substance Abuse and Mental Health Services Administration, *Results from the 2011 National Survey on Drug Use and Health: Summary of National Findings*, NSDUH Series H-44, HHS Publication No. (SMA) 12-4713. Rockville, MD: Substance Abuse and Mental Health Services Administration, 2012.

23. S.V. Dáte (May 30, 2014) "GOP House votes to leave states alone on medical marijuana" *NPR.org*.

24. Ryan Grim (Mar. 29, 2009) "Holder vows to end raids on medical marijuana clubs" *Huff Post Politics*.

25. Richard K. Barry " This day in history - June 8, 1949: George Orwell's Nineteen Eighty-Four is published" (June 08, 2011).

26. "doublespeak" *Merriam-Webster* (2014).

27. National Families in Action (May 28, 2001) "2001: NORML Director Keith Stroup Denies 'Red Herring' Quote".

 Peter Hitchens (July 13, 2011) "Denying Reality. The Red Herring of 'Medical Cannabis' and the Long Goodbye of Mr. 'F'".

28. Janet E. Joy et al. "Marijuana and Medicine: Assessing the Science Base" (Apr. 7, 2003) *Institute of Medicine of the National Academies.*

29. Margaret Haney, PhD et al. "Dronabinol and Marijuana in HIV-Positive Marijuana Smokers: Caloric Intake, Mood and Sleep" (Aug. 15, 2007) *JAIDS: Journal of Acquired Immune Deficiency Syndromes.*

   M.R. Woodward et al. "Dronabinol for the treatment of agitation and aggressive behavior in acutely hospitalized severely demented patients with non-cognitive behavioral symptoms" (Apr. 2014) *American Journal of Geriatric Psychiatry.*

   Z.D. Cooper et al. "Comparison of the analgesic effects of dronabinol and smoked marijuana in daily marijuana smokers" (Sept. 2013) *Neuropyschopharmacology.*

30. National Center for Biotechnology Information "Compound Summary for CID 5284592: Nabilone" *PubChem: Open Chemistry Database.*

   T.D. Reynolds and H.L. Osborn "The use of cannabinoids in chronic pain (July 2013) *BJM Casereports.*

   J. Wissel, T. Haydn, J. Müller, C. Brenneis, T. Berger, W. Poewe, & L.D. Schelosky. (Oct. 2006). Low dose treatment with the synthetic cannabinoid Nabilone significantly reduces spasticity-related pain : a double-blind placebo-controlled cross-over trial. *J Neurol, 253*(10): 1337-41.

31. Shaheen E. Lakhan and Marie Rowland "Whole cannabis extracts in the treatment of spasticity in multiple sclerosis: a systematic review" (Dec. 4, 2009) *BioMedCentral Neurology.*

32. City of Columbia Department of Public Health and Human Services 'Two Options Regarding Epidiolex (CBD)' (Apr. 21, 2014).

33. Johnston, L. D., O'Malley, P. M., Bachman, J. G., Schulenberg, J. E. & Miech, R. A. (2014). *Monitoring the Future national survey results on drug use, 1975–2013: Volume I, Secondary school students.* Ann Arbor: Institute for Social Research, The University of Michigan.

34. NORML Home (Jan. 3, 2014) "Marinol Vs. Natural Plant".

35. Z.D. Cooper et al. "Comparison of the analgesic effects of dronabinol and smoked marijuana in daily marijuana smokers" (Sept. 2013) *Neuropsychopharmacology.*

36. National Center for Biotechnology Information "Compound Summary for CID 5284592: Nabilone" *PubChem: Open Chemistry Database.*

37. M.A. Issa et al. "The subjective psychoactive effects of oral dronabinol studied in a randomized, controlled crossover clinical trial for pain" (June 2014) *The Clinical Journal of Pain.*

38. Mark A. Ware and Emmanuelle St. Arnaud-Trempe "The potential abuse of the synthetic cannabinoid nabilone" (Aug. 11, 2009) *Addiction.*

39. "Dr. Sanjay Gupta's CNN Special 'WEED'" The Putipato Aug. 11, 2013 *youtube.com*

"WEED 2 – Cannabis Madness – Dr. Sanjay Gupta Reports" HDCOLORS Mar. 14, 2014 *youtube.com*

40. GW Pharmaceuticals "Epidiolex" gwpharm.com

41. Dr. Sanjay Gupta "Why I changed my mind on weed" (Aug. 8, 2013) *CNN.com*

42. Dr. Sanjay Gupta "Health : Why I Would Vote No On Pot" (Jan. 8, 2009) *TIME.com*

43. Ibid.

Chapter 12

1. Campaign to Regulate Marijuana Like Alcohol in Alaska "Alaska has ended marijuana prohibition" (Nov. 4, 2014) *regulatemarijuanainalaska.org*

Yes On 91 "Treating Marijuana Use As A Crime Has Failed" (Jan. 15, 2013) *voteyeson91.com*

Casey Michel. (Nov. 19, 2012). The secret ingredients for marijuana legalization: moms and Hispanics. *The Atlantic.*

2. Jeffrey Miron and Katherine Waldock "The Budgetary Impact of Ending Drug Prohibition" (Sept. 27, 2010) *Cato Institute White Paper.*

3. Dale Gieringer, Ph.D, "Revenues From Legalization: Economics of Cannabis Legalization (1994) Detailed Analysis of the Benefits of Ending Cannabis Prohibition" (Apr. 1994) *NORML.org*

4. Beau Kilmer et al. "Altered State? Assessing How Marijuana Legalization In California Could Influence Marijuana Consumption And Public Budgets" (2010) *Rand Drug Policy Research Center.*

5. John Ingold. (Mar. 18, 2014). "Colorado legislature's economists predict smaller marijuana tax haul." *Denver Post.*

6. Katie Lobosco "Colorado's missing marijuana taxes" (Sept. 2, 2014) *money.cnn.com.*

7. Christopher Cadelago "San Diego approves sweeping medical pot limits" (Mar. 28, 2011) *San Diego Union-Tribune.*

8. Craig Gustafson "Momentum builds for new pot shop rules" (Feb. 24, 2014) *San Diego Union-Tribune.*

Esther Rubio-Sheffrey "Medicinal marijuana patients and workers fight back against city's proposed ban" (July 19,2011) San Diego Gay and Lesbian News.

"Southern California—This Just In" (July 25, 2011) *Los Angeles Times.*

Shauntel Lowe "San Diego City Council Repeals Medical Marijuana Restrictions" (July 28, 2011) *Mount Helix Patch, Cannabis Culture Marijuana Magazine.*

9. Center for Science in the Public Interest "The case for alcohol excise tax increases" (Apr. 2007) *cspinet.org*

Chuck Marr and Gillian Brunet "Reversing the erosion in alcohol taxes could help pay for health care reform" (Mar. 27, 2009) *Center on Budget and Policy Priorities.*

10. Bay-Staters Fighting for Alcohol Industry Responsibility "Alcohol Taxes Compared To Inflation 1933-2011" *bfair-mass.org*

11. Bay-Staters Fighting for Alcohol Industry Responsibility "Alcohol Taxes Compared To Inflation 1933-2011" *bfair-mass.org*

12. Joseph Henchman and Scott Drenkard "Cigarette Taxes and Cigarette Smuggling by State" (Jan. 10, 2013) *Tax Foundation.*

David B. Caruso "Higher Cigarette Taxes Lure Buyers To Black Market" (Apr. 18, 2008) *Huff Post Business.*

Carrie Johnson "Trade In Black-Market Cigarettes: Hot, Dangerous" (Sept. 19, 2010) *npr.org*

13. Gabe Silverman "A day in the Colorado marijuana black market" (July 30, 2014) *washingtonpost.com*

Katie Lobosco "Colorado's missing marijuana taxes" (Sept. 2, 2014) *money.cnn.com*

14. Ellen E. Bouchery, Henrick J. Harwood, Jeffrey J. Sacks, Carol J. Simon, & Robert D. Brewer. (Nov. 2011). *Economic costs of excessive alcohol consumption in the U.S., 2006.*

15. See www.ajpmonline.org/article/S0749-3797(11)00538-1/fulltext

16. H. Harwood, D. Fountain, & G. Livermore. (1998). *Economic costs of alcohol and drug abuse in the United States, 1992.* University of Michigan Library

17. H. Harwood, D. Fountain, & G. Livermore. (1998). *Economic costs of alcohol and drug abuse in the United States, 1992.* University of Michigan Library

18. David M. Fergusson & Joseph M. Boden. Cannabis use and later life outcomes. *Addiction, 103*, 969–976

Johnston, L. D., O'Malley, P. M., Bachman, J. G., Schulenberg, J. E. & Miech, R. A. (2014). *Monitoring the Future national survey results on drug use, 1975–2013: Volume I, Secondary school students.* Ann Arbor: Institute for Social Research, The University of Michigan.

Amanda Noss "Household Income 2012: American Community Survey Briefs" (Sept. 2013) *United States Census Bureau.*

U.S. Census Bureau "State & County QuickFacts" (July 8, 2014) *United States Census Bureau.*

19. C. Zwerling et al. "The efficacy of preemployment drug screening for marijuana and cocaine in predicting employment outcome" (Nov. 1990) *Journal of the American Medical Association.*

20. C. Hyggen "Does smoking cannabis affect work commitment?" (July 2012) *Addiction.*

21. E.Q. Wu, H.G. Birnbaum, L. Shi, D.E. Ball, R.C. Kessler, M. Moulis, & J. Aggarwal. (Sept. 2005).

The economic burden of schizophrenia in the United States in 2002. *J Clin Psychiatry, 66*(9):1122-9.

22. Rosalie Liccardo Pacula "Examining the Impact of Marijuana Legalization on Harms Associated with Marijuana Use" (July 2010) *Rand Drug Policy Research Center.*

23. National Center on Addiction and Substance Abuse at Columbia University. (May 2009). Shoveling up II: The impact of substance abuse on federal, state and local budgets. Pages 2 & 4.

24. Casey Michel "The Secret Ingredients for Marijuana Legalization" (Nov. 19, 2012) *The Atlantic.*

25. Beau Kilmer et al. "Altered State? Assessing How Marijuana Legalization In California Could Influence Marijuana Consumption And Public Budgets" (2010) *Rand Drug Policy Research Center.*

26. Ellen E. Bouchery, MS et al. "Economic Costs of Excessive Alcohol Consumption in the U.S., 2006" (Nov. 2011) *American Journal of Preventive Medicine.*

27. Rebecca Joyce Frey (2007) *Fundamentalism: Global Issues* Facts on File.

Chapter 13

1. Christopher Wanjek "Study Suggests Alcohol Ads Target Teens" (August 25, 2009) *livescience.*

   Melissa Davey "Australian and UK alcohol industry lobbyists are hijacking policy – study" *The Guardian* (Dec 10, 2014).

   "Lobbying / Industry: Beer, Wine & Liquor" *Center for Responsive Politics* (2015).

   Anna Quindlen "Alcohol—Mind-altering drug that pretends to be harmless" (Apr 23, 2014) *QCOnlinecom.*

   "The Alcohol Industry Needs Alcoholism to Thrive" The American Interest (Oct 5, 2014).

   Jim & Ed Gogek "The Alcohol and Tobacco Industries Should Have Same Standard" (Aug. 5, 1997) *Lifering* from *1996 New York Times Features Syndicate.*

   Elizabeth Drew "The Quiet Victory of the Cigarette Lobby: How It Found the Best Filter Yet—Congress" *Atlantic* (Sept 1965).

   Michael S Givel, Stanton A Glantz "Tobacco lobby political influence on US state legislatures in the 1990s" *Tobacco Control* (2001).

   Clive Bates & Andy Rowell *Tobacco Explained: The truth about the tobacco industry …in its own words* Action Smoking and Health London (June 25, 1998).

2. Mitch Earleywine "Study Shows Marijuana Often Substituted for Alcohol and Other Drugs" (Dec. 14, 2012) *Marijuana Policy Project's Blog.*

   Steve Elliott "Study: Marijuana Can Help Fight Alcohol and Prescription Drug Abuse" Apr. 15, 2013 *tokesignals.com.*

3. Louisa Degenhardt, PhD et al. "Outcomes of occasional cannabis use in adolescence: 10-year follow-up study in Victoria, Australia" (Apr. 2010) *British Journal of Psychiatry.*

4. Ibid.

5. Louisa Degenhardt , Wayne Hall, &Michael Lynskey. (2001). The relationship between cannabis use and other substance use in the general population. *Drug and Alcohol Dependence, 64*: 319–327.

   L. Degenhardt, PhD et al. Alcohol, tobacco and cannabis use among Australians a comparison of their associations with other drug use and use disorders, affective and anxiety disorders and pyschosis" (Nov. 2001) *Addiction.*

6. Ibid.

7. Ibid.

8. Ibid.

9. Ibid.

10. Ray Stern "Marijuana By Itself Not A Significant Factor In Fatal and Injury Crashes in 2012, DPS Data Shows" (May 17, 2013) *phoenixnewtimes.com*

11. Montana Department of Public Health and Human Services "History of Qualifying Patients, Providers and Doctors" (Jan. 2005-June 2012) *dphhs. mt.gov/*

   Montana Department of Transportation "Overview of Montana's Impaired Driving Problem" (Aug. 2011) *mdt.mt.gov*

12. Ibid.

Chapter 14

1. National Drug Court Resource Center (2012) "How Many Drug Courts Are There?" *ndcrc.org*

   West Huddleston and Douglas B. Marlowe "Painting The Current Picture: A National Report On Drug Courts And Other Problem-Solving Court Programs In The United States" (July 2011) *National Drug Court Institute.*

   Steven Belenko, PhD "Research On Drug Courts: A Critical Review 2001 Update" (June 2001) *The National Center on Addiction and Substance Abuse at Columbia University.*

2. National Association of Drug Court Professionals "How Drug Courts Work" (Jan. 13, 2015) *nadcp.org*

3. Rob Hotakainen "Marijuana is drug most often linked to crime, study finds" (May 23, 2013) *McClatchy Washington Bureau.*

   Office of National Drug Control Policy Executive Office of the President "Arrestee Drug Abuse Monitoring II 2012 Annual Report" (May 2013).

4. Substance Abuse and Mental Health Services Administration, *Results from the 2011 National Survey on Drug Use and Health: Summary of National Findings*, NSDUH Series H-44, HHS Publication No. (SMA) 12-4713. Rockville, MD: Substance Abuse and Mental Health Services Administration, 2012.

5. Stuart Gitlow "How to Achieve an 80 Percent Recovery Rate" (Oct. 16, 2012) *American Society of Addiction Medicine.*

Esperison Martinez "HIMS: Addressing Alcohol Abuse" (Apr. 2004) *Airline Pilots Association.*

Marvin D. Seppala, M.D. and Keith H. Berge, M.D. "Addicated Physician: A Rational Response to an Irrational Disease" *Minnesota Medicine.*

6. UNICEF Office of Research (2013) "Child well-being in rich countries: A comparative overview" *The United Nations Children's Fund* Peter Adamson.

7. The Economist Explains "Why Sweden Has So Few Road Deaths" (Feb. 26, 2014) *The Economist.*

8. Palash Ghosh "Sweden's Happy and Perplexing 'Problem:' Four Prisons Closed Due to Falling Inmate Population" (Nov. 12, 2013) *International Business Times.*

9. R.L. Dupont, B.K. Madras, & P. Johnson. (2011). Chapter 77: Drug policy: A biological science perspective. In Pedro Ruiz & Eric Strain (Eds.), *Substance abuse: A comprehensive textbook.* Philadelphia: Lippincott Williams & Wilkins, pp. 1002–1006

10. *Sweden's Successful Drug Policy: A review of the evidence* United Nations Office on Drugs and Crime (Feb 2007).

11. "What Is SBIRT And Why Use It?" (PowerPoint presentation).

Suneel M. Agerwala, B.A. and Elinore F. McCance-Katz, M.D., PhD "Integrating Screening, Brief Intervention, and Referral to Treatment (SBIRT) into Clinical Practice Settings: A Brief Review" (Sept.-Oct. 2012) *Journal of Psychoactive Drugs.*

B.K. Madras et al. "Screening, brief interventions, referral to treatment (SBIRT) for illicit drug and alcohol use at multiple healthcare sites: comparison at intake and 6 months later" (Jan. 2009) *Drug and Alcohol Dependence.*

12. Carrie Johnson "Criminal Records Keep Creating Obstacles Long After Incarceration" (May 29, 2014) *npr.org*

13. Legal Services of New Jersey "Clearing Your Record" (2012) *lsnjlaw.org*

"Expungement in the United States" Wikipedia: The Free Encyclopedia. Wikimedia Foundation, Inc. (Jan. 9, 2015).

14. Laurie Kellman (Associated Press) "Bush Once Pleaded Guilty To DUI" (Nov. 3, 2000) *washingtonpost.com*

Mike Allen "Rove suspected Gore aide of DUI leak" (Mar. 4, 2010) *Politico*

Ask Factcheck "The Florida Recount of 2000" (Jan. 2008) *factcheck.org*

Martha Raddatz (ABC News) "Bush: I Doubt I'd Be Standing Here If I Hadn't Quit Drinking Whiskey" (Dec. 11, 2007) *ABC News*

15. Christopher James-NYU "U.S. Teens Say They'll Give Marijuana A Try If It's Legal" (Mar. 13, 2014) *futurity.org*

16. The National Center on Addiction and Substance Abuse at Columbia University "Behind Bars II: Substance Abuse and America's Prison Population" (Feb. 2010)

17. Ibid.

18. Rob Hotakainen "Marijuana is drug most often linked to crime, study finds" (May 23, 2013) *McClatchy Washington Bureau*

Office of National Drug Control Policy Executive Office of the President "Arrestee Drug Abuse Monitoring II 2012 Annual Report".

19. Jim Gogek and Ed Gogek. (June 4, 2000). Freedom behind bars. *San Diego Union-Tribune.*

20. Eli Sanders "The War On Drug Courts: King County's drug courts are successful, so why are D.C. progressives against them?" (Aug. 17, 2011) *The Stranger.*

21. Tony Newman and Margaret Dooley-Sammuli "New Report Finds 'Drug Courts Are Not The Answer'" (Mar. 22, 2011) *drugpolicy.org*

22. Eli Sanders "The War On Drug Courts: King County's drug courts are successful, so why are D.C. progressives against them?" (Aug. 17, 2011) *The Stranger.*

23. Tony Newman and Margaret Dooley-Sammuli "New Report Finds 'Drug Courts Are Not The Answer'" (Mar. 22, 2011) *drugpolicy.org*

24. Steven Belenko, PhD "Research On Drug Courts: A Critical Review 2001 Update" (June 2001) *The National Center on Addiction and Substance Abuse at Columbia University.*

25. United States Government Accountability Office "Adult Drug Courts: Evidence Indicates Recidivism Reductions and Mixed Results For Other Outcomes" (Feb. 2005) *gao.gov*

United States Government Accountability Office "Adult Drug Courts: Studies Show Courts Reduce Recidivism, But DOJ Could Enhance Future Performance Measure Revision Efforts" (Dec. 9, 2011) *gao.gov*

26. Theshia Naidoo (Letter to the Editor) "Downside of Drug Courts" (Mar. 10, 2013) *The New York Times*.

27. American Society of Addiction Medicine Policy Statement "Treatment for Prisoners with Addiction to Alcohol or Other Drugs" (Dec. 1, 2000) *asam.org*

28. Marijuana Policy Project "Mission Statement" (Dec. 1, 2008) *mpp.org*

29. Fox Butterfield "California lacks resources for law on drug offenders, experts say" (Feb. 12, 2001) *The New York Times*.

30. Jack Leonard and Megan Garvey "Users kicking Prop. 36, not drugs" (Apr. 1, 2007) *The Los Angeles Times*.

    UCLA Integrated Substance Abuse Programs "Evaluation of the Substance Abuse and Crime Prevention Act: Final Report" (Apr. 13, 2007) *uclaisap.org*

31. UCLA Integrated Substance Abuse Programs "Evaluation of Proposition 36: The Substance Abuse and Crime Prevention Act of 2000 2008 Report" (Oct. 14, 2008) *uclaisap.org*

32. Douglas Young & Steven Belenko, Program Retention and Perceived Coercion in Three Models of Mandatory Drug Treatment, *Journal of Drug Issues;* Winter 2002; 32, 1; ProQuest pg. 297.

33. Amanda B. Cissner and Michael Rempel "The State of Drug Court Research: Moving Beyond 'Do They Work?'" (2005) Center for Court Innovation.

34. Shreema Mehta "Drug-Policy Activists Fight To Peserve Calif. Treatment Program" (Jan. 6, 2007) *The New Standard*.

    Laura Mecoy "Bill to revise Proposition 36 under fire" (July 2, 2006) *Ventura County Star*.

    Meredith J. Cooper "Drug-treatment law gets altered" (July 6, 2006) Chico News and Review.

35. Open Society Foundations "About" (2014) *opensocietyfoundations.org*

    Paige St. John "Prop. 47 puts state at center of a national push for sentencing reform" (Nov. 1, 2014) *The Los Angeles Times*.

36. National Institute on Money in State Politics "Proposition 47" (2013).

37. Jack Leonard and Megan Garvey, "Users kicking Prop. 36, not drugs" Apr. 1, 2007, *Los Angeles Times*.

38. Jack Leonard and Megan Garvey, "Users kicking Prop. 36, not drugs" Apr. 1, 2007, *Los Angeles Times*.

39. Urban Institute Justice Policy Center "The Multi-Site Adult Drug Court Evaluation: Executive Summary" (Nov. 2011) *urban.org*

Simona Combi and Stu Kantor "Drug Courts Can Reduce Substance Use and Crime, Five-Year Study Shows, But Effectiveness Hinges on the Judge" (July 18, 2011) *Urban Institute.*

Urban Institute Justice Policy Center "The Multi-Site Adult Drug Court Evaluation: Final Report: Volume 4" (Nov. 2011) *urban.org*

40. University of Buffalo News Center (Sept. 30, 2014) "Treatment of substance abuse can lessen risk of future violence in mentally ill, study finds" (Press release)

Chapter 15

1. Conor Friedersdorf "Elder Statesmen Declare a War on the 'War on Drugs' (Sept. 10, 2014) *The Atlantic.*

Global Commission on Drug Policy "Taking Control: Pathways to drug policies that work" (Sept. 2014) *globalcommissionondrugs.org*

2. U.S. Legal "Harrison Narcotics Tax Act Law & Legal Definition" (Jan. 14, 2015) *definitions.uslegal.com*

National Alliance of Advocates for Buprenorphine "Learn about the laws concerning opioids from the 1800s until today" (Jan. 14, 2015) *naabt.org*

"Marijuana Timeline" Frontline KCTS 9 *pbs.org*

Tilem & Associates "The Richard Nixon Era – The Comprehensive Drug Abuse Prevention and Control Act of 1970 Eliminates Mandatory Minimums" (Jan. 19, 2009) *New York Criminal Attorney Blog*

3. "The Colombian Cartels" Frontline KCTS 9 *pbs.org*

CNN Library "Mexico Drug War Fast Facts" (Nov. 18, 2014*) cnn.com*

4. Global Commission on Drug Policy "Partners" (2014) *globalcommissionondrugs.org*

Drug Policy Alliance "2013 Annual Report" (2014) *drugpolicy.org*

Canadian Drug Policy Coalition "Partners in Change: Coalition" *drugpolicy.ca*

Open Society Foundations "About Us" (2014) opensocietyfoundations.org

Jane Mayer ""Covert Operations: The billionaire brothers who are waging a war against Obama" *The New Yorker* (Aug 30, 2010)

Chapter 16

1. Psmith "Despite Pot Prohibition Teen Marijuana Use Continues Slight Upward Trend" (Dec. 14, 2010) *The Drug War Chronicle Issue #663.*

2. Johnston, L. D., O'Malley, P. M., Bachman, J. G., Schulenberg, J. E. & Miech, R. A. (2014). *Monitoring the Future national survey results on drug use, 1975–2013: Volume I, Secondary school students.* Ann Arbor: Institute for Social Research, The University of Michigan.

3. TobaccoFreeCA: Tobacco Industry "'Replacement' Customers" (2014) *tobaccofreeca.com*

4. Kimber P. Richter, PhD, M.P.H. and Sharon Levy, M.D., M.P.H. "Big Marijuana: Lessons from Big Tobacco" (July 31, 2014) *New England Journal of Medicine.*

5. Ibid.

6. Kevin A. Sabet (Aug. 27, 2013) *Reefer Sanity: Seven Great Myths About Marijuana* Beaufort Books.

7. SAM Smart Approaches to Marijuana (March 31, 2015).

    GrassIsNotGreener.com (March 31, 2015).

8. Christopher Ingraham "Why marijuana won't become another Big Tobacco" (Aug. 8, 2014) *The Washington Post Wonkblog.*

9. "Marijuana legalization will usher in America's new version of 'Big Tobacco'" (March 31, 2015) GrassIsNotGreener.com

10. Christopher Wanjek "Study Suggests Alcohol Ads Target Teens" (August 25, 2009) *livescience.*

    Jeanette Mulvey "How Alcohol Ads Target Kids" (August 11, 2012) *BusinessNewsDaily.*

    Donna Maldonado-Schullo "Alcohol Industry Targets Latino Teens (August 14, 2008) *Al Dia News.*

    Frank Green "Booze ads target black teens, report finds" (June 20, 2003) San Diego *Union-Tribune.*

11. Garry Trudeau "Doonesbury" (Mar. 9, 2014) *gocomics.*

12. CDC's Office on Smoking and Health "Youth and Tobacco Use" (Feb. 14, 2014) *cdc.gov.*

Substance Abuse and Mental Health Services Administration "The TEDS Report: Marijuana Admissions to Substance Abuse Treatment Aged 18-30: Early vs. Adult Initiation" (Aug. 13, 2013) *archive.samhsa.gov*

13. Garry Trudeau "Doonesbury" (Dec. 21, 2014) *gocomics.com*

14. American Cancer Society "Is smoking tobacco really addictive?" (Feb. 13, 2014) *cancer.org*

15. Miles K. Light et al. (The Marijuana Policy Group) "Market Size And Demand For Marijuana In Colorado" (2014) *Colorado Department of Revenue.*

16. Staci A. Gruber et al. "Age of Onset of Marijuana Use and Executive Function" (Sept. 2012) *Psychology of Addictive Behaviors.*

17. "Our Companies" Altria *altria.com* (Jan 1, 2015).

18. "Ratings and reports," page 1988. (Jan 23, 2015) *Value Line Investment Survey*

Chapter 17

1. Samuel Vickovic (July 22, 2011) *The High Road: A Content Analysis of Newspaper Articles Concerning Medical Marijuana* LAP Lambert Academic Publishing.

2. "Medical Marijuana Vote Days Away: ABC15 Investigators Go Undercover In CA" ABC15 Arizona News ABC Oct. 20, 2010 *youtube.com*

3. David Rookhuyzen "Supporters: Ailing Arizonans would benefit from medical marijuana" (Sept. 20, 2010) *Cronkite News.*

4. Fox10 Phoenix "Medical Marijuana Last Option for Some" (Oc. 14, 2010) *fox10phoenix.com*

5. Amanda Lee Myers (Associated Press) "Arizona voters to vote on medical marijuana" (Sept. 25, 2010) *Deseret News.*

6. Associated Press "Pot Measure Still Trailing At The Polls" (Nov. 9, 2010) *USA Today.*

7. Erik Wemple "Daily Show's Jon Stewart wonders who caused overreaction on religious freedom (Fox News) (Feb. 27, 2014) *The Washington Post.*

8. The Glaucoma Foundation "Marijuana For Glaucoma: Patients Beware!" (Summer 2010) *The Glaucoma Foundation Newsletter.*

9. Henry Jampel, M.D., M.H.S. "Position Statement On Marijuana And The Treatment Of Glaucoma" (Aug. 10, 2009) *American Glaucoma Society.*

Canadian Ophthalmological Society "Medical Use Of Marijuana For Glaucoma: Summary" *cos-sco.ca*

10. Edward Gogek (Opinions) "Medical Pot Just A Smokescreen" (Aug. 5, 2011) *The Arizona Republic.*

11. Brian Dowling "Legal Marijuana: No Market Until 2013" (June 29, 2012) *The Hartford Courant.*

12 Ibid.

13 Ibid.

Bryan Gruley "Medbox: Dawn of the Marijuana Vending Machine" (May 9, 2013) Bloomberg Business.

14. Mary Ellen Clark "Medical Marijuana Legalized in Connecticut" (June 1, 2012) *Reuters: New York.*

15. Bud Foster "Medical marijuana from a doctor's point of view" (Nov. 8, 2010) *tucsonnewsnow.*

Jacques Billeaud (Associated Press) "24 doctors certify most in Ariz.'s pot program" (Nov. 9, 2012) *azcentral.*

16. Timothy B. Wheeler "Maryland Medical Marijuana: O'Malley Administration Withdraws Opposition To Bill" (Mar. 9, 2013) *Huff Post DC.*

17. Associated Press "Illinois Senate approves bill to legalize medical marijuana" (May 19, 2013) *Fox News: Politics.*

18. Massachusetts Patient Advocacy Alliance "State Comparison Infographic" (Jan. 14, 2015) *compassionforpatients.com*

19. Medical Marijuana Commission Laws & Regulations Senate bill 923. (Mar. 31, 2015).

20. Chris Lane "Teen marijuana use common because of Canadian drug policy, says pot activist" (Apr. 16, 2013) *Vancouver Observer.*

21. "Marijuana laws a confusing mess" (July 10, 2007) Montreal *Gazette.*

22. "why are canada's medical marijuana laws so strict??" (Nov. 5, 2008) grasscity.com.

22. Medical Marijuana "Medical Marijuana in Europe" (Jan. 14, 2015) *medicalmarijuana.org*

23. Peter Adamson UNICEF Office of Research "Child well-being in rich countries: A comparative overview" (2013) *UNICEF Office of Research, Florence.*

24. Drugs.com "Methamphetamine" (Jan. 14, 2015) *drugs.com.*

25. Substance Abuse and Mental Health Services Administration, *Results from the 2011 National Survey on Drug Use and Health: Summary of National Findings*, NSDUH Series H-44, HHS Publication No. (SMA) 12-4713. Rockville, MD: Substance Abuse and Mental Health Services Administration, 2012.

26. Crack Facts "How Many People Use Crack?" (2005) *crack-facts.org.*

27. South Central History "Crack Epidemic?" (Jan. 3, 2015) *southcenteralhistory.com*

   Jerry Langton (Apr. 9, 2007) *Iced: The Crystal Meth Epidemic* Key Porter Books

   Celine Gounder "Who Is Responsible Fort he Pain-Pill Epidemic?" (Nov. 8, 2013) *The New Yorker.*

   Mark Potter "America's Heroin Epidemic (17 Stories) (2014)" *nbcnews.com*

28. Substance Abuse and Mental Health Services Administration, *Results from the 2011 National Survey on Drug Use and Health: Summary of National Findings*, NSDUH Series H-44, HHS Publication No. (SMA) 12-4713. Rockville, MD: Substance Abuse and Mental Health Services Administration, 2012.

29. Substance Abuse and Mental Health Services Administration, *Results from the 2011 National Survey on Drug Use and Health: Summary of National Findings*, NSDUH Series H-44, HHS Publication No. (SMA) 12-4713. Rockville, MD: Substance Abuse and Mental Health Services Administration, 2012.

30. Crack Facts "How Many People Use Crack?" (2005) *crack-facts.org.*

   Substance Abuse and Mental Health Services Administration, *Results from the 2011 National Survey on Drug Use and Health: Summary of National Findings*, NSDUH Series H-44, HHS Publication No. (SMA) 12-4713. Rockville, MD: Substance Abuse and Mental Health Services Administration, 2012.Table 1.12a

   Op. cit.

   Op. cit.

31. Op. cit.

32. Op. cit.

33. South Central History "Crack Epidemic?" (Jan. 3, 2015) *southcenteralhistory.com*

   Jerry Langton (Apr. 9, 2007) *Iced: The Crystal Meth Epidemic* Key Porter Books.

Celine Gounder "Who Is Responsible For The Pain-Pill Epidemic?" (Nov. 8, 2013) *The New Yorker.*

34. Arian Campo-Flores and Zusha Elinson "Heroin Use, And Deaths, Rise" (Feb. 3, 2014) *The Wall Street Journal.*

35. Centers for Disease Control and Prevention "Increase in Heroin Overdose Deaths – 28 States, 2010-2012" (Oct. 3, 2014) *cdc.gov.*

36. Joanne E. Brady and Guohua Li "Trends In Alcohol And Other Drugs Detected In Fatally Injured Drivers In The United States, 1999-2010" (Jan. 2014) *American Journal of Epidemiology.*

37. National Highway Traffic Safety Administration (Nov. 14, 2013) "NHTSA Data Confirms Traffic Fatalities Increased In 2012" (Press release).

38. Mark Potter "America's Heroin Epidemic (17 Stories) (2014)" *nbcnews.com.*

DelawareOnline "Delaware's Heroin Crisis: Special Report" (June 14, 2014) *delwareonline.com.*

Ian Pannell "The Horrific Toll of America's Heroin 'Epidemic'" (Mar. 21, 2014) BBC News Chicago.

39. KPBS News "Local Medical Marijuana Propositions Headed Toward Defeat" (Nov. 6, 2012) *kpbs.org.*

Olivia Moore and Justine Moore "Palo Alto medical marijuana measure is defeated" (Nov. 7, 2012) *Peninsula Press.*

Khari Johnson "Pro-Marijuana Group Pulls in Big Green for IB Dispensary Proposition" (Nov. 1, 2012) *Imperial Beach Patch.*

40. National Institute On Money In State Politics "Ask Anything!" (2014) followthemoney.org

41. Ibid.

42. Ibid.

43. Nichola Confessore and Eric Lipton "A Big Check, and Gingrich Gets a Big Lift" Jan. 9, 2012 *The New York Times.*

44. Sean Sullivan "How liberal mega-donor Peter Lewis left his mark on politics" (Nov. 25, 2013) *The Washington Post.*

National Institute On Money In State Politics "Ask Anything!" (2014) followthemoney.org

45. Nick Wing "Here's updated tally of all the people who have ever died from a marijuana overdose" (Jan. 3, 2014) *Huff Post Politics.*

46. "Letter: Marijuana never killed anyone" (Feb. 22, 2015) Freeport *Journal-Standard.*

Danny McDonald "Marijuana never killed anyone" (Mar. 5, 2014) *Bermuda Sun.*

"Marijuana has never killed anyone. MAKE IT LEGAL!" (Mar. 31, 2015) *Facebook*

47. Chris Remington "A Vet Finds PTSD Relief With Pot, Though The Law Creates Hurdles" (Dec. 19, 2013) *npr.org*

48. Amanda Gardner "Prescription Drug Abuse: Who Gets Addicted?" (Mar. 31, 2015) *Webmd.com*

49. Deborah Brauser "Medical Marijuana May Worsen PTSD Symptoms, Increase Violence" (Dec. 15, 2014) *Medscape.com*

50. Wiley-Blackwell "High rates of substance abuse exist among veterans with mental illness, study finds" (Apr. 25, 2011) *ScienceDaily.*

Andrew W. Meisler "Trauma, PTSD and Substance Abuse" (Fall, 1996) *PTSD Research Quarterly.*

51. Amy Miller "Judge rejects key parts of Texas abortion law" (Aug. 29, 2014) *legalinsurrection.com.*

Michael Barajas "How to close abortion clinics under the guise of women's safety" (Mar. 26, 2013) *San Antonio Current.*

Manny Fernandez "Abortion Restrictions Become Law in Texas, but Opponents Will Press The Fight" (July 18, 2013) *The New York Times.*

Wade Goodwyn "A doctor who performed abortions in south Texas makes his case" (Sept. 11, 2014) *npr.org*

52. Kristina Fiore "AMA Reverses Stance on Medical Marijuana" (Nov. 13, 2009) *medpagetoday.com*

American Society of Addiction Medicine Policy Statement "Medical Marijuana" (Apr. 12, 2010) *asam.org*

"The Impact of Marijuana Policies on Youth: Clinical, Research, and Legal Update" *Pediatrics* (January 26, 2015).

53. A.M. Rosenthal "On My Mind; Lean Back Or Fight" (Apr. 14, 1998) *The New York Times.*

Chapter 18

1. Ryan Jaslow "Medical marijuana legalization won't boost teen pot use, study finds" (June 22, 2012) *CBS News*.

2. Katherine Bindley "Medical Marijuana Does Increase Teen Drug Use, Study Finds" (June 19, 2012) *Huff Post Science*.

3. Ted S. Warren (Associated Press) "Study: Legalizing medical pot doesn't boost teen drug use" (June 19, 2012) *nbcnews.com*.

4. D. Mark Anderson et al. "Medical Marijuana Laws And Teen Marijuana Use" (Sept. 2012*) Social Science Research Network*.

5. Montana Department of Public Health and Human Services (Oct. 10, 2014) "History of Qualifying Patients, Providers and Doctors (Jan. 2005-June 2012)" (Reprinted with permission.)

6. Ibid

7. "Medical Marijuana Statistics" (2014) *Colorado Department of Public Health & Environment*.

8. Ibid.

9. Jeff Beeler "Should negative results be treated with the same rigor as positive results?" (Sept. 11, 2012) *researchgate.net*

10. John Ingold "Report shows fewer traffic fatalities after states pass medical-pot laws" (Nov. 30, 2011) *The Denver Post*.

   D. Mark Anderson and Daniel I. Rees "Medical Marijuana Laws, Traffic Fatalities and Alcohol Consumption" (Nov. 2011) *Institute for the Study of Labor*.

11. MADD "Drunk Driving Deaths 1982-2012" (Jan. 14, 2015) madd.org

   Alcohol Problems and Solutions Figure 5: "High school seniors who have consumed 5 or more drinks on an occasion within previous 2 weeks" (Mar 31, 2015).

12. Johnston, L. D., O'Malley, P. M., Bachman, J. G., Schulenberg, J. E. & Miech, R. A. (2014). *Monitoring the Future national survey results on drug use, 1975–2013: Volume I, Secondary school students*. Ann Arbor: Institute for Social Research, The University of Michigan.

13. Clayton Sandell (ABC News) "Driving Stoned: Safer Than Driving Drunk?" (Dec. 2, 2011) *ABC News*.

14. Alcohol Alert "Colorado Drunk Driving Statistics" (2014) *alcoholalert.com* Alcohol Alert "Tennessee Drunk Driving Statistics" (2014) *alcoholalert.com*

15. The Editorial Board "Marijuana and Alcohol" (Nov. 3, 2013) *The New York Times*

    D. Mark Anderson and Daniel I. Rees "The Legalization of Recreational Marijuana How Likely Is The Worst Case Scenario" (July 31, 2013) *dmarkanderson.com*

16. Brian Dowling "Legal Marijuana: No Market Until 2013" (June 29, 2012) *The Hartford Courant.*

17. Ted S. Warren (Associated Press) "Study: Legalizing medical pot doesn't boost teen drug use" (June 19, 2012) *nbcnews.com*

18. Magdalena Cerdá et al. "Medical marijuana laws in 50 states: Investigating the relationship between state legalization of medical marijuana and marijuana usse, abuse and dependence" (Jan. 1, 2012) *Drug and Alcohol Dependence.*

    Melanie M. Wall, PhD et al. "Adolescent marijuana use from 2002 to 2008: higher in states with medical marijuana laws, cause still unclear" (Sept. 1, 2012) *Annals of Epidemiology.*

19. Deborah Hasin et al "Medical marijuana laws and adolescent marijuana use in the USA from 1991 to 2014: results from annual, repeated cross-sectional surveys" (June 15, 2015) *The Lancet.*

20. Carey Goldberg "National Survey Suggests Medical Pot Trickles Down To Teens" (Dec. 18, 2013) *commonhealth.wbur.org*

21. Stacy Salomonsen-Sautel et al. "Medical Marijuana Use Among Adolescents in Substance Abuse Treatment" (May 28, 2012) *Journal of the American Academy of Child & Adolescent Psychiatry.*

22. Ed Gogek, Chapter 11, Figure 11-2, this book.

23. John Ingold "Report shows fewer traffic fatalities after states pass medical-pot laws" (Nov. 30, 2011) *The Denver Post.*

24. T. Huckle, J. Huakau, P. Sweetsur, et al. (2008). Density of alcohol outlets and teenage drinking: Living in an alcogenic environment is associated with higher consumption in a metropolitan setting. *Addiction, 103*:1614–1621. PMID: 18821871. T. Huckle, R.Q. You, & S. Casswell. (2010). Increases in quantities consumed in drinking occasions in New Zealand 1995–2004. *Drug and Alcohol Review, 30*:366–371. PMID: 21355906

25. The Editorial Board "Marijuana And Alcohol" (Nov. 3, 2013) *The New York Times.*

26. Christopher Ingraham "Medical marijuana opponents' most powerful argument is at odds with a mountain of research" (July 29, 2014) *The Washington Post.*

27. Ibid.

28. Jacob Sullum "Economists Predict Marijuana Legalization Will Produce 'Public Health Benefits'" (Nov. 1, 2013) *forbes.com.*

29. Gail Sullivan "Study: Legalizing medical marijuana has not increased teen pot use" (Apr. 24, 2014) *The Washington Post.*

   Esther K. Choo, M.D., M.P.H. et al. "The Impact of State Medical Marijuana Legislation on Adolescent Marijuana Use" (Aug. 2014) *Journal of Adolescent Health.*

30. Laura Kann, PhD et al. "Youth Rish Behavior Surveillance – United States 2013" (June 13, 2014) *Centers for Disease Control and Prevention.*

31. Gail Sullivan "Study: Legalizing medical marijuana has not increased teen pot use" (Apr. 24, 2014) *The Washington Post.*

33. Mark A.R. Kleiman "Don't blame Eric Holder for confusing pot policies: Bloomberg opinion" (Feb. 16, 2014) *oregonlive.com*

34. "cooperate" *Merriam-Webster* (2014).

35. Ivan Semeniuk "Foreign scientists write letter criticizing decline of Canadian federal research" (Oct. 21, 2014) *The Globe and Mail.*

   Ivan Semeniuk "Scientists not shielded from political interference from feds: report" (Oct. 8, 2014) *The Globe and Mail.*

36. The Professional Institute of the Public Service of Canada "Most Federal Scientists Feel They Can't Speak Out, Even If Public Health and Safety at Risk, Says New Survey" *pipsc.ca*

37. Katie Valentine "Stephen Harper's Anti-Labor, Anti-Science Agenda Pushes Union To Speak Out For The First Time" (Nov. 10, 2014) *thinkprogress.org*

38. Centre for Addiction and Mental Health "Cannabis Policy Framework" (Oct. 2014) *camh.ca*

39. Sheryl Ubelacker "Pot should be legalized, addiction centre says" (Oct. 9, 2014) *thestar.com*

40. Centre for Addiction and Mental Health "Cannabis Policy Framework" (Oct. 2014) *camh.ca*

41. Louisa Degenhardt, PhD et al. "Outcomes of occasional cannabis use in adolescence: 10-year follow-up study in Victoria, Australia" (Apr. 2010) *British Journal of Psychiatry*

42. Jean-Francois Crépault *Cannabis Policy Framework* (Oct. 2014) Centre for Addiction and Mental Health *camh.ca*

43. Beau Kilmer et al. "Altered State? Assessing How Marijuana Legalization In California Could Influence Marijuana Consumption And Public Budgets" (2010) *Rand Drug Policy Research Center.*

44. Jurgen Rehm "CAMH's Cannabis Policy Framework: Legalization with regulation" *CAMH Centre for Addiction and Mental Health the official blog for Canada's leading mental health and addictions hospital* (Oct 9, 2014 Q & A on Oct 22 & 23, 2014).

45. Jurgen Rehm et al. *The Costs of Substance Abuse in Canada in 2002* (March 2006) Canadian Centre on Substance Abuse.

46. Jean-Francois Crépault *Cannabis Policy Framework* (Oct. 2014) Centre for Addiction and Mental Health *camh.ca.*

47. Christopher James-NYU "U.S. Teens Say They'll Give Marijuana A Try If It's Legal" (Mar. 13, 2014) *futurity.org.*

48. Marks J: The paradox of prohibition, in Brewer C (ed.) *Treatment Options in Addiction: Medical Management of Alcohol and Opiate Abuse*, The Royal College of Psychiatrists, London, 1993, p 77 – 85.

49. IWB "Dr. John Marks had this same strategy in the UK but it was closed due to US pressure for ideological' reasons" (Feb. 13, 2012) *InvestmentWatchblog.com.*

   Wayne Hall "Controlled Availability: Wisdom Or Disaster?" (Feb. 1989) *National Drug and Alcohol Research Centre.*

50. IWB "Dr. John Marks had this same strategy in the UK but it was closed due to US pressure for 'ideological' reasons" (Feb. 13, 2012) *InvestmentWatchblog.com.*

   Marks J: The paradox of prohibition, in Brewer C (ed.) *Treatment Options in Addiction: Medical Management of Alcohol and Opiate Abuse*, The Royal College of Psychiatrists, London, 1993, p 77 – 85.

51. Jean-Francois Crépault *Cannabis Policy Framework* (Oct. 2014) Centre for Addiction and Mental Health Reprinted with permission. Copyright 2014, Centre for Addiction and Mental Health.

52. Franklin Apfel (2014). *Cannabis: From prohibition to regulation*. AR Policy Brief 5. Barcelona: ALICE RAP (Addictions and Lifestyles in Contemporary Europe – Reframing Addictions Policy).

Transform Drug Policy Foundation "How To Regulate Cannabis: A Practical Guide" (May 2014) *tdpf.org.uk*

Transform Drug Policy Foundation "Our Funding" (2014) *tdpf.org.uk*

Canadian Drug Policy Coalition "Talking to your politician about Drug Policy Abuse" (2014) *drugpolicy.ca*

Canadian Drug Policy Coalition "Getting to Tomorrow: A Report on Canadian Drug Policy" (2014) *drugpolicy.ca*

53. Jean-Francois Crépault *Cannabis Policy Framework* (Oct. 2014) Centre for Addiction and Mental Health *camh.ca*

Chapter 19

1. Bill Keller (Op-Ed Columnist) "How To Legalize Pot" May 19, 2013 *The New York Times*

D. Mark Anderson, Benjamin Hansen and Daniel I. Rees "Medical Marijuana Laws and Teen Marijuana Use" (May 2012) *Institute for the Study of Labor*

2. Ed Gogek, Chapter 11, Figure 11-2, this book.

3. The Editorial Board "Marijuana And Alcohol" (Nov. 3, 2013) *The New York Times*

D. Mark Anderson and Daniel I. Rees "The Legalization of Recreational Marijuana How Likely Is The Worst Case Scenario" (July 31, 2013) *dmarkanderson.com*

4. R.L. Hartman and M.A. Huestis "Cannabis effects on driving skills" (Mar. 2013) *Clinical Chemistry.*

5. Mark Asbridge, Jill A. Hayden, & Jennifer L. Cartwright. (Feb. 2012) "Acute cannabis consumption and motor vehicle collision risk: systematic review of observational studies and meta-analysis" *BMJ, 344.* doi:

6. Joanne E. Brady and Guohua Li "Trends In Alcohol And Other Drugs Detected In Fatally Injured Drivers In The United States, 1999-2010" (Jan. 2014) *American Journal of Epidemiology*

CBS Seattle "Study: Fatal Car Crashes Involving Marijuana Have Tripled" (Feb. 4, 2014) *seattle.cbslocal.com*

7. The Editorial Board "Repeal Prohibition, Again" (July 26, 2014) *The New York Times.*

8. Louisa Degenhardt, PhD et al. "Outcomes of occasional cannabis use in adolescence: 10-year follow-up study in Victoria, Australia" (Apr. 2010) *British Journal of Psychiatry.*

   Drug Policy Research Center "Using Marijuana May Not Raise the Risk of Using Harder Drugs" (2002) *Rand.org*

9. Jesse Wegman "The Injustice of Marijuana Arrests" (July 28, 2014) *The New York Times.*

10. SHouse California Law Group "California Three Strikes Law and Proposition 36 Reforms" (2014) *shouselaw.com*

11. E. Ann Carson and Daniela Golinelli "Prisoners in 2012 – Advance Counts" (July 2013) *Bureau of Justice Statistics.* Table 9 & 10 Prisoners in 2012— Advance Counts, July 2013, NCJ 242467, Table 10

12. Op.cit.

13. Ibid.

14. Kathleen Miles "Just How Much The War On Drugs Impacts Our Overcrowded Prisons In One Chart" (Mar. 10, 2014) *Huff Post Politics.*

15. Ibid.

16. Ibid.

   Federal Bureau of Prisons "Offenses" (2014) *bop.gov*

17. Ibid.

18. "drug of choice" wordnik.com (2015).

19. Mark Motivans, PhD "Federal Justice Statistics 2010 – Statistical Tables" *bjs.gov*

20. Fareed Zakaria "Incarceration Nation" (Apr. 2, 2012) *TIME.*

21. Global Commission on Drug Policy "Partners" (2014) *globalcommissionondrugs.org*

22. "Richard Branson: 'The Virgin Way'" (Sept. 23, 2014) *The Diane Rehm Show.* WAMU

23. Doug Fine "Five Myths About Legalizing Marijuana" (June 7, 2013) *The Washington Post.*

   Kevin A. Sabet, PhD "Five Errors The Washington Post Should Have Caught About Marijuana" (June 10, 2013) *The Washington Post.*

24. "Drug Decriminalization in Portugal: Challenges and Limitations" White House Office of National Drug Control Policy (January 1, 2015).

Maia Szalavitz "Drugs in Portugal: Did Decriminalization Work?" (April 26, 2009) *Time.*

"The difference between legalisation and decriminalization" The *Economist* (June 18 2014).

25. Esther Choo, M.D., M.P.H. et al. "Impact of state-level policy on adolescent marijuana use" (Nov. 2, 2011) *American Public Health Association.*

Magdalena Cerdá et al. "Medical marijuana laws in 50 states: Investigating the relationship between state legalization of medical marijuana and marijuana usse, abuse and dependence" (Jan. 1, 2012) *Drug and Alcohol Dependence.*

26. Katrina vanden Heuvel "Time to end the war on drugs" (Nov. 20, 2012) *The Washington Post.*

27. "Thirty Years of America's Drug War: A Chronology" Frontline KCTS 9 *pbs.org*

28. Michael Massing "The Fix" University of California Press 2000.

29. Katrina vanden Heuvel "Time to end the war on drugs" (Nov. 20, 2012) *The Washington Post.*

30. Ibid.

31. Radley Balko "Since marijuana legalization, highway fatalities in Colorado are at near-historic lows" (Aug. 5, 2014) *The Washington Post.*

32. Australian Transport Safety Bureau (Mar. 2004) "Cannabis and its Effects on Pilot Performance and Flight Safety: A Review" ISBN1 877071 57 9.

33. Ken MacQueen "Why it's time to legalize marijuana" (June 10, 2013) *Maclean's.*

34. A.J. Budney et al. "Review of the validity and significance of cannabis withdrawal syndrome" (Nov. 2004) *American Journal of Psychiatry.*

35. Connie Carter & Donald MacPherson *Getting to Tomorrow: A report on Canadian drug policy* (2013) Canadian Drug Policy Coalition.

Canadian Drug Policy Coalition "About Us" (Mar. 31, 2015).

36. Ken MacQueen "Why it's time to legalize marijuana" (June 10, 2013) *Maclean's.*

37. David Akin "Justin Trudeau high on pot data" (Setp. 9, 2013) *The Toronto Sun.*

38. Jessica Hume "Trudeau sticks to marijuana possession arrest stats" (Sept. 10, 2013) *The Edmonton Sun.*

39. Ed Gogek, Chapter 10, "Evidence that more criminals are carrying marijuana," this book.

40. National Institute of Justice "NIJ's Drug and Crime Research: Arrestee Drug Abuse Monitoring Programs" (June 18, 2014) *National Institute of Justice: Office of Justice Programs.*

41. Rob Hotakainen "Marijuana is drug most often linked to crime, study finds" (May 23, 2013) *McClatchy Washington Bureau.*

42. Justin Peters "New Study Tries, Fails To Show Marijuana Use Is Linked To Crime" (May 24, 2013) *Slate.*

43. Editorial "Pot is a problem only if society decides to make it one" (Sept. 12, 2013) *The Vancouver Sun.*

44. M. Large et al. "Cannabis use and earlier onset of psychosis: a systematic meta-analysis" (June 2011) *Archives of General Psychiatry.*

45. Jodi M. Gilman et al. "Cannabis Use Is Quantitatively Associated With Nucleus Accumbens and Amygdala Abnormalities In Young Adult Recreational Users" (Apr. 16, 2014) *Journal of Neuroscience.*

46. The Economist "How To Stop The Drug Wars" (Mar. 5, 2009) *The Economist.*

47. Ann Boonn "Raising Cigarette Taxes Reduces Smoking, Especially Among Kids (And The Cigarette Companies Know It) (Oct. 11, 2012) *tobaccofreekids.org*

48. Rand Corporation (New Release) "Legalizing Marijuana In California Would Sharply Lower the Price of the Drug" (July 7, 2010) *Rand Drug Policy Research Center.*

49. Jack S. Blocker, Jr. PhD "Did Prohibition Really Work? Alcohol Prohibition As A Public Health Innovation" (Feb. 2006) *American Journal of Public Health.*

   Michael Massing "The Fix" University of California Press 2000.

50. Newsweek staff "Global Warming Deniers Well Funded" (Aug. 12, 2007) *Newsweek.*

51. "23 Legal Medical Marijuana States and DC" Procon.org (May 5, 2015).

   "States That Have Decriminalized" NORML norml.org (2015).

52. Arit John "Big Gulps safe after New York City loses final appeal to ban large sodas" (June 26, 2014) *The Wire.*

53. E.J. Dionne Jr. "The dramatically changing politics of marijuana" (May 29, 2013) *The Washington Post.*

54. Christine Tatum "When Journalists Hide Marijuana Use" (Jan. 3, 2014) *drthurstone.com*

55. "Conflict of Interest" *Business Dictionary* (2014).

56. The Washington Times "Just the circus, and no elephants" (May 11, 2006) *The Washington Times.*

Chapter 20

1. B.A. Primack et al. "Content analysis of tobacco, alcohol and other drugs in popular music" (Feburary 2008) *Archives of Pediatrics & Adolescent Medicine.*

2. Elaina Bergamini et al. "Trends in alcohol and tobacco brand placements in popular US movies, 1996 through 2009" (July 2013) *Journal of the American Medical Association Pediatrics.*

3. Ibid.

4. US Department of Health and Human Services. Preventing Tobacco Use Among Youth and Young Adults: A Report of the Surgeon General. Atlanta, GA: US Dept of Health and Human Services, Centers for Disease Control and Prevention, National Center for Chronic Disease Prevention and Health Promotion, Office on Smoking and Health; 2012, page 602.

5. Genevra Pittman "Fewer tobacco products, but not alcohol, in movies" (May 26, 2013) *Reuters New York.*

6. Elaina Bergamini et al. "Trends in alcohol and tobacco brand placements in popular US movies, 1996 through 2009" (July 2013) *Journal of the American Medical Association Pediatrics.*

7. Substance Abuse and Mental Health Services Administration, *Results from the 2011 National Survey on Drug Use and Health: Summary of National Findings*, NSDUH Series H-44, HHS Publication No. (SMA) 12-4713. Rockville, MD: Substance Abuse and Mental Health Services Administration, 2012.

8. Substance Abuse and Mental Health Services Administration, *Results from the 2011 National Survey on Drug Use and Health: Summary of National Findings*, NSDUH Series H-44, HHS Publication No. (SMA) 12-4713. Rockville, MD: Substance Abuse and Mental Health Services Administration, 2012.

Chapter 21

1. Pew Research Center "Partisans Disagree on Legalization of Marijuana , but Agree on Law Enforcement Policies" (Apr. 30, 2013) *pewresearch.org*

2. Howard Fischer "Kavanagh can't find votes to put medical marijuana back on ballot" (June 7, 2013) *Capitol Media Services/Verde Independent.*

3. Aaron C. Davis and Ed O'Keefe "Congressional spending deal blocks pot legalization in D.C." (Dec. 9, 2014) The *Washington Post.*

4. Aaron C. Davis "With focus elsewhere, GOP Congress shows little interest in blocking pot legalization in D.C." (Nov. 16, 2014) The *Washington Post.*

5. Substance Abuse and Mental Health Services Administration, *Results from the 2011 National Survey on Drug Use and Health: Summary of National Findings*, NSDUH Series H-44, HHS Publication No. (SMA) 12-4713. Rockville, MD: Substance Abuse and Mental Health Services Administration, 2012. Table 1.12A

6. Spencer MacColl "Capital Rivals: Koch Brothers vs. George Soros" (Sept. 21, 2010) *opensecrets.org*

   Reason Foundation "Frequently Asked Questions" (2014) *The Reason Foundation.*

   The Center For Media And Democracy "Mercatus Center" (2014) *sourcewatch.org*

   Doug Bandow "End The Drug War: The American People Are Not the Enemy" (Mar. 3, 2014) *Cato Institute.*

   David Godow "Are Sin Taxes on Marijuana a Price Worth Paying for Reform?" (Oct. 13, 2010) *Reason Foundation.*

   "Paternalism" Mercatus Center (Mar. 31, 2015).

7. Mike Riggs "Want to Go to Drug Court? Say Goodbye to Your Rights" (Aug. 17, 2012) *reason.com*

   "Charles G. Koch Summer Fellow Program" (2014) Institute for Humane Studies at George Mason University *theihs.org*

8. The National Center on Addiction and Substance Abuse at Columbia University "Behind Bars II: Substance Abuse and America's Prison Population" (Feb. 2010).

   Joseph A. Califano, Jr. "High Society: How Substance Abuse Ravages

America And What To Do About It" (Nov. 1, 2008) The National Center on Addiction and Substance Abuse at Columbia University.

William Ruger and Jason Sorens "Paternalism" (2014).

9. Ryan Struyk (ABC News) "Koch Brother Lashes Out Against 'Collectivists'" (Apr. 3, 2014) *ABC News.*

10. Rachel Maddow "Small Victories Seen Among Election Results" (Nov. 5, 2014) *The Rachel Maddow Show.*

11. Kelly Riddell "George Soros' real crusade: Legalizing marijuana in the U.S." (Apr. 2, 2014) *The Washington Times.*

12. Peter Beinart "Mega-Donors Are Now More Important Than Most Politicians" (Apr. 4, 2014) *The Atlantic.*

13. Malik Burnett, M.D. "Legalization Ends Discrimination In Marijuana Enforcement" (Oct.3, 2014) *eNews Park Forest.*

14. Drug Policy Alliance (press release) "Marijuana Initiative Qualifies for Washington, D.C. November Ballot" (Aug. 6, 2014) *drugpolicy.org*

15. Centre for Addiction and Mental Health "Cannabis Policy Framework" (Oct. 2014) *camh.ca*

16. Ryan Gabrielson, Ryann Grochowski Jones and Eric Sagara "Deadly Force, in Black and White" (Oct. 10, 2014) *ProPublica.*

17. Jon Walker "Colorado Democratic Party Platform Supports Marijuana Legalization Initiative" (Apr. 16, 2012) *justsaynow.com*

18. National Institute On Money In State Politics "Marijuana Policy Project" (2014) followthemoney.org

"23 Legal Medical Marijuana States and DC" Procon.org (May 5, 2015).

19. Legal Action Center "The State of State Policy on TANF & Addiction" (June 2002) *lac.org*

20. Legal Action Center "Making Welfare Reform Work" (Sept. 1997) *lac.org*

21. Rukmalie Jayakody et al. Welfare reform, substance use and mental health (2000) *Journal of Health Politics, Policy and Law.*

C. Hyggen "Does smoking cannabis affect work commitment?" (July 2012) *Addiction.*

22. National Association of Drug Court Professionals (Press Release) "Texas Governor Rick Perry Receives NADCP Award For Criminal Justice Reform" (Apr. 2, 2014) *nadcp.org*

23. Reid Wilson "Best state in America: Texas, where both crime and incarceration rates are falling" (Dec. 5, 2014) The *Washington Post*.

24. Ed Gogek, Chapter 11, Figure 11-2, this book.

25. "America withdraws from ABM treaty" (Dec. 13 2001) BBC News.

    Jim Abrams "House Democrats Sue President Bush Over Withdrawal From ABM Treaty" (June 11, 2002) *Associated Press*.

    Single Convention on Narcotic Drugs, 1961 (Mar. 31, 2015) International Narcotics Control Board United Nations Office on Drugs and Crime

26. Public Health Law Center "Master Settlement Agreement" (2010) *publichealthlawcener.org*

27. See http://www.nytimes.com/2014/04/06/us/politics/despite-support-in-party-democratic-governors-resist-legalizing-marijuana.html?hp&_r=0

28. Pew Research Center "Nearly All Tea Party Republicans Distrust The Federal Government" (Oct. 18, 2013) *Pew Research Center For the People & the Press*.

29. Marijuana Policy Project "FDA Approval: You Can't Get There From Here" (2014) *Marijuana Policy Project*.

30. John Cook et al. "Quantifying the consensus on anthropogenic global warming in the scientific literatura" (May 15, 2013) *IOPScience*.

    Pew Research Center "GOP Deeply Divided Over Climate Change" (Nov. 1, 2013) *Pew Research Center For the People & the Press*.

31. Sean Sullivan and Robert Costa "The Tea Party's Senate primary hopes down to one final face-off in Tennessee" (Aug. 7, 2014) The Washington Post.

32. Amanda Sakuma "House blocks feds from going after medical marijuana" (May 30, 2014) *msnbc.com*

    David Ogden *Memorandum for Selected United States Attorneys; Investigations and Prosecutions in States Authorizing the Medical Use of Marijuana* U.S. Department of Justice Office of the Deputy Attorney General (Oct 19, 2009).

33. Amanda Fallin et al. "'To quarterback behind the scenes, third-party efforts:' the tobacco industry and the Tea Party" (Feb. 8, 2013) *Tobacco Control*.

    "Americans for Prosperity" *Factcheck.org* (June 16, 2014).

    Katie Zernike "Shaping Tea Party Passion Into Campaign Force" Aug. 25, 2010 *The New York Times*.

34. Center For The Study Of Carbon Dioxide And Global Change "Fact Sheet" (2014) *exxonsecrets.org*

Douglas Fischer and The Daily Climate "'Dark Money' Funds Climate Change Denial Effort" (Dec. 23, 2013) *Scientific American.*

Greenpeace USA "Koch Industries: Still Fueling Climate Denial" (2014) *greenpeace.org*

Ben Webster "Oil giant gave £1 million to fund climate sceptics" (July 18, 2010) The *Times.*

Phil Plait "The Very, Very Thin Wedge of Denial" (Jan. 14, 2014) *Slate*

350.org "Who Are These Climate Change Deniers?" (July 21, 2011) *nebraskansforpeace.org*

35. Oriana Zill de Granados "The Doubters of Global Warming" in "Hot Politics" (2007) *PBS Frontline.*

Denise Robbins "How The Merchants Of Doubt Push Climate Denial On Your Television" (Mar. 8, 2015) *Media Matters.*

Max Greenberg et al., "STUDY: Media Sowed Doubt In Coverage Of UN Climate Report" (Oct.10, 2013) *Media Matters for America.*

36. Ibid.

Dana Nuccitelli "Conservative media outlets found guilty of biased global warming coverage" (Oct. 11, 2013) *The Guardian.*

Chapter 22

1. Sydney Lupkin (ABC News) "Woman Caught In Cancer Scam To Collect Money To Support Heroin Addiction" (Apr. 11, 2013) *ABC News.*

2. Dean Schabner (ABC News) "ID Theft Linked To Crystal Meth Use" (Mar. 24, 2004) *ABC News.*

3. Margaret Hartmann "Tale of the Barefoot Homeless Man Gets More Depressing" (Dec. 5, 2012 *New York Magazine.*

4. Christopher Ingraham "Where Americans smoke marijuana the most" (Aug. 5, 2014) *The Washington Post.*

5. Substance Abuse and Mental Health Services Administration, *Results from the 2011 National Survey on Drug Use and Health: Summary of National Findings*, NSDUH Series H-44, HHS Publication No. (SMA)

12-4713. Rockville, MD: Substance Abuse and Mental Health Services Administration, 2012.

6. Laura Kann, PhD et al. "Youth Rish Behavior Surveillance – United States 2013" (June 13, 2014) *Centers for Disease Control and Prevention* National Center for HIV/AIDS, Viral Hepatitis, STD and TB Prevention "Trends in the Prevalence of Marijuana, Cocaine and Other Illegal Drug Use National YRBS, 1991-2011" (2012) *Centers for Disease Control and Prevention*.

7. Substance Abuse and Mental Health Services Administration, *Results from the 2011 National Survey on Drug Use and Health: Summary of National Findings*, NSDUH Series H-44, HHS Publication No. (SMA) 12-4713. Rockville, MD: Substance Abuse and Mental Health Services Administration, 2012.

8. Office of National Drug Control Policy Executive Office of the President "Arrestee Drug Abuse Monitoring II 2012 Annual Report".

9. "Arizona Medical Marijuana Act" Full text of Arizona's Proposition 203 (2010).

10. Office of National Drug Control Policy Executive Office of the President "Arrestee Drug Abuse Monitoring II 2012 Annual Report".

11. Garrett Bruno (ABC News) "Hemp Flag To Fly Over Capitol On Fourth Of July" (July 4, 2013) *ABC News*.

Chapter 23

1. Matt Ferner "World Leaders Call For Massive Shift In Global Drug Policy" (Sept. 8, 2014) *Huff Post Politics*.

2. Connie I. Carter and Donald MacPherson "Getting to Tomorrow: A Report on Canadian Drug Policy" (2013) *Canadian Drug Policy Coalition,* page 7.

3. Canadian Drug Policy Coalition "Mission And Vision" drugpolicy.ca

4. Tony Newman "Beyond Marijuana: Gearing Up For the Battle to Decriminalize All Drugs" (June 20, 2013) Huffington Post.

5. Conor Friedersdorf "America Has A Black-Market Problem, Not A Drug Problem" (Mar. 17, 2014) *The Atlantic*.

6. The Economist "How To Stop The Drug Wars" (May 5, 2009) *The Economist*.

Eugene Robinson "Philip Seymour Hoffman's death shows that we're losing this drug war" (Feb. 3, 2014) The *Washington Post*.

7. Doug Bandow "End The Drug War: The American People Are Not the Enemy" (Mar. 3, 2014) *Cato Institute.*

David Godow "Are Sin Taxes on Marijuana a Price Worth Paying for Reform?" (Oct. 13, 2010) *Reason Foundation.*

"Paternalism" Mercatus Center (Mar. 31, 2015).

8. Jeffrey A. Miron and Katherine Waldock "The Budgetary Impact Of Ending Drug Prohibition" (2010) *The Cato Institute.*

9. The National Center on Addiction and Substance Abuse at Columbia University "Behind Bars II: Substance Abuse and America's Prison Population" (Feb. 2010).

10. Office of National Drug Control Policy Executive Office of the President "Arrestee Drug Abuse Monitoring II 2012 Annual Report".

11. The National Center on Addiction and Substance Abuse at Columbia University "Behind Bars: Substance Abuse and America's Prison Population" (Jan. 1998).

The National Center on Addiction and Substance Abuse at Columbia University "Behind Bars II: Substance Abuse and America's Prison Population" (Feb. 2010).

12. Childhelp "Child Abuse Statistics & Facts" (2014) *childhelp.org*

Caroline Wolf Harlow "Prior Abuse Reported by Inmates and Probationers" (April 1999) NCJ 172879 *Bureau of Justice Statistics.*

13. Jason Ryan (ABC News) "Gangs Blamed For 80 Percent of U.S. Crimes" (Jan. 30, 2009) *ABC News.*

14. M.H. Swahn et al. "Alcohol and drug use among gang members: experiences of adolescents who attend school" (July 2010) *Journal of School Health.*

National Gang Center "Frequently Asked Questions" (2014) *nationalgangcenter.gov*

M.H. Swahn et al. "Alcohol and drug use among gang members: experiences of adolescents who attend school" (July 2010) *Journal of School Health.*

15. Joseph A. Califano, Jr. "High Society: How Substance Abuse Ravages America And What To Do About It" (Nov. 1, 2008) The National Center on Addiction and Substance Abuse at Columbia University.

16. Minnesota Advocates for Human Rights "Alcohol And Domestic Violence" (2014).

17. Daniel Brookoff, M.D., PhD "Drugs, Alcohol And Domestic Violence In Memphis" (Oct. 1997) National Institute of Justice.

18. "Buddy T." (Alcoholism Expert) "What Are The Costs of Drug Abuse to Society?" (Feb. 28, 2014) *alcoholism.about.com*

19. H. Richard Lamb, M.D., Frederic I. Kass, M.D. and Leona L. Bachrach, PhD (Eds.) (1992) *Treating The Homeless Mentally Ill American Psychiatric Publishing.*

20. Ibid.

21. Legal Action Center "Making Welfare Reform Work" (Sept. 1997) *lac.org*

22. Kristen W. Springer et al. "Long-term physical and mental health consequences of childhood physical abuse: Results from a large population-based sample of men and women" (May 2007) *Child Abuse & Neglect.*

    D.A. Drossman et al. "Sexual and physical abuse in women with functional or organic gastrointestinal disorders" (Dec. 1990) *Annals of Internal Medicine.*

23. S. Zierler et al. "Adult survivors of childhood sexual abuse and subsequent risk of HIV infection" (May 1991) *American Journal of Public Health.*

24. R.F. Anda et al. "Abused boys, battered mothers, and male involvement in teen pregnancy" (Feb. 2001) *Pediatrics.*

25. Joseph A. Califano Jr. (Letter to the Editor) "Alcohol, Drugs and Abortion" (May 25, 2007) *The New York Times.*

26. S.C. Martino et al. "Exploring the link between substance abuse and abortion: the roles of unconventionality and unplanned pregnancy" (June 2006) *Perspectives on Sexual and Reproductive Health.*

27. Sarah C.M. Roberts et al. "Alcohol, Tobacco and Drug Use as Reasons for Abortion" (Aug. 22, 2012) *Alcohol and Alcoholism.*

28. N.P. Medora et al. "Variables related to romanticism and self-esteem in pregnant teenagers" (Spring 1993) *Adolescence.*

29. Substance Abuse and Mental Health Services Administration "The NSDUH Report: HIV/AIDS and Substance Use" (Dec. 1, 2010) *samhsa.gov.*

30. Mary Ellen Mackesy-Amiti et al. "Symptoms of substance dependence and risky sexual behavior in a probability sample of HIV negative men who have had sex with men in Chicago" (July 1, 2010) *Drug and Alcohol Dependence.*

31. M.H. Silbert et al. "Substance abuse and prostitution" (July-Sept. 1982) *Journal of Pyschoactive Drugs.*

32. Sharna Olfman (editor) "The Sexualization of Childhood" ABC-CLIO 2009 page 158. Or, page 158

33. Annalyn Kurtz "1 in 6 unemployed are substance abusers" (Nov. 26, 2013) *CNN Money.*

34. D. Henkel "Unemployment and substance use: a review of the literature (1990-2010)" (Mar. 2011) *Current Drug Abuse Reviews.*

35. J.W. Bray et al. "The relationship between marijuana initiation and dropping out of high school" (Jan. 2000) *Health Economics.*

36. Christopher Ingraham "Study: Teens who smoke weed daily are 60% less likely to complete high school than those who never use" (Sept. 9, 2014) *The Washington Post.*

37. Substance Abuse and Mental Health Services Administration (Feb. 14, 2013) "12th grade dropouts have higher rates of cigarette, alcohol and illicit drug use" (Press release).

38. Paul R. Amato and Denise Previti "People's Reasons For Divorcing: Gender, Social Class, The Life Course and Adjustment" (July 2003) *Journal of Family Issues.*

39. DeNavas-Walt, C., Proctor, B.D., & Smith, J.C. (Sept. 2010). "Income, Poverty, and Health Insurance Coverage in the United States: 2009." *Current Population Reports – Consumer Income.* Washington, DC: U.S. Government Printing Office.

40. Hon. A. Ellen White and Craig M. Burshem "Problem Solving for Support Enforcement: Virginia's Intensive Case Monitoring Program" (2012) *National Center for State Courts.*

41. Child Welfare Information Gateway "Grandparents Raising Grandchildren" (2006) *childwelfare.gov*

42. American Academy of Child and Adolescent Psychiatry "Grandparents Raising Grandchildren" (Mar. 2011) *aacap.org*

Chapter 24

1. Rocky Mountain High Intensity Drug Trafficking Area "The Legalization of Marijuana in Colorado: The Impact (Vol. 2)" (Aug. 2014) *rmhidta.org*

2. Ibid.

3. Ben Markus "Marijuana public consumption tickets up 471 percent in Denver" (Nov. 14, 2014) *Colorado Public Radio.*

David Sirota "Colorado Governor Says Voters Were 'Reckless' To Legalize Marijuana" (Oct. 6, 2014) International Business Times.

4. "Marijuana Use in Colorado: Results from the Colorado Behavioral Risk Factor Surveillance System" Colorado Department of Public Health and Environment (2015).

Taylor Tyler "Marijuana Legalization in Colorado: New Numbers Hint at Increasingly Unfavorable Views" (Sept. 29, 2014) *hngn.com*

5. Ashley Michels "Study: Legalization of marijuana has not led to increased use among young adults" (Sept. 18, 2014) *FOX31 Denver.*

Rocky Mountain High Intensity Drug Trafficking Area "The Legalization of Marijuana in Colorado: The Impact (Vol. 2)" (Aug. 2014) *rmhidta.org*

6. Substance Abuse and Mental Health Services Administration "National Survey on Drug Use and Health: State Estimates of Substance Use" (2012) *nsduhweb.rti.org*

Substance Abuse and Mental Health Services Administration "National Survey on Drug Use and Health: Comparison of 2011-2012 and 2012-2013 Model-Based Prevalence Estimates (50 States and the District of Columbia)" (Dec. 10, 2014) *samhsa.gov*

7. Christoper Ingraham "Teen marijuana use falls as more states legalize" (Dec. 16, 2014) *The Washington Post.*

8. National Institute on Drug Abuse "Monitoring the Future Study: Trends in Prevalence of Various Drugs" (Jan. 13, 2015) *drugabuse.gov*

9. Peter Adamson UNICEF Innocenti Research Centre "Child Well-Being In Rich Countries: A Comparative Overview" (Apr. 2013) *The United Nations Children's Fund.*

10. Ibid.

11. Neil Swan "California Study Finds $1 Spent On Treatment Saves Taxpayers $7" (Mar./Apr. 1995) *drugabuse.gov*

12. "Monitoring the Future Survey, Overview of Findings 2013." NIDA. Dec. 2013 *drugabuse.gov*

13. *Alcoholics Anonymous* "Chapter 5: How It Works" (2014) Alcoholics Anonymous World Services Inc.

14. *Twelve Steps and Twelve Traditions* (2014) Alcoholics Anonymous World Services, Inc.

15. SMART Recovery "SMART Ideas" (2014) *trianglesmartrecovery.org*

CPSIA information can be obtained at www.ICGtesting.com
Printed in the USA
LVOW04*1045300815

452088LV00013B/132/P

APPLIED SYMBOLIC LOGIC

APPLIED SYMBOLIC LOGIC

EDWARD P. LYNCH, PE

Consulting Chemical Engineer
Fellow, A.I.Ch.E.

A Wiley-Interscience Publication

JOHN WILEY & SONS

New York · Chichester · Brisbane · Toronto

Library of Congress Cataloging in Publication Data

Lynch, Edward P   1919-
    Applied symbolic logic.

    Includes index.
      1. Chemical engineering—Mathematics.   2. Logic,
Symbolic and mathematical.   I. Title.

TP149.I96   511.3′24′02466   79-29718
ISBN 0-471-06256-1

Printed in the United States of America

10 9 8 7 6 5 4 3 2 1

ERRATA

for

Lynch: Applied Symbolic Logic

Figure 11.6.8, "Digraph for the tank filling system—two tanks only," appears opposite page 124. This figure should appear opposite page 224.

To

THE RT. REV. MSGR. JOHN J. DOYLE, Ph.D.

Professor Emeritus of Philosophy
Marian College
Indianapolis, Indiana

PREFACE

This book is intended for use primarily by chemical and mechanical engineers in the chemical process industries. It could also serve as a text at the undergraduate or graduate level for students in chemical or mechanical engineering. I hope that this presentation gives these engineers and students a basic foundation in applied symbolic logic as it relates to the real world they will encounter. For those whose milieu is electronics, computer science, telemetry, and so on, this book is completely inadequate.

It has been my experience that most chemical and mechanical engineers are blissfully unaware that such a powerful communications tool as symbolic logic exists, particularly in the graphic form of logic diagrams. The most common reaction I have heard is "Who needs it?" My answer to that is "Who needs a pocket calculator?" After all, we got along for a few thousand years without them. Yet, if someone decreed that pocket calculators were illegal, the wailing and gnashing of teeth would be awesome indeed. To a somewhat lesser extent the same thing is true of logic diagrams. Once you start using them you wonder how you ever got by without them. However, logic diagrams may be misapplied.

For this reason the basic material on set theory and propositional calculus (one form of the algebra of logic) is presented first. If the reader understands these, the probability of making errors is greatly reduced.

The logic presented here differs in many respects from the logic that would be taught as part of a course in philosophy. We are not concerned with emphasizing such things as "modus ponens," "modus tollens," "the square of opposition," whether arguments are strong or weak, and so on. The emphasis here is on the development and use of the various Boolean algebras and the concept of sequential logic as distinguished from combinational logic.

Appendix A contains exercises covering some of the topics presented. These exercises range from the very simple to the absolutely fiendish. I will leave it to the reader to find out which is which.

EDWARD P. LYNCH

Downers Grove, Illinois
January 1980

ACKNOWLEDGMENTS

Portions of this work previously appeared in *Chemical Engineering* (August 19, 1974; September 16, 1974; October 14, 1974) in the series of articles entitled "Using Boolean Algebra and Logic Diagrams," copyright © 1974. This material is reprinted by special permission of McGraw-Hill, Inc., New York, NY 10020.

The logic symbol cross-reference chart, Figure 9.1.2, is reproduced by courtesy of the ARO Corporation, Bryant, Ohio.

The quotation from Kamke given in the introduction is excerpted from *Theory of Sets* by E. Kamke (Dover, 1950) by special permission of the Dover Publishing Company, New York, NY.

Special thanks are due Dr. Gary J. Powers and Dr. Stephen A. Lapp of Carnegie Mellon University for permission to draw rather heavily on their work in fault tree analysis.

E. P. L.

CONTENTS

PART ONE   SETS, LOGIC, AND BOOLEAN ALGEBRA

1	Basic Set Theory	3
2	Set Theoretic Algebras	23
3	The Logic of Propositions	29
4	The Algebra of Logic	50
5	The Boolean Algebra of On–Off Events	59
6	Extension of the Algebra	70
7	Canonical Forms	81
8	Simplification of Boolean Functions	92

PART TWO   APPLICATIONS

9	Logic Diagrams	115
10	Analysis of Diagnostic Systems	158
11	Fault Trees	175
	References	229
	Appendix A Selected Problems	231
	Appendix B Polish Notation	237
	Appendix C Reliability Data Sources	239
	Author Index	255
	Subject Index	257

Part One

SETS, LOGIC, AND BOOLEAN ALGEBRA

ONE
BASIC SET THEORY

INTRODUCTION

One of the most basic concepts in mathematics is that of a "set" or "class." It has been argued by some mathematicians that the postulates of set theory are the only postulates in mathematics that must be accepted without proof—all of the other postulates may be reduced to these although such a reduction would be an awesome chore. From earliest times people have had at least an intuitive grasp of the concept of "class." The earliest numbering system used cardinal (natural) numbers, which indicate the number of members in a class. The positive integers are an abstraction of the cardinal numbers. It is interesting to note that one of the most ancient languages known, one still in use today, makes a definite distinction between the positive integers and the cardinal numbers. This language is Gaelic.

In this chapter a brief history of logic is presented. It is also shown how "sets" evolved from "classes." Two fundamental differences between them are the concept of the empty set and the concept of a set of dissimilar elements. The major portion of the chapter is concerned with the development of set theoretic techniques.

1.1 HISTORICAL BACKGROUND

Logic as we know it today originated with Aristotle in the fourth century B.C. This logic is referred to as "Aristotelian," "classical," "traditional," or "syllogistic," and it dominated the field until late in the nineteenth century. Megarian and Stoic logic* originated about the same time, but never attained a preeminent position. From the time of Aristotle until the nineteenth century the only notable contribution to logic was the *Summa Theologica* of St. Thomas Aquinas.

In the seventeenth century an attempt was made by Gottfried Wilhelm von Leibniz (the concurrent originator, along with Sir Isaac Newton, of the

---

*For an insight into Stoic–Megarian logic see Benson Mates, *Stoic Logic*, University of California Press, Berkeley, CA (1961)

differential and integral calculus) to reduce classical logic to symbols that would permit a mathematical approach to the subject. Leibniz' contributions were not profound enough to challenge the preeminent position of classical logic, and it was not until 1854, when George Boole published his major work *An Investigation of the Laws of Thought, on Which are Founded the Mathematical Theories of Logic and Probability*, that a viable symbolic logic was formulated.

During the nineteenth century many other contributions were made to the formulation of symbolic logic by such men as Augustus DeMorgan, John Venn, and Ernst Schröder. DeMorgan's major work, *Formal Logic, or the Calculus of Inference, Necessary and Probable*, published in 1847, predated that of George Boole; but Boole's name is associated with the algebra of logic (although this is sometimes referred to as the Boole–Schröder algebra).

One of the greatest contributions to symbolic logic is the theory of sets. In the introduction to Kamke's[1] *Theory of Sets* he states:

The theory of sets, which was founded by G. Cantor (1845–1918) and already developed by him into an admirable system, is one of the greatest creations of the human mind. In no other science is such bold formulation of concepts found, and only the theory of numbers, perhaps, contains methods of proof of comparable beauty. It is no wonder, then, that everyone who studies the theory of sets is indescribably fascinated by it. Over and above that, however, this theory has become of the very greatest importance for the whole of mathematics. It has enriched nearly every part of mathematics, and lent it a new appearance. It has given rise to new branches of mathematics, or at least first rendered possible their further development, such as the theory of sets of points, the theory of real functions, and topology. Finally, the theory of sets has had particular influence on the investigation of the foundations of mathematics, acting in this respect, as well as through the generality of its concepts, as a connecting link between mathematics and philosophy.

In 1905 E. V. Huntington[2] published a paper outlining a set of postulates for the algebra of logic. These postulates are widely used today in the construction of the various Boolean algebras.

Until 1938 symbolic logic was used only as another tool of philosophy and mathematics. In that year Claude E. Shannon[3] published a paper entitled "A Symbolic Analysis of Relay and Switching Circuits." This paper was based on Shannon's thesis presented at the Massachusetts Institute of Technology for the Master of Science degree, and it firmly established symbolic logic, in the form of Boolean algebra, as a communications tool. Since then, the design and development of digital computers, data processing systems, programmed automatic control systems, and similar complex systems has been made feasible by the in-depth application of symbolic logic.

1.2 CLASSES AND SETS

The distinction between classes and sets, if such a distinction truly exists, is a matter for disagreement among logicians and the terms are frequently used interchangeably. Roullard[4] has defined a class by saying, "A class consists of everything of one kind which exists in the Universe." Kamke[1] attributes to Cantor this definition of a set: "A collection into a whole of definite well-distinguished objects (called the 'elements' of the set) of our perception or of our thought." From these definitions a class may be considered to be one form of a set, but these definitions are by no means accepted by all logicians.

In classical logic there are two major divisions: the logic of classes and the logic of propositions. In the logic of classes the units are nouns or adjectives that are known as class or term variables. The logic of classes investigates the bearing of these variables on the meaning of arguments. The logic of propositions is quite a different matter. An explanation of what this logic consists is deferred until Chapter 3.

To classical logicians these were two disparate logics. Cantor's development of the theory of sets shows that there is a definite connection between these logics through the algebra of the conditions of sets. This connection is shown in Chapter 2.

The logic of classes was developed before the logic of propositions. Considerable effort has been expended over the centuries since the time of Aristotle on one type of argument, the categorical syllogism—so much effort in fact that this logic is frequently referred to as "syllogistic logic." The classical example of a syllogism is this:

> Socrates is a man.
>
> All men are mortal.
>
> Therefore, Socrates is mortal.

We will have more to say about syllogisms later. In particular we will show that the categorical syllogism is not quite as sacred as it once was and can be converted by some fancy semantic footwork into another type of syllogism. (This of course is considered pure heresy by classical logicians.)

In our use of logic we are not concerned with such things as "the square of opposition," "immediate inference," "mediate inference," and so on, although these are a part of the traditional approach to this logic. We are interested in developing a symbolic logic from which we can derive a valid Boolean algebra. Excellent presentations of the traditional approach are given by Johnstone,[5] and Langer.[6] Thomas[7] has stated that set theory procedures are not a part of traditional logic. This is true not only because set theory is a symbolic logic but also because it embodies certain basic concepts unheard of in traditional logic. It does however include within its scope the logic of classes, albeit in symbolic form.

1.3   THE STRUCTURE OF SETS

A set may consist of anything we wish it to consist of and may be finite or infinite. Sets are made up of elements that may or may not be similar either physically or in concept. The set of all automobiles is a finite set of physically similar elements. The set of natural numbers is an infinite set whose elements are similar in concept. The set consisting of a pencil, a collie dog, and the planet Mars is a finite set of dissimilar elements. These are all completely valid sets. Some sets, both finite and infinite, may be completely described by listing their elements. The set of natural numbers from 1 through 8 may be described by $\{1,2,3,4,5,6,7,8\}$. (It is customary to use the brace notation to isolate sets.) An element may appear more than once in any given set but it need be listed only once. The set of letters in the word Mississippi is simply $\{m,i,s,p\}$. An example of an infinite set that can be listed is {the real numbers, the complex numbers}. This of course is the set of all numbers. Here our elements are also sets but an element may be defined as a member of a set, which does not preclude sets from being members of other sets. When it is impossible or impractical to list the members of a set, we have available a technique for describing the set. Before developing this we need to develop some symbology.

Uppercase letters such as A, B, C, and so on are used to symbolize sets—sometimes specific sets, other times unspecified sets. The symbol $\in$ is used to indicate the relation of membership in a set and the symbol $\notin$ indicates nonmembership. If A is the set of natural numbers from 1 through 8, $2 \in A$ and $9 \notin A$. The symbol $\in$ is read "is an element of" and the symbol $\notin$ is read "is not an element of."

As was mentioned above, elements can in themselves be sets. If $R\#$ is the set of real numbers, then the set of rational numbers, the set of integers, the set of irrational numbers, and so on, are all elements of $R\#$. Since the most convenient, but by no means exclusive, way of representing and working with sets is with numbers, we show here the "number tree" and assign specific symbols to the various sets of numbers:

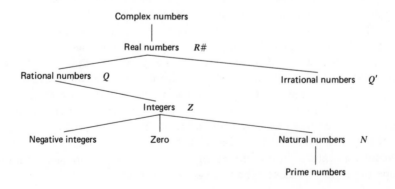

No symbols are assigned to the negative integers, zero, prime numbers, and complex numbers. For the first three of these, symbols are unnecessary. Complex numbers we ignore since they take us into fields of mathematics and set theory that are beyond the scope of this book.

A further classification of infinite sets may be made on the basis of whether or not they are enumerable. An infinite set S is enumerable if and only if it can be written as a sequence $\{s_1, s_2, s_3, \ldots\}$, that is, if and only if the mapping of the set of natural numbers, N, into the set S is a one–one and onto function. It is obvious that the set of natural numbers is enumerable. If a set is finite or enumerable it is said that it is at most enumerable. If it is neither finite nor enumerable it is designated as nonenumerable.

Georg Cantor proved the enumerability of several other infinite sets. One of these is the set of rational numbers. If we consider first the positive rational numbers we may list those with a denominator of 1, then those with a denominator of 2, and so on. This gives us the rows of numbers

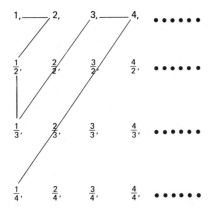

If we write down the numbers in the order of succession shown by the line drawn, leaving out numbers that have already appeared, every positive rational number will appear once and only once. Thus we have

$$1, 2, \tfrac{1}{2}, \tfrac{1}{3}, 3, 4, \tfrac{3}{2}, \tfrac{2}{3}, \tfrac{1}{4}, \ldots$$

If we denote this sequence by $s_1, s_2, s_3, s_4, \ldots$ it becomes obvious that the set of all rational numbers is

$$\{0, -s_1, s_1, -s_2, s_2, -s_3, s_3, \ldots\}$$

and that this set is enumerable. For other examples of such sets refer to Kamke.[1]

If A and B are sets such that every element of A is also an element of B, then A is included in B, that is, A is a subset of B. This is shown symbolically as $A \subset B$ which is read as "A is a subset of B" or as "A is properly included in B," which means that A is a proper subset of B. If $A = B$ then A is an improper subset of B and B is an improper subset of A. This is shown as $A \subseteq B$ and $B \subseteq A$. For our purpose this is relatively unimportant and we shall use the symbol $\subset$ to indicate both proper and improper subsets. A word of caution is needed here. The fact that two (or more) sets may be equal does not necessarily mean that they are identical. If A is the set $\{2,3,9\}$ and B is the set $\{2,3,9\}$, $A = B$ but A is not identical with B if A represents the set of digits in the telephone number 223-3299 and B represents the set of digits in the telephone number 299-2323. In passing, we must mention superset notation. This is shown as $B \supset A$ and is read as "B properly includes A." This notation is rarely encountered and its use should be discouraged since the same symbol is used by some authors to indicate implication between propositions.

Every set is considered to be a subset of itself and is by definition the only improper subset of itself. One set of particular interest is the "Universe set," sometimes referred to as the "Universal set." By strict definition this set contains everything that exists in the Universe. For our purposes this is much too broad a classification. If we are working with the set of natural numbers we have no interest in a Universe that contains such things as the set of one-eyed cats in Bangkok. Therefore we will omit the capital letter and assume "a universe of discourse" and define the universe set as the set of all things that are contained in that universe. The symbol used for the universe set is $\mathscr{U}$. For sets where the elements are natural numbers we could choose $\mathscr{U}$ as the set of all natural numbers (N), the set of positive integers (Z), or the set of real numbers ($R\#$).*

One other special set must be considered. This is the "null" or "empty" set whose symbol is $\{\ \}$ or $\varnothing$. Note that the set $\{0\}$ is not the empty set. It contains one element, the number zero. The empty set has no elements. According to Christian[8] the empty set is a "convenient fiction, like the number zero." This set is of great importance in set theory and is considered to be a subset of every set and, in particular, is a subset of itself. It is interesting to note that the concept of the empty set was unknown in traditional logic. However, the number zero was unknown in the Roman numeral system. The introduction of the concept of the empty set is as important to set theoretic computations as the introduction of the number zero is to mathematical computations.

---

*We use the symbol $R\#$ for the set of real numbers because R is reserved as the symbol for relationship.

With the empty set defined we may now define the "power set." We have said that every set is a subset of itself and that the empty set is a subset of every set. If we consider the set $M = \{a,b\}$ the possible subsets are $\{a,b\}$, $\{a\}$, $\{b\}$, and $\varnothing$. For the set $S = \{x,y,z\}$ the subsets are $\{x,y,z\}$, $\{x\}$, $\{y\}$, $\{z\}$, $\{x,y\}$, $\{x,z\}$, $\{y,z\}$, and $\varnothing$. It is evident that the number of possible subsets is 2^n where n is the number of elements in the set. For the set M we have $2^2 = 4$ subsets and for the set S we have $2^3 = 8$ subsets. If we let A be any set with n elements, the set of all subsets of A (which will number 2^n) is known as the "power set" of A and is denoted as 2^A. As the number of elements in a set increases the power set can become very large.

1.4 THE SET BUILDER

Every element of a set must satisfy a condition—the condition of being a member of the set. In sets of dissimilar elements this may be the only thing they have in common and all of the elements must be listed to describe the set. For sets of similar elements it is usually possible to ascribe some attribute to the element that assures it of inclusion. This is known as the "set-builder technique." If p is a given condition (or attribute) and x is a general term describing any element of a given set, we may designate $p(x)$ as an abbreviation for the statement "x satisfies the condition p." Given a set A and a condition p, the set of all things that satisfy this condition and are therefore elements of A is shown by

$$\{x \in A \,|\, p(x)\}$$

This is read as "the set of all elements x of A for which $p(x)$ is true." This is called the "truth set" in A of the condition p. The symbol $\{\,|\,\}$ is called the set builder. Some examples of the use of the set builder are:

Example 1.4.1 Consider the universe set and let p be the condition that x is blue. Then

$$\{x \in \mathfrak{U} \,|\, p(x)\}$$

completely describes the set of all blue things in the universe of discourse.

Example 1.4.2 Consider the set N and let p be the condition that x is a prime number less than 10. Then

$$\{x \in N \,|\, p(x)\}$$

completely describes the set $\{1,2,3,5,7\}$.*

---

*There is some controversy over whether or not 1 is a prime number. It depends on the book you read.

Example 1.4.3 In the set N, if p is the condition that "$x = 2^n$ where n is all of the elements of N taken successively in ascending order," then

$$\{x \in N \,|\, p(x)\}$$

describes the infinite set $\{2, 4, 8, 16, 32, \ldots, 2^n\}$.

Where it is convenient to do so $p(x)$ is made specific in the set builder. In Example 1.4.3 it is not convenient to do so. The set builder could be shown as $\{x \in N \,|\, x = 2^n\}$ but an explanation of n would still be required. It is convenient, however, in:

Example 1.4.4 In the set N let $p(x)$ be "x is less than 8." Then

$$\{x \in N \,|\, x < 8\} = \{1, 2, 3, 4, 5, 6, 7\}$$

Example 1.4.5 In the set Z let $p(x)$ be "$2x = 8$." Then

$$\{x \in Z \,|\, 2x = 8\} = \{4\}$$

Example 1.4.6 In the set Z let $p(x)$ be "$x = (25)^{1/2}$." Then

$$\{x \in Z \,|\, x = (25)^{1/2}\} = \{-5, 5\}$$

The set builder may determine the empty set.

Example 1.4.7 In the set of natural numbers let $M = \{1, 2, 3\}$ and $p(x)$ be $x = 5$. Then

$$\{x \in M \,|\, x = 5\} = \varnothing$$

In all of these examples $p(x)$ defines a condition that x must fulfill. The expression $p(x)$ can become abiguous if p is a proposition instead of a condition. (We will have more to say about this in subsequent sections.) If C is the set of all states of the United States of America and $p(x)$ reads "x is the easternmost state," then $\{x \in C \,|\, p(x)\} = \{\text{Maine}\}$, or is it $\{\text{Alaska}\}$? This depends upon the point of reference. If this point is Chicago then $\{\text{Maine}\}$ is the correct answer. If the reference point is the zero meridian, which passes through Greenwich, England, then $\{\text{Alaska}\}$ is the correct answer since the 180th degree meridian passes through the Aleutian Islands.* Propositions are subject to change but conditions are invariant. Ambiguities can and do arise when propositions are accepted as conditions. Such ambiguities frequently arise in mathematics but are tolerated for convenience.

*This also makes Alaska the westernmost state. It is also the northernmost. Three out of four isn't bad!

We have shown that a condition completely determines its truth set. However, more than one condition may determine the same truth set. In the set N the conditions $p(x$ is odd) and $q(x$ is the sum of two consecutive numbers) define the same truth set—the set of odd natural numbers. When two conditions describe the same truth set they are said to be equivalent and are shown as $p \Leftrightarrow q$. This symbology is identical to that we encounter in the logic of propositions. The reader by now should be aware that there is a very definite connection between set theory and the logic of propositions. This connection is through the logic of conditions of sets and will be developed later.

1.5 QUANTIFIERS

Any word or expression involving the idea of "how many" is called a quantifier. The most common of these quantifiers involve the words "all" or "some." The universal quantifiers are "all," "for every," "for all," and so on. A standard example involving a universal quantifier is a condition from our familiar syllogisim: "All men are mortal." This is a condition applied to the set (or class) of men—namely that men are mortal. If M is the set of all men, then

$$\{x \in M \,|\, q(x)\} \qquad \text{or} \qquad \{x \in M \,|\, x \text{ is mortal}\}$$

defines the truth set Q of $q(x)$ in M. However, the truth set Q and the set M are in this case equal. When this occurs we have a universally quantified set builder, which is usually shown as

$$(\forall x \in M)q(x)$$

and is read "for all $x, q(x)$." Numerous examples of universal quantifiers can be cited from ordinary algebra using a function with one variable. One of these is:

Example 1.5.1 Let $R\#$ denote the set of real numbers and $p(x)$ denote $(x+2)(x-2)=x^2-4$. The truth set for $p(x)$ is the entire set of real numbers so

$$(\forall x \in R\#)p(x)$$

The other type of quantifier we use is the existential quantifier. Words or expressions involving "some" used in the sense of "there is at least one" are this type of quantifier. The existential quantifier assures that a truth set is not empty, that is, if we have a set M and a condition $p(x)$, at least one $x \in M$ satisfies the condition $p(x)$. If P is the truth set for $p(x)$ in M,

$$P = \{x \in M \,|\, p(x)\} \neq \varnothing$$

This is usually written as

$$(\exists x \in M)p(x)$$

and is read "for at least one x, $p(x)$." Here again numerous examples could be taken from ordinary algebra. One of these is:

Example 1.5.2 Let N denote the set of natural numbers and $q(x)$ denote $nx - (n-1) = x^2$. The truth set Q in N is

$$Q = \{x \in N \,|\, nx - (n-1) = x^2\} = \{1, n-1\}$$

Since $\{1, n-1\} \neq \varnothing$,

$$(\exists x \in N)q(x)$$

1.6 BASIC OPERATIONS WITH SETS

Sets may be combined in two different ways. If the sets $\{2,4,6,8,10\}$ and $\{1,2,3,4,5\}$ are combined to give only those elements that are common to both sets, the resulting set is $\{2,4\}$. This operation is known as "intersection" and the symbol used for it is $\cap$. Intersection may be visualized easily through the use of a Venn diagram (sometimes called a Venn–Euler diagram). If we let A represent the set $\{2,4,6,8,10\}$, B the set $\{1,2,3,4,5\}$, and C the set $\{2,4\}$, the intersection of A and B is represented diagrammatically by Figure 1.6.1. In this diagram the circles represent the sets A and B, the shaded area represents set C, and the rectangle represents the universe of discourse.

If sets A and B are combined to give all of the elements in both sets the resulting set is $\{1,2,3,4,5,6,8,10\}$, which we will denote as set D. This operation is known as "union" and the symbol used for it is $\cup$. The union of sets A and B is shown in Figure 1.6.2. The shaded area there represents the set D.

The third and last basic operation with sets is that of complementation. The complement of set A is everything in the universe of discourse that is not included in set A. The complement of set A is denoted as "not A" and is symbolized variously as $\sim A$, $-A$, $\overline{A}$, and A'. This is shown on a Venn diagram in Figure 1.6.3, where the shaded area is A'.

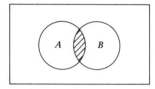

Figure 1.6.1 Venn diagram for intersection of sets: $A \cap B$ $= C$ or $\{2,4,6,8,10\} \cap \{1,2,3,4,5\} = \{2,4\}$.

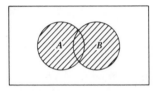

Figure 1.6.2 Venn diagram for union of sets: $A \cup B = D$ or $\{2,4,6,8,10\} \cup \{1,2,3,4,5\} = \{1,2,3,4,5,6,8,10\}$.

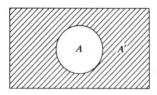

Figure 1.6.3 Venn diagram for complementation.

We may of course have more than two sets involved in an operation and may show the results on a Venn diagram. The intersection of A, B, and C would be as shown in Figure 1.6.4. We may also have various combinations of operations that, when combined with a multiplicity of sets, can make diagramming an awesome chore. The Venn diagram for $(A \cap B) \cup (C \cap D') \cap (E \cap F)' = G$ would be formidable indeed. There are, however, other situations that should be illustrated with Venn diagrams. If we have the sets $A = \{1,2,3\}$ and $B = \{7,8,9\}$, then $A \cap B = \varnothing$. In this case A and B are "disjoint sets"; the Venn diagram is shown in Figure 1.6.5. It should be noted that although $A \cap B = \varnothing$, $A \cup B \neq \varnothing$. It is somewhat pointless to show this on a Venn diagram. Thomas[7] has devised a method for showing the empty set on a Venn diagram but this is not necessary for our purposes.

Two other common operations with sets are "difference" and "symmetric difference." These are not basic operations because they can be

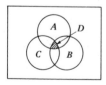

Figure 1.6.4 Ven diagram for multiple intersection: $A \cap B \cap C = D$.

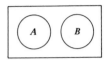

Figure 1.6.5 Venn diagram for disjoint sets: $A \cap B = \emptyset$.

presented in terms of the three basic operations. The "difference" of sets A and B is the set of all elements that belong to A but not to B. This is denoted as $A - B$ and is defined precisely as $A - B = \{x \mid x \in A, x \notin B\}$. The Venn diagram for this is shown in Figure 1.6.6. This is also known as the "relative complement" and may be shown in terms of the basic operations as $A \cap B'$.

The symmetric difference of two sets A and B is denoted as $A \Delta B$ and is defined as $(A \cup B) - (A \cap B)$. The Venn diagram for this is shown in Figure 1.6.7. This may be shown in terms of the basic operations as

$$(A \cup B) \cap (A \cap B)'$$

This is quite similar in form to one version of the "exclusive or" encountered later.

All of these operations have simple properties when applied to comparable sets, that is, sets where one is a proper subset of another. If $X \subset Y$ we have these theorems, all of which can be proved.

Theorem 1.6.1

$$X \subset Y \rightarrow X \cap Y = X$$

The Venn diagram for this is shown in Figure 1.6.8.

Theorem 1.6.2

$$X \subset Y \rightarrow X \cup Y = Y$$

The Venn diagram for this is shown in Figure 1.6.9.

Theorem 1.6.3

$$X \subset Y \rightarrow Y' \subset X'$$

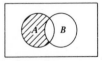

Figure 1.6.6 Venn diagram for difference of sets: $A - B$ is shaded.

Figure 1.6.7 Venn diagram for symmetric difference: $A \triangle B$ is shaded.

Figure 1.6.8 Venn diagram for Theorem 1.6.1: $X \cap Y$ is shaded.

Figure 1.6.9 Venn diagram for Theorem 1.6.2: $X \cup Y$ is shaded.

We will illustrate this with two Venn diagrams, Figures 1.6.10 and 1.6.11. From inspection of these diagrams it is seen that $Y' \subset X'$.

Theorem 1.6.4

$$X \subset Y \rightarrow X \cup (Y - X) = Y$$

It was previously shown that $Y - X = Y \cap X'$. The Venn diagram for $Y \cap X'$ is shown in Figure 1.6.12. From this it should be obvious that $X \cup (Y \cap X') = Y$.

Figure 1.6.10 Venn diagram for Theorem 1.6.3—Y' only: Y' is shaded.

Figure 1.6.11 Venn diagram for Theorem 1.6.3—X' only: X' is shaded.

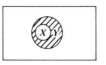

Figure 1.6.12 Venn diagram for difference of set and subset: $Y \cap X'$ is shaded.

1.7 INDEXED SETS

We have stated that the elements of sets may in themselves be sets. Although the superset is sometimes called a set of sets it is usually known as a family of sets. Consider the set $A = \{1,2,3,4,5,6,7,8,9\}$. This could be written as $A = \{\{1,7,10\}, \{4,5,7,9\}, \{3,6,9\}, \{2,4,8,10\}, \{4,9\}\}$. A now represents a family of sets. We may represent the sets in this family as

$$A_1 = \{1,7,10\} \qquad A_4 = \{2,4,8,10\}$$
$$A_2 = \{4,5,7,9\} \qquad A_5 = \{4,9\}$$
$$A_3 = \{3,6,9\}$$

The family may now be shown as $A = \{A_1, A_2, A_3, A_4, A_5\}$. The subscripts are called indexes (or indices) and the set $I = \{1,2,3,4,5\}$ is the index set. The sets A_1, A_2, A_3, A_4, A_5 are known as indexed sets. If i stands for any of the indices, $i \in I$, the entire indexed family of sets is denoted by $\{A_i\}_{i \in I}$.

We have already defined the operations of union and intersection for two sets. Through the use of indexed sets we may extend these operations to an infinite number of sets. If we let $I = N =$ the set of natural numbers, we have

$$\{B_i\}_{i \in I} = \{B_1, B_2, B_3, B_4, \ldots, B_n\}$$

and

$$\cup_{i \in I} B_i = B_i \cup B_2 \cup B_3 \cup B_4 \ldots B_n$$

also

$$\cap_{i \in I} B_i = B_1 \cap B_2 \cap B_3 \cap B_4 \ldots B_n$$

where $=$ means "by definition." Since $\cup$ and $\cap$ are both associative operations, which will be shown later, the union or intersection of the sets may be taken in any order and parentheses are not required.

In the above family of sets consider A_2, A_4, and A_5. The index numbers for these sets are obviously 2, 4, and 5. We may call this set of index numbers anything we please, so let's call it J. Then $J = \{2,4,5\}$ and since $\{2,4,5\}$ is a subset of the index set $\{1,2,3,4,5\}$, J is a subset of I. Since subsets may be considered as elements we may say that J is an element of I. In symbolic notation what we have said is

$$\{2,4,5\} \subset \{1,2,3,4,5\}$$
$$J \subset I$$
$$J \in I$$

Now, if i is any of the index numbers of the family of sets, we wish to know what results from the union and from the intersection of all sets where the index number is one of the numbers appearing in the set J. The union is $A_2 \cup A_4 \cup A_5$. This is equal to $\{4,5,7,9\} \cup \{2,4,8,10\} \cup \{4,9\} = \{2,4,5,7,9,8,10\}$. The short notation for this is $\cup_{i \in J} A_i$. The intersection is $A_2 \cap A_4 \cap A_5 = \{4,5,7,9\} \cap \{2,4,8,10\} \cap \{4,9\} = \{4\}$. The short notation for this is $\cap_{i \in J} A_i$. This procedure is summarized in:

Example 1.6.1 Let

$$
\begin{aligned}
P_1 &= \{a,c\} & P_4 &= \{g\} \\
P_2 &= \{d,e,f\} & P_5 &= \{b,h\} \\
P_3 &= \{a,b,c,d\} & P_6 &= \{b,c,f\}
\end{aligned}
$$

Then $I = \{1,2,3,4,5,6\}$. Let $j \in I = \{3,5,6\}$. Then

$$\cup_{i \in j} P_i = P_3 \cup P_5 \cup P_6 = \{a,b,c,d,f,h\}$$

and

$$\cap_{i \in j} P_i = P_3 \cap P_5 \cap P_6 = \{b\}$$

1.8 PARTITIONS OF SETS

We frequently encounter sets that naturally divide or partition into two or more sets. The set of all human beings, H, divides into the set of all males, M, and the set of all females, F. The set of chessmen in a chess match divides into the set of white chessmen, W, and the set of black chessmen, B. The set of natural numbers, N, divides into the set of even numbers, E, and the set of odd numbers, D. All of these sets have two things in common—the union of the partial sets gives the partitioned set and the intersection of the partial sets gives the empty set. We have

$$
\begin{aligned}
M \cup F &= H & M \cap F &= \varnothing \\
W \cup B &= C & W \cap B &= \varnothing \\
E \cup D &= N & E \cap D &= \varnothing
\end{aligned}
$$

The partition of a set may give more than two partial sets and these may or may not have the same number of members. It is also not necessary that the intersection of the partial sets give the empty set. Consider the set $A = \{a,c,e,h,k,l,m,n,o,r,s,t,w\}$ and let y_1, y_2, y_3, and y_4 be respectively the words "settle," "whom," "crank," and "lest." Define $P_i = \{x | x \text{ is a}$

letter in the word y_i}. Then $\{P_1, P_2, P_3, P_4\}$ is a partition of A. The partial sets are

$$P_1 = \{s, e, t, t, l, e\} = \{s, e, t, l\}$$
$$P_2 = \{w, h, o, m\}$$
$$P_3 = \{c, r, a, n, k\}$$
$$P_4 = \{l, e, s, t\}$$

and

$$P_1 \cup P_2 \cup P_3 \cup P_4 = A$$

The possible intersections are

$$
\begin{array}{ll}
P_1 \cap P_2 = \varnothing & P_2 \cap P_3 = \varnothing \\
P_1 \cap P_3 = \varnothing & P_2 \cap P_4 = \varnothing \\
P_1 \cap P_4 = P_1 = P_4 & P_3 \cap P_4 = \varnothing
\end{array}
$$

Since $P_1 = P_4$ we may eliminate one of them in $\{P_1, P_2, P_3, P_4\}$ to give either $\{P_1, P_2, P_3\}$ or $\{P_2, P_3, P_4\}$. Using $\{P_1, P_2, P_3\}$ we have $P_1 \cup P_2 \cup P_3 = A$, $P_1 \cap P_2 = \varnothing$, $P_1 \cap P_3 = \varnothing$, and $P_2 \cap P_3 = \varnothing$. This proves that $\{P_i\}_{i \in y_i}$, which is another way of saying the set $\{P_1, P_2, P_3, P_4\}$ is a partition of A.

We may now illustrate the concept of partition by this example.

Example 1.8.1 Let β be a family of nonempty subsets of A so that $\beta = \{B_1, B_2, B_3, B_4\}$, and let $A = B_1 \cup B_2 \cup B_3 \cup B_4$. If for any sets B_i, B_j either $B_i \cap B_j = \varnothing$ or $B_i = B_j$, then β is a partition of A.

We may define a partition exactly by using the concept of indexed sets.

Definition 1.8.1 If $\{P_i\}_{i \in I}$ is a nonempty family of subsets of A and if $\cup_{i \in I} P_i = A$ and for any P_i, P_j either $P_i \cap P_j = \varnothing$ or $P_i = P_j$, then $\{P_i\}_{i \in I}$ is a partition of A. Also, each P_i is called an equivalence class of A.

1.9   EQUIVALENCE RELATIONS AND PARTITIONS

The customary symbol for a relation is R. So far we have avoided using this symbol, even to the extent of using $R \#$ to symbolize the real numbers. An excellent presentation of relations and functions has been given by Lipschutz[9]. Here we present only the absolute minimum necessary to define "relation" and will studiously ignore "function." The theory of functions, which is based on the theory of sets, is a vast and mind-boggling branch of mathematics in itself.

Defining an equivalence relation presents difficulties in a work such as this which gives a very elementary introduction to set theory and has not even touched on relations and functions. It would not even be attempted if it were not necessary to lay the foundation for one method of the reduction of Boolean functions, which is covered in Chapter 8. Certain statements must be accepted without proof since we have not developed the background necessary to prove them. We call these statements "definitions" with the understanding that they are defined here in a very narrow and limited sense.

Definition 1.9.1 The product set, $A \times B$, is the familiar Cartesian plane, that is, the rectangular coordinates we usually refer to as the x, y coordinates. The product set may be referred to as $A \times A$, $B \times B$, and so on if the range of x equals the range of y.

Definition 1.9.2 An ordered pair is a set of two elements, say a and b, in which one of them, say a, is designated as the first element and the other as the second. By this definition $\{a,b\} \neq \{b,a\}$. In the Cartesian plane $(2,3)$ and $(3,2)$ are not the same point.

Definition 1.9.3 A propositional function defined on the product set $A \times B$ is an expression denoted by $P(x,y)$ that has the property that $P(a,b)$, where a and b are constants substituted for the variables x and y respectively in $P(x,y)$, is true or false for any ordered pair $(a,b) \in (A \times B)$. $P(x,y)$ is called an open sentence in two variables, or, more simply, an open sentence. (Note that product sets and ordered pairs are not usually isolated by braces.) Some examples of open sentences are

$$x \text{ is more than } y.$$
$$x \text{ divides } y.$$
$$x \text{ is the husband of } y.$$
$$x^2 + y^2 = 25.$$

Definition 1.9.4 A relation R consists of:

1. A set A.
2. A set B.
3. An open sentence $P(x,y)$ that may be true or false for any $(a,b) \in (A \times B)$.

Definition 1.9.5 A relation R is reflexive if $R = [A, A, P(x,y)]$, that is, if R is a relationship in the set $A \times A$, and if, for every $a \in A$, $(a,a) \in R$.

Example 1.9.1 If B is a family of sets and $P(x,y)$ is "x is a subset of y," then $R = [B, B, P(a,a)]$ is reflexive since every set is a subset of itself.

Example 1.9.2 If T is the set of triangles in the Cartesian plane $A \times A$ and $P(x,y)$ is "x is similar to y," then $R = [A,A,P(t,t)]$ is reflexive since every triangle is similar to itself.

Example 1.9.3 If N is the set of natural numbers and $P(x,y)$ is "x is less than y," then $R = [N,N,P(a,a)]$ is not reflexive since $a \not< a$ for any natural number.

Definition 1.9.6 If $R \subset (A \times A)$ and $(a,b) \in R \rightarrow (b,a) \in R$, then R is symmetric.

Definition 1.9.7 If $R \subset (A \times A)$ and $[(a,b) \in R$ and $(b,a) \in R] \rightarrow (a,c) \in R$, then R is transitive.

We may now define an equivalence relation.

Definition 1.9.8 Let A be a product set (unspecified) and R be a relation in that set. Then, if R is reflexive, symmetric, and transitive, it is an equivalence relation in A.

The fundamental theorem on equivalence relations follows.

Theorem 1.9.1

If R is an equivalence relation in set A and for every $a \in A$, $B_a = \{X | (x,a) \in R\}$, then $\{B_a\}_{a \in A}$ is a partition of A. This may also be denoted by A/R, which is called the quotient set.

As an example of this, consider the set of ordered pairs of real numbers, $R\# \times R\#$, and let the ordered pairs (x,y) and (z,w) be any elements of this set. [This does not preclude (x,y) and (z,w) from being the same ordered pair but we shall assume they are not.] Let R be an equivalence relation such that (x,y) is related to (z,w) if and only if $xw = zy$. Since R is by definition reflexive, symmetric, and transitive, the ordered pairs (x,y) and (z,w) exhibit this relation if and only if $x/y = z/w$. This is the familiar relation that establishes the equality of fractions. This partitions the set $R\#$ into the set of equal fractions and the set of unequal fractions. It also partitions it into the set of rational numbers and the set of irrational numbers since only rational numbers may be expressed as fractions.

The converse of Theorem 1.9.1 is:

Theorem 1.9.2

Let $\{P_i\}_{i \in I}$ be a partition of A and let R be the relation "x is in the same set (of the family $\{P_i\}_{i \in I}$) as y." Then R is an equivalence relation in A.

There is a one to one correspondence between all partitions of a set and all equivalence relations in the set.

Example 1.9.4 Similarity of triangles is an equivalence relation. In the Cartesian plane $A \times B$ the set of all triangles is partitioned into disjoint sets of similar triangles.

Example 1.9.5 In the set of integers one relation, which we shall call $R3$, is $x = y \pmod 3$, which is read as "x is congruent to y modulo 3." This means that $x - y$ is divisible by 3. Consider the subset of Z, $\{-6, -5, -4, -3, -2, -1, 0, 1, 2, 3, 4, 5, 6\}$. If each element is divided by 3 we have

$$
\begin{array}{ll}
-6/3 = -2 + 0 & \text{remainder} \\
-5/3 = -2 + 1 & '' \\
-4/3 = -2 + 2 & '' \\
-3/3 = -1 + 0 & '' \\
-2/3 = -1 + 1 & '' \\
-1/3 = -1 + 2 & '' \\
0/3 = 0 + 0 & '' \\
1/3 = 0 + 1 & '' \\
2/3 = 0 + 2 & '' \\
3/3 = 1 + 0 & '' \\
4/3 = 1 + 1 & '' \\
5/3 = 1 + 2 & '' \\
6/3 = 2 + 0 & '' \\
\end{array}
$$

It is apparent that $R3$ partitions the integers into three distinct classes: a class where the remainder is 0, a class where the remainder is 1, and a class where the remainder is 2. The remainder classes, whose general designation may be given as C_R, are called "residue" classes and may be shown as

$$
\begin{aligned}
C_0 &= \{\ldots, -6, -3, 0, 3, 6, \ldots\} \\
C_1 &= \{\ldots, -5, -2, 1, 3, \ldots\} \\
C_2 &= \{\ldots, -4, -1, 2, 5, \ldots\}
\end{aligned}
$$

This is a true partition since $C_0 \cup C_1 \cup C_2 = Z$ and $C_0 \cap C_1 \cap C_2 = \varnothing$. $R3$ is reflexive, symmetric, and transitive so it is an equivalence relation and C_0, C_1, and C_2 are equivalence classes. The quotient set is $Z/R = \{C_0, C_1, C_2\}$.

The modulo relation is very important and is frequently encountered in various branches of mathematics.

SUMMARY

Although set theory finds great use in purely mathematical applications, it is of equal value in describing the relationships between physical objects. We are concerned with sets of valves, sets of switches, and so on, and we frequently partition these sets although we may not think of it as such at the time. A knowledge of the basic operations with sets as well as techniques such as partitioning, indexing, and so on can be of great value in analyzing a complex physical network. In the next chapter we develop the set theoretic algebras, particularly the algebra of conditions, and show that these are Boolean algebras.

TWO
SET THEORETIC ALGEBRAS

INTRODUCTION

At the risk of incurring the wrath of many mathematicians, I shall state that set theory is not a branch of mathematics. It is a bridge between philosophy and mathematics. The same may be said of propositional calculus (the algebra of logic). As we proceed you will see that the algebras we develop are homomorphous but based on different philosophical concepts. Two such algebras are presented here—the algebra of conditions of sets and the algebra of sets. They are presented in that order because the latter may be derived from the former. It may seem odd that the actual derivation of the laws of the algebra of conditions of sets is deferred until we develop the laws of the algebra of propositions in Chapter 4. The reason for this will become evident.

The algebra of sets, while useful in itself, is not of great value in the applications we consider. The algebra of conditions of sets, however, is of great value in that it serves as a bridge between set theory and the logic of propositions. In actual applications it is supplanted by other algebras, particularly the algebra of on–off events.

2.1 CONDITIONS OF SETS

In Chapter 1 we defined a condition as being a statement $p(x)$ involving an unspecified term x. The symbol $p(x)$ stands for the statement "x satisfies the condition p." The relation of equivalence of conditions corresponds to that of equality of sets. Other relations between sets also hold between conditions. If A and B are subsets of $\mathfrak{U}$ and $A \subset B$, then every element of A belongs to B, that is, if $x \in A$, then $x \in B$. The relation of inclusion between sets is an "if...then" relation between conditions, which is a relation of implication. A condition p implies a condition q if the truth set of p is a subset of the truth set of q, that is, if

$$\{x \in \mathfrak{U} \,|\, p(x)\} \subset \{x \in \mathfrak{U} \,|\, q(x)\}$$

This is a precise definition of one kind of implication—implication between conditions—and applies only to that one kind. This is symbolized as $p \Rightarrow q$ or $q \Leftarrow p$. If P is the truth set of the condition p and Q is the truth set of the condition q, then $P = Q$ whenever $P \subset Q$ and $Q \subset P$. Therefore $p \Leftrightarrow q$ whenever $p \Rightarrow q$ and $q \Rightarrow p$. The relation $p \Leftrightarrow q$ is expressed by "p if and only if q." Also, if A is the truth set of condition a, then $A \subset D$ whenever $A \subset B$ and $B \subset D$ so if $a \Rightarrow b$ and $b \Rightarrow d$, then $a \Rightarrow d$.

If the truth set of a condition p is the complement of the truth set of a condition q, that is, $P = Q'$, then p and q are complementary conditions and each is the negation or complement of the other. The negation of a condition p is denoted as $-p$ and when the notation $p(x)$ is used the negation is $(-p)(x)$. In general, the negation of $\{x \in \mathfrak{U} \,|\, p(x)\}$ is $\{x \in \mathfrak{U} \,|\, (-p)(x)\}$.

Example 2.1 If $\mathfrak{U}$ is the set of all people, the set of all engineers is $\{x \in \mathfrak{U} \,|\, x$ is an engineer$\}$ and the set of all nonengineers is $\{x \in \mathfrak{U} \,|\, -(x$ is an engineer$)\}$.

2.2 THE ALGEBRA OF CONDITIONS

Two conditions in a set $\mathfrak{U}$ may be combined by means of the word *and* to yield another condition p *and* q. This is symbolized by $p \wedge q$ and is known as conjunction. This defines the set of elements in $\mathfrak{U}$ that satisfy both condition p and condition q. Conditions may also be combined by the word *or* to give p *or* q, which is symbolized by $p \vee q$. This defines the set of elements in $\mathfrak{U}$ that satisfy condition p or condition q or both.

The expression $(p \wedge q)(x)$ is read as "x satisfies the condition $(p \wedge q)$." This is equivalent to "x satisfies the condition p and x satisfies the condition q." We may show this as

$$(p \wedge q)(x) = p(x) \wedge q(x)$$

Similarly

$$(p \vee q)(x) = p(x) \vee q(x)$$

and

$$(-p)(x) = -p(x)$$

We may consider the $\wedge$ and $\vee$ symbols on the left-hand side of the above equivalences as combining conditions. This is not quite true for the symbols on the right-hand side. If we redefine $p(x)$ as a propositional function or "open sentence" on a set A, then $p(x)$ has the property that $p(a)$ is true or false for every $a \in A$ (see Definition 1.9.3). Although we defer defining a proposition until Chapter 3, we state here that $p(x)$ is a propositional function on A if $p(x)$ becomes a proposition whenever any element $a \in A$ is substituted for the variable x.

The laws for the algebra of conditions are the same as those for the algebra of propositions. The former may be proved from the latter by use of the above listed equivalences. We content ourselves here with merely listing the laws of the algebra of conditions. In Chapter 4 we derive and prove the algebra of propositions. In the listing the symbols t and f represent true and false.

1	(a)	$-t \Leftrightarrow f$	
	(b)	$-f \Leftrightarrow t$	
2	(a)	$p \wedge -p \Leftrightarrow f$	
	(b)	$p \vee -p \Leftrightarrow t$	
	(c)	$--p \Leftrightarrow p$	*complement laws*
3	(a)	$p \wedge t \Leftrightarrow p$	
	(b)	$p \wedge f \Leftrightarrow f$	
	(c)	$p \vee t \Leftrightarrow t$	
	(d)	$p \vee f \Leftrightarrow p$	*identity laws*
4	(a)	$p \wedge p \Leftrightarrow p$	
	(b)	$p \vee p \Leftrightarrow p$	*idempotent laws*
5	(a)	$p \wedge q \Leftrightarrow q \wedge p$	
	(b)	$p \vee q \Leftrightarrow q \vee p$	*commutative laws*
6	(a)	$-(p \wedge q) \Leftrightarrow -p \vee -q$	
	(b)	$-(p \vee q) \Leftrightarrow -p \wedge -q$	*DeMorgan's rules*
7	(a)	$(p \wedge q) \wedge r \Leftrightarrow p \wedge (q \wedge r)$	
	(b)	$(p \vee q) \vee r \Leftrightarrow p \vee (q \vee r)$	*associative laws*
8	(a)	$p \wedge (q \vee r) \Leftrightarrow (p \wedge q) \vee (p \wedge r)$	
	(b)	$p \vee (q \wedge r) \Leftrightarrow (p \vee q) \wedge (p \vee r)$	*distributive laws*

2.3 THE ALGEBRA OF SETS

We have already defined (Section 1.6) the three basic operations with sets: intersection, union, and complementation. These are analogous to the operations of conjunction, disjunction, and negation, which were developed for the algebra of conditions. In practice these terms are rather freely interchanged as are similar terms that we develop later for the algebra of propositions and the algebra of on–off events. Usually we do not encounter difficulties in using these terms rather loosely but it must be remembered that, although they are similar or identical in usage, they represent different logical concepts.

The intersection of two sets, P and Q, has been defined as the set of all elements in $\mathcal{U}$ that belong to both P and Q. We may state this as

$$P \cap Q = \{x \in \mathcal{U} | (P \vee Q)(x)\}$$
$$= \{x \in \mathcal{U} | (x \in P) \wedge (x \in Q)\}$$

The union of two sets, P and Q, has been defined as the set of all elements in $\mathcal{U}$ that belong to either P or Q or both. We may state this as

$$P \cup Q = \{x \in \mathcal{U} | (P \vee Q)(x)\}$$
$$= \{x \in \mathcal{U} | (x \in P) \vee (x \in Q)\}$$

The complement of a set P has been defined as all elements of $\mathcal{U}$ that do not belong to P. We may state this as

$$\text{if} \qquad P = \{x \in \mathcal{U} | p(x)\}$$
$$\text{then} \qquad P' = \{x \in \mathcal{U} | -p(x)\}$$

These three equations

$$P \cap Q = \{x \in \mathcal{U} | (x \in P) \wedge (x \in Q)\}$$
$$P \cup Q = \{x \in \mathcal{U} | (x \in P) \vee (x \in Q)\}$$
$$P' = \{x \in \mathcal{U} | -p(x)\}$$

permit us to construct the laws of the algebra of sets, which may be proved from the corresponding laws of the algebra of conditions.

It may seem odd to the reader that proofs for the two algebras we have encountered are deferred until we develop the proof for the algebra of propositions. This could have been avoided by developing the logic of propositions first. However, in my opinion it is highly desirable to proceed from sets to propositions to on–off events. The deferral of these proofs is a small price to pay for maintaining this sequence.

The laws for the algebra of sets are:

1	(a)	$\mathfrak{U}' = \varnothing$	
	(b)	$\varnothing' = \mathfrak{U}$	
2	(a)	$P \cap P' = \varnothing$	
	(b)	$P \cup P' = \mathfrak{U}$	
	(c)	$(P')' = P$	*complement laws*
3	(a)	$P \cap \mathfrak{U} = P$	
	(b)	$P \cap \varnothing = \varnothing$	
	(c)	$P \cup \mathfrak{U} = \mathfrak{U}$	
	(d)	$P \cup \varnothing = P$	*identity laws*
4	(a)	$P \cap P = P$	
	(b)	$P \cup P = P$	*idempotent laws*
5	(a)	$P \cap Q = Q \cap P$	
	(b)	$P \cup Q = Q \cup P$	*commutative laws*
6	(a)	$(P \cap Q)' = P' \cup Q'$	
	(b)	$(P \cup Q)' = P' \cap Q'$	*DeMorgan's rules*
7	(a)	$(P \cap Q) \cap R = P \cap (Q \cap R)$	
	(b)	$(P \cup Q) \cup R = P \cup (Q \cup R)$	*associative laws*
8	(a)	$P \cap (Q \cup R) = (P \cap Q) \cup (P \cap R)$	
	(b)	$P \cup (Q \cap R) = (P \cup Q) \cap (P \cup R)$	*distributive laws*

2.3   POSTULATES OF THE ALGEBRA

The Huntington[2] postulates have been widely, even universally, accepted as the basic postulates for the various algebras of logic, including the algebra of sets. Before considering these postulates we must know something more about our basic operations. Union and intersection are binary operations since, when applied to two members of a system, they yield a third and unique member of the system. Complementation is a unary operation since it is applied to a single member of a system to yield the same member with its value or meaning inverted. With this understood we may proceed to the postulates.

Postulate I.   In a set S composed of the elements $x \in S$ and employing two binary operations $\cap$ and $\cup$, the operations $\cap$ and $\cup$ are commutative.

Postulate II. The two operations ∩ and ∪ are associative.

Postulate III. Each of the binary operations ∩ and ∪ is distributive over the other.

Postulate IV. The identity element ∅ is associated with the operation ∪.

Postulate V. The identity element 𝒰 is associated with the operation ∩.

Postulate VI. For every element $x \in S$ there exists an element x' such that $x \cup x' = \mathscr{U}$ and $x \cap x' = \varnothing$.

Postulate VII. In any algebra of this type, if the operation ∩ and the operation ∪ and the identity element 𝒰 and the identity element ∅ are interchanged throughout the expression, the validity of the expression remains unchanged.

Since both the algebra of sets and the algebra of conditions of sets fulfill these postulates they are, by definition, Boolean algebras.

SUMMARY

The most important feature of this chapter lies in showing the connection between conditions of sets and propositional functions even though we have not as yet defined propositional functions. It is sufficient to know at this point that a condition becomes a proposition when it is applied to a specific member of a set. We will see how useful this relationship is when we derive the Boolean algebra of on–off events in Chapter 5.

The algebra of sets, although useful in itself and essential in set theoretic computations, is of little value to us in working with on–off events. It is presented here for completeness.

THREE
THE LOGIC OF PROPOSITIONS

INTRODUCTION

The logic of propositions is, by definition, a "conversational" logic. Here we are working with declarative sentences known as propositions. The work done by Boole, DeMorgan, Schröder, Euler, and others was most notable in that it abstracted these propositions to symbols. Before this could be done, however, it was necessary to determine the basic laws of the logic by analyzing the meanings of propositional arguments. Once the basic relationships were established, symbols could be introduced.

In establishing these relationships many concepts were introduced that added to the depth and richness of classical logic—such concepts as "modus ponens," "modus tollens," "the square of opposition," and strong versus weak arguments. These are not included in this work. The purpose here is not to present a treatise on classical logic but to derive a viable Boolean algebra that can be used in the solution of scientific and engineering problems.

In arriving at our goal we derive from the logic of propositions the algebra of propositions, the algebra of truth-value functions, and the Boolean algebra of on–off events. All of these algebras, as well as those previously encountered, are Boolean algebras. However, it has become customary to reserve the term "Boolean algebra" for on–off events and to use a special symbology for this algebra.

3.1 DEFINITION OF LOGIC

The word logic has different meanings for different people and is one of the more widely misused words in the English language. The units of logic are propositions, which are statements considered to be true or false but not both true and false. They may be any statements we wish to consider provided they are made by complete declarative sentences. Exclamatory, hortative, optative, and imperative sentences do not express propositions. The sentence "Block that kick!" is not a proposition since it is not a declarative sentence. The statement "Cincinnati is on the Mississippi river" is a proposition since it is a declarative sentence and is demonstrably false.

Other branches of reasoning are frequently (and, it is argued by some, validly) called logic. Two of these are rhetoric and inductive inference. Rhetoric is the discipline that attempts to investigate and classify the meaning of nonpropositional statements. This is a somewhat archaic word and today this discipline is considered to lie within the field of general semantics. Inductive inference, which is usually given the misleading name "inductive logic," is an attempt to justify scientific or other generalizations that are based upon limited data. The statement "All salts are soluble" is an example of such a proposition in inductive inference. The truth or falsity of such a statement is probable at best. Even more illustrative is the statement "Candy is dandy but liquor is quicker".* This, after all, is a matter of opinion and/or personal experience. Either way it is inductive inference.

The theory of sets is often referred to as the "logic of sets" or "the logic of classes." Sets, per se, do not fit into the logic of propositions. However, the logic of conditions of sets is very definitely related to the logic of propositions. This was very strongly hinted at in the previous chapters. The connection between the two will be demonstrated frequently throughout the balance of this work. In particular, it will be shown that the logic of conditions of sets is a necessary precursor to the logic of on–off events. We may thus include of conditions of sets in our definition of logic, which is *the study of the propositional meanings of declarative sentences.* Later we shall define logic in a different and more precise way.

3.2 PROPOSITIONS

There are two kinds of propositions, factual and logical. Factual propositions are true or false by virtue of some fact or circumstance. The proposition "Today is Tuesday" is true if today happens to be Tuesday and false otherwise. Whether or not we can determine the truth or falsity of a factual proposition does not affect its being factual—only the potential for proof need exist. "The rings of Saturn are composed of diamonds, the smallest of which weighs 250 carats" is a factual proposition. The probability of it being true is small but probability does not enter into the logic of propositions (even though probability is based on the algebra of propositions). What is important is that the potential for ascertaining the truth or falsity of the proposition could exist. We could give countless examples of propositions of this type: "At this moment it is raining on Mars", "The girl I dated thirty years ago is now living in Kalamazoo," and so on. These are all factual, but trivial, propositions. (That woman in

(*With suitable apologies to Ogden Nash).

Kalamazoo may take a dim view of this!) Of much more importance to us are factual propositions, the truth or falsity of which are apparent or immediately ascertainable. Some examples:

3.2.1 Dogs are mammals.

3.2.2 It is snowing.

3.2.3 The Earth is the center of the solar system.

3.2.4 The capital of the United States is in Canada or Cincinnati is on the Ohio river.

That proposition 3.2.1 is always true is a fact established by zoology. Proposition 3.2.2 may or may not be true depending upon existing meteorological conditions. Proposition 3.2.3 is false according to our present knowledge of astronomy. It should be noted that these are simple propositions in that each is composed of just one declarative sentence. Proposition 3.2.4, however, is composed of two declarative sentences joined by the word "or." This is a complex, or compound, proposition, which is true because one of its components is true. We shall go into more detail on this later.

Logical propositions are another matter. These are true or false by virtue of their form. "It is either raining or not raining" is one example. Who could possibly dispute that statement? Let's rearrange it to read "It is raining or it is not raining." This is a true logical proposition. It is also a complex proposition. However, the most important thing to notice is that the components of the true logical proposition are both factual propositions. Although this is not a requirement we find that most of our complex logical propositions have factual propositions as components. One exception would be "It is raining or not raining and all squares are square." The proposition "All squares are square" is not a factual proposition. We could just as easily have said "All dogs are dogs" or "All men are men" or "All --- are ---" without affecting the original proposition.

So far these examples have been of true logical propositions. What of false logical propositions? "It is both raining and not raining" is one example. "Jones is both a human and a nonhuman" is another. In either of these "both...and" may be replaced by its correlative "and" just as "either...or" may be replaced by its correlative "or." The difference is one of semantics, not logic. Semantics is of course important in ordinary discourse. Consider these two propositions: "Darling you look lovely tonight" and "Darling! And isn't it lovely you look tonight?" Anyone who cannot appreciate the semantic difference between those two has spent far too much time reading books like this one.

Now we shall examine some other true logical propositions.

3.2.5 Dogs are either mammals or not mammals.

3.2.6 Socrates is a man and all men are mortal; therefore, Socrates is mortal.

3.2.7 All red roses are red.

The truth or falsity of these resides in their form. Since this is so it is essential that a word must have the same meaning wherever it occurs in a logical proposition. Nuances, shades of meaning, and play on words are not permitted. Unless we adopt this rule there can be no such thing as a logical proposition. If by "It is raining and it is not raining" we mean "It is raining in Cincinnati and it is not raining in Louisville", we must so state. Then we have a factual, not a logical, proposition.

3.3 THE STRUCTURE OF LOGICAL PROPOSITIONS

Most propositions with which we are concerned are complex propositions constructed from simple factual propositions. An analysis of some of these shows the difference between logical and factual propositions. "Dogs are either mammals or not mammals" is a true complex logical proposition. Please note the phraseology used here. We could have said that "..." is a logically true complex proposition, and this wording is frequently used. There is, however, a shade of difference in meaning between the two and "true logical" is more correct. In this proposition we could substitute any plural noun, or some adjectives, for mammals and the result would still be a true logical proposition. "Dogs are either birds or not birds" and "Dogs are either gray or not gray" are examples of such substitutions. We can generalize this proposition by writing it as

"Dogs are either --- or not ---."

This generalized proposition would also apply to cats, mice, men, and so on, so a further generalization may be made. This is

"*** are either --- or not ---."

By using the correlative of "either...or" this may be reduced to

"*** are --- or not ---."

Our original proposition has now been completely stripped of its content and only the words "are," "or," and "not" are left. These words are "constants" or "essential" words and cannot be replaced without transforming the proposition from a true logical to a false logical proposition or from a logical to a factual proposition. The words stripped from the proposition are known as "variable" or "nonessential" words.

In this proposition, or any similar one, substituting "both...and" or its correlative "and" for "or" would result in the false logical proposition:

"∗∗∗ are --- and not ---."

which is obviously false no matter which variable words are inserted. A substitution for "not" however would usually convert it to a factual proposition. If we used the word "indeed" in place of "not" we would have

"∗∗∗ are --- or indeed ---."

This of course reduces to simply

"∗∗∗ are ---."

If something is green or indeed green, it is green. Inserting grammatically incorrect words would give us a nonsense phrase.

Replacing the word "are" in our sample proposition is something to be approached with care. There are approximately thirty-six variations of the verb "to be," many of which would fit nicely into our proposition without affecting it. Most other verbs would convert it from a logical to a factual proposition.

Proposition 3.2.6 is of special interest to us and is one we use frequently in our development of logic. It is also of interest historically since it is the famous syllogism of Aristotle and is probably the most widely quoted of the categorical syllogisms. When this proposition is stripped of its contents we have

"∗∗∗ is a --- and all --- are ///;
therefore, ∗∗∗ is ///.

This is now a universally true logical proposition. It is also the basic form for all categorical syllogisims, which we touch upon later.

The word "logic" may now be defined more precisely as *the analysis of logical propositions*. This is not a circular definition since we have defined a logical proposition quite independently of any definition of logic.

It should now be apparent that the difference between factual and logical propositions is the form in which the proposition appears. All of the above logical propositions are in a form that happens to exclude them from the logic of propositions but is the basis for the logic of conditions of sets. An example of this is our famous syllogisim. If we let $p(x)$ read "x is a man" and $q(x)$ read "x is mortal," then we have

$$\{x \in M \mid p(x)\} \quad \text{and} \quad \{\forall x \in M \mid q(x)\}$$

which completely defines this syllogism for all members of the set M (including Socrates). There is another form for logical propositions that provides the basis for the logic of propositions. To develop this form it is necessary to have some understanding of implication and logical argument.

3.4 IMPLICATION AND LOGICAL ARGUMENT

We have already made a distinction between single and complex propositions. This permits us to define the fundamental concepts of "argument." The word is not used here in the sense of debate or controversy. Rather it means "a complex proposition one of whose constituent propositions is represented as a conclusion following from the others."[4] An argument involves at least one proposition argued from and another one argued to. The former is the premise and the latter is the conclusion. Some familiar examples of arguments:

3.4.1 Because the volume of a gas is proportional to its temperature at constant pressure, increasing the temperature will increase the volume.

3.4.2 Because the pressure drop of a flowing fluid varies as the square of the mass velocity, doubling the flow rate will quadruple the pressure drop.

The premise of an argument makes certain claims that result in the conclusion. We may say that the premise implies the conclusion. Not only that, the premise asserts that the conclusion is true.

Implication is essential to argument. It serves to erect a bridge between premise and conclusion. Crossing this bridge is another matter. Such a crossing means that we have accepted the premise as being true and therefore accept the conclusion as being true. This is known as inference. It is possible to have more than one premise in an argument but there may be only one conclusion. (This is not quite true. Certain arguments may lead to more than one conclusion. This unhappy result is known as a dilemma. For more details on dilemmas see any standard text on logic.) In some arguments, if more than one premise is involved, one is designated as the major premise while the others are minor premises. In case of the categorical syllogism, which is one form of argument, we are limited to two premises. In our classical example our minor premise is "Socrates is a man," our major premise is "All men are mortal," and our conclusion is "Socrates is mortal." Technically a categorical syllogism must meet these qualifications:

1. There may be only two premises, a major and a minor.
2. The minor premise must contain the subject of the conclusion and the major premise must contain the predicate.
3. Only three major nonessential words may be used, two of which must appear in the conclusion.
4. The syllogism applies, as written, only to the logic of sets.

At this point it may be asked "Why such stress on something limited to the logic of sets when we are supposed to be working with the logic of propositions?" Before we are through we shall give this syllogism the classical engineering treatment—cut to shape, beat to fit, and paint to match—and see how beautifully it fits into the logic of propositions. Ordinarily, we are more concerned with another type of syllogism known as a hypothetical syllogism. This usually called a chain argument and may have more than two premises. The chain argument applies only to the logic of propositions.

In English usage it is sometimes difficult to distinguish between the premises and the conclusion of an argument. This is particularly true of chain arguments. A reliable, but not infallible, way of making such a distinction is through the choice of certain words that often appear in argument. Words such as "since," "for," and "because" usually precede the premise. "Therefore," "hence," "thus," and "so" are usually followed by the conclusion.

It is much easier to work with symbols for propositions than with the propositions themselves. Lowercase letters are used as such symbols. The symbols are an abstraction, much as the positive integers are an abstraction of the natural numbers. When we use the letters p, q, r, and so on as symbols, the propositions they may represent are limited only by our imagination. Two things must be borne in mind: any given symbol represents a simple proposition, and when symbols are reused in complex propositions, such as chain arguments, they must always represent the same simple proposition. We adopt two other symbols at this point. An arrow is usually used as the symbol for implication. We may write "p implies q" as $p \rightarrow q$. This may also be read as "If p, then q" or "p only if q." The other symbol is that for the negaton, or denial, of a proposition. This symbol is usually $\sim$ or the minus sign, $-$. The minus sign is more often used since very few typewriters are equipped with a $\sim$ key. The proposition "If not p, then q" may now be written as $-p \rightarrow q$.

Any proposition containing implication is called a conditional proposition, or a conditional for short. An argument that has at least one conditional as a premise is known as a conditional argument. A conditional has three related propositions, all of which are very important. They are:

the conditional	$p \rightarrow q$
the converse	$q \rightarrow p$
the contrapositive	$-q \rightarrow -p$
the contradictory	$-(p \rightarrow q)$

Certain statements may be made in respect to the related propositions.

1. The converse is independent of the conditional. If the conditional is true the converse may or may not be true.
2. The contrapositive of a conditional is the exact equivalent of it.
3. The contradictory of a conditional is the exact opposite of it. If the conditional is true the contradictory is false and vice versa.

In a conditional such as $p \rightarrow q$ the first term is the antecedent and the second is the consequent. With one exception we may regard these as being true or false as we please. Thus

3.4.3 $p \rightarrow q$

3.4.4 $-p \rightarrow q$

3.4.5 $-p \rightarrow -q$

The exception is

3.4.6 $p \rightarrow -q$

No true antecedent may imply a false consequent. It was pointed out in our definition of implication that a true premise (antecedent) implies a true conclusion (consequent). As we see from propositions 3.4.4 and 3.4.5, a false antecedent may imply either a true or a false consequent. In fact, it may imply anything we wish it to imply regardless of how ridiculous this may be. For example we may say "$2+2=5 \rightarrow$ I am the greatest lover in the world." It would be difficult to get more ridiculous than that.

There may be some confusion at this point on the usage of the words "premise," "antecedent," "conclusion," and "consequent." "Premise" and "conclusion" usually refer to arguments that have more than one proposition implying another. "Antecedent" and "consequent" refer to simple conditionals, that is, one simple proposition implying another.

So far we have not paid much attention to the truth or falsity of arguments. An argument may be factually true, factually false, logically true, or logically false. However, only a true logical argument is considered to be valid. The others are invalid. A true logical argument may consist of all factual propositions, all logical propositions, or may have a mixture of logical and factual propositions as its premises. If, however, a true logical argument has a factual proposition as its conclusion, it must have at least one factual proposition in its premises. Logical propositions imply only other logical propositions. Most of the arguments we are interested in consist of factual propositions only. It is the form of the argument that makes it a true logical, or valid, argument. In the argument

3.4.7 Since it is either raining or snowing and it is not raining, it is snowing.

all of the propositions are factual and, because of its form, the argument is valid. Here again the propositions may be stripped to give

3.4.8 Since it is --- or *** and it is not ---, it is ***.

Stripping the proposition in this manner shows that we have a valid argument.

Valid chain arguments have the form

3.4.9 $(p \rightarrow q)$ and $(q \rightarrow r)$ and $(r \rightarrow s) \rightarrow (p \rightarrow s)$

They may sometimes be shown in this form:

3.4.10
$$p \rightarrow q$$
$$q \rightarrow r$$
$$r \rightarrow s$$
$$\overline{}$$
$$p \rightarrow s$$

The confusion that can arise in chain arguments is well illustrated by this example:

3.4.11 If I can get my car repaired today I shall drive to Florida.
If I do not leave on Monday I shall not drive to Florida.
If I get paid today I can get my car repaired.

If I get paid today I shall leave on Monday.

To analyze this we will put it into symbolic form.

Symbol	Proposition
p	I can get my car repaired
q	I shall drive to Florida
r	I shall leave on Monday
s	I shall get paid today

Therefore

$$p \rightarrow q$$
$$-r \rightarrow -q$$
$$s \rightarrow p$$
$$\overline{}$$
$$s \rightarrow r$$

If we substitute the contrapositive for the second premise in the above we have

$$p \longrightarrow q$$
$$q \longrightarrow r$$
$$s \longrightarrow p$$
$$\overline{}$$
$$s \longrightarrow r$$

Rearranging the premises gives

$$s \longrightarrow p$$
$$p \longrightarrow q$$
$$q \longrightarrow r$$
$$\overline{}$$
$$s \longrightarrow r$$

We see that the antecedent of the second premise is the consequent of the first and the antecedent of the third premise is the consequent of the second. The antecedent of the conclusion is the antecedent of the first premise and the consequent of the conclusion is the consequent of the third premise. All of this is necessary and sufficient to establish argument 3.4.11 as valid. The form used above, where the horizontal line replaces the final arrow in the argument, is frequently used for chain arguments and sometimes used for simple implication. The form shown in argument 3.4.9 can become quite cumbersome if a chain argument has more than three premises.

The example used above may strike you as extremely simple—too simple to require the analysis given. It is used merely to illustrate the method of analysis. Now that you know the method of analysis try it on some of the more advanced Lewis Carroll problems (which are presented as exercises). Lots of luck.

One special type of conditional, and the one with which we shall be mostly concerned, is the biconditional. This is any conditional containing the words "if and only if." The proposition "Today is Thursday if and only if tomorrow is Friday" is a biconditional. This could be reversed to read "Tomorrow is Friday if and only if today is Thursday." In one case we are reading the proposition from left to right and in the other case from right to left. A biconditional is known in some contexts as an equivalence and various symbols are used for it. Some of these are:

$$\leftrightarrow$$
$$\Leftrightarrow$$
$$\leftrightarrow$$
$$\equiv$$

A biconditional represents double implication because each side implies the other. The two conditionals involved (vectored conditionals, if you prefer) may be true or false just as any other conditional may be. An example of a false biconditional is "Today is Wednesday if and only if tomorrow is Friday." Biconditionals are not in themselves arguments but a method of stating that two propositions are equivalent. The convention we follow with biconditionals is:

1. The symbol $\leftrightarrow$ will represent any biconditional such as $p \leftrightarrow q$.
2. The symbol $\Leftrightarrow$ will represent true (equivalent) biconditionals. True biconditionals are the basis for the propositional calculus, that is, that part of the algebra of logic that applies to the logic of propositions. In a true biconditional we are stating that a conditional and its converse are equivalent. Making this assumption when it is not warranted probably results in more fallacies than does any other error in logic.

3.5 BASIC OPERATIONS WITH PROPOSITIONS

We have defined a simple proposition as a complete declarative sentence that may be either true or false but not both. A proposition may be said to have a truth value of T if it is true and F if it is false. The relationship between a proposition and its truth value is known as the truth-value function and is designated by the Greek letter tau (τ). If we have the proposition "Cincinnati is in Ohio," we may say

$$\tau(\text{Cincinnati is in Ohio}) = T$$

where the equals sign means identical with. Also, if we say "Cincinnati is in Kentucky" we have

$$\tau(\text{Cincinnati is in Kentucky}) = F$$

Now let p symbolize "Cincinnati is in Ohio" and q symbolize "Cincinnati is on the Ohio River." Obviously $\tau(p) = T$ and $\tau(q) = T$. We may combine these to give $\tau(p \text{ and } q) = T$. This operation is known as conjunction and the symbol used for it is $\wedge$ so we may write $\tau(p \wedge q) = T$. By convention two or more conjoined propositions yield a true complex proposition when all of the component propositions are true and otherwise yield a false proposition.

Why did we combine these propositions as $\tau(p \wedge q) = T$ and not as $\tau(p) \wedge \tau(q) = T$? Because these forms have different meanings. In $\tau(p \wedge q) = T$ we are stating that the truth-value function of the conjoined propositions is T. In $\tau(p) \wedge \tau(q) = T$ we are stating that the conjoined truth-value functions of the propositions is T. A more correct way to show $\tau(p)\wedge\tau(q)$ $= T$ is $\tau[\tau(p)\wedge\tau(q)] = T$. In the one case we are conjoining propositions and in the other conjoining truth-value functions. In Chapter 4 it will be shown that the systems represented by these cases are analogous and homomorphous.

Propositions may also be connected by the operator "or," which is known as disjunction. The complex proposition "Cincinnati is in Ohio or Rome is the capital of Italy" is an example. If we let p symbolize "Cincinnati is in Ohio" and q symbolize "Rome is the capital of Italy," we have $\tau(p$ or $q) = T$. The symbol used for disjunction is $\vee$ (from the Latin, vel). The "or" operator used here is the "nonexclusive or" in that it means "--- or *** or both." The exclusive or means "--- or *** but not both." For example, an object may be all white or all black but it cannot be both at any given time. No separate symbol is used here for the "exlusive or" since it can be handled very readily with the symbols we are developing in this section. The "exclusive or" will be considered in more detail later. As of now, whenever the operator "or" is used it is the "nonexclusive or."

Again by convention, two or more disjoined propositions yield a false complex proposition whenever all of the component propositions are false and yield a true complex proposition otherwise. We may also have disjunction of propositions or disjunction of truth-value functions similar to that encountered with the operation of conjunction. We shall give some examples of disjunction but first we tabulate some propositions with assigned symbols.

Symbol	Proposition
q	Cincinnati is in Ohio
r	Rome is the capital of Italy
s	Cincinnati is in Kentucky
t	Los Angeles is the capital of Italy
x	$2+2=5$
y	Today is Friday the thirteenth

Some examples are

$$\tau(q\vee r) = T$$
$$\tau(q\vee s) = T$$
$$\tau(s\vee t) = F$$
$$\tau(s\vee x) = F$$
$$\tau(y\vee \qquad\qquad \text{Hold it!}$$

We now have a small problem. It was previously stated that our symbols would represent simple propositions but here y represents a complex proposition. At first glance this proposition does not appear to be complex but it is. It should be written as "Today is Friday and it is the thirteenth day of this month." In ordinary discourse many complex propositions are shortened by assuming that certain things are too well known to require inclusion. Another example of this is "Because today is a holiday I do not have to go to school." Here the proposition "And there is no school on holidays" is tacitly assumed to be included. If all people affected by a shortened argument do not assume the same proposition for tacit inclusion, the result can be a breakdown in communication. Tacit inclusion cannot be tolerated in the logic of propositions. We could use our complex proposition, y, as it stands but it is safer to work with the complete proposition and assign separate symbols to its components.

We may also use our tabulated propositions in examples for the operation of conjunction. Some of these are

$$\tau(q \wedge r) = T$$
$$\tau(q \wedge t) = F$$
$$\tau(t \wedge x) = F$$
$$\tau(q \wedge s) = F$$

We may of course wish to use conjunction and disjunction simultaneously. Some examples of this, using the same list of propositions, are

$$\tau[(q \wedge r) \vee x] = T$$
$$\tau[(q \wedge t) \vee x] = T$$
$$\tau[(s \wedge t) \vee r] = T$$
$$\tau[(s \vee r) \wedge q] = T$$
$$\tau[(x \vee r) \wedge t] = F$$
$$\tau[(x \vee r) \wedge (q \vee t)] = T$$

In these examples it is easy to determine the value of τ. The combination of these operations, plus the next operation we consider, can be so complex as to defy analysis by examination. An easy method for making such analyses is the subject of our next section.

The third and final operation we consider is negation. We covered this briefly in the previous section in our discussion of biconditionals. We will repeat only that negation is the denial of a proposition and the symbol for it is $-$. If s symbolizes "Cincinnati is in Kentucky," $-s$ would be read as "It is false that Cincinnati is in Kentucky," Individual propositions, conjoined propositions, disjoined propositions, or any combination of these may be negated. Using our tabulation we could have, for instance

$$\tau\big[-(s\vee t)\wedge(q\wedge-x)\big]=T \quad \text{and} \quad \tau\big[(q\wedge-t)\wedge(-x\vee s)\big]=T$$

From here on we dispense with the truth-value function symbol, τ. Continued use of this symbol in what follows would be unwieldly. However, it is absolutely essential to realize that we shall be working with the truth values of various combinations of propositions, not just the propositions themselves.

So far the basic operations—conjunction, disjunction, and (to a certain extent) negation—and the concept of implication seem to be unrelated. It would be more correct to say that we have not yet established a relationship. Implication may be expressed completely in terms of the basic operations. We may go a bit farther and state that that implication may be established completely in terms of disjunction and negation only, which is the basis for NOR ("not or") logic, or in terms of conjunction and negation only, which is the basis for NAND ("not and") logic. NOR logic is used extensively in electronics work and will be covered briefly in Chapter 9.

To establish the relationship between implication and the basic operations let us first examine the biconditional. We have said that $p\leftrightarrow q$ means that a proposition implies its converse and vice versa. Therefore $p\leftrightarrow q$ may be defined as $(p\rightarrow q)\wedge(q\rightarrow p)$. Next, let us symbolize the proposition "Smith comes" by x and the proposition "Jones goes" by y. We may symbolize the argument "Smith comes implies Jones goes" (or more elegantly "If Smith comes, Jones will go") by $x\rightarrow y$. However, this statement is equivalent to "Either Smith will not come or Jones will go," which may be symbolized by $-x\vee y$. Since $x\rightarrow y$ and $-x\vee y$ symbolize equivalent statements, one may be substituted for the other.

It may also be shown that $p\wedge q$ means precisely $-(-p\vee-q)$. The proposition "It is not the case either that it is not snowing or that Jones is not an American" is an example of this. The expression $-p\vee-q$ is the contradictory of $p\wedge q$ since it permits precisely the possibilities that $p\wedge q$ rules out, that is, that either or both p and q are false, and rules out the one possibility that $p\wedge q$ permits, that is, that both p and q are true. But if $-p\vee-q$ is the contradictory of $p\wedge q$, then $-(-p\vee-q)$ is equivalent to $p\wedge q$ and one may be substituted for the other. This is the basis for DeMorgan's rules, which we shall find to be of great value in applying the algebra of logic.

We have defined the symbol $\leftrightarrow$ in terms of $\rightarrow$ and $\wedge$, that is, $p \leftrightarrow q$ is the same as $(p \rightarrow q) \wedge (q \rightarrow p)$. Since $\rightarrow$ and $\wedge$ are reducible to $\vee$ and $-$, we see that $\leftrightarrow$ is also reducible. The steps in this reduction are:

1. $p \leftrightarrow q$
2. $(p \rightarrow q) \wedge (q \rightarrow p)$
3. $(-p \vee q) \wedge (-q \vee p)$
4. $-(-((-p \vee q) \vee (-q \vee p)))$

The fourth step shows the biconditional relationship in terms of $\vee$ and $-$ only, which is NOR logic. This is cumbersome compared to the relationship shown in Step 3, which is in terms of $\vee$, $-$, and $\wedge$ and has been referred to as "English" logic. Later we shall see just how important this difference in form is and the circumstances under which each form should be used.

We are now in position to beat our favorite syllogism into shape. We will rewrite this as "Socrates is a man and all men are mortal implies that Socrates is mortal." Let us define the symbols:

p	Socrates is a man
q	All men are mortal
r	Socrates is mortal

We may now show this as $(p \wedge q) \rightarrow r$. We have shown that this form is the equivalent of $-(p \wedge q) \vee r$, which in turn is equivalent to $(-p \vee -q) \vee r$. This may now be read as "(Either it is false that Socrates is a man or it is false that all men are mortal) or Socrates is mortal."

There is a very definite reason for our playing games with this syllogism. It indicates the relationship, through propositions, between the logic of propositions and the logic of conditions of sets.

3.6 TRUTH TABLES

The operations of conjunction, disjunction, and negation are usually referred to as AND, OR, and NOT. Since these operations are completely nonambiguous, we may determine the truth value of any given complex proposition if we know the truth values of its components. The proposition $x \wedge -y$ is true if $x = T$ and $y = F$. However, in this proposition, and in every proposition involving two components, there are four possible combinations of the truth values of the components. These are (using x and y as the components)

$$x = F, \quad y = F$$
$$x = F, \quad y = T$$
$$x = T, \quad y = F$$
$$x = T, \quad y = T$$

We may analyze any complex proposition by incorporating all of the possibilities in a "truth table."

Step 1 To construct such a table we list the possibilities in a tabular array:

x	y
F	F
F	T
T	F
T	T

Any sequence of F's and T's could be used in such an array, providing all of the possibilities are listed. The reason for choosing the sequence shown will become apparent in Chapter 6. To analyze the proposition $x \wedge -y$ we continue with the following steps:

Step 2

x	y	$-y$
F	F	T
F	T	F
T	F	T
T	T	F

Step 3

x	y	$-y$	$x \wedge -y$
F	F	T	F
F	T	F	F
T	F	T	T
T	T	F	F
			*

The column indicated by the asterisk completes the analysis. The truth-value symbols in this column are usually placed under the operative symbol (see also the column headed $-y$).

Any proposition expressed in terms of AND, OR, and NOT, or any combination of these, may be analyzed by using a truth table. Propositions such as $p \lor q$ may be analyzed at a glance without resorting to a table. This proposition is obviously true if either p or q or both are true. As we have stated, this is the definition of the operation of disjunction. A proposition such as $(-p \land q) \lor (p \land -q)$ is by no means obvious. The truth table for this is

p	q	$-p$	$-q$	$(-p \land q)$	$(p \land -q)$	$(-p \land q) \lor (p \land -q)$
F	F	T	T	F	F	F
F	T	T	F	T	F	T
T	F	F	T	F	T	T
T	T	F	F	F	F	F

If we are lazy, but cautious, we may shortcut this procedure a bit:

$(-$	p	$\land$	$q)$	$\lor$	$(p$	$\land$	$-$	$q)$
T	F	F	F	F	F	F	T	F
T	F	T	T	T	F	F	F	T
F	T	F	F	T	T	T	T	F
F	T	F	T	F	T	F	F	T
3	1	5	2	7	1	6	4	2

The numbers below the columns indicate the sequence in the development of the truth table. Columns 5 and 6 are the ones disjoined to arrive at the answer in column 7.

So far we have considered complex propositions involving only two simple propositions. A truth table for these may always be constructed with just four rows, since we have only four possible combinations of truth values. A complex proposition involving three simple propositions would require eight rows, since we have eight possible combinations. The truth table for a proposition involving, say, p, q, and x would start with

p	q	x
F	F	F
F	F	T
F	T	F
F	T	T
T	F	F
T	F	T
T	T	F
T	T	T

In general, if we have n simple propositions involved we will need 2^n rows to express all of the possible combinations.

The primary use of truth tables is in the comparison of two or more complex propositions. If these propositions have the same truth values in comparable rows of a truth table they are said to be equivalent. This, in fact, is our definition of equivalence. For example, are the propositions $(p \wedge q) \wedge x$ and $p \wedge (q \wedge x)$ equivalent? The truth tables are

(p	$\wedge$	q)	$\wedge$	x	p	$\wedge$	(q	$\wedge$	x)
F	F	F	F	F	F	F	F	F	F
F	F	F	F	T	F	F	F	F	T
F	F	T	F	F	F	F	T	F	F
F	F	T	F	T	F	F	T	T	T
T	F	F	F	F	T	F	F	F	F
T	F	F	F	T	T	F	F	F	T
T	T	T	F	F	T	F	T	F	F
T	T	T	T	T	T	T	T	T	T
1	4	2	5	3	1	5	2	4	3
			*			*			

The columns marked with an asterisk have identical truth values, row for row. Therefore the propositions are equivalent. Note again that the numbers below the columns indicate the sequence used in constructing the truth tables. These numbers are usually omitted. The above example is a proof of one of the theorems we encounter in the algebra of logic. All of the theorems of this algebra may be proved in this manner, which is known as "proof by perfect induction."

3.7 TAUTOLOGY

A tautology is a complex proposition that is true for all combinations of truth values of its component propositions. All tautologies are true logical propositions, but all true logical propositions are not tautologies. However, every valid propositional argument is a tautology.

Some examples of simple tautologies are:

3.7.1

$p \vee -p$

T	T	F T
F	T	T F

3.7.2

$-(p \wedge -p)$

T	T	F F T
T	F	F T F

3.7.3

$p \rightarrow p$

T	T	T
F	T	F

These are distinct but equivalent propositions. The form shown in 3.7.3 bears closer examination. In Section 3.4 we stated that the premise and the conclusion of a logical argument may be variously true or false, except that a true premise cannot imply false conclusion. In the argument $p \rightarrow q$ we have these possibilities:

3.7.4

$$p \rightarrow q$$

F	T	F
F	T	T
T	F	F
T	T	T

The only possibility that can render the argument invalid is shown in row three. In dealing with more involved arguments we need examine them only to see if this form appears:

3.7.5

$$p \rightarrow q$$

T	F	F

If this form does not appear the argument is a tautology. The argument shown in 3.7.3 is obviously a tautology because the form in question does not appear. The examples shown in 3.7.1, 3.7.2, and 3.7.3 are not as trivial as they seem to be. They establish the proof of three related laws in traditional logic—the law of the excluded middle (3.7.1), the law of contradiction (3.7.2), and the law of sterility (3.7.3). Another example of tautology, using implication, is

3.7.6

$$(p \wedge q) \rightarrow (p \vee q)$$

F	F F	T	F	F F		
F	F T	T	F	T T		
T	F F	T	T	T F		
T	T T	T	T	T T		

We could have shortcut this example by using the rule developed in 3.7.5. The only row that needs to be examined in the truth table for implication is that which contains an F under the implied proposition. This is row 1 in the above example. Another example is

3.7.7

$[(p$	$\rightarrow q)$	$\wedge$	$(q$	$\rightarrow r)]$	$\rightarrow$	$(p$	$\rightarrow r)$	Row Number
F		F	F		F T F		F	1
F		F	F		T T F		T	2
F		T	T		F T F		F	3
F		T	T		T T F		T	4
T F F F		F	T	F T T	F		F	5
T		F	F		T T T		T	6
T T T F		T	F	F T T	F		F	7
T		T	T		T T T		T	8
1	6	2	7	2	5	3 8	1	4 3

In this example we first establish the basic columns 1, 2, and 3. Next we evaluate column 4. Only rows 5 and 7 in column 4 exhibit the form

$$\frac{p \longrightarrow r}{T \ F \ F}$$

Therefore we evaluate only these rows in columns 5 and 6. Column 7 is determined by the conjunction of rows 5 and 7 in columns 5 and 6. Rows 5 and 7 in column 7 and in column 4 are now compared. This results in the solid column of *T*'s in column 8, which proves that 3.7.7 is a tautology. All of this makes the procedure seem to be much more involved than it really is. With a little practice the test for tautology can be performed easily and rapidly.

The biconditional may be tested for tautology in a similar manner. Here, however, we have two forms to watch out for. They are

3.7.8 $$\frac{p \longleftrightarrow q}{\begin{array}{c} T \ F \ F \\ F \ F \ T \end{array}}$$

An example of a biconditional was given in Section 3.6. In this we were asked to determine if the two forms were equivalent and concluded that they were. We now show that the equivalence of these forms makes the biconditional relationship between them a tautology.

3.7.9

(p	∧	q)	∧	x	↔	p	∧	(q	∧	x)
F	F	F	F	F	T	F	F	F	F	F
F	F	F	F	T	T	F	F	F	F	T
F	F	T	F	F	T	F	F	T	F	F
F	F	T	F	T	T	F	F	T	T	T
T	F	F	F	F	T	T	F	F	F	F
T	F	F	F	T	T	T	F	F	F	T
T	T	T	F	F	T	T	F	T	F	F
T	T	T	T	T	T	T	T	T	T	T
			*				*			

The columns marked with an asterisk are compared from left to right and from right to left for the combinations indicated in 3.7.8. Since these combinations do not appear, 3.7.9 is a tautology.

We may now make a general statement: if any two, or more, propositions are compared by means of a truth table, and if the truth values (*T* or *F*) of these propositions are comparable row for row, the propositions form a tautology. Establishing the tautology means that the propositions are equivalent, and more importantly, means that the truth-value functions (τ) of the propositions are equal. This is the definition of "proof by perfect induction," which was mentioned in Section 3.6.

The denial of a tautology is called a contradiction. The main column in the truth table for a contradiction consists entirely of F's. Any contradiction is false logically because its falsity is independent of the factual truth or falsity of its components. In example 3.7.2 we showed that $-(p \wedge -p)$ is a tautology. The contradictory of 3.7.3 is $p \wedge -p$. If we examine this we see

3.7.10

$$p \wedge - p$$
$$\overline{T \quad F \quad FT}$$
$$F \quad F \quad TF$$

which is a contradiction of the tautology in 3.7.2. If, however, we have two complex propositions, $f(p,q)$ and $f(x,y)$, both of which are contradictions, each will have in its truth table a solid column of F's, so that $f(p,q) \leftrightarrow f(x,y)$ is still a tautology.

All tautologies are equivalent and all true logical propositions are equivalent since they are true under all circumstances. Similarly, all contradictions and all false logical propositions are equivalent since they are false under all circumstances. We may therefore adopt a single symbol to represent the former and another single symbol to represent the latter. The symbol "t" will be used to represent all tautologies and all true logical propositions. The symbol "f" will be used to represent all contradictions and all false logical propositions. With these symbols defined, our basic operations defined, and a working knowledge of implication and logical argument, we are in a position to develop the algebra of logic.

SUMMARY

This chapter could be considered the heart of this book in that it is absolutely essential to master the material presented here if one is to have a good understanding of the development of the logics that follow. The concepts advanced may be unfamiliar but they are not difficult to master. The ones which may give the most trouble are "tautology" and "contradiction." An extra effort to master these will be well worthwhile because they form the basis for the algebra of truth-value functions, which is presented in the next chapter.

FOUR
THE ALGEBRA OF LOGIC

INTRODUCTION

The term "algebra of logic" is used somewhat loosely by most authors. There are two algebras presented in this chapter, each of which is referred to by some authors as an algebra of logic. A rigorous definition would place both of these under the heading of propositional calculus. Thus we have

propositional calculus

algebra of propositions   Algebra of truth-value functions

The algebra of truth-value functions is the one usually referred to when the term "algebra of logic" is used. This is the first two-variable algebra we encounter and is the immediate precursor of the Boolean algebra of on–off events. Note that I said two-variable, not two-valued. All Boolean algebras are, by definition, two-valued.

4.1 RELATIONSHIPS AMONG PROPOSITIONS

The various relationships that may be established among propositions by using the basic operators AND, OR, and NOT, and the manipulation of these relationships, is known as the algebra of logic. Although we included the logic of sets in our definition of logic (Section 3.1) the term "algebra of logic" is restricted to propositions. For this reason this algebra is sometimes referred to as "propositional calculus." The algebra of sets involves different concepts and symbology and, although it is analogous to the algebra of logic, is a distinctly different subject.

The basic propositional form used in this algebra is the biconditional, $p \leftrightarrow q$. Since it is possible to have a false biconditional, the notation used in this algebra is $p \Leftrightarrow q$. This is defined as

    "$p \Leftrightarrow q$ if and only if $p \leftrightarrow q$ is a tautology."

Hohn[10] points out that $\leftrightarrow$ is a logical connective between propositions, whereas $\Leftrightarrow$ designates a relationship existing between logical functions. Distinctions of this type become apparent in Section 4.2 A logical function is any relationship or relationships between propositions that involves the basic operations. Such a relationship may be generalized as $f(p,q,r), \phi(x,y), \Theta(q,b,c)$ or any other of the commonly used notations found in ordinary algebra. In the algebra of logic we develop a system to determine if a relationship such as

$$f(p,q,r) \Leftrightarrow \phi(x,y,z)$$

is valid.

In Section 3.7 we stated that all tautologies and all true logical propositions could be symbolized by "t," and all contradictions and all false logical propositions by "f." A relationship that is immediately apparent is

1(a) $-t \Leftrightarrow f$

(b) $-f \Leftrightarrow t$

These state merely that the denial of a true proposition is false and the denial of a false proposition is true. By definition a proposition cannot be both true and false. This, along with the definition of the basic operations results in

2(a) $p \wedge -p \Leftrightarrow f$

(b) $p \vee -p \Leftrightarrow t$

(c) $--p \Leftrightarrow p$

These are known as the "complement laws" and state that a proposition or its negation must be true but both cannot be true. Form 2(c) is put in here for convenience. It is the familiar "law of double negation" in rhetoric and is sometimes called the "law of involution" in logic.

Another set of laws is known as the "identity laws." These are

3(a) $p \wedge t \Leftrightarrow p$

(b) $p \wedge f \Leftrightarrow f$

(c) $p \vee t \Leftrightarrow t$

(d) $p \vee f \Leftrightarrow p$

In laws 3(a) and 3(d) the truth value of the proposition depends only on the truth value of p. This establishes t as an identity element for conjunction and f as an identity element for disjunction.

The fourth set of laws we may establish are

4(a) $p \wedge p \Leftrightarrow p$

(b) $p \vee p \Leftrightarrow p$

These are the "indempotent laws" and appear on casual consideration to be of no value. The proposition

"Cincinnati is in Ohio and Cincinnati is in Ohio."

is of course true—slightly hysterical, but true. It will be seen later that these laws are of great value in manipulating relationships.

Our next set of laws is

$$5(a) \quad p \wedge q \Leftrightarrow q \wedge p$$
$$(b) \quad p \vee q \Leftrightarrow q \vee p$$

These are the "commutative laws" and show that the order in which propositions are taken in conjunction and disjunction is immaterial. In Section 3.5 we developed the basis for DeMorgan's rules, which are

$$6(a) \quad -(p \wedge q) \Leftrightarrow - p \vee -q$$
$$(b) \quad -(p \vee q) \Leftrightarrow - p \wedge -q$$

These laws are probably the most useful ones we shall encounter. The laws as written, or variations and extensions of them, provide a powerful tool for manipulating relationships in the algebra of logic.

Although we have defined conjunction and disjunction in Section 3.5 as applying to two or more propositions, we find it more convenient to work with pairs of propositions, especially when we are working with truth tables. If we have the propositions $p \wedge q \wedge r$ or $p \vee q \vee r$ we have a choice in how we group the individual propositions. Thus

$$7(a) \quad (p \wedge q) \wedge r \Leftrightarrow p \wedge (q \wedge r)$$
$$(b) \quad (p \vee q) \vee r \Leftrightarrow p \vee (q \vee r)$$

These are the associative laws, which hold for any number of simple propositions. The proposition $p \vee q \vee r \vee s \vee \cdots$ may be grouped in any combination of pairs we see fit to use.

The last set of fundamental laws are the "distributive laws." These are

$$8(a) \quad p \wedge (q \vee r) \Leftrightarrow (p \wedge q) \vee (p \wedge r)$$
$$(b) \quad p \vee (q \wedge r) \Leftrightarrow (p \vee q) \wedge (p \vee r)$$

These are a bit trickier than the others. We can readily see that 8(a) is similar in form to the ordinary algebraic equation $a(b+c) = ab + ac$. However 8(b) is similar to $a + bc = (a+b)(a+c)$, which is definitely not permissible in ordinary algebra. An example of 8(b) is

"Cincinnati is in Ohio or (Rome is in Italy and London is in England)"⇔"(Cincinnati is in Ohio and Rome is in Italy) or (Cincinnati is in Ohio and London is in England)."

To remove any doubts about the validity of 8(a) and 8(b) the truth tables for each are presented. For 8(a):

```
p ∧ (q ∨ r) ⇔ (p ∧ q) ∨ (p ∧ r)
F F F F F T F F F F F F F
F F F T T T F F F F F F T
F F T T F T F F T F F F F
F F T T T T F F T F F F T
T F F F F T T F F F T F F
T T F T T T T F F T T T T
T T T T F T T T T T T F F
T T T T T T T T T T T T T
        *             *
```

For 8(b):

```
p ∨ (q ∧ r) ⇔ (p ∨ q) ∧ (p ∨ r)
F F F F F T F F F F F F F
F F F F T T F F F F F T T
F F T F F T F T T F F F F
F T T T T T F T T T F T T
T T F F F T T T F T T T F
T T F F T T T T F T T T T
T T T F F T T T T T T T F
T T T T T T T T T T T T T
        *             *
```

In each of the above tables we compare the columns marked with an asterisk and find that, find that, from the procedure given in Section 3.7, in each case we have a tautology. In fact, we have proved 8(a) and 8(b) by perfect induction. All of the laws given in this section can be proved by this method. This exercise is, naturally, left to the reader.*

For convenience all of the laws of this algebra are summarized:

1 (a) $-t \Leftrightarrow f$
  (b) $-f \Leftrightarrow t$

2 (a) $p \wedge -p \Leftrightarrow f$
  (b) $p \vee -p \Leftrightarrow t$
  (c) $--p \Leftrightarrow p$ *complement laws*

3 (a) $p \wedge t \Leftrightarrow p$
  (b) $p \vee f \Leftrightarrow f$
  (c) $p \vee t \Leftrightarrow t$
  (d) $p \vee f \Leftrightarrow p$ *identity laws*

---

*All authors of scientific or semiscientific works take a solemn vow to do this at least once in each work.

$$4 \ (a) \quad p \wedge p \Leftrightarrow p$$
$$\quad (b) \quad p \vee p \Leftrightarrow p \qquad\qquad\qquad\qquad \textit{idempotent laws}$$

$$5 \ (a) \quad p \wedge q \Leftrightarrow q \wedge p$$
$$\quad (b) \quad p \vee q \Leftrightarrow q \vee p \qquad\qquad\qquad \textit{commutative laws}$$

$$6 \ (a) \quad -(p \wedge q) \Leftrightarrow -p \vee -q$$
$$\quad (b) \quad -(p \vee q) \Leftrightarrow -p \wedge -q \qquad\qquad \textit{DeMorgan's rules}$$

$$7 \ (a) \quad (p \wedge q) \wedge r \Leftrightarrow p \wedge (q \wedge r)$$
$$\quad (b) \quad (p \vee q) \vee r \Leftrightarrow p \vee (q \vee r) \qquad\quad \textit{associative laws}$$

$$8 \ (a) \quad p \wedge (q \vee r) \Leftrightarrow (p \wedge q) \vee (p \wedge r)$$
$$\quad (b) \quad p \vee (q \wedge r) \Leftrightarrow (p \vee q) \wedge (q \vee r) \qquad \textit{distributive laws}$$

Now that we have developed all of these laws, what do we do with them? Nothing. These laws are for the algebra of propositions, which is one version of the algebra of logic. The algebra of propositions is based on implication and equivalence and can be very difficult to work with. Fortunately there is another version that is much easier to use. This is known as the algebra of truth-value functions but to develop it we need to make a closer examination of the truth-value function.

4.2 THE TRUTH-VALUE FUNCTION

In Section 3.5 we stated that the relationship between a proposition and its truth value, T or F, is known as the truth-value function. In Section 3.7 we stated that all true logical propositions could be symbolized by t and all false logical propositions by f. This is another way of saying that the truth-value function, τ, may be symbolized by t or f. However, *all* propositions, whether logical or factual, must by definition be true or false but not both. The truth-value function of *any* proposition, therefore, may be symbolized by t or f, providing the propositions are used in a complex proposition that is either a tautology or a contradiction. The relationships between truth-value functions may be expressed in a miniature system, which has been aptly described by Christian[8] as the system $\{t,f\}$. In this system we are working with equalities, not equivalences. Propositions and/or the truth values of propositions are equivalent or not equivalent. Truth-value functions of propositions are equal or not equal. It should be stressed that when we equate truth-value functions we establish either a tautology or a contradiction, so that our analysis of truth-value functions of propositions is just as valid as our analysis of the truth values of propositions.

As an example of the system $\{t,f\}$ consider the propositions p and q and the truth-value functions $\tau(p)$, $\tau(q)$, and $\tau(p \wedge q)$. Each of these functions may be replaced by the symbols t or f. The relationships between these functions are

4.2.1
$$\tau(p \wedge q) = \tau(p) \wedge \tau(q)$$

t	$=$	t	t
f	$=$	f	f
f	$=$	t	f
f	$=$	f	t

In 4.2.1 the first $\wedge$ refers to a conjunction of propositions while the second $\wedge$ refers to a conjunction of truth-value functions. The left-hand side is an operation in the system of propositions, while the right-hand side is an operation in the system $\{t,f\}$. The equality sign shows that these systems are analogous and homomorphous.*

Now let's turn our attention to the system $\{t,f\}$. We may let x, y, z, and so on stand for t or f just as we let such letters stand for numbers in ordinary algebra. A proposition will stand for t while the negation of a proposition will stand for f. The algebra of this system is

1	(a)	$x \wedge -x = -x \wedge x = f$	
	(b)	$x \vee -x = -x \vee x = t$	
	(c)	$--x = x$	*complement laws*
2	(a)	$x \wedge t = t \wedge x = x$	
	(b)	$x \wedge f = f \wedge x = f$	
	(c)	$x \vee t = t \vee x = t$	
	(d)	$x \vee f = f \vee x = x$	*identity laws*
3	(a)	$x \wedge x = x$	
	(b)	$x \vee x = x$	*idempotent laws*
4	(a)	$x \wedge y = y \wedge x$	
	(b)	$x \vee y = y \vee x$	*commutative laws*
5	(a)	$-(x \wedge y) = -x \vee -y$	
	(b)	$-(x \vee y) = -x \wedge -y$	*DeMorgan's rules*
6	(a)	$(x \wedge y) \wedge z = x \wedge (y \wedge z)$	
	(b)	$(x \vee y) \vee z = x \vee (y \vee z)$	*associative laws*
7	(a)	$x \wedge (y \vee z) = (x \wedge y) \vee (x \wedge z)$	
	(b)	$x \vee (y \wedge z) = (x \vee y) \wedge (x \vee z)$	*distributive laws*

This algebra, which is the algebra of truth-value functions (or the system $\{t,f\}$), is the one usually referred to as the algebra of logic. It is much more concise than the algebra of propositions since it is a two-variable algebra (t and f) only.

*Homomorphous means "having the same form."

4.3 MANIPULATIONS

We present a few examples to show how the various laws are used in manipulating (not necessarily simplifying) complex expressions.

4.3.1 Simplify $p \vee (-p \wedge p)$.

$$
\begin{aligned}
p \vee (-p \wedge p) &= p \vee f &&\text{by 1(a)} \\
p \vee f &= p &&\text{by 2(d)}
\end{aligned}
$$

4.3.2 Simplify $p \vee (-p \vee q)$.

$$
\begin{aligned}
p \vee (-p \vee q) &= (p \vee -p) \vee q &&\text{by 6(b)} \\
&= t \vee q &&\text{by 1(b)} \\
&= t &&\text{by 2(c)}
\end{aligned}
$$

4.3.3 Simplify $-q \wedge [p \wedge (-p \vee q)]$.

$$
\begin{aligned}
-q \wedge [p \wedge (-p \vee q)] &= -q \wedge [(p \wedge -p) \vee (p \wedge q)] &&\text{by 7(a)} \\
&= -q \wedge [f \vee (p \wedge q)] &&\text{by 1(a)} \\
&= -q \wedge (p \wedge q) &&\text{by 2(d)} \\
&= (-q \wedge q) \wedge p &&\text{by 6(a)} \\
&= f \wedge p &&\text{by 1(a)} \\
&= f &&\text{by 2 (b)}
\end{aligned}
$$

4.3.4 Manipulate $(p \wedge -q) \vee (-p \wedge q)$.

$$
\begin{aligned}
&(p \wedge -q) \vee (-p \wedge q) \\
=&[(p \wedge -q) \vee -p] \wedge [(p \wedge -q) \vee q] &&\text{by 7(b)} \\
=&[(p \vee -p) \wedge (-q \vee -p)] \wedge [(p \vee q) \wedge (q \vee -q)] &&\text{by 7(a)} \\
=&[t \wedge (-p \vee -q)] \wedge [(p \vee q) \wedge t] &&\text{by 4(b), 1(b)} \\
=&(-p \vee -q) \wedge (p \vee q) &&\text{by 2(a)} \\
=&-(p \wedge q) \wedge (p \vee q) &&\text{by 5(a)}
\end{aligned}
$$

Example 4.3.4 is interesting in that it involves the "exclusive or." The given proposition

$$(p \wedge -q) \vee (-p \wedge q)$$

and

$$(-p \vee -q) \wedge (p \vee q)$$

as well as

$$-(p\wedge q)\wedge(p\vee q)$$

are all forms of this that are put into practical use, as we shall see in Chapter 5.

These examples serve to show that this algebra can be manipulated to give a wide variety of results. All of our manipulations have involved simple relationships and could be performed by inspection. There are several methods available for performing these manipulations in a more scientific manner, but the relationships encountered in the logic of truth-value functions are usually not sufficiently complex to justify their use. These methods will be explained and used in Chapter 8.

4.4 POSTULATES OF THE ALGEBRA

In Section 2.3 we defined unary and binary operations and presented the Huntington postulates for the algebra of sets. These postulates, with different notation, hold for all of the algebras we consider. For the algebra of logic, conjunction and disjunction are the binary operations and negation is the unary. The postulates, with the proper notation for this algebra, are:

Postulate I. In system P composed of the elements p, q, r and so on and employing two binary operations $\vee$ and $\wedge$, the operations $\vee$ and $\wedge$ are communtative.

Postulate II. The two operations $\vee$ and $\wedge$ are associative.

Postulate III. Each of the binary operations $\vee$ and $\wedge$ is distributive over the other.

Postulate IV. The identity element f is associated with the operation $\vee$.

Postulate V. The identity element t is associated with the operation $\wedge$.

Postulate VI. For every element p in the system P there exists an element $-p$ such that $p \vee -p = t$ and $p \wedge -p = f$.

Postulate VII. In any algebra of this type, if the operation $\vee$ and the operation $\wedge$ and the identity element t and the identity element f are interchanged throughout the expression, the validity of the expression remains unchanged.

This algebra is, then, by definition a Boolean algebra.

SUMMARY

The most important procedure in this chapter is that of deriving a two-variable algebra (the algebra of truth-value functions) from a multivariable algebra (the algebra of propositions). It is important the reader have a good understanding of how this was accomplished. The applications presented in this book are all based on a two-variable algebra. There are other applications that are not and it is possible to make a serious error by assuming a two-variable algebra applies when it does not. Working with a multivariable algebra usually requires a much more extensive treatment of implication than has been given here.

FIVE
THE BOOLEAN ALGEBRA OF ON–OFF EVENTS

INTRODUCTION

By definition a Boolean algebra consists of a set of variables, three operators, two identity elements, and conforms to the Huntington postulates. If the set of variables consists of two members only and if these are the same as the identity elements, we have the simplest algebra that it is possible to construct.

In the Boolean algebra presented here we have the set $\{1, 0\}$ and the identity elements $1, 0$. In neither case are these to be interpreted as the numbers one and zero. They are abstract symbols. The use of these symbols will become evident.

In this chapter we define on–off events and derive the algebra both rigorously and intuitively.

5.1 ON–OFF EVENTS

In our everyday experience we encounter many things that can exist in only one of two mutually exclusive states or conditions at any given time. You are either at home or not at home, a door is open or closed, you are either sleeping or not sleeping, and so on. All of these may be classified as events. Webster defines an event as "Something that happens: Occurrence." In chemical and mechanical process plants there are many devices that can exist in only one of two states at any given time. A motor may be running or not running, a solenoid may be energized or deenergized, a valve may be open or closed. The state of a device is not in itself an event. Starting or stopping a motor, energizing or deenergizing a solenoid, and opening or closing a valve are events. All devices that may exist in only one of two states at any given time are called bistable devices and they all have one thing in common—the state they are in is the result of an event. These states may be detected by appropriate sensors, which may be electrical, fluidic, mechanical, optical, magnetic, ultrasonic, and so on. The signals from these sensors may be used for control, interlocking, warning, or shutdown, and are also bistable in that they either exist or do not exist.

For our purposes an event is defined as an occurrence that results in the change of the state of a bistable device with a resulting generation or cancellation of a signal. (These may be internal, nonapparent signals in a system.) A signal is defined as information transmitted and *received* concerning the state of a bistable device, or the cancellation (negation, inversion) of a signal. If, for example, a position switch is trying to signal that a valve is closed, and a wire between this switch and the receiving device is broken, there is no signal that the valve is closed. In fact there is a false signal that the valve is *not* closed. A signal may be as simple as an operator observing the liquid level in a gauge glass or as complicated as modern instrumentation can devise. If the liquid level in a tank is rising, this is not an event by our definition unless there is a device to transmit a signal and even then it is not an event unless the signal is bistable. If the liquid reaches a certain level and a device signals that it has attained that level, then we have an event. The liquid may rise above that level but it cannot drop below it without creating another event resulting in a signal that the liquid is below that level, which is a cancellation of the previous signal. We must make this distinction in situations that are not inherently bistable such as the level in a tank or a valve being open or closed. Our signal can only indicate that a level is "high or not high" or "low or not low" if it is to be bistable. Similarly, a valve is "open or not open" or "closed or not closed." The choice of which state will transmit or cancel a signal is completely arbitrary. If the signal is transmitted electrically we may equip the sensing device with normally open or normally closed contacts as we please.

5.2   OPERATIONS WITH ON–OFF EVENTS

The symbology used for on–off events is similar to that used in set theory. Capital letters indicate bistable devices and lowercase letters designate signals that indicate the state a device is in as the result of an event. Since these signals are usually involved in some type of circuit, we say that a signal such as q has a circuit value of 1 and q' has a circuit value of 0. These are abstract symbols, not the numbers one and zero.

Some further explanation of the term "device" is required. We define three different types of devices:

1. A piece of equipment, such as a valve, pump, screw conveyor, or elevator, with a sensing element as an auxiliary part of the equipment. These elements may be position switches, proximity sensors, motion switches, tachometer generators, and so on.

2. An instrument that transmits information such as pressure, temperature, flow, pH, density, or viscosity, in the sense of "high or not high," "low or not low," and so on.

3. In electrical switching circuits switches, relays and so on that may require auxiliary contacts but not auxiliary sensors.

All devices are elements of sets. If we let $\mathfrak{U}$ be the set of devices in a given system, then $A \in \mathfrak{U}$, $B \in \mathfrak{U}$, and so on. An individual device may be represented as a set in itself such as $\{A\}$. For this reason we may use set theory notation and let capital letters represent these sets, that is, the device itself. An event may now be defined as an occurrence resulting in a condition applying to a set. In the expression $\{Q \in \mathfrak{U} | Q(q)\}$ or $\{Q \in \mathfrak{U} | Q(q')\}$, $Q(q)$ is read "device Q is in the state that yields a circuit value of 1" and $Q(q')$ is read "device Q is in the state that yields a circuit value of 0." In Section 2.2 we stated that a condition becomes a proposition when it is applied to an individual member of a set. Since $Q = \{Q\}$ has only one member,* $Q(q)$ and $Q(q')$ are propositions. It is customary to consider q as the event although in reality q is the condition resulting from the event. Since we must assume that any event results in a bistable device being in one or the other of its states we may equate the event with the condition. Thus the algebra of on–off events is really the algebra of circuit values of bistable signals but is rarely, if ever, referred to as such. In working with the algebra the lowercase letters used to denote events are frequently referred to as variables.

Events may be combined in the same way as propositions. The symbology used for events is:

Conjunction	$\cdot$	(expressed or implied as in $p \cdot q$ or pq)
Disjunction	$+$	
Negation	$'$	

Here again, conjunction and disjunction are binary operations and negation is a unary operation.

5.3 RIGOROUS DERIVATION OF THE ALGEBRA

It could be demonstrated that the algebra of on–off events is completely analogous to the algebra of truth-value functions where the system $\{1,0\}$ is comparable to the system $\{t,f\}$. It is not necessary to do this. With the other algebras we first derived them and then demonstrated that they were Boolean algebras. In this case we start by stating that the algebra of on–off

---

*Because the empty set $\varnothing$ is a subset of all sets our set $\{Q\}$ really has two elements, or members; $Q \subseteq \{Q\}$ and $\varnothing \subset \{Q\}$. The empty set indicates the absence of a device.

events *is* a Boolean algebra and we construct it by using the Huntington postulates. These postulates in event notation (usually called Boolean notation) are:

Postulate I. In a class E composed of elements a, b, c, and so on and employing two binary operations $+$ and $\cdot$, the operations $+$ and $\cdot$ are commutative.

Postulate II. The two operations $+$ and $\cdot$ are associative.

Postulate III. Each of the binary operations $+$ and $\cdot$ is distributive over the other.

Postulate IV. The identity element 0 is associated with the operation $+$.

Postulate V. The identity element 1 is associated with the operation $\cdot$.

Postulate VI. For every element a in the class E there exists an element a' such that $a + a' = 1$ and $aa' = 0$.

Postulate VII. In any Boolean algebra, if the operation $+$ and the operation $\cdot$, and the identity element 1 and the identity element 0 are interchanged throughout the expression, the validity of the expression remains unchanged.

The laws of the algebra of on–off events are:

	$1' = 0$	
	$0' = 1$	*by definition*
1 (a)	$aa' = 0$	
(b)	$a + a' = 1$	
(c)	$(a')' = a$	*complement laws (Postulate VI)*
2 (a)	$a1 = a$	
(b)	$a0 = 0$	
(c)	$a + 1 = 1$	
(d)	$a + 0 = a$	*identity laws (Postulates IV and V)*
3 (a)	$aa = a$	
(b)	$a + a = a$	*idempotent laws (Self-evident from the logic of propositions)*
4 (a)	$ab = ba$	
(b)	$a + b = b + a$	*commutative laws (Postulate I)*
5 (a)	$(ab)' = a' + b'$	
(b)	$(a + b)' = a'b'$	*DeMorgan's rules (Postulate VII)*
6 (a)	$(ab)c = a(bc)$	
(b)	$(a + b) + c = a + (b + c)$	*associative laws (Postulate II)*
7 (a)	$a(b + c) = ab + ac$	
(b)	$a + bc = (a + b)(a + c)$	*distributive laws (Postulate III)*

It is evident that this algebra is analogous to and homomorphous with the algebra of truth-value functions. The derivation is completely rigorous because it was made independently of any reliance upon specific types of devices or circuits and is valid for all systems of on–off events. Such a derivation could be made only by using the principles of logic and set theory presented in previous chapters.

5.4 INTUITIVE DERIVATION OF THE ALGEBRA

There is another method for deriving this algebra that is based on an intuitive consideration of simple electrical switching circuits. This method is the one most often presented and results in deriving the "algebra of switching circuits." The assumption is then made that, since switching circuits are based on one system of on–off events, the algebra is valid for all systems of on–off events. This is an excellent example of inductive inference. We will derive the algebra of switching circuits by this method and show that it is identical to the algebra of on–off events so the inference in this case is justified.

The switching circuits we consider are two-terminal, hard wired, relay circuits. We wish to conduct electrons from one terminal to the other without being concerned about the source of these electrons. In between the terminals we may have various devices. The simplest of these would be a single pole single throw (SPST) switch, as shown in Figure 5.4.1. If A is closed the circuit is completed and electrons flow from one terminal to the other. We define this condition of the circuit by the symbol 1. If we open switch A electrons cease to flow. We define this condition of the circuit by the symbol 0. Here again, these are symbols, not the numbers one and zero. The assignment of these symbols to the circuit conditions is completely arbitrary but is conventional. Opening and closing switch A are events. We symbolize the opening of switch A by a' and the closing of the switch by a. We may now say $a = 1$ and $a' = 0$. These equations are not read "a equals one" and "a' equals zero." Rather they mean "Event a results in the state of device A that gives a circuit value of 1" and "Event a' results in the state of device A that gives a circuit value of 0." Now we put another SPST switch into the circuit. If we put it in series with switch A we have the device shown in Figure 5.4.2. We now have four possible combinations, which are

A is open, B is open

A is open, B is closed

A is closed, B is open

A is closed, B is closed

Figure 5.4.1 SPST switch.

Figure 5.4.2 Switches in series.

We may restate these combinations as

$$a' \text{ and } b' = 0$$
$$a' \text{ and } b = 0$$
$$a \text{ and } b' = 0$$
$$a \text{ and } b = 1$$

Now we can see at a glance that only one combination will give us a closed circuit. To make this completely symbolic we will replace the word "and" by the symbol $\cdot$, expressed or implied. Our combinations are now

$$a'b' = 0$$
$$a'b = 0$$
$$ab' = 0$$
$$ab = 1$$

An expression such as ab is known as a logical product.

If we put switch B in parallel with switch A as shown in Figure 5.4.3, we again have four possible combinations, which are

$$a' \text{ or } b' = 0$$
$$a' \text{ or } b = 1$$
$$a \text{ or } b' = 1$$
$$a \text{ or } b = 1$$

Now we see that we have only one combination that gives us an open circuit. If we replace the word "or" by the symbol $+$, we have

$$a' + b' = 0$$
$$a' + b = 1$$
$$a + b' = 1$$
$$a + b = 1$$

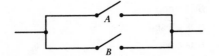

Figure 5.4.3 Switches in parallel.

An expression such as $a+b$ is known as a logical sum. The symbol $+$ stands for the nonexclusive *or* in that it means "--- or *** or both." The exclusive *or*, "--- or *** but not both," is covered later.

We now have all the symbols needed for our algebra. They are

$\cdot$	AND	(conjunction)
$+$	OR	(disjunction)
$'$	NOT	(negation)
$=$	gives as a result	

The AND and OR are binary operations, while the NOT is a unary operation. With our symbols defined it is now possible to determine certain relationships between events. The first of these may seem trivial but isn't. In the circuit shown in Figure 5.4.4 we have electrons flowing through a permanently closed junction, which we shall designate as 1 since it always gives 1 as a circuit value. If we introduce switch A into this circuit, as shown in Figure 5.4.5, we come up with these interesting relationships:

$$a \cdot 1 = 1 \quad \text{and} \quad a' \cdot 1 = 0$$

This means that the circuit value depends entirely on the state of switch A and shows that 1 is an identity element for the operation AND.

Similarly, if we have a permanently open junction, as in Figure 5.4.6, we may call it 0 since it always yields 0 as a circuit value. If we introduce switch A into this circuit, as in Figure 5.4.7, we have $a + 0 = 1$ and $a' + 0 = 0$. This shows that 0 is an identity element for the operation OR. These are the identity laws of the algebra of switching circuits.

In Figure 5.4.8 we show two sets of normally open (NO) or normally closed (NC) contacts on a relay, both sets designated as A. Now if A is closed, A is certainly closed so $aa = a$ and if A is open $a'a' = a'$. If these two sets of NO or NC contacts are in parallel, as shown in Figure 5.4.9, we have $a + a = a$ and $a' + a' = a'$. These are the idempotent laws of the algebra and may seem a bit hysterical at first glance but are extremely useful in manipulating Boolean functions. If in Figures 5.4.8 and 5.4.9 one

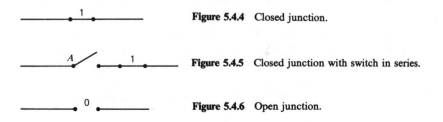

Figure 5.4.4　Closed junction.

Figure 5.4.5　Closed junction with switch in series.

Figure 5.4.6　Open junction.

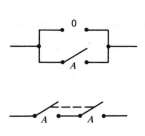

Figure 5.4.7   Open junction with switch in parallel.

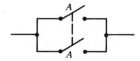

Figure 5.4.8   Gang switch, series circuit.

Figure 5.4.9   Gang switch, parallel circuit.

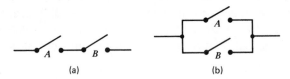

(a)   (b)

Figure 5.4.10   (a) Series circuit with SPST switches. (b) Parallel circuit with SPST switches.

set of contacts was NO while the other was NC we would have $aa' = 0$ and $a + a' = 1$. These are the complement laws.

In the circuits shown in Figure 5.4.10(a) and (b), the sequence in which the switches are opened or closed makes no difference. Therefore $ab = ba$ and $a + b = b + a$, which are the commutative laws.

Two somewhat difficult concepts to grasp intuitively from circuit diagrams are $(ab)' = a' + b'$ and $(a + b)' = a'b'$. These are DeMorgan's rules, which can be illustrated much more easily with logic diagrams than with circuit diagrams. However, a careful study of Figure 5.4.11 will show that this diagram does illustrate DeMorgan's rules. The functions $(ab)'$ and $(a + b)'$ are extremely important from the standpoint of logic hardware. The first is known as the NAND gate and the second as the NOR gate.*

We have two more sets of laws to derive but they require three devices. From Figure 5.4.12 it is evident that $(a + b) + c = a + (b + c) = a + b + c$. Also, from Figure 5.4.13, $(ab)c = a(bc) = abc$. These are the associative laws.

If we now consider Figure 5.4.14(a) and (b) it is evident that $a(b + c) = ab + ac$. From Figure 5.4.15(a) and (b) it is seen that $a + bc = (a + b)(a + c)$. These are the distributive laws and complete the set of basic laws for the

*This is imprecise but generally accepted terminology. NAND is not a gating function.

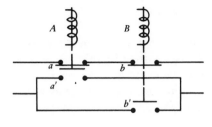

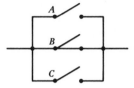

Figure 5.4.11 Relay circuit illustrating DeMorgan's rules.

Figure 5.4.12 Multiple switches in parallel.

Figure 5.4.13 Multiple switches in series.

algebra of switching circuits. A listing of these laws would be the same as the list given in Section 5.3. This indicates that the intuitive derivation of this algebra is valid. It is also a very simple system to work with in that it involves well-known devices and is, as presented, a system of two-terminal combinational circuits. Some systems of on–off events would be very difficult to analyze intuitively, particularly if they were inherently sequential.

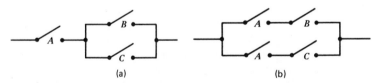

(a)   (b)

Figure 5.4.14 (a) Series/parallel circuit illustrating $a(b+c)$. (b) Parallel circuit illustrating $ab+ac$.

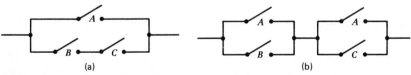

(a)   (b)

Figure 5.4.15 (a) Series/parallel circuit illustrating $a+bc$. (b) Parallel/series/parallel circuit illustrating $(a+b)(a+c)$.

5.5   MULTIPLE VARIABLE BOOLEAN ALGEBRAS

The various Boolean algebras we have encountered are frequently referred to as "two-valued Boolean algebras." This is correct in that all Boolean algebras are by definition two-valued. The statement is, however, misleading because what is meant is that these algebras are two-variable as well as two-valued algebras. The strict definition of any Boolean algebra is

$$\beta(S, \text{Oper}, \text{Oper}, \text{Oper}, \text{Ident}, \text{Ident})$$

where S = the set of variables
        Oper = one of the three basic functions
        Ident = one of the identity elements

In on–off events symbols this becomes

$$\beta(S, \cdot, +, ', 1, 0)$$

Because $S = \{1,0\}$, this is a two-variable algebra. In algebra of logic symbols we have

$$\beta(S, \wedge, \vee, \sim, t, f)$$

If we are dealing with the logic of propositions the set S may have more than two elements, which is one reason why we do not use it. In the algebra of truth-value functions $S = \{t, f\}$ so we have a two-variable algebra.

An example of a multivariable algebra has been given by Mendelson.[11] This is

$$(S, \wedge, \vee, ', 1, 70)$$

Let $x \in S, y \in S$
      $x \wedge y$ = greatest common divisor
      $x \vee y$ = least common multiple
      S = integer divisors of $70 = 1, 2, 5, 7, 10, 14, 35, 70$
      x' = $70/x$
      $1'$ = 70
      $70'$ = 1

This is a multivariable two-valued Boolean algebra based on the number 70.

There are also multivalued algebras that, by definition, are not Boolean algebras. In these algebras there are more than two identity elements. Brown[12] gives an example of one of these and has developed a computer program to investigate such algebras.

SUMMARY

The use of the abstract symbols for members of the set 1, 0 and for the identity elements tends to be confusing. In each case the symbols represent a circuit condition (not necessarily an electrical circuit). This, however, is more easily explained by reference to electrical switching circuits. In Figure 5.4.7 it is readily seen that closing switch A (condition = a) results in a circuit condition of 1. Opening this switch (condition = a') gives a circuit condition of 0. Thus we may say that a has a circuit value of 1 and a' has a circuit value of 0.

    In the parallel circuit shown in Figure 5.4.10(b) the same analogy may be used. In this case the circuit values for a, a' and b, b' apply to the branch of the circuit in which they appear.

SIX

EXTENSION OF THE ALGEBRA

INTRODUCTION

The Boolean algebra we are considering is essentially a very simple algebra in that it involves only two variables and three operations. However, the number of terms (a, b, c, d, ...) which may be involved is unlimited. There can be a bewildering number of combinations of terms and operators. There are methods to reduce such a maze to manageable expressions. These methods may involve dualities, identities, and basic functions. Truth tables are of great assistance in checking the validity of various expressions that may be derived.

Here we also introduce the concept of the Boolean matrix. It will become evident that all truth tables are Boolean matrices but all Boolean matrices are not truth tables.

6.1 DUALITIES AND IDENTITIES

An important but frequently misunderstood relationship in Boolean algebra is the principle of duality. This is based on Huntington's seventh postulate, which is repeated here for convenience.

Postulate VII. In any Boolean algebra, if the operation + and the operation ·, and the identity element 1 and the identity element 0 are interchanged throughout the expression, the validity of the expression remains unchanged.

The principle of duality is well illustrated by laws 1(a) and 1(b), which are

$$1(a) \qquad aa' = 0$$
$$1(b) \qquad a + a' = 1$$

These are known as dual laws since either can be derived from the other through the use of the seventh postulate. This is so evident with laws 1(a) and 1(b) that they are also known as the "axioms of duality." The principle of duality tells us that if the expression $aa' = 0$ is valid, the expression $a + a' = 1$ is equally valid. It does *not* tell us that $aa' = a + a'$. Although this is obvious in the case of laws 1(a) and 1(b), it is not so obvious in laws such as DeMorgan's rules and misinterpretation of this principle can and does create confusion. All of the laws listed in Section 5.3, with the exception of law 1(c), are grouped as dual pairs. Law 1(c) is its own dual. The great utility of the principle of duality is that if any given law is proved, its dual is automatically proved.

The laws of Boolean algebra may be used to derive an unlimited number of identities but only a few of these are important to us. These are listed here without proof but later it will be shown that these and all of the laws may be proven through the use of truth tables. The identities are:

1. Extension of the distributive laws:
   a) $a(b + c + d) = ab + ac + ad$
   b) $\quad a + bcd = (a + b)(a + c)(a + d)$
2. Extension of DeMorgan's rules:
   a) $(a + b + c)' = a'(b'c') = a'b'c'$
   b) $\quad (abc)' = a' + b' + c'$
3. Variation of DeMorgan's rules:
   a) $(a'b')' = a + b$
   b) $(a' + b')' = ab$
4. The absorption laws:
   a) $\quad\quad\quad\quad a + ab = a$
   b) $\quad\quad\quad\quad a(a + b) = a$
   c) $\quad\quad\quad\quad a + a'b = a + b$
   d) $\quad\quad\quad\quad a(a' + b) = ab$
   e) $(a + b)(a' + c)(b + c) = (a + b)(a' + c)$
   f) $\quad\quad\quad ab + a'c + bc = ab + a'c$

All of these identities are arranged as dual pairs.

6.2 TRUTH TABLES

In Chapter 5 it was shown that the algebra of on–off events is a propositional algebra applied to sets and is analogous to the algebra of truth-value functions. This may therefore be analyzed by truth tables where 1 and 0 are substituted, respectively, for t and f. A Boolean truth table is known more correctly as a Boolean matrix or, in switching circuits, a circuit matrix. In subsequent chapters we will use the term "matrix" and it will become evident that while all truth tables are matrices all matrices are not, by strict definition, truth tables.

The truth table for the operation of conjunction is:

a	b	$a \cdot b$
0	0	0
0	1	0
1	0	0
1	1	1

Because $ab = 1$ only if $a = 1$ and $b = 1$, we can have only one 1 in the column under the conjoined events. For the operation of disjunction we have

a	b	$a + b$
0	0	0
0	1	1
1	0	1
1	1	1

Here we have three combinations where the disjoined events have a circuit value of 1.

Compound forms are those which involve more than one of the operations AND, OR, and NOT. Some examples of these are

Example 6.2.1 ab'.

Example 6.2.2 $a'b + ab'$.

Example 6.2.3 $a(a' + b)' + b$.

The truth table for Example 6.2.1 is

a	b	b'	$a \cdot b'$
0	0	1	0
0	1	0	0
1	0	1	1
1	1	0	0

For Example 6.2.2 we have

a	b	a'	b'	$a' \cdot b$	$a \cdot b'$	$a' \cdot b + a \cdot b'$
0	0	1	1	0	0	0
0	1	1	0	1	0	1
1	0	0	1	0	1	1
1	1	0	0	0	0	0

This may be done in abbreviated form as was shown in Section 1.7. For Example 6.2.2 this is

a'	$\cdot$	b	$+$	a	$\cdot$	b'
0 1 0 0	0	0 0 0 1
0 1 1 1	1	0 0 1 0
1 0 0 0	1	1 1 0 1
1 0 0 1	0	1 0 1 0

Example 6.2.3 is shown in abbreviated form as

[a	$\cdot$	(a	$'$	$+$	b)	$'$]	$+$	b
0	0	0	1	1	0		1	0
0	0	0	1	1	1		1	1
1	0	1	0	0	0		1	0
1	1	1	0	1	1		1	1
							*	

(The asterisk indicates the final operation.)

It is readily seen that these truth tables are, except for symbols, the same type as given in Section 1.7. Here again two events require four rows, three events require eight rows, and n events require 2^n rows. Now we can say that this is true because the power set of n elements in a set of devices, $\mathcal{U}$, is composed of the 2^n subsets of $\mathcal{U}$ (see Section 3.2). In setting up a truth table for three events and for four events we would have

a	b	c
0	0	0
0	0	1
0	1	0
0	1	1
1	0	0
1	0	1
1	1	0
1	1	1

a	b	c	d
0	0	0	0
0	0	0	1
0	0	1	0
0	0	1	1
0	1	0	0
0	1	0	1
0	1	1	0
0	1	1	1
1	0	0	0
1	0	0	1
1	0	1	0
1	0	1	1
1	1	0	0
1	1	0	1
1	1	1	0
1	1	1	1

These are of particular interest in that the former lists, from top to bottom, the numbers zero through seven and the latter the numbers zero through fifteen in binary notation. This is the reason that all of the possible combinations are listed in the manner chosen, as was hinted in Section 3.6. Arrays such as these are known as codes (they are also matrices) and are essential in constructing counters, adders, comparators, and so on in digital computers. The arrays shown represent the standard binary code. Many other codes have been developed for special purposes, particularly for telemetry. For our purposes the standard binary code will usually suffice, although we will encounter the reflected binary code (Gray code) in Chapter 7.

To demonstrate the power of truth tables we use them to prove some of the theorems and identities. The duals of these are automatically proven. The columns in the truth tables to be compared for the proof are denoted by asterisks.

Proof of Theorem 5(a)

$$(ab)' = a' + b'$$

$$(a \cdot b)' = a' + b'$$

0	0	0	1	0	1	1	0	1
0	0	1	1	0	1	1	1	0
1	0	0	1	1	0	1	0	1
1	1	1	0	1	0	0	1	0
			*			*		

Proof of Theorem 7(b)

$$a + bc = (a+b)(a+c)$$

$$a + (b \cdot c) = (a + b) \cdot (a + c)$$

0	0	0	0	0	0	0	0	0	0	0	0
0	0	0	0	1	0	0	0	0	0	1	1
0	0	1	0	0	0	1	1	0	0	0	0
0	1	1	1	1	0	1	1	1	0	1	1
1	1	0	0	0	1	1	0	1	1	1	0
1	1	0	0	1	1	1	0	1	1	1	1
1	1	1	0	0	1	1	1	1	1	1	0
1	1	1	1	1	1	1	1	1	1	1	1
	*						*				

Proof of Identity 4(a)

$$a + ab = a$$

$$a + (a \cdot b) = a$$

0	0	0	0	0	0
0	0	0	0	1	0
1	1	1	0	0	1
1	1	1	1	1	1
	*				*

Proof of Identity 4(c)

$$a + a'b \quad = \quad a + b$$

a	+	(a	'	·	b)	=	a	+	b
0	0	0	1	0	0		0	0	0
0	1	0	1	1	1		0	1	1
1	1	1	0	0	0		1	1	0
1	1	1	0	0	1		1	1	1

　　　　*　　　　　　　*

Proof of Identity 4(f)

$$ab + a'c + bc \quad = \quad ab + a'c$$

(a	·	b)	+	(a	'	·	c)	+	(b	·	c)	=	(a	·	b)	+	(a	'	·	c)
0	0	0	0	0	1	0	0	0	0	0	0		0	0	0	0	0	1	0	0
0	0	0	1	0	1	1	1	1	0	0	1		0	0	0	1	0	1	1	1
0	0	1	0	0	1	0	0	0	1	0	0		0	0	1	0	0	1	0	0
0	0	1	1	0	1	1	1	1	1	1	1		0	0	1	1	0	1	1	1
1	0	0	0	1	0	0	0	0	0	0	0		1	0	0	0	1	0	0	0
1	0	0	0	1	0	0	1	0	0	0	1		1	0	0	0	1	0	0	1
1	1	1	1	1	0	0	0	0	1	0	0		1	1	1	1	1	0	0	0
1	1	1	1	1	0	0	1	1	1	1	1		1	1	1	1	1	0	0	1

　　　　*　　　　　　　*

All of these proofs are "proofs by perfect induction." These proofs may be made by algebraic manipulation of the Boolean functions. Law 7(b) will be proven in this manner for illustration. It will be assumed that all of the other laws have been proven.

$$a + bc = (a + b)(a + c) \qquad \qquad \textit{Law 7(b)}$$

Step 1　$a + bc = a1 + bc$
　　　　since by 2(a) $a1 = a$.

Step 2　$a + bc = a[1 + (b + c)] + bc$
　　　　since by 2(c) $1 + (b + c) = 1$.

Step 3　$a + bc = [a1 + a(b + c)] + bc$
　　　　from 7(a).

Step 4　$a + bc = [a + (ab + ac)] + bc$
　　　　from 2(a) and 7(a).

Step 5　$a + bc = [(a + ab) + ac] + bc$
　　　　from 6(b).

Step 6　$a + bc = (a + ab) + (ac + bc)$
　　　　from 6(b).

Step 7　$a + bc = (aa + ab) + (ac + bc)$
　　　　since from 3(a) $aa = a$.

Step 8 $a + bc = a(a + b) + c(a + b)$
from 7(a).

Step 9 $a + bc = (a + b)(a + c)$ Q.E.D.

It is obvious that proof by perfect induction is faster and easier if the number of variables (events) does not exceed four. The above proof by manipulation was given in great (and unnecessary) detail to show how the functions can be manipulated and in particular to show the usefulness of the idempotent law (Step 7). Such manipulations should be practiced to attain facility in working with Boolean functions.

6.3   THE BASIC BOOLEAN FUNCTIONS

There are four primary Boolean functions in two variables. These are xy, xy', $x'y$, and $x'y'$. The disjunction of these functions yields all of the basic, nonequivalent Boolean functions and all other functions in two variables may be reduced to these. The function $xy + xy' + x'y + x'y' = 1$ is one of the two "canonical forms" and is known as the "disjunctive normal form." If we apply the principle of duality this becomes

$$(x + y)(x + y')(x' + y)(x' + y') = 0.$$

This is the other canonical form and is known as the "conjunctive normal form." The former is also called the "sum of the product terms (or P-terms)" and the latter the "product of the sum terms (S-terms)." The canonical forms are covered in more detail in Chapter 7. The disjunctive form is the easier of the two to work with so it is used to derive the basic functions.

The primary P-terms comprise a set of functions that has 4 elements so the power set is composed of 16 subsets. Disjunction of the elements of these subsets yields the basic functions. For convenience let

$$x'y' = a$$
$$x'y = b$$
$$xy' = c$$
$$xy = d$$

where the symbol $=$ means "is defined as." The sixteen subsets of the set $\{a,b,c,d\}$ are

$$
\begin{array}{cccc}
\{a,b,c,d\} & \{b,c,d\} & \{b,c\} & \{b\} \\
\{a,b,c\} & \{a,b\} & \{b,d\} & \{c\} \\
\{a,b,d\} & \{a,c\} & \{c,d\} & \{d\} \\
\{a,c,d\} & \{a,d\} & \{a\} & \varnothing
\end{array}
$$

Starting with the first listed subset, $\{a,b,c,d\}$, the disjunction of the elements gives

$$
\begin{aligned}
a+b+c+d &= x'y' + x'y + xy' + xy \\
&= x'(y'+y) + x(y'+y) \\
&= x'(1) + x(1) \\
&= x' + x \\
&= 1 \\
a+b+c &= x'y' + x'y + xy' \\
&= x'(y+y') + xy' \\
&= x' + xy' \\
&= (x'+x)(x'+y') \\
&= x' + y' \\
a+b+d &= x'y' + x'y + xy \\
&= x'(y+y') + xy \\
&= x' + xy \\
&= (x'+x)(x'+y) \\
&= x' + y
\end{aligned}
$$

This procedure could be repeated for all of the subsets. However, we may assume that the dual of a basic function is also a basic function so we have

Function	Dual function
$x'y'$	$x'+y'$
$x'y$	$x'+y$
xy'	$x+y'$
xy	$x+y$

We may also assume that x, x', y, and y' as well as the two canonical forms are basic functions. This gives a total of 14. We can verify that all of these functions are basic by constructing a matrix that shows all of the possible disjunctions of the primary P-terms. In this matrix a 1 under a P-term indicates that it is present in the disjunction while a 0 indicates that it is absent. It should be noted that this is a Boolean matrix which is not a truth table. The matrix is:

P	a	b	c	d	$f_{(+)}(a,b,c,d)$
0	0	0	0	0	0
1	0	0	0	1	xy
2	0	0	1	0	xy'
3	0	0	1	1	x
4	0	1	0	0	$x'y$
5	0	1	0	1	y
6	0	1	1	0	$xy' + x'y$
7	0	1	1	1	$x+y$
8	1	0	0	0	$x'y'$
9	1	0	0	1	$xy + x'y'$
10	1	0	1	0	y'
11	1	0	1	1	$x+y'$
12	1	1	0	0	x'
13	1	1	0	1	$x'+y$
14	1	1	1	0	$x'+y'$
15	1	1	1	1	1

This verifies that the 14 forms we selected *are* basic functions. The other two are $P6$ and $P9$. The reader should perform all of these disjunctions and, in particular, verify that $P0$ and $P15$ are the canonical forms. It is excellent practice in manipulating Boolean functions.

If we had used the conjunctive form to develop our basic functions the primary functions would be

$$x' + y' = e \qquad \text{(by definition)}$$

$$x' + y = f \qquad \text{(by definition)}$$

$$x + y' = g \qquad \text{(by definition)}$$

$$x + y = h \qquad \text{(by definition)}$$

Using the same matrix method we used for disjunction gives the basic functions in different order.

S	e	f	g	h	$f_{()}(e,f,g,h)$
0	0	0	0	0	1
1	0	0	0	1	$x+y$
2	0	0	1	0	$x+y'$
3	0	0	1	1	x
4	0	1	0	0	$x'+y$
5	0	1	0	1	y
6	0	1	1	0	$xy+x'y'$
7	0	1	1	1	xy
8	1	0	0	0	$x'+y'$
9	1	0	0	1	$xy'+x'y$
10	1	0	1	0	y'
11	1	0	1	1	xy'
12	1	1	0	0	x'
13	1	1	0	1	$x'y$
14	1	1	1	0	$x'y'$
15	1	1	1	1	0

To arrive at the $S0$ through $S15$ terms it is only necessary to take the duals of the corresponding $P0$ through $P15$ terms.

6.4 ADDITIONAL SYMBOLOGY

Functions $P9$ ($S6$) and $P6$ ($S9$) are of particular interest. $P9$ is the "both-or-neither" and is found in the well-known "hall light switch" circuit. $P6$ is, at long last, the "exclusive or." This is also called the "ring sum" because the symbol usually used for it is $\oplus$. The "both-or-neither" and the "exclusive or" are dual functions. (Wiring a hall light switch with an "exclusive or" circuit is an excellent but frustrating way of demonstrating that dual functions are not equal.) The "exclusive or" may be implemented in these ways:

$xy'+x'y$	basic function
$(x+y)(xy)'$	from DeMorgan's rules
$(x+y)(x'+y')$	dual of the both-or-neither function (first step)

Any of these may be used but the second one has the least number of logical operations (four versus five) and should be the most economical to implement.

Function $P14$ ($S8$) is $x' + y'$. This function is of sufficient importance to have acquired a special symbol, which is $x|y$. The vertical line is known as the "Scheffer stroke." From DeMorgan's rules $x' + y' = (xy)'$, which is the NAND function. The Scheffer stroke usually designates this function. All logical functions in two variables can be expressed in terms of the NAND, or stroke, function.

Function $P8$ ($S14$) is $x'y'$. This also has a special symbol, $x\|y$, known as the "double stroke." From DeMorgan's rules $x'y' = (x+y)'$, which is the NOR function. All logical functions in two variables may also be expressed in terms of the NOR, or double stroke function. The NOR function (which is covered briefly in Chapter 9) is used more widely than the NAND function. It should be noted that NAND and NOR are dual functions.

The two-variable matrix for the above functions is

x	y	$x \oplus y$	$x\|y$	$x\|\|y$
0	0	0	1	1
0	1	1	1	0
1	0	1	1	0
1	1	0	0	0

SUMMARY

Although all of the material presented in this chapter is used in later chapters, the most important concepts introduced are the principle of duality and the Boolean matrix (as distinguished from a truth table). We will see how important these are in the following chapter, which deals with canonical forms.

SEVEN
CANONICAL FORMS

INTRODUCTION

The canonical (or standard) forms of Boolean functions are essential in circuit design. This applies not just to switching circuits but also to pneumatic, hydraulic, fluidic, and mechanical circuits. There are two different canonical forms—disjunctive normal and conjunctive normal. A very slight amount of practice in manipulating Boolean functions will convince you that disjunctive functions are much easier to work with than conjunctive functions. The easiest way to work with the conjunctive form is to convert it to the disjunctive by using the principle of duality. However, each form has its advantages, as you will see.

Conversion of a disjunctive function to disjunctive normal form (dnf) may be done by manipulating the function through the various laws of the algebra. Here the idempotent laws, which were described as seeming somewhat hysterical, are put to good use.

Conversion by manipulation is widely used and is usually the only method presented. It will become apparent that matrix conversion is much easier, faster, and less subject to error.

We also introduce the concept of the "don't care" variable (or term). This will be of great use to us, particularly in the material covered in Chapter 10.

7.1 DISJUNCTIVE NORMAL FORM

Boolean functions may appear in many different forms. A function such as $f(a,b,c)$ may appear for example as

7.1.1 $a'b'c' + a'bc + ab'c + abc' = 1$

7.1.2 $ac + ab' + b + c + ab = 1$

7.1.3 $ab + bc + c + ac = 1$

All of these functions are in disjunctive form because they are disjunctions (logical sums) of conjunctive (logical product) terms. Such a form is usually called a "sum of the P-terms," as was noted in the previous chapter.

For the sake of illustration we assume that the above functions represent different switching circuits involving three switches, A, B, and C. The circuit values of these switches are symbolized by a,a', b,b', and c,c'. We wish to design circuits corresponding to these functions, using all three switches, where each term in the function represents a path through the circuit that results in a circuit value of 1. In the terms where not all of the switches are represented we must know the state (circuit value) of the missing switches to design the circuit. When an expression exists for all of the switches in all of the terms the function is said to be in canonical, or standard, form.

In function 7.1.1 all of the switches are represented in each term so this function is in canonical form. Since the function is composed solely of the sum of P-terms it is said to be in disjunctive normal form (dnf). Function 7.1.1 may be simplified from

$$a'b'c' + a'bc + ab'c + abc' = 1$$

to

$$a'(b'c' + bc) + a(b'c + bc') = 1$$

which, although in canonical form, is not in normal form since both P-terms and S-terms are involved. The circuit for this function in the simplified form is shown in Figure 7.1.1.

Functions 7.1.2 and 7.1.3 are not in canonical form. However, they may be put into dnf by applying laws 1(b), 2(a), 3(b), and 7(a) given in Chapter 5. Function 7.1.2 would be converted by

$$ac + ab' + b + c + ab = 1$$
$$ac(b + b') + ab'(c + c') + b(a + a') + c(a + a') + ab(c + c') = 1$$
$$abc + ab'c + ab'c + ab'c' + ab + a'b + ac + a'c + abc + abc' = 1$$
$$abc + ab'c + ab'c' + abc' + ab(c + c') + a'b(c + c') + ac(b + b') + $$
$$a'c(b + b') = 1$$
$$abc + ab'c + ab'c' + abc' + abc + abc' + a'bc + a'bc' + abc + ab'c + $$
$$a'bc + a'b'c = 1$$
$$abc + ab'c + ab'c' + abc' + a'bc + a'bc' + a'b'c = 1$$

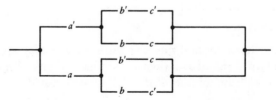

Figure 7.1.1   Circuit diagram for function 7.1.1.

An easier way to do this is with a circuit matrix. In using such a matrix we consider only the P-terms given in the function, that is, only those terms that have a circuit value of 1. The others have a circuit value of 0. For function 7.1.2 the matrix, shown constructed in two steps, is shown below.

Table 7.1.1   Circuit matrix for function 7.1.2—Step 1

P	a	b	c	P-terms in function 7.1.2
0	0	0	0	
1	0	0	1	c
2	0	1	0	b
3	0	1	1	bc
4	1	0	0	ab'
5	1	0	1	$ab'c$
6	1	1	0	ab
7	1	1	1	abc

Step 1   See Table 7.1.1. Function 7.1.2 is $ac + ab' + b + c + ab = 1$. The first term, where $a = 1$ and $c = 1$, appears in $P5$ and $P7$. The second term, where $a = 1$ and $b' = 1$ ($b = 0$), appears in $P4$ and $P5$. The third term, b, appears in $P2$, $P3$, $P6$, and $P7$. The fourth term, c, appears in $P1$, $P3$, $P5$, and $P7$. The fifth term, where $a = 1$ and $b = 1$, appears in $P6$ and $P7$. It is apparent that $P5$ and $P7$ are complete terms in that all three switches are represented. The completion of the other terms is shown in Table 7.1.2.

Table 7.1.2   Circuit matrix for function 7.1.2—Step 2

P	a	b	c	P-terms in Function 7.1.2	Completed P-terms
0	0	0	0		
1	0	0	1	c	$a'b'c$
2	0	1	0	b	$a'bc'$
3	0	1	1	bc	$a'bc$
4	1	0	0	ab'	$ab'c'$
5	1	0	1	$ab'c$	$ab'c$
6	1	1	0	ab	abc'
7	1	1	1	abc	abc

Step 2   See Table 7.1.2. The dnf is then

$$P1 + P2 + P3 + P4 + P5 + P6 + P7 = 1$$

which is

$$a'b'c + a'bc' + a'bc + ab'c' + ab'c + abc' + abc = 1$$

This may be simplified as shown:

$$a'b'c + a'b(c' + c) + ab'(c' + c) + ab(c' + c) = 1$$
$$a'b'c + a'b + ab' + ab = 1$$
$$a'b'c + b(a' + a) + ab' = 1$$
$$a'b'c + b + ab' = 1$$
$$b'(a'c + a) + b = 1$$
$$b'(a + c) + b = 1 \qquad \text{(by absorption law)}$$

The circuit for this is shown in Figure 7.1.2.

Table 7.1.3   Circuit matrix for function 7.1.3

P	a	b	c	P-terms in function 7.1.3	P-terms
0	0	0	0		
1	0	0	1	c	$a'b'c$
2	0	1	0		
3	0	1	1	bc	$a'bc$
4	1	0	0		
5	1	0	1	$a\ c$	$ab'c$
6	1	1	0	ab	abc'
7	1	1	1	abc	abc

The dnf for function 7.1.3 may be determined from Table 7.1.3. The dnf is

$$P1 + P3 + P5 + P6 + P7 = 1$$

which is

$$a'b'c + a'bc + ab'c + abc' + abc = 1$$

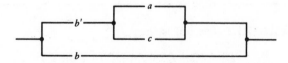

Figure 7.1.2   Circuit diagram for function 7.1.2.

The simplification of this is

$$a'b'c + a'bc + ab'c + ab(c' + c) = 1$$
$$a'c(b' + b) + ab'c + ab = 1$$
$$a'c + a(b'c + b) = 1$$
$$a'c + a(b + c) = 1$$
$$a'c + ab + ac = 1$$
$$c(a' + a) + ab = 1$$
$$c + ab = 1$$

This circuit is, of course, as shown in Figure 7.1.3.

We may also determine the expression for a circuit that gives a particular circuit characteristic, that is, that has a specific circuit matrix. If we are given

x	y	z	$f(x,y,z)$
0	0	0	0
0	0	1	1
0	1	0	0
0	1	1	0
1	0	0	1
1	0	1	0
1	1	0	1
1	1	1	1

the expression is $x'y'z + xy'z' + xyz' + xyz$. A practical example of this is the design of the three-position hall lamp switch circuit. In this circuit we wish to switch a lamp on or off from any of three locations. We will stipulate that $abc = 1$ and that this completes the circuit and lights the lamp. Putting any one (or all three) of these switches in their other state will turn the lamp off. The circuit matrix for this is best shown by use of the reflected binary (or Gray) code. The standard binary code and the Gray code are compared in Table 7.1.4. The first column in each of these codes is the same. In the second column of the Gray code the lower half is a reflection of the upper half. In the third column of the Gray code the second quarter is a reflection of the first quarter and the fourth quarter is a

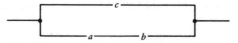

Figure 7.1.3 Circuit diagram for function 7.1.3.

reflection of the third quarter. The advantage of the Gray code is that as we proceed down the array, only one binary value changes in successive rows.

Table 7.1.4   Standard binary and Gray codes

Standard binary code			Gray code		
a	b	c	a	b	c
0	0	0	0	0	0
0	0	1	0	0	1
0	1	0	0	1	1
0	1	1	0	1	0
1	0	0	1	1	0
1	0	1	1	1	1
1	1	0	1	0	1
1	1	1	1	0	0

In our hall lamp problem we stipulated that the lamp would be on when $abc = 1$. Using the Gray code, as in Table 7.1.5, we see that the lamp will go off and on alternately as we proceed up or down the array from $abc = 1$. Therefore $f(a,b,c) = a'b'c + a'bc' + abc + ab'c' = 1$. The circuit for this is shown in Figure 7.1.4. Here B is a special, but available, switch. This circuit could be extended to include n switches, $n-2$ of which would be special.

Table 7.1.5   Circuit matrix for the three-position hall light switch problem

a	b	c	$f(a,b,c)$	
0	0	0	0	
0	0	1	1	$a'b'c$
0	1	1	0	
0	1	0	1	$a'bc'$
1	1	0	0	
1	1	1	1	abc
1	0	1	0	
1	0	0	1	$ab'c'$

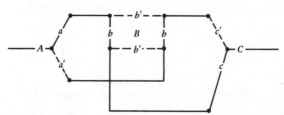

Figure 7.1.4   Circuit diagram for the three-position hall light switch problem.

7.2 CONJUNCTIVE NORMAL FORM

A Boolean function that appears as the conjunction (logical product) of disjunctive (logical sum) terms, usually called the product of the S-terms, is in conjunctive form. If all of the variables (either primed or unprimed) appear in all of the terms the function is in conjunctive normal form—cnf for short. Since the cnf and the dnf are dual functions, the dnf function

$$f(a,b,c) = ab'c + abc' + a'bc = 1$$

when converted to cnf becomes

$$(a+b'+c)(a+b+c)(a'+b+c) = 0$$

In using matrices to analyze functions in conjunctive form we may use the standard binary code and invert the value of the variables or we may invert the binary code and proceed as we did for the disjunctive form. Each method has its advantages. The inverted binary code for three variables is shown in Table 7.2.1.

Table 7.2.1   Matrix for the inverted binary code

a	b	c	Binary value
1	1	1	0
1	1	0	1
1	0	1	2
1	0	0	3
0	1	1	4
0	1	0	5
0	0	1	6
0	0	0	7

Table 7.2.2   Matrix for a function in S-terms using inverted binary code

S	a	b	c	S-terms in function	Completed S-terms
0	1	1	1	$a+c$	$a+b+c$
1	1	1	0	$b+c'$	$a+b+c'$
2	1	0	1	$a+b',a+c$	$a+b'+c$
3	1	0	0	$a+b'$	$a+b'+c'$
4	0	1	1		
5	0	1	0	$b+c'$	$a'+b+c'$
6	0	0	1		
7	0	0	0		

If we have, for example, $f(a,b,c) = (a+b')(a+c)(b+c') = 0$ we convert this to cnf as shown in Table 7.2.2. Therefore $f(a,b,c) = (S0)(S1)(S2)(S3)(S5)$. If we wished to use the standard binary code we would invert the values of the variables by assigning a primed letter to correspond to 1 and an unprimed letter to correspond to 0. Thus we would have Table 7.2.3. Here again $f(a,b,c)=(S0)(S1)(S2)(S3)(S5)$.

Table 7.2.3 *Matrix for a function in S-terms using standard binary code with inverted values*

S	a	b	c	S-terms in function	Completed S-terms
0	0	0	0	$a+c$	$a+b+c$
1	0	0	1	$b+c'$	$a+b+c'$
2	0	1	0	$a+b', a+c$	$a+b'+c$
3	0	1	1	$a+b'$	$a+b'+c'$
4	1	0	0		
5	1	0	1	$b+c'$	$a'+b+c'$
6	1	1	0		
7	1	1	1		

Table 7.2.4 *Specific circuit matrix*

a	b	c	d	f_{cnf}
0	0	0	0	0
0	0	0	1	0
0	0	1	1	0
0	1	1	1	0

$f(a,b,c,d)=1$ otherwise

Either one of the canonical forms may be used in analyzing or designing a system of on–off events. If we are given a matrix for a certain function and the number of 0-entries is less than the number of 1-entries in the function-value column, the cnf is preferred. If the reverse were true we would use the dnf. For example, in Table 7.2.4, we would design the circuit using cnf since we would have only four terms to consider. If we used the dnf we would have twelve terms. The expression for Table 7.2.4 is (inverting the value of the variables for the cnf)

$$f(a,b,c,d)=(a+b+c+d)(a+b+c+d')(a+b+c'+d')(a+b'+c'+d')$$
$$=a+(b+c+d)(b+c+d')(b+c'+d')(b'+c'+d')$$
$$=a+(b+c)(c'+d')$$
$$=a+bc'+bd'+cd'$$

The circuit for this is shown in Figure 7.2.1.

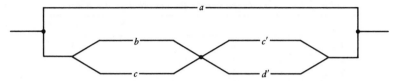

Figure 7.2.1   Diagram for the circuit derived from Table 7.2.4. The values are inverted.

7.3   DON'T CARE COMBINATIONS

In certain circuits a variable may appear that can have the value of either 0 or 1 without affecting the circuit. These are "don't care" variables and two are found in Figure 7.2.1. It is obvious from this diagram that switch A and/or switch C may be open or closed under certain circumstances without affecting the ability of the circuit to conduct current. This is shown clearly by an examination of Table 7.2.4. In the rows marked by the bracket the variables a and c may be either 0 or 1 as we please, since in both cases the circuit is made through bd'. We indicate this on the matrix by putting the letter d (for don't care) in place of the 1 or 0 as shown in Table 7.3.1.

Table 7.3.1   *"Don't care" variables substituted in Table 7.2.4; the values are inverted*

a	b	c	d	f_{cnf}
0	0	0	0	0
d	0	d	1	0
d	0	d	1	0
0	1	1	1	0

Table 7.3.2   *Matrix for the function $a + b = b + c$*

Row	a	b	c	$a+b$	$b+c$
0	0	0	0	0	0
1	0	0	1	0	1
2	0	1	0	1	1
3	0	1	1	1	1
4	1	0	0	1	0
5	1	0	1	1	1
6	1	1	0	1	1
7	1	1	1	1	1

Table 7.3.3   *Condensed matrix for the function* $a + b = b + c$

Row	a	b	c	$a+b$	$b+c$
0	0	0	0	0	0
2	0	1	0	1	1
3	0	1	1	1	1
5	1	0	1	1	1
6	1	1	0	1	1
7	1	1	1	1	1

Table 7.3.4   *"Don't care" variables substituted in Table 7.3.3*

a	b	c	$a+b$	$b+c$
0	d	0	$\begin{cases} 0 \\ 1 \end{cases}$	$\begin{cases} 0 \\ 1 \end{cases}$
0	1	1	1	1
1	0	1	1	1
1	1	d	1	1

Table 7.3.5   *Condensed matrix with "don't care" variables for the function* $ab = bc$

a	b	c	$a{\cdot}b$	$b{\cdot}c$
0	0	d	0	0
0	1	0	0	0
1	0	d	0	0
1	1	1	1	1

Table 7.3.6   *Alternate matrix for the function* $ab = bc$

a	b	c	$a{\cdot}b$	$b{\cdot}c$
0	0	d	0	0
0	1	0	0	0
1	0	0	0	0
			0	0
1	d	1	1	1

Another example is the relation $a + b = b + c$. Here we have the matrix shown in Table 7.3.2. Rows 1 and 4 may be eliminated since in these rows $a + b \neq b + c$. The array may be condensed as shown in Table 7.3.3. In Rows 0 and 2 b is a "don't care" since $a + b = b + c$, regardless of the value of b. Similarly, in Rows 6 and 7 c is a "don't care." This array may now be written as shown in Table 7.3.4. In a similar manner it can be shown that the relation $ab = bc$ may be written as in Table 7.3.5 or alternately, as in Table 7.3.6. If "don't care" combinations appear in a switching circuit they are assigned a value of 1 or 0, whichever will result in the simplest circuit.

It should be remembered that "don't care" combinations may be found in any type of circuit, not just in electrical circuits.

SUMMARY

We have now seen one application of Boolean algebra—that of circuit design. This, and variations of it, are widely used by electrical and electronic engineers. We do not pursue this subject because it is left more properly to a work devoted to switching circuits.

Circuit design techniques can be used for nonhardware applications such as decision trees. These applications are also beyond the scope of this book.

Now that we know how to put a function into a canonical form we are prepared to address the problem of simplification of the functions. In every such method I know of the disjunctive normal form is used. Simplification is the subject of the next chapter.

EIGHT

SIMPLIFICATION OF BOOLEAN FUNCTIONS

INTRODUCTION

This chapter covers in a very condensed manner a subject about which books have been written. There are many approaches to the simplification problem, only five of which are presented here. These were chosen because they cover a wide range of methods. Briefly, these are: algebraic; modified algebraic using P-terms; numerical, suitable for computerization; graphical; and graphical/ algebraic.

The material presented requires careful study if you wish to have a real understanding of these methods. It is not easy to assimilate because the subject of simplification methods is one of the most difficult topics encountered in Boolean algebra. It is essential that these methods be mastered, particularly the numerical method (McCluskey's second method), because the entire analytical system presented in Chapter 10 depends upon this method.

8.1 PRIME IMPLICANTS

The Boolean functions we have considered thus far have all been combinational rather than sequential or a mixture of the two. Sequential and sequential/combinational functions will be covered in Chapter 9. Many combinational forms may be simplified by inspection or by simple algebraic manipulation of the disjunctive normal form of the function. (This could also be done with the cnf but the dnf, as has been pointed out previously, is much easier to work with.) Quine[13] has shown that application of law 1(b), which is $a + a' = 1$, in the form $ab + a'b = b(a + a') = b$ simplifies a function in dnf to terms that are known as "prime implicants."

In Chapter 7 the method of arriving at the dnf was explained. It was also shown that a dnf function could be expressed by listing the decimal designation of the *P*-terms rather than writing out the terms themselves. An example of this is (from Figure 7.1.5)

$$a'b'c + a'bc + ab'c + abc' + abc = 1$$

or

$$P1 + P3 + P5 + P6 + P7 = 1$$

This is, of course, in dnf and the standard binary matrix for it is shown in Figure 7.1.5. The simplification of this using Quine's method (although it is not identified as such) was given in Section 7.1 as a purely algebraic manipulation. This could also be done in this manner:

$$
\begin{array}{lllll}
a'b'c & +\,a'bc & +\,ab'c & +\,abc' & +\,abc & = 1 \\
001 & 011 & 101 & 110 & 111 \\
P1 & P3 & P5 & P6 & P7 \\
a'\!-\!c & +\!-\!bc+ & -\!b'c & +\,ab\!-\! & +\,a\!-\!c = 1 \\
P1 & P3 & P1 & P6 & P5 \\
P3 & P7 & P5 & P7 & P7 \\
a'\!-\!c & & +\!-\!-\!c & +\,ab & a\!-\!c = 1 \\
P1 & & P1,P3 & P6 & P5 \\
P3 & & P5,P7 & P7 & P7 \\
-\!-\!c & & +\!-\!-\!c & +\,ab\!-\! & = 1 \\
P1,P3 & & P1,P3 & P6 \\
P5,P7 & & P5,P7 & P7
\end{array}
$$

or

$$ab + c = 1$$

Variables that are eliminated by applying Quine's method are indicated by blanks in the various terms. The *P* numbers under the terms show which terms were combined to make the elimination. In the final expression *ab* and *c* are prime implicants. Since the expression cannot be further simplified it is called a minimum sum.

8.2 THE QUINE–McCLUSKEY METHOD

Although Quine's method applies to functions with any finite number of variables, it can become cumbersome and tedious if four or more variables are involved. McCluskey[14] developed a simplified approach to Quine's method, which makes it easier to use. This simplification has been widely used and results in what is now called the Quine–McCluskey method. We show how this method is used for four-variable functions and how to test the results for nonessential prime implicants.

In applying the Quine–McCluskey (or Q–M) method the standard binary matrix is rearranged as shown in Table 8.2.1. In this arrangement the matrix is divided into five groups. These are:

Group number	P-term	Number of 1's in P-term
0	0	0
1	1, 2, 4, 8	1
2	3, 5, 6, 9, 10, 12	2
3	7, 11, 13, 14	3
4	15	4

The terms in each group are compared with each term in the next higher group to see which variables, if any, may be eliminated. This is better demonstrated than explained. Consider the function

$$f(a,b,c,d) = P1 + P2 + P3 + P4 + P6 + P7 + P8 + P9 + P11$$
$$+ P12 + P13 + P14$$

Table 8.2.1 Matrix segregation by number of 1's in P-terms

P-term	a	b	c	d
0	0	0	0	0
1	0	0	0	1
2	0	0	1	0
4	0	1	0	0
8	1	0	0	0
3	0	0	1	1
5	0	1	0	1
6	0	1	1	0
9	1	0	0	1
10	1	0	1	0
12	1	1	0	0
7	0	1	1	1
11	1	0	1	1
13	1	1	0	1
14	1	1	1	1
15	1	1	1	1

Table 8.2.2 Segregated matrix for $F1$

Group	P-term	a	b	c	d
1	1	0	0	0	1
	2	0	0	1	0
	4	0	1	0	0
	8	1	0	0	0
2	3	0	0	1	1
	6	0	1	1	0
	9	1	0	0	1
	12	1	1	0	0
3	7	0	1	1	1
	11	1	0	1	1
	13	1	1	0	1
	14	1	1	1	0

Since we will be using the dnf only this is usually written as

$$f(a,b,c,d) = (1,2,3,4,6,7,8,9,11,12,13,14) = F1$$

The matrix for this using the Q–M grouping is shown in Table 8.2.2. In this matrix we have only three groups represented. If we now disjoin each

Table 8.2.3 First step in reduction and regrouping of matrix for $F1$

P-terms	a	b	c	d
1, 3	0	0	—	1
1, 9	—	0	0	1
2, 3	0	0	1	—
2, 6	0	—	1	0
4, 6	0	1	—	0
4, 12	—	1	0	0
8, 9	1	0	0	—
8, 12	1	—	0	0
3, 7	0	—	1	1
3, 11	—	0	1	1
6, 7	0	1	1	—
6, 14	—	1	1	0
9, 11	1	0	—	1
9, 13	1	—	0	1
12, 13	1	1	0	—
12, 14	1	1	—	0

term in Group 1 with each term in Group 2, each term in Group 2 with each term in Group 3, and eliminate variables where possible by law 1(b), we have the array in Table 8.2.3. The blanks in this table indicate variables that were eliminated. This matrix also divides into two groups in the first of which the combined P-terms contain one blank and one 1. In the second group we have one blank and two 1's in each P-term combination. We now disjoin terms from the first group of this matrix with terms from the second group *which have a blank in the same position* to see if we can eliminate more variables by law 1(b). This results in Table 8.2.4.

Table 8.2.4   Second step in reduction and regrouping of matrix for $F1$

P-terms	a	b	c	d
1,3,9,11	—	0	—	1
2,3,6,7	0	—	1	—
4,6,12,14	—	1	—	0
8,9,12,13	1	—	0	—

Table 8.2.5   Summary of procedure for reduction of matrix for $F1$

	(a)					(b)					(c)				
P	a	b	c	d	P	a	b	c	d	P	a	b	c	d	
1	0	0	0	1√	1,3	0	0	—	1√	1,3,9,11	—	0	—	1	$= b'd$
2	0	0	1	0√	1,9	—	0	0	1√	2,3,6,7	0	—	1	—	$= a'c$
4	0	1	0	0√	2,3	0	0	1	—√	4,6,12,14	—	1	—	0	$= bd'$
8	1	0	0	0√	2,6	0	—	1	0√	8,9,12,13	1	—	0	—	$= ac'$
					4,6	0	1	—	0√						
3	0	0	1	1√	4,12	—	1	0	0√						
6	0	1	1	0√	8,9	1	0	0	—√						
9	1	0	0	1√	8,12	1	—	0	0√						
12	1	1	0	0√						1,9,3,11	—	0	—	1	
					3,7	0	—	1	1√	2,6,3,7	0	—	1	—	
7	0	1	1	1√	3,11	—	0	1	1√	4,12,6,14	—	1	—	0	
11	1	0	1	1√	6,7	0	1	1	—√	8,12,9,13	1	—	0	—	
13	1	1	0	1√	6,14	—	1	1	0√						
14	1	1	1	0√	9,11	1	0	—	1√						
					9,13	1	—	0	1√						
					12,13	1	1	0	—√						
					12,14	1	1	—	0√						

Now we have only one grouping, where each of the combined *P*-terms contains two blanks and one 1. Since we have only one group no further simplification is possible. The procedure is summarized and completed in Table 8.2.5. Here each term in (a) appears in (b) and each term in (b) appears in (c). This is noted by the check marks following the terms in (a) and (b). If any term in (a) or (b) were not checked *it would be a prime implicant*. In this example only the terms in Table 8.2.5(c) are prime implicants. It will also be noted that in (c) four comparable redundant terms appear. For reasons that become evident the terms we use are those in which the *P*-terms are in ascending order, for example, $1, 3, 9, 11$ rather than $1, 9, 3, 11$.

The expressions in Table 8.2.5(c) are all prime implicants but not necessarily essential prime implicants. To check which of these are essential we first rewrite the matrix for the function. We then determine where each of the prime implicants *could* appear in incomplete form in the various rows. This is shown in Table 8.2.6. Each of the prime implicants appears in four rows of the table as indicated by the *x*'s in each column. Where more than one prime implicant appears in the same row (such as in *P*3, *P*6, *P*9, and *P*12), the entries may be ignored. The prime implicants that are unique to a row are indicated by circling the *x* entered in that row. These are the essential prime implicants. In this example all of the prime implicants are essential.

Table 8.2.6 Determination of prime implicants for *F*1

P-term	*a*	*b*	*c*	*d*	*b′d*	*a′c*	*bd′*	*ac′*
1	0	0	0	1	⊗			
2	0	0	1	0		⊗		
3	0	0	1	1	*x*	*x*		
4	0	1	0	0			⊗	
6	0	1	1	0		*x*	*x*	
7	0	1	1	1	⊗			
8	1	0	0	0				⊗
9	1	0	0	1	*x*			*x*
11	1	0	1	1	⊗			
12	1	1	0	0			*x*	*x*
13	1	1	0	1				⊗
14	1	1	1	0			⊗	

*Table 8.2.7   Reduction of matrix for F*2

(a)					(b)					(c)					
P	a	b	c	d	P	a	b	c	d	P	a	b	c	d	Implicants
0	0	0	0	0	0,1	0	0	0	—	0,1,2,3	0	0	—	—	a'b'
					0,2	0	0	—	0	0,1,8,9	—	0	0	—	b'c'
1	0	0	0	1	0,4	0	—	0	0	0,2,1,3	duplicate				
2	0	0	1	0	0,8	—	0	0	0	0,2,4,6	0	—	—	0	a'd'
4	0	1	0	0						0,4,2,6	duplicate				
8	1	0	0	0	1,3	0	0	—	1	0,8,1,9	duplicate				
					1,9	—	0	0	1						
3	0	0	1	1	2,3	0	0	1	—	1,3,9,11	—	0	—	1	b'd
6	0	1	1	0	2,6	0	—	1	0	1,9,3,11	duplicate				
9	1	0	0	1	4,6	0	1	—	0	2,3,6,7	0	—	1	—	a'c
					8,9	1	0	0	—	2,6,3,7	duplicate				
7	0	1	1	1											
11	1	0	1	1	3,7	0	—	1	1	3,7,11,15	—	—	1	1	cd
					3,11	—	0	1	1	3,11,7,15	duplicate				
15	1	1	1	1	6,7	0	1	1	—						
					9,11	1	0	—	1						
					7,15	—	1	1	1						
					11,15	1	—	1	1						

An example which shows nonessential prime implicants is

$$f(a,b,c,d) = (0,1,2,3,4,6,7,8,9,11,15) = F2$$

The Q–M matrix for this and the various steps in the simplification are shown in Table 8.2.7. The test for essential prime implicants is shown in Table 8.2.8. From this it is seen that they are

$$a'd' + b'c' + cd$$

However, we must find out if the disjunction of these represents a complete function. To do this we cross out the rows in Table 8.2.8 in which the essential primes appear. These are

	Essential prime implicant		
	a'd'	b'c'	cd
	P0	P0	P3
Rows	P2	P1	P7
	P4	P8	P11
	P6	P9	P15

All of the rows are crossed out so no terms must be accounted for. Thus the disjunction of the essential prime implicants represents a complete, minimal function. (For a thorough treatment of minimal functions see McCluskey[14].)

Table 8.2.8 *Determination of essential prime implicants for F*2

P	a b c d	a'b'	a'd'	b'c'	b'd	a'c	cd
0	0 0 0 0	x———x———x					
1	0 0 0 1	x—————————x———x					
2	0 0 1 0	x———x———————————x					
3	0 0 1 1	x———————————x———x———x					
4	0 1 0 0		⊗				
6	0 1 1 0		x———————————x			
7	0 1 1 1					x———x	
8	1 0 0 0			⊗			
9	1 0 0 1			x———x			
11	1 0 1 1			x———————————x		
15	1 1 1 1						⊗

Another function we consider is $f(a,b,c,d) = (0,2,4,6,8,9,13,15) = F3$. The determination of the prime implicants for this is shown in Table 8.2.9 and the essential prime implicants in Table 8.2.10. The prime implicants are $a'd'$, $b'c'd'$, $ab'c'$, $ac'd$, and abd. The essential prime implicants are $a'd'$ and abd. If we cross out all of the rows in which these appear we have left only $P8$ and $P9$. The prime implicants that appear in these rows are $b'c'd'$, $ab'c'$, and $ac'd$. We have two complete terms to account for ($P8$ and $P9$) and three prime implicants to do it with. However, $ab'c'$ accounts for both of them because it appears in both rows. Therefore, the minimal complete function we can have is

$$f(a,b,c,d) = a'd + abd + ab'c'$$

If this function is converted back to the canonical dnf we will have the original eight terms we started with.

Table 8.2.9 *Reduction of matrix for F*3

(a)					(b)					(c)					Prime
P	a	b	c	d	P	a	b	c	d	P	a	b	c	d	Implicants
0	0	0	0	0	0,2	0	0	—	0	0,2:4,6	0	—	—	0	a'd
2	0	0	1	0	0,4	0	—	0	0	0,4:2,6	0	—	—	0	duplicate
4	0	1	0	0	0,8	—	0	0	0						b'c'd'
8	1	0	0	0	2,6	0	—	1	0						
					4,6	0	1	—	0						
6	0	1	1	0	8,9	1	0	0	—						ab'c'
9	1	0	0	1											
					9,13	1	—	0	1						ac'd
13	1	1	0	1											
					13,15	1	1	—	1						abd
15	1	1	1	1											

Table 8.2.10 *Determination of prime implicants for F3*

P	a	b	c	d	a'd'	b'c'd'	ab'c'	ac'd	abd
0	0	0	0	0	x————x				
2	0	0	1	0	⊗				
4	0	1	0	0	⊗				
6	0	1	1	0	⊗				
8	1	0	0	0		x————x			
9	1	0	0	1			x————x		
13	1	1	0	1				x————x	
15	1	1	1	1					⊗

8.3   McCLUSKEY'S SECOND (NUMERICAL) METHOD

In using the Q–M method it is relatively easy to become confused in matching blanks and 1's as you go from row to row. McCluskey devised a method that eliminates this procedure. If two P-terms may be combined by the Q–M method the decimal label of one term may be derived from

Table 8.3.1   *First step in numerical method for simplification of F2*

		$f(a,b,c,d) = (0,1,2,3,4,6,7,8,9,11,15) = F2$	
Group	P-term	First Combination[a]	First Combination (Continued)[a]
0	0	0,1	3,4 *
		0,2	3,5 *
		0,4	3,7
		0,8	3,11
			6,7
1	1	1,2 *	6,8 *
	2	1,3	6,10*
	4	1,5 *	6,14*
	8	1,9	9,10*
		2,3	9,11
2	3	2,4 *	9,13*
	6	2,6	
	9	2,10*	7,8 *
		4,5 *	7,9 *
3	7	4,6	7,11*
	11	4,8 *	7,15
		4,12*	11,12*
4	15	8,9	11,13*
		8,10*	11,15
		8,12*	

[a]The asterisks denote nonvalid combinations.

the decimal label of the other by adding some power of two to each number in the first P-term. The power of two to be added is determined by the decimal weight of the position in which the two P-terms differ. We will rework the example shown in Table 8.2.7 by this method.

The P-terms of the original function must, as before, be put into a McCluskey grouping but now we may eliminate the matrix. The P-terms are listed and a power of two (which for a four-variable function would be 1, 2, 4, or 8) is added to the term or terms in each group. If the result is a P-term in an immediately succeeding group, the combination is a valid one in the Q–M method. The first step in this procedure is shown in Table 8.3.1.

In the second step of the procedure a power of two is added to each digit in the combined P-terms from the first step. If the resulting digits appear in the immediately succeeding group the combination is valid. Only combinations where the digits are in ascending order are recorded. Those combinations with the same digits not in ascending order are duplicates. Step 2 is shown in Table 8.3.2 with the nonvalid combinations from Step 1 omitted. It is seen that no further valid combinations are possible so the combined P-terms from the second step are prime implicants. These are identified as shown in Table 8.3.3.

Table 8.3.2 Second step in numerical method of simplification of F2

Combined Groups	First Combination	Combined Groups	Second Combination
0+1	0,1	0+1, 1+2	0,1,2,3
	0,2		0,1,8,9
	0,4		0,2,4,6
	0,8		
		1+2, 2+3	1,3,9,11
1+2	1,3		2,3,6,7
	1,9		
	2,3	2+3, 3+4	3,7,11,15
	2,6		
	4,6		
	8,9		
2+3	3,7		
	3,11		
	6,7		
	9,11		
3+4	7,15		
	11,15		

Table 8.3.3   Conversion of numerical to binary to literal values

P	abcd	P	abcd	P	abcd	P	abcd	P	abcd	P	abcd
0	0000	0	0000	0	0000	1	0001	2	0010	3	0011
1	0001	1	0001	2	0010	3	0011	3	0011	7	0111
2	0010	8	1000	4	0100	9	1001	6	0110	11	1011
3	0011	9	1001	6	0110	11	1011	7	0111	15	1111
	$a'b'$		$b'c'$		$a'd'$		$b'd$		$a'c$		cd

Table 8.3.4   Summary of procedure for numerical simplification of F2

	$f(a,b,c,d) = (0,1,2,3,4,6,7,8,9,11,15) = F2$	
P	$\Sigma_1 P$	$\Sigma_2 P$
0	0,1	0,1,2,3
	0,2	0,1,8,9
1	0,4	0,2,4,6
2	0,8	
4		1,3,9,11
8	1,3	2,3,6,7
	1,9	
3	2,3	3,7,11,15
6	2,6	
9	4,6	
	8,9	
7		
11	3,7	
15	3,11	
	6,7	
	9,11	
	7,15	
	11,15	

In identifying the prime implicant variables in Table 8.3.3 only those with a solid column of 0's or 1's below them remain in the various terms of the function. The essential prime implicants are identified as shown previously in Table 8.2.8. For clarity the procedure is summarized in Table 8.3.4 with group designations and nonvalid combinations omitted, and P-term combinations indicated by ΣP.

Another example of the use of this method is the simplification of $f(a,b,c,d) = (1,2,3,4,6,7,8,9,11,12,13,14) = F1$. This is shown in Table 8.3.5.

Table 8.3.5 *Numerical simplification procedure for* $F1$
(See Table 8.2.6 for essential prime implicants)

P	$\Sigma_1 P$	$\Sigma_2 P$
	$f(a,b,c,d)=(1,2,3,4,6,7,8,9,11,12,13,14)=F1$	
1	1,3	1,3,9,11
2	1,9	
4	2,3	2,3,6,7
8	2,6	
	4,6	4,6,12,14
3	4,12	
6	8,9	8,9,12,13
9	8,12	
12		
	3,7	
7	3,11	
11	6,7	
13	6,14	
14	9,11	
	9,13	
	12,13	
	12,14	

P	$abcd$	P	$abcd$	P	$abcd$	P	$abcd$
1	0001	2	0010	4	0100	8	1000
3	0011	3	0011	6	0110	9	1001
9	1001	6	0110	12	1100	12	1100
11	1011	7	0111	14	1110	13	1101
	$b'd$		$a'c$		bd'		ac'

8.4 SCHEINMAN'S METHOD

Scheinman[15] devised a charting method for determining prime implicants based upon the expansion theorem. This theorem states that any Boolean function, say $f(x_1,\ldots,x_n)$ for example, may be expanded in the form

$$f(x_1, x_2, \ldots, x_n) = x_1 f(1, x_2, \ldots, x_n) + x_1' f(0, x_2, \ldots, x_n)$$

The usual explanation for making such an expansion is, to say the least, obtuse. The explanation presented here is a complete departure from those usually encountered.

Any Boolean function in disjunctive normal form expressed in decimal P-term notation may be expanded around its variables in succession

Table 8.4.1   Matrix for F2

P	a	b	c	d
0	0	0	0	0
1	0	0	0	1
2	0	0	1	0
3	0	0	1	1
4	0	1	0	0
6	0	1	1	0
7	0	1	1	1
8	1	0	0	0
9	1	0	0	1
11	1	0	1	1
15	1	1	1	1

starting with the variable that has the highest decimal weight. Each expansion results in a multiple partition of the set of P-terms involved. The partition is based on the modulo relation presented in Chapter 1. Consider the function

$$f(a,b,c,d) = (0,1,2,3,4,6,7,8,9,11,15) = F2$$

which is written more correctly as

$$f(a,b,c,d) = P0 + P1 + P2 + P3 + P4 + P6 + P7 + P8 + P9 + P11 + P15$$

The standard Boolean matrix for this function is shown in Table 8.4.1. If we now determine the residue classes modulo 8 for the decimal values of the P-terms we have Table 8.4.2.

It is obvious that the residue classes shown in Table 8.4.2(a) are associated with a' (circuit value 0) and those in Table 8.4.2(b) are associated with a (circuit value 1). It is also evident that the residue classes R_0, R_1, R_3, and R_7 are associated with either a or a' or both. Thus we have partitioned the set of P-terms into:

1. The residue classes $R_0, R_1, R_2, R_3, R_4, R_6, R_7$.
2. A family of residue classes associated with a.
3. A family of residue classes associated with a'.
4. A family of residue classes associated with $a + a'$.

This is an expansion of the original function around the variable a to give $f(a,b,c,d) = a'(0,1,2,3,4,6,7) + a(0,1,3,7) + (a+a')(0,1,3,7)$. The resulting families of residue classes (or residues) may now be expanded around b

Table 8.4.2   Residue classes modulo 8 for F2

(a)		(b)
0 + 0		1 + 0
0 + 1		1 + 1
0 + 2		1 + 3
0 + 3	AND	1 + 7
0 + 4		
0 + 6		
0 + 7		

(modulo 4). Since the family associated with a in this example is completely included in the family associated with $a + a'$ it may be omitted in the expansion around b.

The first step in Scheinman's application of the expansion theorem is to list the decimal values of the P-terms of the function in vertical array and indicate the first expansion as shown in Figure 8.4.1. (We usually list the decimal values of the P-terms in horizontal array to save space.) In the tabulation of Figure 8.4.1 "—" represents $a + a'$ and all of the entries appearing under both a and a' (and therefore under the blank) are checked. The complete expansion of the function is shown in Figure 8.4.2. In making this chart the first expansion is as shown in Figure 8.4.1. Each

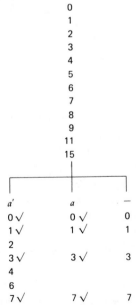

Figure 8.4.1   Modulo 8 expansion for $F2$.

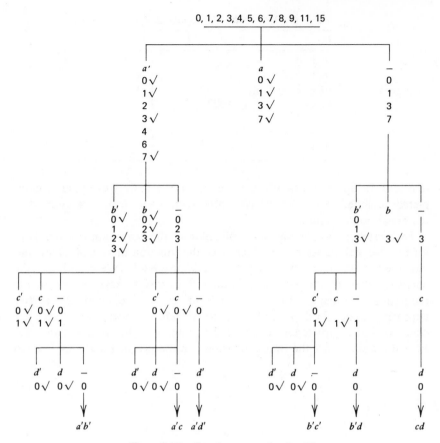

Figure 8.4.2　Complete expansion for $F2$.

branch of the first expansion is then expanded, if necessary, around b. It is not necessary to expand a branch where every entry is followed by a check mark as is the case for the branch headed by the variable a in this example. (Expanding a branch that is completely checked off would give redundant answers.) Every branch resulting from the second expansion is, unless completely checked off, expanded around the variable c. This is repeated as necessary for the variable d. All branches must end in a 0 for the expansion to be complete.

Other examples of Scheinman's method are shown in Figures 8.4.3, 8.4.4, and 8.4.5. The first two of these are straightforward but Figure 8.4.5, which is the expansion of

$$f(a,b,c,d) = (1,2,3,4,6,7,8,9,11,12,13,14) = F1$$

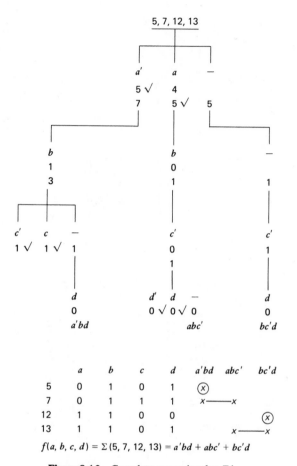

$$f(a, b, c, d) = \Sigma(5, 7, 12, 13) = a'bd + abc' + bc'd$$

Figure 8.4.3 Complete expansion for *F*4.

requires some explanation. In the expansion of the *a'* family of residues around *b*, the *b'* family and the *b* family contain residues that are not common, to wit:

b'	b	—
1	0	
2	2	2
3	3	3

However, these residues are checked off as though they were common. In the modulo 8 expansion we obtained

$$a'(1,2,3,4,6,7) + a(0,1,3,4,5,6) + (a + a')(1,3,4,6)$$

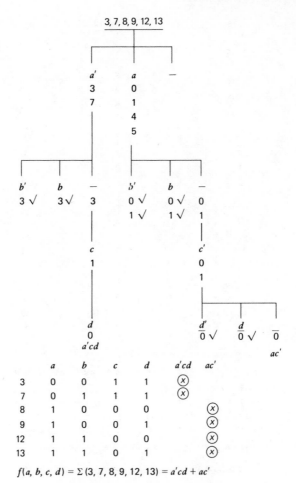

$$f(a, b, c, d) = \Sigma\,(3, 7, 8, 9, 12, 13) = a'cd + ac'$$

Figure 8.4.4 Complete expansion for $F5$.

We could write this as

$$a'(2,7) + a(0,5) + (a + a')(1,3,4,6)$$

If we expand $a'(2,7)$ around b we have $b'(2) + b(3)$. However, if we use the redundant residues in the a' family, that is, expand $a'(1,2,3,4,6,7)$ around b, we obtain

$$b'(1,2,3) + b(0,2,3) + (b + b')(2,3)$$

Since the nonredundant residues, $(2,3)$, form the family of residues associated with $(b + b')$ we need only to expand this family. Scheinman

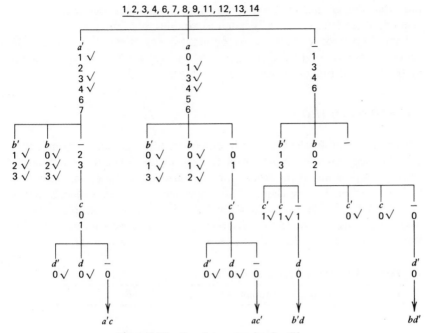

Figure 8.4.5 Complete expansion for $F1$.

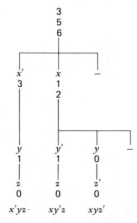

$$f(x, y, z) = x'yz + xy'z + xyz' = \text{original function}$$

Figure 8.4.6 Complete expansion for $F6$.

indicates this in his article by checking all residues that derive from redundant residues of a family when expanding that family.

Some functions cannot be simplified by any method. Consider the function $f(x, y, z) = (3, 5, 6) = x'yz + xy'z + xyz' = F6$. The Scheinman method for this function gives Figure 8.4.6.

8.5 HYBRID METHOD

All of the simplification methods described thus far suffer from being cumbersome. Another approach is to expand the function as necessary, usually not more than twice for a four-valued function, and use Quine's method by inspection. This approach is applied to $f(a,b,c,d) = (0,1,2,3,4,6,7,8,9,11,15)$ as shown in Table 8.5.1. In this example it is seen that the expansion around the variables a and b is carried out exactly as in Scheinman's method although the results are recorded in a different way.

Table 8.5.1   Hybrid expansion for F2

P	Modulo 8	Modulo 4	c	d	
0	⎧ 0√				
1	⎪ 1√				
2	⎪ 2	⎧ 0√			
3	a'⎨ 3√	b'⎨ 1√			
4	⎪ 4	⎪ 2√			
6	⎪ 6	⎩ 3√			
7	⎩ 7√				
		⎧ 0√			
		b⎨ 2√			
		⎩ 3√			
		⎧ 0√	0	0	
		−⎨ 2√	1	0	$a'd$
		⎩ 3√	1	1	$a'c$
8	⎧ 0√				
9	a⎨ 1√				
11	⎪ 3√				
15	⎩ 7√				
	⎧ 0		0	0	
	−⎨ 1	b'⎨ 0	0	0	$b'c'$
	⎪ 3	⎪ 1	1	1	$b'd$
	⎩ 7	⎩ 3√			
		b{3√			
		−{3	1	1	cd

Table 8.5.2   Essential prime implicants for F2 by hybrid expansion

P	a	b	c	d	a'd'	b'c'	b'd	a'c	cd
0	0	0	0	0	x	x			
1	0	0	0	1		x	x		
2	0	0	1	0	x			x	
3	0	0	1	1			x	x	x
4	0	1	0	0	⊗				
6	0	1	1	0	x			x	
7	0	1	1	1				x	x
8	1	0	0	0			⊗		
9	1	0	0	1		x	x		
11	1	0	1	1			x		x
15	1	1	1	1					⊗

$$f(a,b,c,d) = a'd' + b'c' + cd$$

The expansions around c and around d are omitted. Instead the binary values for c and d are listed and Quine's method applied to see which of the variables, if either, may be eliminated. Note that $a'b'$, which appeared in the Q–M method (Tables 8.2.7 and 8.3.4), does not appear here because it is a nonessential prime implicant. So are $a'c$ and $b'd$, which would have disappeared in an expansion around c or d. The overlapping rectangles in Table 8.5.1 indicate that one of the prime implicants in each case is nonessential but does not tell us which one. The test for nonessential prime implicants for this example is shown in Table 8.5.2. This of course is the same as Table 8.2.8 with $a'b'$ eliminated.

Table 8.5.3   Hybrid expansion for F1

P	Modulo 8	Modulo 4	c	d	
1	1√				
2	2				
3	a′ { 3√	b′ { 1√			
4	4√	2√			
6	6√	3√			
7	7				
		b { 0√			
		2√			
		3√			
		− { 2	1	0	a′c
		3	1	1	

Table 8.5.3   (*Continued*)

$$
\begin{array}{c}
\begin{array}{c}
8 \\ 9 \\ 11 \\ 12 \\ 13 \\ 14
\end{array}
\quad
a\left\{
\begin{array}{l}
0 \\ 1\surd \\ 3\surd \\ 4\surd \\ 5 \\ 6\surd
\end{array}
\right.
\quad
b'\left\{
\begin{array}{l}
0\surd \\ 1\surd \\ 3\surd
\end{array}
\right.
\end{array}
$$

$$
b\left\{
\begin{array}{l}
0\surd \\ 1\surd \\ 2\surd
\end{array}
\right.
$$

$$
-\left\{
\begin{array}{l}
0 \\ 1
\end{array}
\right.
\qquad
\begin{array}{c} 0 \\ 0 \end{array}
\qquad
\boxed{\begin{array}{c} 0 \\ 1 \end{array}}
\qquad ac'
$$

$$
-\left\{
\begin{array}{l}
1 \\ 3 \\ 4 \\ 6
\end{array}
\right.
\qquad
b'\left\{
\begin{array}{l}
1 \\ 3
\end{array}
\right.
\qquad
\boxed{\begin{array}{c} 0 \\ 1 \end{array}}
\qquad
\begin{array}{c} 1 \\ 1 \end{array}
\qquad b'd
$$

$$
b\left\{
\begin{array}{l}
0 \\ 2
\end{array}
\right.
\qquad
\boxed{\begin{array}{c} 0 \\ 1 \end{array}}
\qquad
\begin{array}{c} 0 \\ 0 \end{array}
\qquad bd'
$$

Another example of the use of this method is in the simplification of $f(a,b,c,d)=(1,2,3,4,6,7,8,9,11,12,13,14)=F1$, which is shown in Table 8.5.3. The test for nonessential prime implicants is shown in Table 8.2.6. That there are none is also indicated by the nonoverlapping of the rectangles in Table 8.5.3.

The hybrid method and the Scheinman method have the advantage that no special grouping of the P-terms is required, which is not true of the Q–M method. All of them are valid.

SUMMARY

The simplification methods given here are very basic. Continuing effort is being made by many researchers to develop more sophisticated approaches. Such approaches usually require a computer solution although a simple method to handle a complex system without a computer would be of much greater use. So far as I know, such a method has not been developed. The nature of the problem may preclude such a development.

Part Two

APPLICATIONS

Most of the inputs to our diagrams are indicated by signals in state 1, as shown in Figure 9.1.3. The arrow represents the signal from the device. If we wish to use a signal in state 0 it will be inverted, as shown in Figure 9.1.4. Although the arrow symbol is also used for inputs, it is not readily confused with the symbol for "gives as a result". The latter symbol is *always* the output of a logic operation. In Figures 9.1.3(a) and 9.1.4(a) these are unary operations. In the other figures they are binary operations.

In Figures 9.1.3 and 9.1.4 it is seen that these symbols represent these Boolean functions:

Figure	Boolean Function
9.1.3(a)	$a = 1$
9.1.3(b)	$ab = 1$
9.1.3(c)	$a + b = 1$
9.1.4(a)	$a' = 0$
9.1.4(b)	$ab' = 0$
9.1.4(c)	$a + b' = 1$
9.1.4(d)	$a' + b' = 0$

We see how these symbols are used to represent the theorems given in Chapter 5.

Complement laws   These are shown in Figure 9.1.5.

Identity laws   These are obvious and require no diagrams.

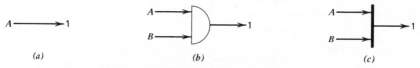

(a)   (b)   (c)

Figure 9.1.3   Examples of signals in state 1.

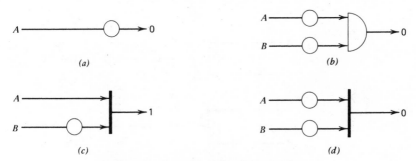

(a)   (b)

(c)   (d)

Figure 9.1.4   Examples of signals in state 0.

1 (a)

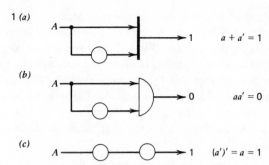

$a + a' = 1$

(b)

$aa' = 0$

(c)

$(a')' = a = 1$

Figure 9.1.5 Complement laws in graphic form.

3 (a)

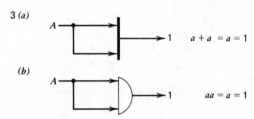

$a + a = a = 1$

(b)

$aa = a = 1$

Figure 9.1.6 Idempotent laws in graphic form.

5 (a) (left side)

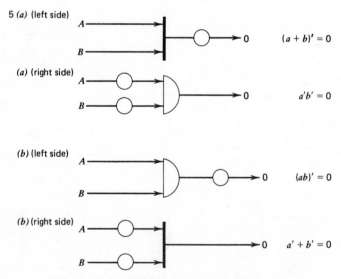

$(a + b)' = 0$

(a) (right side)

$a'b' = 0$

(b) (left side)

$(ab)' = 0$

(b) (right side)

$a' + b' = 0$

Figure 9.1.7 DeMorgan's rules in graphic form.

Idempotent laws   These are diagrammed in Figure 9.1.6.

Commutative laws   These are obvious and require no diagrams.

DeMorgan's rules   These are shown in Figure 9.1.7. It might seem that 5(a) (left) is also equivalent to $a'b$ and to ab' but this is not the case. Check it out with truth tables.

Associative laws   These are show in Figure 9.1.8. With diagrams similar to those used in 6(a) of that figure it can be shown that either side may be shown as in 6(b).

Distributive laws   These are diagrammed in Figure 9.1.9.

The identities given in Chapter 6 can, of course, be presented graphically just as the theorems were. This exercise is left to the reader.

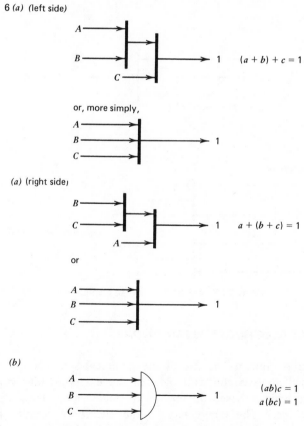

Figure 9.1.8   Associative laws in graphic form.

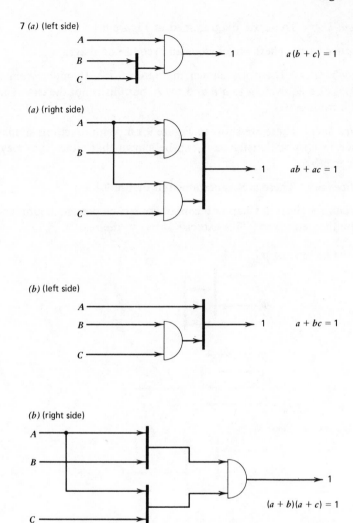

Figure 9.1.9   Distributive laws in graphic form.

9.2   SIMPLE ELECTRICAL APPLICATIONS

For an introduction to the use of the graphical symbols we use simple electrical switching circuit examples. In the examples involving control circuits, the logic is based on the use of relays rather than a solid-state "logic machine." The complexity of the electronic circuits in such a machine would unnecessarily complicate the presentation. We will also follow the electrical convention of using ✦ to indicate a connection between lines and ✛ to indicate no connection.

The simplest electrical circuits used in the intuitive derivation of our algebra and the logic diagrams for them are those corresponding to the theorems. A more involved, but commonly encountered, circuit that we have not covered is the "hall light switch" circuit, which involves turning a light on or off from two different locations. This is shown schematically as in Figure 9.2.1. The Boolean algebra equation for this circuit is $ab + a'b'$ or, by applying DeMorgan's rules, $ab + (a + b)' = 1$. The corresponding logic diagrams are shown in Figures 9.2.2 and 9.2.3. This is a departure from some of our previous concepts. In this example both switches are single pole double throw so they may conduct current in either state. The a and b symbols mean that A and B are closed to conductor 1. The a' and b' mean that A and B are closed to conductor 0. Situations such as this are frequently encountered in relay circuits and analogous situations may be found in piping systems where three- and four-way valves are used. In complex systems we clarify this by proper labeling of our signals. Remember that we cannot handle more than two conductor paths (or flow paths) for any one device: otherwise we would be working with signals that were not bistable.

Another commonly encountered circuit is the control circuit for starting and stopping a motor by using momentary contact pushbuttons. Figure 9.2.4 is a partial elementary wiring diagram for this circuit. M represents the relay activating the power circuit, R is a holding relay, and $R1$ represents the control circuit sealing contacts on R. When the "start" pushbutton is depressed, R is energized and the circuit is sealed through $R1$. When the "stop" pushbutton is depressed, R is deenergized and the

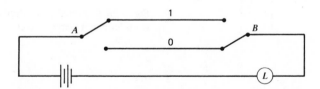

Figure 9.2.1 Circuit diagram for a two-position hall light switch.

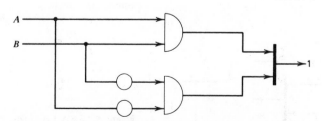

Figure 9.2.2 Logic diagram for a two-position hall light switch.

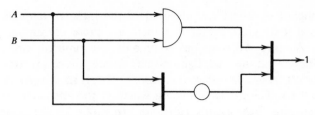

Figure 9.2.3   Variation of the logic diagram for a two-position hall light switch.

circuit through $R1$ is broken. The equation for this circuit is deceptively simple and does not tell the entire story. It is $ab' = 1$. Note that b is a nonexistent signal (or, if you prefer, a signal in state 0) until the "stop" pushbutton is depressed and $(0)' = 1$ so $ab' = 1$. The logic diagram in Figure 9.2.5 would be correct if we were using switches instead of momentary contact pushbuttons and relays. The actual logic diagram is shown in Figure 9.2.6, where x represents the holding circuit. Figure 9.2.7 is the customary way of showing this. We have labeled the input signals and the output signal rather than showing them as devices or events $A, B, C, \ldots$ in state $a, b, c, \ldots$ or as a circuit condition 1 or 0. The signal x in Figure 9.2.6 is not labeled in Figure 9.2.7. This is an internal signal and these are not labeled except in unusual circumstances.

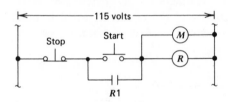

Figure 9.2.4   Partial elementary wiring diagram for motor starter circuit.

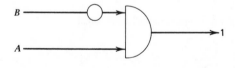

Figure 9.2.5   Simplified logic diagram for motor starter circuit.

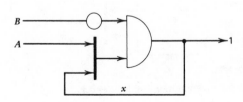

Figure 9.2.6   Actual logic diagram for motor starter circuit.

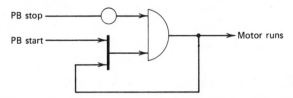

Figure 9.2.7   Labeled logic diagram for motor starter circuit. PB = pushbutton.

Some further explanation is needed for 0 signals. A signal may have a circuit value of 0 because it is nonexistent at a given time or because it is *defined* as having a 0 circuit value under certain conditions, for example the "hall light switch" circuit. Another example is a tank equipped with a high level switch. We could have high level either make or break a circuit. In the first case high level would give a circuit value of 1. In the second case it would give a circuit value of 0. The choice of make or break on high level could be dictated by process or safety requirements, or it could be completely arbitrary. The NOT operator in Boolean algebra and in logic diagrams is a signal inverter, regardless of the state of the signal.

From here on the Boolean algebra equations corresponding to the logic diagrams are usually omitted. We are primarily interested in the diagrams rather than the manipulation and simplification of the equations.

More examples of simple switching circuits are shown in Figures 9.2.8 through 9.2.11.

In Figure 9.2.9 note that if both control circuits are energized, both stop buttons must be pushed to stop the motor. In Figure 9.2.10 energizing the control circuit on either panel deactivates the control circuit on the other panel. And in 9.2.11 if a local audible alarm is energized by two or more alarm signals it may be silenced, and still be prepared to accept another signal, by this method (shown for two signals).

It is convenient at this point to give further attention to the logic operator OR, that is, the operation of disjunction. By the definition previously given, we see that an input *a* or an input *b*, or both, will give an

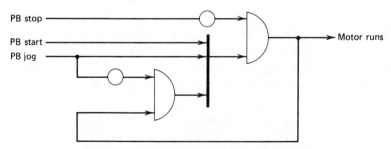

Figure 9.2.8   Motor starter with "jog only" control.

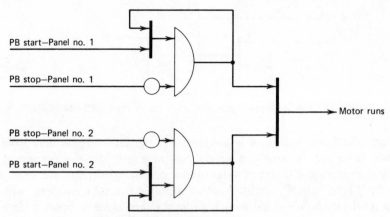

Figure 9.2.9   Motor start from two locations.

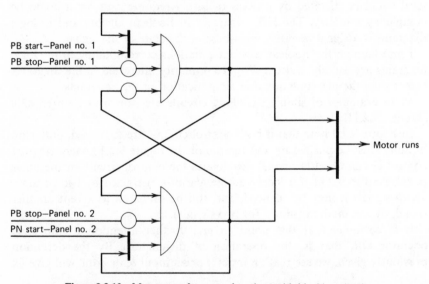

Figure 9.2.10   Motor start from two locations with blocking circuit.

output of 1. (This may be expanded to any number of inputs for a given output.) The condition of having an input *a* or an input *b*, but not both, is called the "exclusive or." No separate symbol is used for this since it can be expressed in three separate ways using the symbols already given. These ways are

$$(a+b)(ab)' = 1$$
$$(a+b)(a'+b') = 1$$
$$ab' + a'b = 1$$

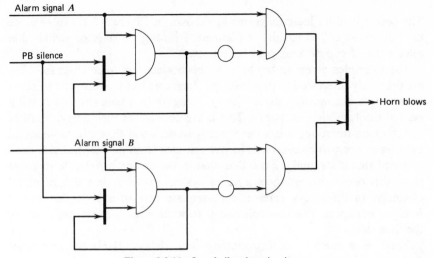

Figure 9.2.11 Local silencing circuit.

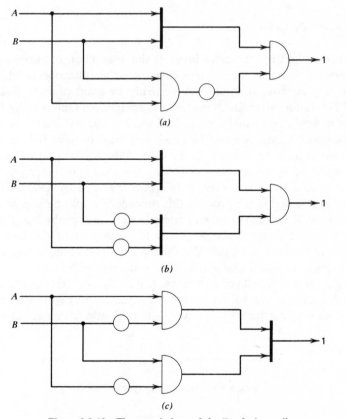

(a)

(b)

(c)

Figure 9.2.12 Three variations of the "exclusive or."

The corresponding logic diagrams are shown in Figure 9.2.12. In practice the "exclusive or" is usually implemented through a selector switch that selects one of two or more possible inputs.

The examples given so far have all been electrical logic diagrams. We are primarily interested in process logic diagrams but it is difficult to show even simple examples of these without bringing in a concept that is not a part of Boolean algebra, per se. This is the concept of time delay. In all of our Boolean functions it has been tacitly understood that a bistable signal exists *now*, not two picoseconds or five minutes from now. It has also been assumed that if a signal is cancelled, that is, the device switches to its other state, this occurs instantaneously. If a system involves time delays, either on-delays or off-delays, there is no adequate way to express this with a Boolean equation. The best solution is to write equations on each side of the time delay.

There is a method of introducing time delays painlessly into logic diagrams. This is the subject of our next section.

9.3   TIME DELAYS

A process plant by its nature involves the interaction of various pieces of equipment. Some of these interactions occur simultaneously while others occur sequentially. It would not normally be good practice to have two 1000 HP motors start simultaneously. If an agitated tank is being filled, the agitator would not usually be started until it was sufficiently submerged. Many other examples could be cited, but they all have this in common: some event must be delayed. In the case of the agitated tank this could be accomplished by an operator observing the level and starting the agitator at the proper time. However, if this tank was one of several tanks in a highly automated batch process, this procedure would be impractical. The signal to start the agitator could come from a level probe but it is simpler to use a time delay. Since we know the feed rate to the tank and the volume of the tank, we know that the liquid will be at the proper level after t minutes. The signal that started the feed flow to the tank can also start the agitator if it is delayed t minutes. A time delay of this type is called an on-delay and the symbol we use for it is $\subset\!\!\!\supset$. In Figure 9.3.1 a 1 signal at x does not become a 1 signal at y until t minutes have elapsed.

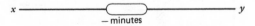

Figure 9.3.1   Time delay symbol—on delay.

A simple example of the use of a time delay is found in starting a piece of rotating or reciprocating equipment that is supplied with lubricating oil from a pump driven by the same motor. The equipment must run but should shut down automatically if the oil is not up to a specified pressure within a given time interval. The logic diagram for this is shown in Figure 9.3.2.

A more involved example is one in which pump *A* starts and is interlocked with pump *B*, which pumps ingredient *x*, and pump *C*, which pumps ingredient *y*. The flow valves for ingredients *x* and *y* must also open. If, within a given time interval, ingredients *x* and *y* are not within set flow limits as determined by flow measuring devices, the entire system must shut down. The logic diagram for this is shown in Figure 9.3.3.

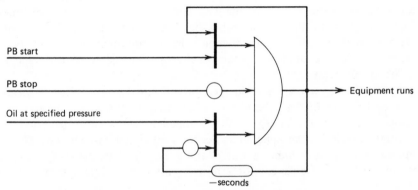

Figure 9.3.2 Equipment start with time delayed holding circuit.

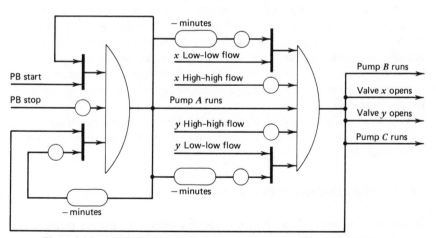

Figure 9.3.3 Interlocked equipment start with time delayed override cutouts.

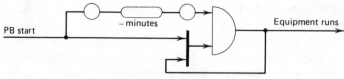

PB start

− minutes

Equipment runs

Figure 9.3.4   Self-extinguishing circuit.

x_1 x_2 y_1 y_2

Figure 9.3.5   Time delay symbol—off delay.

There are other cases where we wish to retain a signal after the original impulse has been cancelled or disappears. One common example of this is retaining the signal from a momentary contact pushbutton for a set time. Figure 9.3.4 shows the use of such a delay in a self-extinguishing circuit. Here we wish to have a piece of motor driven equipment start, run for a given time, and shut down automatically. A time delay of this type is called an off-delay.

In an off-delay a 1 signal is delayed but a 0 signal is not. In the off-delay shown in Figure 9.3.5 a 1 signal at x_1 becomes a 0 signal at x_2 and y_1 and a 1 signal at y_2 immediately. If the 1 signal at x_1 is cancelled, that is, becomes a 0 signal, the signal at x_2 becomes a 1 signal immediately. After t minutes the signal becomes a 1 at y_1 and a 0 at y_2. Thus the signal at y_2 is maintained, or off-delayed, for t minutes after the original signal at x_1 disappears.

Delay times may range from nanoseconds to minutes. In process plants they are usually in the seconds to minutes range. Most time delay devices are adjustable over a given range. When the delay times required are in the range of several minutes (or even hours) timers are used. These may usually be treated the same as time delay devices but caution should be exercised because you could run into a device that is not bistable. Also, many timers have the disadvantage of requiring manual reset, which is not true of time delay devices.

You will notice we have deliberately avoided using the expression "time delay relay." There are also fluidic, pneumatic, hydraulic, and mechanical time delay devices.

9.4   SIMPLE PROCESS APPLICATIONS

In the development of the Boolean algebra of on–off events through the use of switching circuits, all of the circuits we used were combinational. The results obtained depended only upon the combination of the variables.

The time delay concept introduced in the previous section shows that the results obtained depend not only on the combination of the variables but also on the sequence in which the combinations occur. Such sequential logic occurs when time delays are used, when interlocking is used, or when devices having a "memory" are used. Devices that can remember the state to which they were last set will be discussed later.

A flow diagram for an interlocked system is shown in Figure 9.4.1. This is an extremely simple system and could be operated manually with no interlocking of equipment. Such interlocking is, however, usually required. This system could also be equipped with instrumentation of various degrees of sophistication until we finally arrive at a system that is completely automatic. Logic diagrams for the simple interlocked manual system, a semiautomatic system, and a full automatic system are shown in Figures 9.4.2, 9.4.3, and 9.4.4. In developing this logic it is assumed that the loading equipment can fill the bins at several times the withdrawal rate.

Assume the system shown in Figure 9.4.1 is handling a free-flowing granular solid that is to be transferred from a three-hopper car to one of two bins. The car is in position, hopper No. 1 is open, and the track hopper is full. Assume also that the only instruments in the system are locally mounted high and low level indicators for the bins. (Note that LS in the instrument symbol stands for level signal.) For manual operation the logic diagram is shown in Figure 9.4.2.

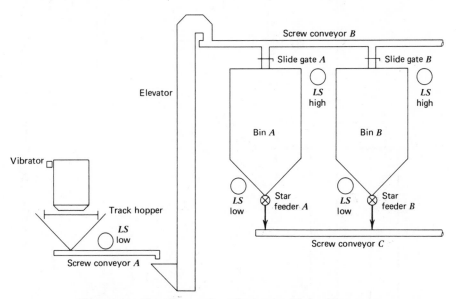

Figure 9.4.1 Flow diagram for a simple materials handling system.

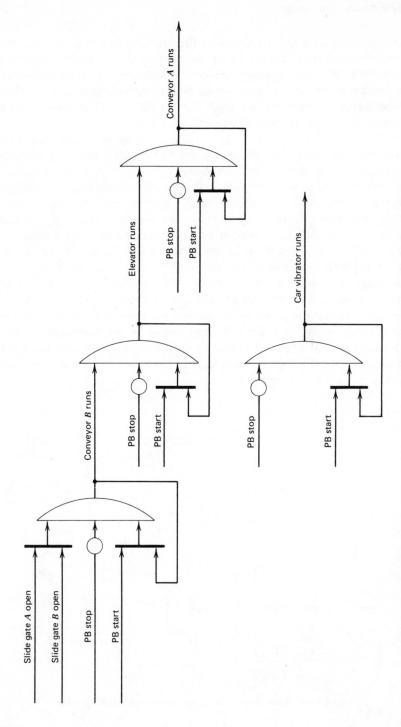

Figure 9.4.2 Logic diagram for flow diagram Figure 9.4.1—interlocked system with manual operation.

For the semiautomatic case we again assume that the car is in position, hopper No. 1 is open, and the track hopper is full. The instruments in use are high and low level controllers on the bins and a low level controller on the track hopper. All controllers are remotely located and panel mounted but there are local start–stop pushbutton stations for all of the equipment. Assume that screw conveyor C is feeding material from bin A and the level in the bin drops to the low level point, actuating an annunciator drop. The system is in the automatic mode through selector switch No. 1. The operator pushes the pushbutton marked "fill bin A" and the sequence of events is:

1. Slide gate A opens.
2. Screw conveyor B starts.
3. Elevator starts.
4. Screw conveyor A starts.
5. If the level in the track hopper drops to the low level position the car vibrator starts. If this level remains low for a given period (set by the time delay) an annunciator drop is actuated to indicate that the car is empty and the vibrator stops. The operator stops the sequence, repositions the car, and opens hopper No. 2. He then pushes the start button to reinitiate the sequence.
6. When bin A is full slide gate A closes shutting down conveyor B, the elevator, and conveyor A.

The logic diagram for this is shown in Figure 9.4.3. A similar sequence and logic diagram would apply for filling bin B. The manual mode is not shown since this would be the same as in Figure 9.4.2.

In the fully automatic system, everything except repositioning the car and opening the car hopper is taken out of the operator's hands. We again assume that the car is in position with number 1 hopper open, the track hopper is full, the system is in the automatic mode, conveyor C is feeding material from bin A, and the level in bin A drops to the low level position. The instrumentation is the same as for the semiautomatic case. The sequence of events is:

1. Star feeder B starts and star feeder A stops.
2. Slide gate A opens.
3. Conveyor B starts.
4. Elevator starts.
5. Conveyor A starts.

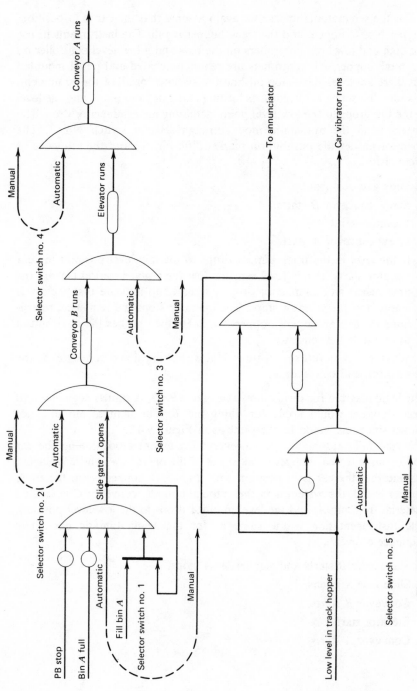

Figure 9.4.3 Logic diagram for flow diagram Figure 9.4.1—interlocked system with semiautomatic operation.

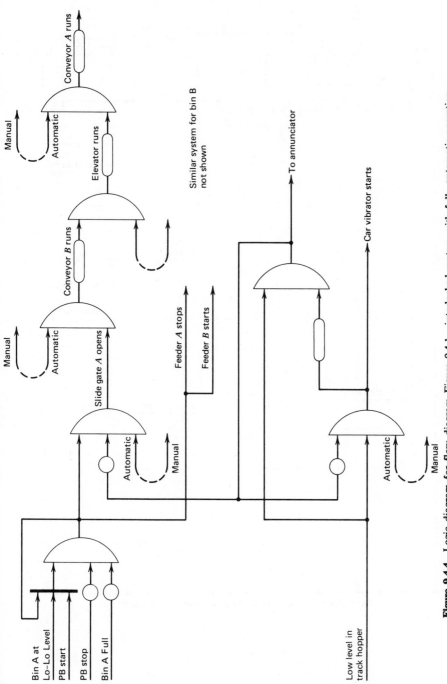

Figure 9.4.4 Logic diagram for flow diagram Figure 9.4.1—interlocked system with fully automatic operation.

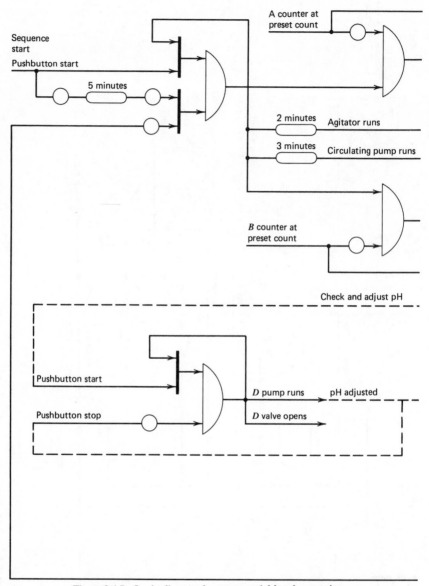

Figure 9.4.5 Logic diagram for a sequential batch operation.

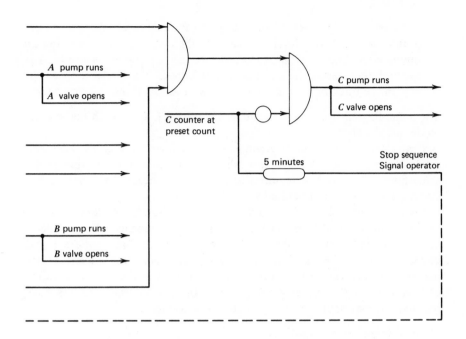

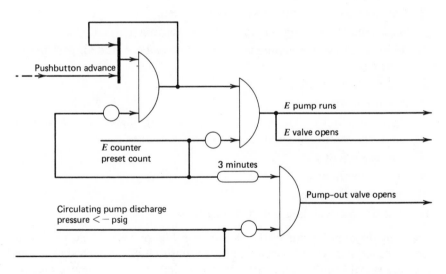

6. If the level in the track hopper drops to the low level position the car vibrator starts. If this level remains low the system shuts down and an annunciator drop is actuated to indicate the car hopper is empty. The operator repositions the car and opens hopper No. 2. As soon as the level in the track hopper is above the low level point the system restarts.

The logic diagram for this is shown in Figure 9.4.4, again with the manual mode not shown.

Time delays in the starting sequence are shown in Figures 9.4.3 and 9.4.4. These are necessary to keep all of the motors from starting at the same time. They are not required in Figure 9.4.2 because the operator is starting these motors individually.

Another simple example is a batch mixing system where several ingredients must be fed to the mixer in a particular sequence. We consider a mixer equipped with an agitator and a circulating pump where liquid ingredients A, B, C, D, and E are added. All ingredients except D are metered by integrating flow controllers which close their control valves and shut down the corresponding feed pumps when the counters have reached a preset count. The sequence of operations is:

1. Add ingredients A and B.
2. Start agitator two minutes after start of feed.
3. Start circulating pump one minute after starting agitator.
4. After all of both ingredients A and B have been added, add ingredient C.
5. Mix for five minutes.
6. Signal operator.
7. Operator checks pH and adjusts by adding ingredient D with a manually controlled pump while mixing continues.
8. Add ingredient E.
9. Mix three minutes.
10. Pump out to storage.
11. Shut down circulating pump and agitator.

The logic diagram for this system is shown in Figure 9.4.5. The off-delay in the sequence start circuit permits the start pushbutton to override the low pressure signal from the circulating pump so that another sequence may be initiated.

9.5 MULTIPLE SEQUENCING

There are many batch systems where it is necessary to stop the process more than once to check and adjust such things as pH, density, viscosity, color, and so on. Multiple sequencing such as this could be shown on a logic diagram using techniques we have developed to this point. Since this could become quite cumbersome it is more convenient to use a logic device that is a variation of the "flipflop."

A flipflop is a very simple logic device with a memory. It can remember which of its two outputs was last energized. An ordinary flipflop is shown in Figure 9.5.1. As you can see, this is two NOR gates, which have been labeled as L and R, with the output from each gate feeding a signal back as an input to the other gate. To follow the operation of this flipflop assume that we have a 1 output at Y and a 0 input at A and B. At gate L we have a 0 input from A and a 1 input from Y feedback. This gives a 1 output from this gate, which is inverted to a 0 signal by the NOT, giving a 0 signal at X. At gate R we have a 0 input from B and a 0 input from X feedback, giving us a 0 output from the gate that is inverted to a 1 signal by the NOT. Thus the 1 signal at Y is locked in and stable.

Now let us put in a momentary signal at B. The output of gate R becomes a 1, which is inverted to a 0 at Y. Since the signal A at gate L is 0 and Y feedback is 0, the output of gate L is 0, which is inverted to 1 at X and X feedback. The 1 signal at X is now locked in and stable. The signals at X and Y have thus flipflopped. Alternate momentary signals at A and B cause the X and Y outputs to alternate between 1 and 0.

A refinement of the flipflop is the triggered flipflop shown in Figure 9.5.2. Assume we have a locked in, stable signal 1 at X. Since the X feedback signal is 1, the output of gate R is 1, which is inverted to 0. The output of gate L is 0, which is inverted to 1. Since the system is stable we have a 1 input to the left AND from the NOT and a 0 signal to both

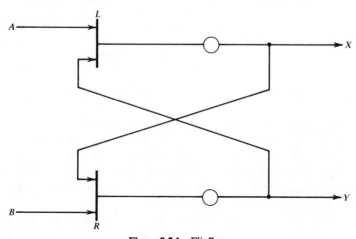

Figure 9.5.1 Flipflop.

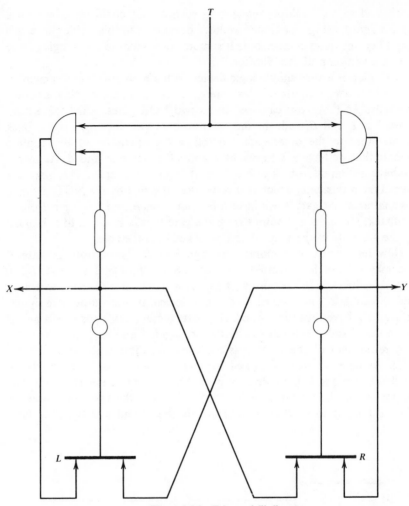

Figure 9.5.2   Triggered flipflop.

AND's from the trigger. The right AND also has a 0 signal from the right NOT.

Now we put in a momentary 1 signal at T. X immediately goes to 0 and Y immediately goes to 1. The 1 signal at Y is fed through the right time delay to the right AND. However, this signal is delayed long enough to insure that the signal at T has disappeared so the right AND is not activated to produce a 1 signal. Another momentary signal at T causes the device to flipflop to the original condition.

A sustained signal at T would cause the device to flipflop continuously. For this device to be of any use to us, the duration of the signal at T must

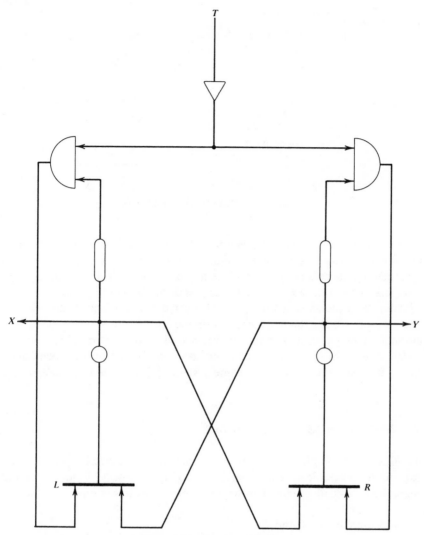

Figure 9.5.3 Standard binary.

be less than the on-delay time set on the time delay units. To insure this condition the trigger signal is fed through a time differentiator, which converts the signal, regardless of its duration, to a single burst, usually (for electrical signals) in the microsecond range. A triggered flipflop with a time differentiator is known as a "standard binary." The logic diagram for this is shown in Figure 9.5.3 where the symbol $\bigtriangledown$ stands for the time differentiator. For brevity, the symbol we use for a standard binary is as shown in Figure 9.5.4.

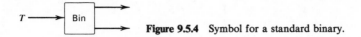

Figure 9.5.4 Symbol for a standard binary.

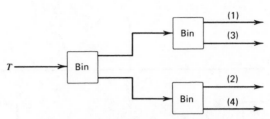

Figure 9.5.5 Cascaded standard binaries.

We can show as many sequential operations as we wish in a logic diagram by cascading standard binaries. A four-sequence operation programmed by successive pulses on one trigger is shown in Figure 9.5.5. The numbers in parentheses indicate the sequence of the output signals.

Multiple sequencing is encountered most often in batch processes but can be used to advantage in some continuous processes. A complex, highly automated materials handling system involving automatic calibration of weigh belts, purging of conveyors, and so on lends itself to this technique. In the next section we consider some systems using multiple sequencing.

9.6 MORE PROCESS APPLICATIONS

To illustrate a simple use of multiple sequencing in a batch operation we expand the example given in Section 9.4 (Figure 9.4.5) by adding seven ingredients instead of five. The sequence of operations is now:

1. Add ingredients *A* and *B*.
2. Start agitator two minutes after start of feed.
3. Start circulating pump one minute after starting agitator.
4. After all of both ingredients *A* and *B* have been added, add ingredient *C*.
5. Mix for five minutes.
6. Stop sequence, signal operator

7. Operator checks pH and adjusts by adding ingredient D with a manually controlled pump while mixing continues.

8. Operator pushes "Advance" button.

9. Add ingredient E.

10. Mix three minutes.

11. Stop sequence, signal operator.

12. Operator checks viscosity and sets ingredient F counter to proper value.

13. Operator manually starts ingredient F pump.

14. When the F counter reaches its preset count, the pump stops and the valve closes. The standard binary is automatically pulsed to start the ingredient G pump.

15. Add ingredient G.

16. Mix five minutes.

17. Pump out to storage.

18. Close pump-out valve, shut down circulating pump and agitator.

The logic diagram for this is shown in Figure 9.6.1

More complex interlocking and sequencing is involved when several different products, usually with certain raw materials in common, can be made in the same reactor, mixer, and so on. The logic diagram for such a system involving two products is shown in Figure 9.6.2. No verbal description of this system is given. A process logic diagram is meant to replace a description of process and the reader should be able to follow the procedure indicated in this diagram without difficulty, except for the starting circuit, which is a bit tricky. A blow-up of this circuit with the time delays labeled is shown in Figure 9.6.3. Time delay A is an off-delay that maintains the pushbutton signal for five minutes to override the pump-out low pressure signal when starting another batch. Time delay B is an off-delay that maintains the pushbutton signal long enough to insure that all counters are reset. Time delay C is an on-delay that insures that nothing else happens until the counters are reset. Time delay D is an on-delay that deactivates the pushbutton after ten seconds so that accidental pushing of this button will not reset the counters in the course of making a batch.

Another example of multiple sequencing is the case where several tanks containing the same liquid have their low level alarm signals connected to the same annunciator drop. In case of an alarm more than one tank may

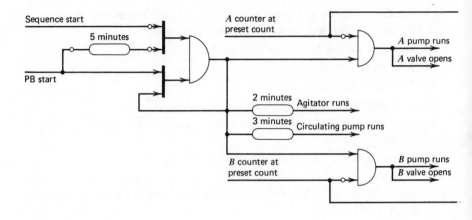

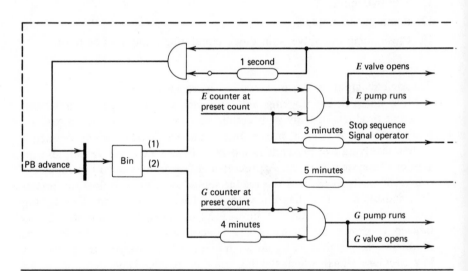

Figure 9.6.1 Batch process with multiple sequencing.

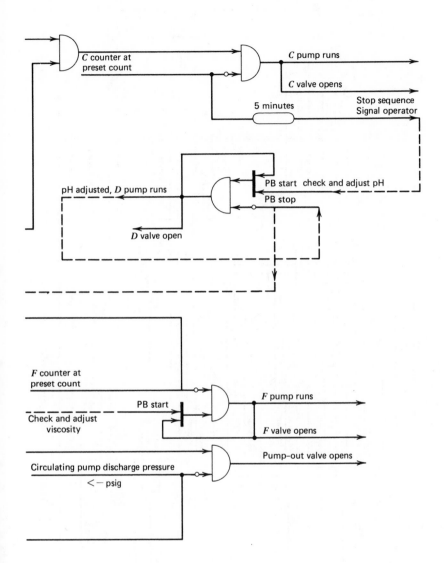

C counter at preset count

C pump runs

C valve opens

5 minutes

Stop sequence
Signal operator

pH adjusted, D pump runs

PB start   check and adjust pH

PB stop

D valve open

F counter at
preset count

F pump runs

PB start

Check and adjust
viscosity

F valve opens

Pump-out valve opens

Circulating pump discharge pressure
< – psig

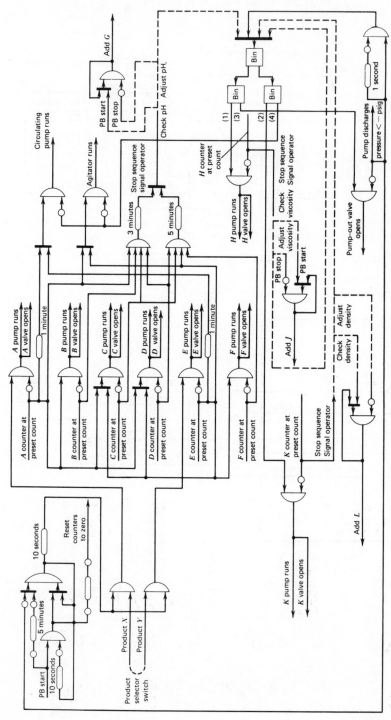

Figure 9.6.2 Batch process with cascaded standard binaries.

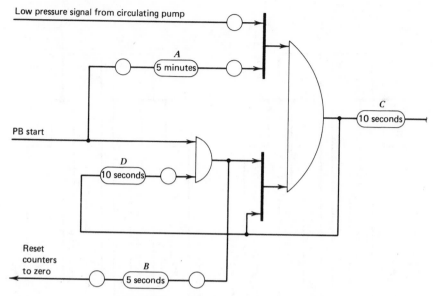

Low pressure signal from circulating pump

A
(5 minutes)

C
(10 seconds)

PB start

D
(10 seconds)

Reset
counters
to zero

B
(5 seconds)

Figure 9.6.3 Initiating circuit for Figure 9.6.2.

have a low level so we wish to check all of them automatically and fill the tanks that are low. In Figure 9.6.4 we show the logic diagram for a four-tank system fed by gravity from a supply tank. The sequence could be started by the operator or by the signal that activated the annunciator drop.

Our final logic diagram is for an operation seldom found in process plants but often encountered on construction projects. It is included here because:

1. All operations in the system are mechanical.
2. All signals are visual and/or audible.
3. It is an excellent example of multiple sequencing in a semicontinuous operation.
4. It illustrates the astonishing versatility of process logic diagrams.

This diagram is shown in Figure 9.6.5

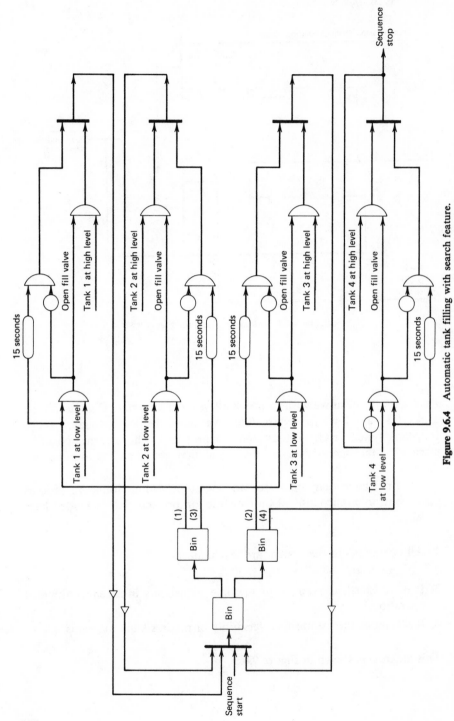

Figure 9.6.4 Automatic tank filling with search feature.

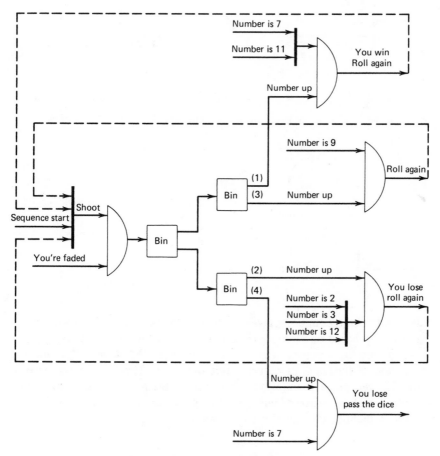

Figure 9.6.5 The Las Vegas syndrome.

9.7 NOR LOGIC

All of the basic logic operations can be implemented with NOR gates. The symbol we have used for NOR is shown in Figure 9.7.1. This represents the circuit shown in Figure 9.7.2 so you can see that negating an OR operation converts it from a parallel to a series circuit. Similarly, negating an AND operation converts it from a series to a parallel circuit. To conserve space the NOR and NAND symbols are drawn as in Figure 9.7.3.

A NOR gate with one input is a NOT or, as it is usually referred to in logic hardware terms, an inverter (see Figure 9.7.4). The OR operation, using NOR gates, is shown in Figure 9.7.5. The AND operation is shown in Figure 9.7.6 and the NAND operation is shown in Figure 9.7.7. The flipflop, which is covered in Section 9.5, is illustrated in Figure 9.7.8. You

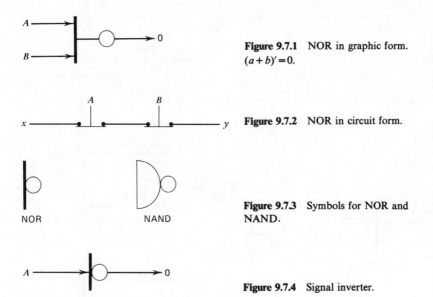

Figure 9.7.1 NOR in graphic form. $(a+b)'=0$.

Figure 9.7.2 NOR in circuit form.

Figure 9.7.3 Symbols for NOR and NAND.

Figure 9.7.4 Signal inverter.

can see that the equations given with the OR, AND, and NAND operations are all based on DeMorgan's rules or variations of these rules.

It should be obvious why we do not use "NOR gates" (with the exception of flipflops) in process logic diagrams. They are shown here so you will recognize them if you run across them. Every now and then someone making process logic diagrams becomes enamored of NOR gates and uses them freely, thereby confusing the hell out of the rest of us.

Figure 9.7.5 OR operation using NOR gates. $[(a+b)']' = (a'b')' = a+b = 1$.

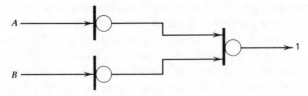

Figure 9.7.6 AND operation using NOR gates. $(a'+b') = ab = 1$.

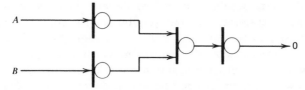

Figure 9.7.7 NAND operation using NOR gates. $[(a' + b')']' = a' + b' = (ab)' = 0$.

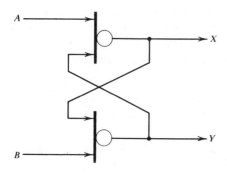

Figure 9.7.8 The flipflop as an illustration of NOR gates.

9.8 LADDER DIAGRAMS

A logic diagram is essentially a communications tool. An example that is encountered in switching circuits illustrates this well. The logic diagram in Figure 9.4.2, in conjunction with the flow diagram in Figure 9.4.1, tells the electrical designer exactly what the process design engineer wants to happen in this part of the system. That is:

1. Conveyor B may be started manually if and only if slide gate A or slide gate B or both are open.*
2. The elevator may be started manually if and only if conveyor B is operating.
3. Conveyor A may be started manually if and only if the elevator is running.
4. The car vibrator may be started and stopped independently of the rest of the system.

A system such as this is treated as a combinational logic system even though it appears to be inherently sequential. If two operators depressed

---

*By convention, in a device that is not inherently bistable, such as this, "open" means fully open as distinguished from "not closed."

and held the start pushbuttons for the elevator and conveyor *A*, and a third operator depressed the start pushbutton for conveyor *B*, all units would start simultaneously. An unlikely situation, but it could happen. True sequential systems usually require built-in time delays.

It is now the job of the electrical designer to design a hardware system to accomplish what is desired. The first step in doing this is to draw a ladder diagram (elementary wiring diagram). Such a diagram is shown in Figure 9.8.1. This diagram is for relay circuitry and is incomplete in that safety fuses, overload relays, and so on are not shown. Junction numbers are also omitted. We follow this diagram in detail starting at the top. The various circuits have been labeled as *A, B, C...* for convenience. Such labels are not used in practice. (Ladder diagram symbols are shown in Section 11.7.)

1. Note that the voltage applied across the busbars (the stringers of the ladder) is 115 bolts (110 to 120 volts range). Using a higher voltage than this would be hazardous. A 24 volt system would be preferable but is rarely found in process plants.

2. Circuit *A* is the starting circuit for conveyor *B*. When the start pushbutton is depressed, relays *R*1 and *M*1 are energized; the contacts on *R*1 close and seal the circuit if and only if the contacts on *R*2 or *R*3 or both are closed. *M*1 operates a relay, or relays, in a power circuit (not shown). When the stop pushbutton is depressed the circuit is deenergized and the contacts on *R*1 open. The circuit stays deenergized until the start pushbutton is again depressed.

3. In circuits *B* and *C*, *R*2 is energized if the position (limit) switch *LS*1 is closed and *R*3 is energized if *LS*2 is closed. These limit switches indicate the "open" position of the slide gates. The contacts on *R*2 and *R*3 close when the relays are energized.

4. Circuit *D*, the starting circuit for the elevator, is energized and the contacts on *R*4 close when the start pushbutton is depressed if and only if circuit *A* is energized and the contacts on *R*1 are closed. Depressing the stop pushbutton results in action similar to that described for circuit *A*.

5. Circuit *E* is similar to circuit *D* and can be energized only when circuit *D* is energized and the contacts on *R*4 are closed.

6. Circuit *F* is a simple, noninterlocked starting circuit.

This all seems very simple and leads to the question: "So who needs logic diagrams?" This example is simple. If, however, you have 150 full size sheets of ladder diagrams—not uncommon for even medium size plants—you will soon discover who needs logic diagrams. If a multiple contact relay, say relay number 320, is shown on drawing 79 and its various contacts are shown on drawings 11, 29, 87, 109, 121, and 143—all

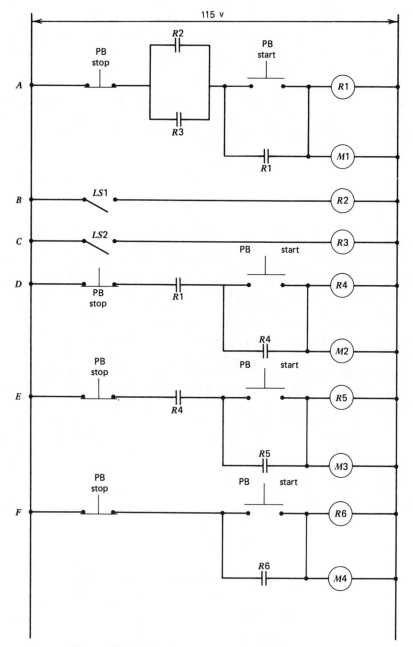

Figure 9.8.1 Ladder diagram for logic diagram Figure 9.4.2.

identified as $R320$—you will spend a great amount of time trying to determine just what this relay does. The answer is obvious immediately on a logic diagram or diagrams. One fairly complex logic diagram can result in a large number of ladder diagrams.

Synthesizing a logic diagram from ladder diagrams that were drawn without benefit of logic diagrams is usually a very time consuming task. It is also a very constructive operation. The number of outright errors and the examples of generally poor circuit design that will be uncovered will amaze you.

9.9 INTERLOCKING

Interlocking may be required in process plants for many reasons. The process may require a sequential step that can be implemented with a time delayed interlock. Starting a tank agitator x minutes after a tank has started to fill is a very simple example of this and is shown in Figure 9.9.1. Notice that a one-shot relay has been incorporated into this interlock. Without this the agitator could not be shut down as long as the pump was running. Process interlocks are usually of this type and may be considered as automatic pushbuttons. Although the circuit shown is for starting a motor, a similar circuit could be used for stopping.

Process interlocks are the *only* type permitted in the holding circuit of a starter. Safety interlocks should never be installed this way. A great many horror stories could be written to illustrate what happens when safety interlocks are designed incorrectly. Such designs usually occur when a process group gives a written schedule of interlocks to an electrical design

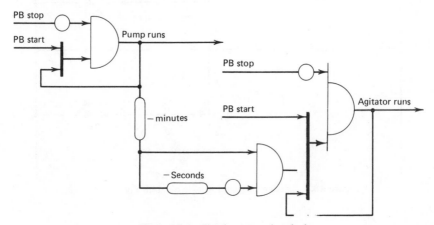

Figure 9.9.1 Simple process interlock.

group, which then makes the ladder diagrams. Unfortunately the electrical group has no way of knowing which are process and which are safety interlocks. This is one problem in communications that the logic diagram is designed to solve.

An example of incorrect design is given in Figure 9.9.2. Unfortunately, this is not a hypothetical example; in the particular plant where this design was done, most of the safety interlocks were designed incorrectly.

The number of errors incorporated into the simple circuit shown in Figure 9.9.2 would be laughable if they were not so potentially deadly. These errors are:

1. If both interlocks are energized, motor *A* can be energized with a defective starter, that is, one where the holding relay does not operate.
2. If the starter is not defective, interlock 1 is worthless. It is a "don't care" variable.
3. Both interlocks can be overridden by "matchstick" operation, that is, keeping the start pushbutton depressed by mechanical means such as jamming a matchstick into it.

The interlock system shown in Figure 9.9.2 should have been designed as shown in Figure 9.9.3. This would have been obvious if logic diagrams had been prepared for this installation. Matchstick operation can be applied to most noninterlocked starting circuits and to interlocked circuits if the interlocks are energized. The most hazardous use of this idiotic practice occurs with jogging circuits where interlocks are of necessity bypassed. Such a circuit, with interlock bypassing, is shown in Figure 9.9.4.

The circuit shown in Figure 9.9.5 will prevent matchstick operation from either pushbutton start or pushbutton jog. If you really wish to frustrate

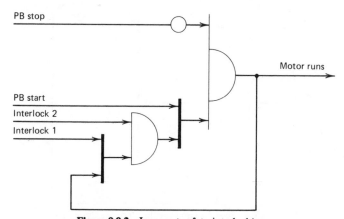

Figure 9.9.2 Incorrect safety interlocking.

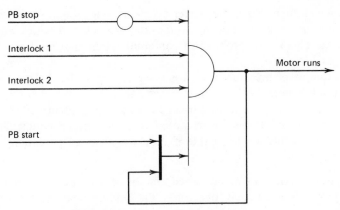

Figure 9.9.3   Correct safety interlocking.

the operator, use a manual reset type one-shot relay in the pushbutton jog circuit and locate this relay as far away from the control room as possible. Of course you might also frustrate yourself this way.

There are many ways of making interlock systems foolproof but no way of making them damn foolproof. An operator with the knowledge, the desire, and access to the relay panels can undo all the precautions you have taken. The only solutions I know to this problem are illegal, immoral, and drastic.

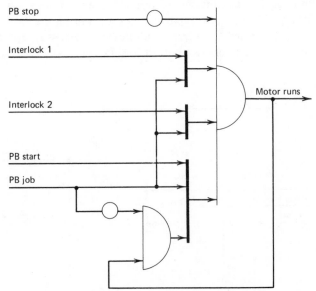

Figure 9.9.4   Jogging circuit with interlocks bypassed.

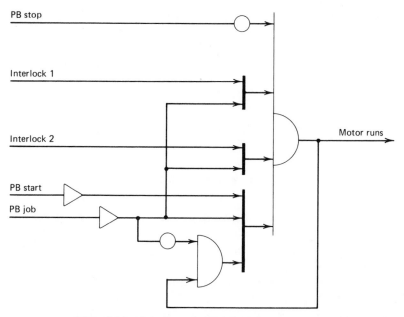

Figure 9.9.5 One-shot relays in start and jog circuits.

The easiest and cheapest way to transmit signals concerning the status of equipment powered by electric motors is through contacts in the starters and this is usually where signals originate for interlocking. This is also the least satisfactory way. The fact that a motor is running gives no assurance that the equipment it is connected to is running. Couplings, shafts, chains, and V-belts have all been known to fail frequently. A safer, but more expensive, way to transmit signals is by using motion switches, tachometer generators, pressure switches, and so on. Too often the choice is not up to the process design engineer but to whoever is paid to watch the budget. As with most other things, you get what you pay for.

9.10 GATING FUNCTIONS

One common error committed by people who use on–off logic and logic devices is referring to AND, OR, NAND, and NOR functions as "gates." AND and NOR are gating functions; the others are not. The simplest gate that could be considered is a telegraph key, which may be looked upon as a single input AND gate. The signal is transmitted only when the circuit is closed by the key (not the message—the signal. The message is transmitted by the time interval between signals). An AND gate of much more interest

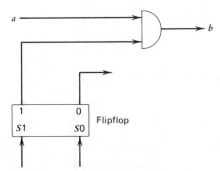

Figure 9.10.1   AND gate with flipflop input.

to us is shown in Figure 9.10.1. Here we are using a flipflop to open and close the gate. The input signal a appears as the output signal b only when the $S1$ input of the flipflop is energized. This gate may be turned on or off permanently by the flipflop.

Another use of a flipflop is shown in Figure 9.10.2. The contents of the first flipflop are copied into the second when the signal x is energized.

This leads us to a practical, although extremely elementary, application in telemetry. Suppose we have four flipflops, the contents of which we wish to copy into four similar flipflops at a remote location. This can be done very readily and rapidly by making a parallel-to-series conversion at the sending location, transmitting this serial by radio, and making a series-to-parallel conversion at the receiver. The parallel-to-series conversion is shown in Figure 9.10.3. In this figure a,b,c and d are signals from a timer. We assume that a is energized during only the first second (or millisecond or microsecond) from time zero, b is energized during only the second second, c during the third, and d during the fourth. We also assume that these timing signals are transmitted as they are energized. These time signals activate the gates so the contents of our flipflops are in serial form.

We will need a counterpart of this device at the receiver to make a series-to-parallel conversion. This is shown in Figure 9.10.4. By combining these we transmit and receive the contents of the original flipflop, which in

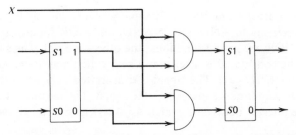

Figure 9.10.2   Copying the contents of a flipflop with AND gates.

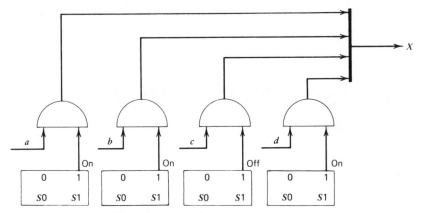

Figure 9.10.3 Parallel-to-series conversion.

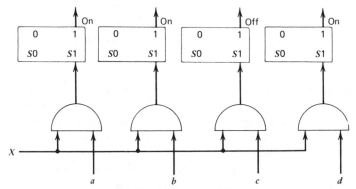

Figure 9.10.4 Series-to-parallel conversion.

this example are 1101. We can do exactly the same thing using NOR gates. In fact, in an application such as this, NOR gates would probably be used.

SUMMARY

The material presented should enable you to both read and make logic diagrams. With practice you can become adept at both. Some companies insist that their process engineers, plant supervisors, operators, and instrument technicians all become thoroughly familiar with these diagrams and do not consider a set of engineering flow diagrams to be complete unless it contains the applicable logic diagrams.

In making logic diagrams do not use freehand drawing. Sloppy drawing leads to sloppy thinking, which is the antithesis of logical thinking.

One more word of caution about interlocking. Mistakes in interlocking can cause serious injuries or deaths.

TEN

ANALYSIS OF DIAGNOSTIC SYSTEMS

INTRODUCTION

The material presented in this chapter is unique. Nothing similar to this has ever appeared in the literature to the best of my knowledge.

The first step in the construction of this system takes us away from a two-variable logic and into a multivariable one—the logic of propositions. With the elimination of nonpermissable implications, that is,

$$p \rightarrow -q$$

we have nothing left but tautologies. This permits us to revert to two-variable logic and simplify the resulting functions. The simplified functions are then converted back to multivariable logic, that is, one using implication. Proving that all of this constitutes a valid procedure required a great deal of background work that is not presented here.

This technique is published here for the first time. Unfortunately, it has never been tested in a real-life situation. It is hoped that this will be remedied in the near future.

10.1 IMPLICATION AND INFERENCE

In Section 3.4 we discussed the relationship between implication and inference. In particular it was pointed out that a conditional could be shown as

$$p \rightarrow q$$
$$-p \rightarrow q$$
$$-p \rightarrow -q$$

But that

$$p \rightarrow -q$$

is not permitted. No true antecedent may imply a false consequent.

An extremely interesting application of symbolic logic may be derived from this.* If, for any given situation, we have a number of implications, which may or may not be combined by our basic operations, giving a number of inferences, which also may or may not be combined by our basic operations, just what do we have? Quite obviously we cannot have a condition where $p \to -q$. But how do we analyze this? Consider these relationships for a particular situation:

10.1.1a $xy \to a + bc'$

10.1.2a $y \to a + c$

10.1.3a $z \to b + c$

10.1.4a $x \to ac'$

10.1.5a $xz \to bc'$

10.1.6a $xyz \to ac$

Just what conclusion may be drawn from the above equations? The answer is by no means obvious even though we have only six terms (not variables —here we are working with a two-variable two-valued algebra) involved in conditionals.

Now let's complicate it a bit:

10.1.1b $xy \leftrightarrow a + bc'$

10.1.2b $y \leftrightarrow a + c$

10.1.3b $z \leftrightarrow b + c$

10.1.4b $x \leftrightarrow ac'$

10.1.5b $xz \leftrightarrow bc'$

10.1.6b $xyz \leftrightarrow ac$

Now we have our six terms involved in biconditionals. We could complicate things even more by assuming we have a mixture of conditionals and biconditionals in any combination you care to take.

Let's assume that x, y, and z are observations we have made and a, b, and c are conclusions we have come to from our observations. This is a classical example of implication and inference that can and does arise in many fields of scientific and/or social endeavor. In the field of archeology we may have, for example, "This bone is x centimeters long by y centimeters in diameter and shows evidence of double articulation at both ends. From this we conclude that this is a --- bone from the species ***." One social context would be the field of criminal investigation: "Jones was

---

*This application was originally presented for a very simple case by Irving Adler in his book *Thinking Machines*, Signet Science Library (1962). Nothing further was done with this, possibly because of the need for a sophisticated digital computer for more complex cases.

seen in Fountain Square at 2:00 AM on Friday the 13th; this implies that Jones was in Cincinnati at that time." Another technical field to consider is that of chemical analysis: "If ion x and ion y are identified in a --- solution at a pH of ***, we infer that compound a is present." Many other situations can and do arise in a vast variety of applications.

Possibly the most fertile field that comes to mind is that of medical diagnostics. This is also the one that could have the greatest possibility of giving biconditionals. If the presence of symptoms x and y implies that a patient has disease b and not disease c, it is quite probable that if he has disease b and not disease c he will exhibit symptoms x and y. This situation would rarely occur in a criminal investigation: "Jones was in Cincinnati at 2:00 AM on Friday the 13th" does not imply that Jones was seen on Fountain Square. He could have been at my house drinking beer.

10.2 BASIC RELATIONSHIPS

So what do we do with this? First we consider the relationship

$$p \rightarrow q$$

This may be expressed as $p \rightarrow q \equiv p \leftrightarrow pq$. (Check this with a truth table if you don't believe it.) $p \leftrightarrow pq$ is a tautology for all conditions except pq'. (Again, check this out with a truth table.) Therefore, for all conditions except pq' we may write this as $p \Leftrightarrow pq$. Using the truth value function we have

$$\tau(p) = \tau(p)\tau(q)$$

which for simplicity is written as

$$p = pq$$

Also, since $p \rightarrow pq$ and $pq \rightarrow p$, we have

$$p \rightarrow pq = pq \rightarrow p$$

But

$$p \rightarrow pq = p' + pq$$

and

$$pq \rightarrow p = (pq)' + p$$

Therefore

$$p' + pq = (pq)' + p$$
$$pp' + ppq = p(pq)' + pp$$
$$0 + pq = p(p' + q') + p$$
$$pq = pp' + pq' + p$$
$$pq = 0 + p(q' + 1)$$
$$pq = p$$
$$pqq' = pq'$$
$$pq' = 0$$

This could have been done more simply, of course, by using just the last three steps since we had already established that $p = pq$. Or we could have used

$$p \rightarrow q$$
$$p' + q = 1$$

and, by the principle of duality,

$$pq' = 0$$

The first derivation is, however, more informative.

Applying this to the first equation listed in Section 10.1 we have

10.1.1a
$$xy \rightarrow a + bc'$$
$$xy(a + bc')' = 0$$
$$xy(a'(bc')') = 0$$
$$xy(a'(b' + c)) = 0$$
$$xy(a'b' + a'c) = 0$$
$$xya'b' + xya'c = 0$$

therefore

$$xya'b' = 0$$

and

$$xya'c = 0$$

All of the equations in Section 10.1 may be manipulated in a similar manner.

10.3   MATRIX REDUCTION

If we set up a Boolean matrix (not a truth table) in six terms we have

x	y	z	a	b	c
0	0	0	0	0	0
0	0	0	0	0	1
0	0	0	0	1	0
0	0	0	0	1	1

and so on for 64 rows. In this matrix a 1 entry indicates the positive presence of a term and a 0 entry indicates the negative presence of a term. A d (for don't care) entry indicates that the term is not involved. If we take the two answers given in Section 10.2 for Equation 10.1.1a and scan the matrix row by row for the combinations $11d00d$ and $11d01d$, we may eliminate any row that contains these forms since the conjunction of the terms of these forms is 0. Remember that the don't care (d) entries may be either 1 or 0 in the matrix—the row is still eliminated.

If we take Equation 10.1.1a, $xy \rightarrow a + bc'$, and rewrite it as a biconditional we have

10.1.1b $xy \leftrightarrow a + bc'$

If we manipulate this equation we have for the left to right conditional the results we obtained when we manipulated Equation 10.1.1a. For the right to left conditional we have

10.1.1b (right to left)

$$(xy)'(a + bc') = 0$$
$$(xy)'a + (xy)'bc' = 0$$
$$(x' + y')a + (x' + y')bc' = 0$$
$$x'a + y'a + x'bc' + y'bc' = 0$$

therefore

$$x'a = 0$$
$$y'a = 0$$
$$x'bc' = 0$$
$$y'bc' = 0$$

For the biconditional situation we now have these results

$$xya'b' = 0 \qquad 11d00d$$

$$xya'c = 0 \qquad 11d01d$$

$$x'a = 0 \qquad 1dd0dd$$

$$y'a = 0 \qquad d0d1dd$$

$$x'bc' = 0 \qquad 0ddd10$$

$$y'bc' = 0 \qquad d0dd10$$

It should be unnecessary to present the manipulations for all of the equations given in Section 10.1, as the reader can perform these manipulations for himself. Only the results are presented here.

Equation number	Conditional	Biconditional
10.1.1	$xya'b' = 0$	$xya'b' = 0$
	$xya'c = 0$	$xya'c = 0$
		$x'a = 0$
		$y'a = 0$
		$x'bc' = 0$
		$y'bc' = 0$
10.1.2	$ya'c' = 0$	$ya'c' = 0$
		$y'a = 0$
		$y'c = 0$
10.1.3	$zb'c' = 0$	$zb'c' = 0$
		$z'b = 0$
		$\dot{z}'c = 0$
10.1.4	$xa' = 0$	$xa' = 0$
	$xc = 0$	$xc = 0$
		$x'ac' = 0$
10.1.5	$xzb' = 0$	$xzb' = 0$
	$xzc = 0$	$xzc = 0$
		$x'bc' = 0$
		$z'bc' = 0$
10.1.6	$xyza' = 0$	$xyza' = 0$
	$xyzc' = 0$	$xyzc' = 0$
		$x'ac = 0$
		$y'ac = 0$
		$z'ac = 0$

In the context of medical diagnostics we may add two more equations. We may assume that the absence of all symptoms cannot imply the presence of a disease so $x'y'z' = 0$, and the absence of all diseases cannot imply the presence of symptoms so $a'b'c' = 0$. My medical friends may hotly dispute these two assumptions, in which case I must bow to their superior knowledge. Remember, however, that this is a purely hypothetical example. We use the above two assumptions in both the conditional and biconditional cases.

Scanning the matrix for all of the above forms and eliminating the rows in which they appear will result in an amazing reduction in the number of rows in the matrix. This could be done by hand at the cost of many hours of work. In fact, a 6-term system was chosen because it could be done by hand since there are only 64 rows in the matrix. If a 16-term system had been used the matrix would have 2^{16} or 65,536 rows! Obviously a computer approach is desirable.

The matrix for any given diagnostic system can be reduced very readily on a digital computer. However, reduction of the matrix is only the first step. It is desirable to simplify the resulting Boolean functions by using McCluskey's second method, described in Section 8.3. This requires segregation of the reduced matrix into groups and combination of the groups to find the prime implicants. A determination of the essential prime implicants is also made and the p-terms associated with these essential prime implicants are listed. The disjunction of all of the prime implicants gives the final equation, which may be subject to further simplification.

A computer program for reducing and segregating the matrix and combining the resulting Boolean functions has been written in FORTRAN IV by the author. Computer runs were made at the University of Cincinnati using an IBM system 360/370 model 168 computer. These runs were made for:

1. The biconditional case.
2. An arbitrary mix of conditionals and biconditionals.
3. The conditional case

10.4   THE BICONDITIONAL CASE

The results of the run for the biconditional case are shown in Table 10.4.1. The combination (disjunction) of $P25$ and $P27$ is

p	x	y	z	a	b	c	
25	0	1	1	0	0	1	
27	0	1	1	0	1	1	
	0	1	1	0	—	1	or $x'yza'c$

The final result is the disjunction of this with $P52$:

10.4.1 $$x'yza'c + xyz'ab'c' = 1$$

Both of these terms are essential prime implicants. Since Equation 10.4.1 is a disjunction using the nonexclusive or, one or both terms must equal 1.

Table 10.4.1   Computer results for the biconditional case

| P-term | Reduced matrix | | | | | |
	x	y	z	a	b	c
25	0	1	1	0	0	1
27	0	1	1	0	1	1
52	1	1	0	1	0	0

| Combinations | |
First	Second
25, 27	None

Consider the first term:

$$x'yza'c = 1$$

and let $x'yz = p$ and $a'c = q$. Then $pq = 1$. The truth table for the conjunction of p and q is:

p	$\cdot$	q
0	0	0
0	0	1
1	0	0
1	1	1

The truth table for the biconditional, $p \leftrightarrow q$, is:

p	$\leftrightarrow$	q
0	1	0
0	0	1
1	0	0
1	1	1

If, and only if (IFF), $pq = 1$, the last row of the truth table for the biconditional is the only valid row. We may therefore replace pq with $p \leftrightarrow q$. This same reasoning also applies to $p \rightarrow q$ and $q \rightarrow p$. We may now rewrite Equation 10.4.1 as

10.4.2 $\qquad (x'yz \leftrightarrow a'c) + (xyz' \leftrightarrow ab'c') = 1$

Therefore either

10.4.3 $\qquad x'yz \leftrightarrow a'c$

10.4.4 $\qquad xyz' \leftrightarrow ab'c'$

or both. In a medical context we may state:

1. If the patient exhibits symptoms y and z but not symptom x, he has disease c but not disease a. The status of disease b is indeterminate.

2. If the patient exhibits symptoms x and y but not symptom z, he has disease a but not disease b or c.

3. At least two symptoms must be present. Therefore, the original Equations 10.1.2b, 10.1.3b, and 10.1.4b represent faulty diagnoses.

This is a considerable simplification of the six original equations. Again, it must be emphasized that we are dealing with a hypothetical situation.

10.5 THE MIXED CASE

An arbitrary mixture of conditionals and biconditionals was chosen as

Conditional	Biconditional
Equation 10.1.1a	Equation 10.1.2b
Equation 10.1.3a	Equation 10.1.4b
Equation 10.1.5a	Equation 10.1.6b

The reduced matrix and the combinations determined by the computer run are shown in Table 10.5.1. Note the checkmarks that have been placed after the terms in the reduced matrix and in the first combination. This indicates that these terms were used in either the first or second combination.

Table 10.5.1　Computer Results for the mixed case

	Reduced matrix					
P-term	x	y	z	a	b	c
10—	0	0	1	0	1	0
17√	0	1	0	0	0	1
19√	0	1	0	0	1	1
25√	0	1	1	0	0	1
27√	0	1	1	0	1	1
52√	1	1	0	1	0	0
54√	1	1	0	1	1	0

Combinations	
First	Second
17, 19√	17, 19, 25, 27
17, 25√	
19, 27√	
25, 27√	
52, 54—	

To obtain the final equation we have

52	1 1 0 1 0 0
54	1 1 0 1 1 0
	1 1 0 1 — 0
	$xyz'ac'$

17	0 1 0 0 0 1
19	0 1 0 0 1 1
25	0 1 1 0 0 1
27	0 1 1 0 1 1
	0 1 — 0 — 1
	$x'ya'c$

These must be combined with $P\,10$ (since it has no check mark after it) to give

10.5.1 $$x'y'za'bc' + xyz'ac' + x'ya'c = 1$$

All of these terms are essential prime implicants. Using the same reasoning we used for the biconditional case we may write this as

10.5.2 $$(x'y'z \rightarrow a'bc') + (xyz' \rightarrow ac') + (x'y \rightarrow a'c) = 1$$

Notice that here we must use conditional notation rather than biconditional. In a mixed case we have no way of knowing that our results are biconditional so we must take the safest course and assume that they are not.

Relisting the terms in Equation 10.5.1 we have

$$x'y'z \longrightarrow a'bc'$$

$$xyz' \longrightarrow ac'$$

$$x'y \longrightarrow a'c$$

In a medical context this tells us:

1. If the patient exhibits symptom z but not symptoms x and y, he has disease b but not diseases a and c.
2. If the patient exhibits symptoms x and y but not symptom z he has disease a but not disease c.
3. If the patient exhibits symptom y but not symptom x he has disease c but not disease a.

10.6 THE CONDITIONAL CASE

This case becomes quite involved because there are 22 p-terms in the reduced matrix and we have first, second, and third combinations of these *p*-terms. It also gives nonessential as well as essential prime implicants. It is the most instructive of the three cases in that the development illustrates a different method of determining the essential prime implicants and determines whether or not the concept of an essential prime implicant is meaningful in this context. The fact that it is meaningful in electrical circuit theory does not necessarily mean that it is here.

The computer run results for this case are shown in several tables: Table 10.6.1, reduced matrix; Table 10.6.2, first combination; Table 10.6.3, second combination; Table 10.6.4, third combination. All of these tables are laid out in the groupings required by McCluskey's second method for the simplification of Boolean functions. We collect in Table 10.6.5 those combinations that are not checked off in Tables 10.6.1 through 10.6.4. In Table 10.6.6 we list the *p*-terms of the reduced matrix and the sets *A* through *K* of Table 10.6.5 in which they are found.

Table 10.6.1 Matrix reduction and segregation for the conditional case

P-term	x y z a b c	0	1	2	3	4	5	6
9√	0 0 1 0 0 1			9				
10√	0 0 1 0 1 0			10				
11√	0 0 1 0 1 1				11			
13√	0 0 1 1 0 1				13			
14√	0 0 1 1 1 0				14			
15√	0 0 1 1 1 1					15		
17√	0 1 0 0 0 1			17				
19√	0 1 0 0 1 1				19			
20√	0 1 0 1 0 0			20				
21√	0 1 0 1 0 1				21			
22√	0 1 0 1 1 0				22			
23√	0 1 0 1 1 1					23		
25√	0 1 1 0 0 1				25			
27√	0 1 1 0 1 1					27		
29√	0 1 1 1 0 1					29		
30√	0 1 1 1 1 0					30		
31√	0 1 1 1 1 1						31	
36√	1 0 0 1 0 0			36				
38√	1 0 0 1 1 0				38			
46√	1 0 1 1 1 0					46		
52√	1 1 0 1 0 0				52			
54√	1 1 0 1 1 0					54		

Table 10.6.2 First combination for the conditional case

9,11√	11,15√	15,31√
9,13√	11,27√	23,31√
9,25√	13,15√	27,31√
10,11√	13,29√	29,31√
10,14√	14,15√	30,31√
17,19√	14,30√	
17,21√	14,46−	
17,25√	19,23√	
20,21√	19,27√	
20,22√	21,23√	
20,52√	21,29√	
36,38√	22,23√	
36,52√	22,30√	
	22,54√	
	25,27√	
	25,29√	
	38,46−	
	38,54√	
	52,54√	

Table 10.6.3 Second combination for the conditional case

9,11,13,15√	11,15,27,31√
9,11,25,27√	19,23,27,31√
9,13,25,29√	13,15,29,31√
10,11,14,15−	14,15,30,31−
17,19,21,23√	21,23,29,31√
17,19,25,27√	22,23,30,31−
17,21,25,29√	25,27,29,31√
20,21,22,23−	
20,22,52,54−	
36,38,52,54−	

Table 10.6.4 Third combination for the conditional case

11,15,27,31,	9,13,25,29
19,23,27,31,	17,21,25,29

*Table 10.6.5 Summary of final combinations
for the conditional case*

Sets	Combinations
A	14, 46
B	38, 46
C	10, 11, 14, 15
D	14, 15, 30, 31
E	20, 21, 22, 23
F	20, 22, 52, 54
G	22, 23, 30, 31
H	36, 38, 52, 54
J	11, 15, 27, 31, 9, 13, 25, 29
K	19, 23, 27, 31, 17, 21, 25, 29

In Table 10.6.6 those sets that appear as singletons beside a P-term are the sets that form the essential prime implicants. They are C, H, J, and K. We determine the value of these sets in the usual manner:

Set C

10	0 0 1 0 1 0
11	0 0 1 0 1 1
14	0 0 1 1 1 0
15	0 0 1 1 1 1

$$0\ 0\ 1 - 1 -$$

$$x'y'zb$$

Set H

36	1 0 0 1 0 0
38	1 0 0 1 1 0
52	1 1 0 1 0 0
54	1 1 0 1 1 0

$$1 - 0\ 1 - 0$$

$$xz'ac'$$

Set J

11	0 0 1 0 1 1
15	0 0 1 1 1 1
27	0 1 1 0 1 1
31	0 1 1 1 1 1
9	0 0 1 0 0 1
13	0 0 1 1 0 1
25	0 1 1 0 0 1
29	0 1 1 1 0 1

$$0 - 1 - - 1$$

$$x'zc$$

Set K

19	0 1 0 0 1 1
23	0 1 0 1 1 1
27	0 1 1 0 1 1
31	0 1 1 1 1 1
17	0 1 0 0 0 1
21	0 1 0 1 0 1
25	0 1 1 0 0 1
29	0 1 1 1 0 1

$$0\ 1 - - - 1$$

$$x'yc$$

Table 10.6.6 *Allocation of P-terms to sets*

P-term	Sets	P-term	Sets	P-term	Sets
9	J	20	E,F	30	D,G
10	C	21	E,K	31	D,G,J,K
11	C,J	22	E,F,G	36	H
13	J	23	E,G,K	38	B,H
14	A,C,D	25	J,K	46	A,B
15	C,D,J	27	J,K	52	F,H
17	K	29	J,K	54	F,H
19	K				

The four essential prime implicants are, therefore:

$$x'y'zb \qquad xz'ac' \qquad x'zc \qquad x'yc$$

We have no assurance that the disjunction of the four essential prime implicants is the complete Boolean function we seek. They are necessary but may not be sufficient. If we examine Table 10.6.6 we see that all of the P-terms except four are included in one or more of the essential prime implicant sets. These four are $P20$, $P22$, $P30$, and $P46$. Therefore, the necessary and sufficient function contains the essential prime implicants plus the prime implicants in which these P-terms appear. They are

$$
\begin{array}{ll}
P20 & EF \\
P22 & EFG \\
P30 & DG \\
P46 & AB
\end{array}
$$

If we construct a matrix for these P-terms and the nonessential prime implicants we have Table 10.6.7.

Table 10.6.7 *Nonessential prime implicants for the conditional case*

Nonessential Prime Implicants	P- terms			
	20	22	30	46
A				x
B				x
D			x	
E	x	x		
F	x	x		
G		x	x	

From this we see that A and B include $P46$. (Expanding either A or B to its canonical dnf will give $P46$ as one of the terms.) D and G include $P30$. G also includes $P30$ and E and F include both $P20$ and $P22$. Therefore, there are eight possible combinations of disjunctions that include all of these P-terms. Using any one of these combinations disjoined with the essential prime implicants would give a minimal function if this were a switching circuit. However, we are not working with a switching circuit so all of the prime implicants must be considered.

We determine the values of A, B, D, E, F, G:

	A			B			D
14	0 0 1 1 1 0		38	1 0 0 1 1 0		14	0 0 1 1 1 0
46	1 0 1 1 1 0		46	1 0 1 1 1 0		15	0 0 1 1 1 1
—	$-\ 0\ 1\ 1\ 1\ 0$			$1\ 0\ -\ 1\ 1\ 0$		30	0 1 1 1 1 0
	$y'zabc'$			$xy'abc'$		31	0 1 1 1 1 1
							$0\ -\ 1\ 1\ 1\ -$
							$x'zab$

	E			F			G
20	0 1 0 1 0 0		20	0 1 0 1 0 0		22	0 1 0 1 1 0
21	0 1 0 1 0 1		21	0 1 0 1 1 0		23	0 1 0 1 1 1
22	0 1 0 1 1 0		52	1 1 0 1 0 0		30	0 1 1 1 1 0
23	0 1 0 1 1 1		54	1 1 0 1 1 0		31	0 1 1 1 1 1
	$0\ 1\ 0\ 1\ -\ -$			$-\ 1\ 0\ 1\ -\ 0$			$0\ 1\ -\ 1\ 1\ -$
	$x'yz'a$			$yz'ac'$			$x'yab$

The prime implicants can be combined to give

$$E + C + (A + B) + (F + H) + (G + D + J + \overset{\text{\tiny\textbf{,}}}{K}) = 1$$

$$A + B = (x + z)y'abc'$$

$$F + H = (x + y)z'ac'$$

$$G + D + J + K = x'(y + z)(ab + c)$$

The complete function is

$$x'yz'a + x'y'zb + y'(x + z)abc' + z'(x + y)ac' + x'(y + z)(ab + c) = 1$$

The truth tables for conjunction and implication are, for variables p and q

$p \cdot q$			$p \rightarrow q$		
0	0	0	0	1	0
0	0	1	0	1	1
1	0	0	1	0	0
1	1	1	1	1	1

Because we have stipulated that $pq = 1$, both $p = 1$ and $q = 1$ must be true. When this is true $p \rightarrow q$ is valid. Therefore we may list the terms of our function as

1. $x'yz' \rightarrow a$
2. $x'y'z \rightarrow b$
3. $y'(x + z) \rightarrow abc'$
4. $z'(x + y) \rightarrow ac'$
5. $x'(y + z) \rightarrow ab + c$

In a medical context we may say:

1. If the patient has symptom y but not symptoms x or z he has disease a.
2. If the patient has symptom z but not symptoms x or y he has disease b.
3. If the patient has symptoms x or z (or both) but not symptom y, he has diseases a and b but not c.
4. If the patient has symptoms x or y (or both) but not symptom z, he has disease a but not disease c.
5. If the patient has symptoms y or z (or both) but not symptom x, he has disease c or all three.

At least one of the above five conditions must be true because the function is equal to 1.

From a medical standpoint it is possible to pick holes in the results of the above analysis. For example, in all of the terms of the function the presence or absence of all of the symptoms is accounted for. This is not so for the diseases. If the term $x'yz' \rightarrow a$ is true, what is the status of diseases b and c? We cannot state definitely that they are absent. In switching circuits these would be "don't care" variables. It must be reemphasized that we are working with a *hypothetical* situation. The initial logical relationships are based on abstract variables. In a real-life situation it could be that all diseases would be accounted for, that one disease could mask another, or that "don't care" variables are permissable.

A summary of the three cases in tabular format is:

1. Biconditional case
   a. $x'yz \leftrightarrow a'c$
   b. $xyz' \leftrightarrow ab'c'$

2. Mixed case
   a. $x'y'z \rightarrow a'bc'$
   b. $xyz' \rightarrow ac'$
   c. $x'y \rightarrow a'c$

3. Conditional case
   a. $x'yz' \rightarrow a$
   b. $x'y'z \rightarrow b$
   c. $y'(x+z) \rightarrow abc'$
   d. $z'(x+y) \rightarrow ac'$
   e. $x'(y+z) \rightarrow ab+c$

One might be tempted to manipulate functions between the three cases. For example, it is obvious that $2a + 3b = 3b$. Lots of luck. This could open up a real can of worms, which is beyond the scope of the present effort.

SUMMARY

All of the work required to arrive at these results can be done on a digital computer. Unfortunately, the author's program covers only matrix reduction and segregation plus simplification of the Boolean functions. A complete workup of the program would be an excellent project for a computer science class.

There is a definite danger that the technique presented in this chapter will be misunderstood, particularly by members of the medical profession. This is not a technique for performing medical diagnostics on a computer or with the aid of a computer. Computer aided diagnostic techniques do exist, many of them based on Bayesian probability, but have fallen into disfavor because they have proved far less useful than originally anticipated.

The technique presented here is designed to analyze any complex system of implication and inference, not to create such a system. Some individuals will undoubtedly assume that they can analyze any system they encounter without resorting to this technique. It is possible that they can—if they have several months of free time in which to arrive at the answer. This would rarely be the case in a medical context where time is usually of the essence.

It must be emphasized that this is a novel technique, untried in the "real" world. The application of this technique to real-life situations could be an excellent research project. It would require an individual or group well-versed in Boolean algebra working in close cooperation with a large medical institution.

ELEVEN

FAULT TREES

INTRODUCTION

A fault tree is a formalized method for predicting the possibility of an equipment or system failure when the failure itself is postulated and the system is analyzed to determine what events could have caused this failure. Such an analysis results in creating, or synthesizing, the tree. This is only part of the job. The probability of failure of any subsystem or piece of equipment must then be determined. The two together pinpoint weaknesses in design and show where corrective action in respect to the design must be taken.

In this chapter we consider only synthesis of fault trees but we extend this synthesis to systems that are inherently sequential. A complete fault tree for even relatively simple systems can be quite complex. For complex systems they can require thousands or tens of thousands of man-hours if they are done manually. Fortunately there are several computer programs available to both synthesize and analyze fault trees for complex systems. Lapp and Powers[22] have developed such a program for the synthesis method described in this chapter.

The analysis of fault trees is primarily an exercise in statistical probability—a subject we do not cover in this book. Any good text on this will enable you to make such an analysis. Unfortunately, the data available for probability calculations are very scanty. The major sources of these data are listed in Appendix C.

11.1 BACKGROUND

Over the past 10 to 15 years there has been a definite trend in those sectors of the chemical industry dealing with high tonnage production to adopt the single-train approach to plant design. Nowhere has this been more evident than in the production of anhydrous ammonia. It is not uncommon today (1979) to have single-train units which produce 1500 to 2000 tons per day of product.

This trend started with ammonia plants and attracted considerable attention throughout the chemical industry. The approach was definitely novel—at the time some said foolhardy. Also, there is probably no industry that has expended more time, effort, and money on plant safety than the ammonia industry. Grave doubts were raised in the minds of many knowledgeable people as to the effect of single-train design on plant safety.

The reason for going to single-train design is simple. It is much cheaper to build a single train of large components than it is to build multiple trains of smaller components. But the question "what if...?" keeps coming up. There are two approaches to answering this question, both of which have been used successfully in the aerospace and electronics industries. These are failure modes and effects analysis (FMEA) and fault tree analysis (FTA). It is only quite recently that these methods have been applied to the chemical industry.

Failure modes and effects analysis (FMEA) is a formalized method for asking the question "what if...?" All of the possible component failures such as valves leaking, pump couplings or shafts breaking, line blockages, instrument failure, or operator error, are hypothesized and possible effects on the system are determined by investigating the system response to each failure or combination of failures. This can be done quite readily with a digital computer, providing an adequate model of the system is available. The key word is "adequate." Rarely will a model adequate for FMEA exist for a chemical plant, particularly in the design stage where FMEA is most useful. Changes in process conditions, process constraints, physical constraints, and so on make the process flow diagrams ever-changing documents—sometimes to the point where one thinks that order will never be brought out of the chaos.

Fault tree analysis (FTA) is a method of determining the possibility and/or probability of a specific designated failure occurring. A complete logic diagram is constructed which identifies the immediate precursor events leading to the failure, the precursors of these events, and so on until a pyramid structure or "tree" is generated. A probability is assigned to each event in the tree and the overall probability of the designated failure occurring is calculated.

The primary difference between FMEA and FTA is that the former starts with the primal precursor events and works forward (or upward) to detect possible failures while the latter identifies a specific failure and works backward (or downward) to identify the precursor events that could cause the failure to occur.

Both FMEA and FTA are systems approaches. To use either one it is necessary to have complete engineering flow diagrams (usually referred to as P&ID's) and complete logic diagrams. It is also necessary to define the system adequately. Although this may seem elementary it is sometimes the most difficult part of the analysis.

11.2 FAILURE PREVENTION

The failure of an individual item of equipment does not necessarily imply that a system failure will occur. Automatic control devices are usually capable of operating in the manual mode so a failure in the automatic mode may be compensated for by switching to manual. If process pumps are paralleled with operable spares, a failure of one pump will not shut down the system. However, as the complexity of a process increases, the probability of an individual failure causing a system failure also increases. The present trend in the design of chemical plants shows an increase in computerized operation, minimization of intermediate storage, complex recycle systems for energy conservation, and so on. The result is that the time available to take corrective action in the event of the failure of an individual item is being cut to a minimum. The existence of operable spares cannot prevent a system failure if they cannot be put on-stream fast enough. Theoretically a plant could be automated to the point where operable spares could be brought into service without human action but the resulting increase in the complexity of the system might create more problems than it solves.

System failures may be grouped into several categories. They are:

1. Normally nonhazardous.
2. Hazardous.
3. Disastrous.
4. Catastrophic.

An example of a normally nonhazardous failure would be the loss of electrical power to an electrolytic chlorine plant. This is frequently caused by a lightning strike on the substation feeding the plant. The entire plant goes down and generation of the chlorine gas ceases immediately, which eliminates the source of a potential hazard. Only economic losses are incurred.

An example of a hazardous failure is one where a temperature controller on a reactor fails, resulting in a runaway condition that causes an explosion. This could result in personnel injury or death and always results in financial loss.

The above example could result in a disastrous hazard if units adjacent to the one that exploded also explode. The result could be widespread loss of life and severe financial loss. Nearby communities could also be severely affected.

The rupture of a large liquid chlorine storage vessel (e.g., a 1000 ton capacity sphere) would be catastrophic. The potential loss of life would depend upon the location of the vessel.

Two methods of failure prevention are currently in widespread use. The first of these is the protective systems approach. This is essentially an after-the-fact attempt to limit the effect of the failure, that is, to keep a hazard from becoming a disaster. Sprinkler systems, explosion vents, fire doors, breakaway walls, and so on are examples of this approach. The second method is the systems safety approach. An attempt is made to predict the possible failure pathways in a system and to eliminate them or at least reduce the probability of their occurrence by proper design techniques, adequate spacing of equipment, and so on. A combination of both methods should always be applied to a process that is potentially hazardous.

The systems safety approach, as it has been used until recently, has been a somewhat haphazard method. No technique has been available by which all failure modes can be predicted and it is usually an unforseen failure that results in hazardous events. Attempts to make all items of equipment as failure-proof as possible soon run afoul of the economic facts of life. You just can't afford to do this. FMEA and FTA are methodologies applied to the systems safety approach to make it possible to weigh the benefits of measures taken against the cost of those measures. Of the two methodologies, FTA is, in my opinion, the more powerful.

11.3 FAILURE PREDICTION AND ANALYSIS

Not too many years ago failure analysis was just that—the analysis of failures that had already occurred. This led to systems of preventive maintenance which became more and more sophisticated over the years. No one argues that preventive maintenance is not required. However preventive maintenance systems are based to a great extent on an analysis of previous failures and do not take into account the unforseen failure. There is no doubt that the more highly sophisticated systems of preventive maintenance could benefit from a FMEA or FTA of the plant being maintained.

Most process design engineers attempt to predict failure pathways through the process they are designing. These predictions are usually based on experience or a "gut feeling" for a particular pathway. While this approach is not all bad it is definitely inadequate. The preparation of detailed process logic diagrams would in itself be of considerable assistance in predicting failure pathways. Unfortunately it appears that the great majority of engineers engaged in the design of chemical and/or mechanical process plants are blissfully unaware that such a powerful tool as the logic diagram exists. The intuitive approach now used will invariably not consider all failure modes except for the simplest processes. The FTA system is a far superior, but by no means infallible, approach.

11.4 FAULT TREE SYNTHESIS—COMBINATIONAL

The material presented in this and subsequent sections is not designed to give the reader an in-depth knowledge of the synthesis and analysis of fault trees. Many approaches have been made to this subject and the body of literature associated with fault trees is growing rapidly. Among the more recent publications are those of Vesely,[16] Vesely and Narum,[17] Lambert,[18, 19] Powers and Tompkins,[20] Fussell,[21] Lapp and Powers,[22] and Shaeiwitz, Lapp, and Powers.[23] The intent here is to show how logic diagrams may be used in fault tree work. In my opinion, this can be demonstrated most adequately using the techniques developed by Lapp and Powers. Only the simplest systems are considered here and the use of statistical probability in the analysis is only touched upon. FTA is a vast field and it would require a book at least the size of this one to give an adequate introduction to the subject. The first systems we consider are those which involve combinational logic only. Although various time lags may be encountered, everything is assumed to happen in the logical "now." Later we consider sequential logic systems where one or more events cannot occur until one or more previous events have been completed.

Any given chemical or mechanical process plant is built from basic components that may interact in many ways. Some type of control instrumentation is almost invariably required for proper operation of the system. This instrumentation may involve open-loop control, closed-loop feedback control, closed-loop feedforward control, or various combinations of any or all of these loops. All of this must be considered in synthesizing a fault tree.

We consider only simple systems containing few components and develop the trees for these. One of the simplest that could be selected is shown in Figure 11.4.1. Here we have a shell and tube cooler with no control instrumentation. Assume that the top event in our tree is a high temperature in stream 4, designated as $T4(+1)$. [A low temperature would

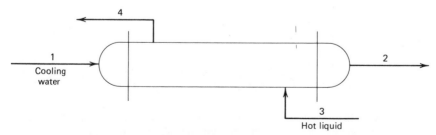

Figure 11.4.1 Shell and tube heat exchanger with no control.

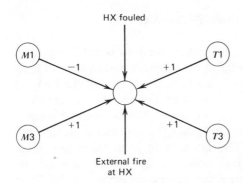

Figure 11.4.2 Digraph for exchanger shown in Figure 11.4.1. HX=heat exchanger. Courtesy of Lapp and Powers.*

be designated as $T4(-1)$.] What could cause this? The possible causes are:

$M1(-1)$	Mass flow in stream 1 decreases.
$M3(+1)$	Mass flow in stream 3 increases.
$T3(+1)$	Inlet temperature of hot fluid increases.
$T1(+1)$	Inlet temperature of cooling water increases.
	Heat exchanger fouled.
	External fire at heat exchanger.

These conditions are shown graphically in Figure 11.4.2. This is a vectored diagram, usually referred to as a digraph (which is a coined word for directed graph). The fault tree for this example is shown in Figure 11.4.3. It is evident that occurrence of any of these events would result in the top event.

We now complicate this system by adding a simple feedback control loop, as shown in Figure 11.4.4. Now the number of events that can cause the top event is considerably increased. These could be listed but it is much easier to indicate them on the digraph, Figure 11.4.5.

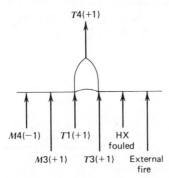

Figure 11.4.3 Fault tree for exchanger shown in Figure 11.4.1. Courtesy of Lapp and Powers.

*References to Lapp and Powers without a reference number refers to unpublished information presented in their short course on fault trees given at Carnegie-Mellon University.

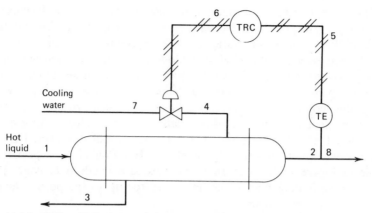

Figure 11.4.4 Shell and tube heat exchanger with feedback control loop. TRC = temperature recording controller; TE = temperature element. Courtesy of Lapp and Powers.

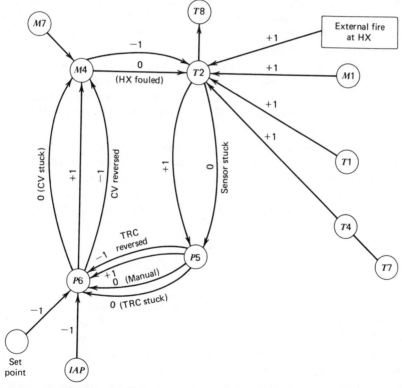

Figure 11.4.5 Digraph for exchanger shown in Figure 11.4.4. CV = control valve; IAP = instrument air pressure. Courtesy of Lapp and Powers.

The symbols used on a digraph are completely arbitrary. Because they are easily drawn, circles are usually used to designate discreet conditions such as flow rate, temperature, pressure, concentration, and so on. Lapp and Powers refer to these circles as "nodes," which is as good terminology as any and the one we use here. Inputs to a node are indicated by directed lines. Lapp and Powers use the term "edge" to describe these lines. We will adopt this terminology also. If a relationship between two nodes, shown by an edge, depends upon another relationship the edge is known as a conditional edge. A node that has no input is called a primal node or prime event. (Note that in Figure 11.4.2 "HX Fouled" is a prime event while in Figure 11.4.5 it is an event causing a conditional edge. In the second case fouling may be compensated for up to the point where the control valve is wide open.)

A gain is always connected with an edge. Gain is Δ output/Δ input. If the gain is greater than 1 it is defined as positive and if it is less than 1 it is defined as negative. If the ratio stays the same with change in input, the gain is zero. In a hypothetical system we have no way of knowing what the absolute value of the gain is. We can refer to gains only as zero, small, or large. For comparison purposes we can arbitrarily assign values to these, for example, large $= \pm 1000$, small $= \pm 100$. Lapp and Powers use ± 10, ± 1, and 0. These are convenient numbers to use so we adopt them. It must be emphasized that these values are arbitrary. For example, a small external fire at a heat exchanger would be assigned a $+1$, and a large external fire a $+10$. How about a medium fire? We are only allowing values of 10, 1, and 0. When in doubt call it a large fire.

All of the information needed to analyze the system is given on the digraph. It is not, however, in a readily usable form. The information is put into usable form through the use of a logic diagram. Before we can do this we must learn more about loops, gains, and deviations.

In Figure 11.4.5 we have a control loop that must be classified. The elements of the loop are

$$T2 \overset{-1}{\leftarrow} M4 \overset{+1}{\leftarrow} P6 \overset{+1}{\leftarrow} P5 \overset{+1}{\leftarrow} T2$$

The gains for normal operation are shown above the arrows. The net gain is $(-1)(+1)(+1)(+1) = -1$ so this is a negative feedback loop (NFBL). We must now consider the magnitude of the disturbances that could occur. We have used $(+1)$ and (-1) to indicate normal disturbances. For big and/or fast disturbances we use $(+10)$ and (-10). Could our loop handle such disturbances? To answer this we must analyze the interior elements of the loop.

$M4(-10)$ Severe decrease in flow rate or loss of flow from supply. Neither big nor fast disturbances could be handled. Opening the control valve would not increase the flow.

$M4(+10)$ Large increase in flow rate from supply. Both large and fast disturbances could be handled by throttling the control valve.

$P6(-10)$ Loss of instrument air pressure to valve. Neither large nor fast disturbances could be handled unless the valve were the lock-last-position-on-air-failure type.

$P5(-10)$ Loss of instrument air pressure to the temperature recording controller. Neither large nor fast disturbances could be handled. The temperature recording controller would cause the valve to go fully open or fully closed, depending upon its design.

Large and/or fast disturbances external to the loop that cause the top event are:

$$M1(+10)$$
$$T1(+10)$$
$$T4(+10) \text{ or } T7(+10)$$

Large external fire at heat exchanger

It is obvious that the fault tree for this system is much more complex than that shown in Figure 11.4.3, which is a system without feedback. An excellent methodology for synthesizing such a tree has been developed by Lapp and Powers. This is best described by the Lapp—Powers fault tree synthesis algorithm, which is presented as part of the short course in FTA given at Carnegie-Mellon University. This algorithm is shown in Figures 11.4.6(a) through (d) and is presented here through the courtesy of Dr. Lapp and Dr. Powers. For simple cases such as we are considering, a fault tree may be synthesized manually by using this method. For more complex systems the computer approach developed by Lapp and Powers is recommended.

We will now construct the fault tree step by step for the system shown in Figure 11.4.4.* We will select $T8(+1)$, that is $T8$ is high, as the top event. We have already complied with the first four steps of the algorithm. The

---

*This development is that of Lapp and Powers (Figures 11.4.7 through 11.4.14). However, they do not use ANSI symbols such as are used here.

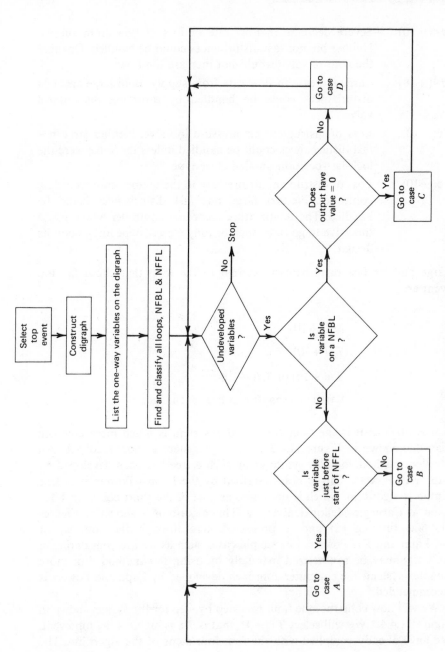

Figure 11.4.6a Lapp–Powers algorithm. Overall.

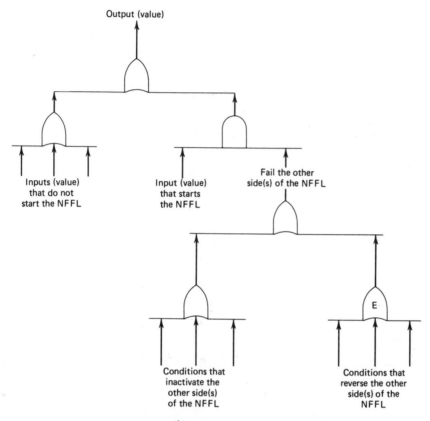

Figure 11.4.6b Case A (E) is the symbol for the EXCLUSIVE OR.

only variable directly affecting $T8$ is $T2$ so this is chosen as our undeveloped variable. We now ask, and answer, these questions:

Is $T2$ on a NFBL?   Yes.

Does the output have value $=0$?   No.

This indicates that for Step 1 we should go to Case D, which is shown on Figure 11.4.6(d). The result of this step is shown on Figure 11.4.7. In this step we have developed the variables $T2$, $M1$, $T1$, $T4$, external fire, and heat exchanger fouled. All of these are primal events because they are not subject to control within the system as defined. The variables remaining to be developed are $M4$, $P6$, and $P5$. We develop them in that order, which

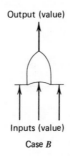

Output (value)

Inputs (value)

Case *B*

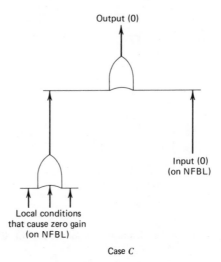

Output (0)

Input (0)
(on NFBL)

Local conditions
that cause zero gain
(on NFBL)

Case *C*

Figure 11.4.6c Cases *B* and *C*.

is the sequence in which they appear in the loop. In respect to $M4$ we
again ask, and answer, these questions:

Is $M4$ on a NFBL?   Yes.

Does the output have value=0?   Note that $M4$ appears twice, once with
                                      value=0 and once with value=−1. We
                                      consider the value=0 condition first.

When $M4$ has the output value=0 we go to Case *C*. Step 2 is shown on
Figure 11.4.8. When $M4$ has the output value=−1 we go to Case *D*. Step
3 is shown on Figure 11.4.9. Note the area on this figure enclosed by the
dashed line. This area was developed in Figure 11.4.8 and it is unnecessary
to show it twice. In our final diagram we directly connect this area to its
multiple destinations if it is convenient to do so. Otherwise, we will

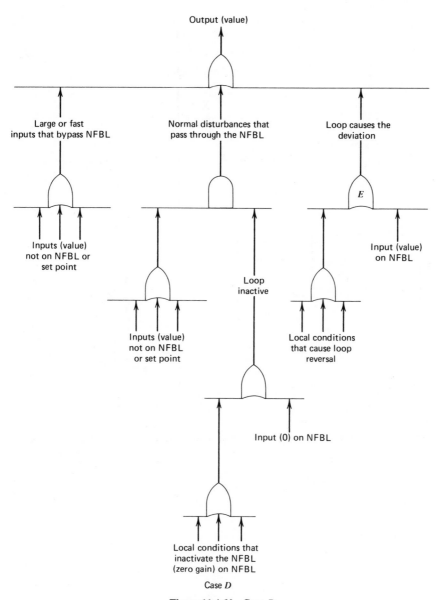

Case *D*

Figure 11.4.6d Case *D*.

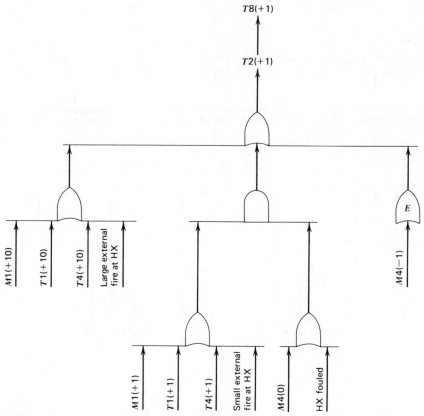

Figure 11.4.7 Partial fault tree derived from algorithm—variable $T2$. Courtesy of Lapp and Powers.

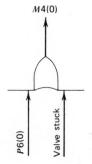

Figure 11.4.8 Partial fault tree derived from algorithm—variable $M4(0)$. Courtesy of Lapp and Powers.

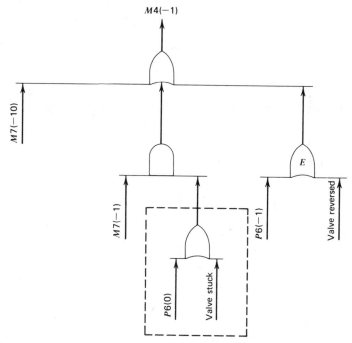

Figure 11.4.9 Partial fault tree derived from algorithm—variable $M4(-1)$. Courtesy of Lapp and Powers.

indicate duplicate areas by match marking as $\triangle$ $\triangle$, $\triangle$ $\triangle$, and so on.

We must now develop $P6$. Again we have two output values, $P6(0)$ and $P6(-1)$. We will consider $P6(0)$ first. $P6$ is on the NFBL so the algorithm directs us to use Case C. Step 4 is shown on Figure 11.4.10. For the condition where the output value $= -1$ we are referred to Case D. Step 5 is shown on Figure 11.4.11. This leaves only $P5$ to be developed. This also has two values. Step 6, for $P5(0)$ is shown on Figure 11.4.12. In this figure, the x across the input $T2(0)$ means that this is not an allowable input. We have already established that $T2$ has the value $= +1$. Step 7 for $P5(-1)$ is shown on Figure 11.4.13.

We now combine Figures 11.4.7 through 11.4.13 in Figure 11.4.14, with duplications omitted. At this point there will be a natural desire to "collapse" the tree somewhat. It is obvious that several OR functions could be combined and single input functions could be eliminated. It is also

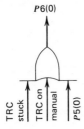

Figure 11.4.10 Partial fault tree derived from algorithm—variable $P6(0)$. Courtesy of Lapp and Powers.

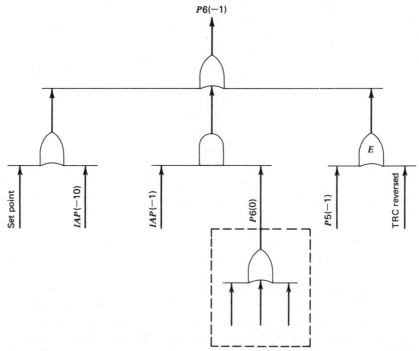

Figure 11.4.11 Partial fault tree derived from algorithm—variable $P6(-1)$. Courtesy of Lapp and Powers.

possible that certain Boolean manipulations may be made to simplify the diagram. Resist the temptation to do either. A relatively minor change in the process or in the instrumentation could cost many man-hours to find how such "simplifications" would affect the tree.

In this example we are dealing only with a NFBL. We now consider a feedforward loop. A simple example of such a loop is shown in Figure 11.4.15 and the digraph for the system in Figure 11.4.16. This example is

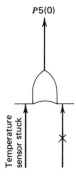

$P5(0)$

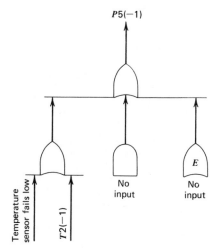

Figure 11.4.12 Partial fault tree derived from algorithm—variable $P5(0)$. Courtesy of Lapp and Powers.

$P5(-1)$

Figure 11.4.13 Partial fault tree derived from algorithm—variable $P5(-1)$. Courtesy of Lapp and Powers.

the simple but widely encountered case of diluting an acid with water where the acid stream is the "wild" flow and the water stream is the controlled flow. As our top event we will choose $C3(+1)$, that is, the concentration of acid in the outlet stream is too high. The feedforward loop will be negative if the sign of the product of the normal gains in one branch is different from that of the other branch or branches. In this example we have:

Branch 1 $\qquad M1 \xrightarrow{+1} C3 \qquad$ product $= +1$

Branch 2 $\quad M1 \xrightarrow{+1} P4 \xrightarrow{+1} P5 \xrightarrow{+1} M6 \xrightarrow{-1} C3 \qquad$ product $= -1$

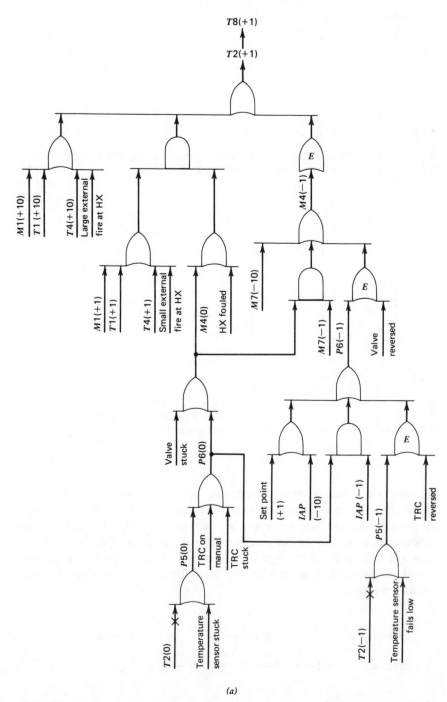

Figure 11.4.14 (a) Combined fault tree using Figures 11.4.7 through 11.4.13. Courtesy of Lapp and Powers. (b) Simplification of (a). (c) Further simplification of (a).

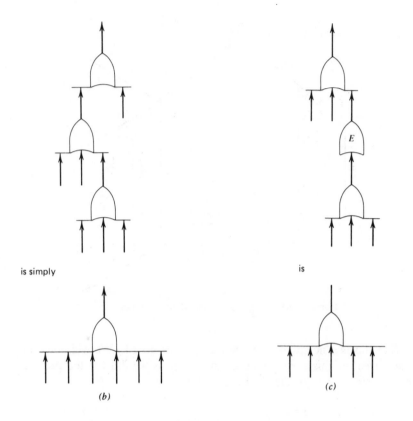

is simply

is

(b)

(c)

Figure 11.4.14 (*Continued*)

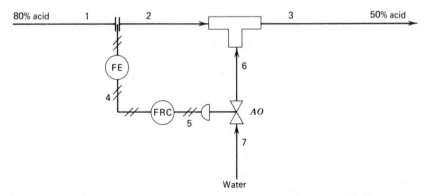

Figure 11.4.15 Acid dilution system with feedforward control loop. FE=flow element; FRC=flow recording controller; AO=air to open.

193

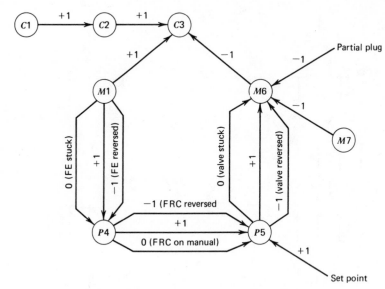

Figure 11.4.16 Digraph for acid dilution system.

Therefore this is a negative feedforward loop, or NFFL. We will construct the fault tree for this system step by step, just as we did for the previous example, using the algorithm in Figure 11.4.6.

Step 1	Is C3 on a NFBL?	No.
	Is C3 just before the start of a NFFL?	Yes.
	Go to Case A.	
	Step 1 is shown in Figure 11.4.17.	
Step 2	$P5(0)$	
	Is $P5$ on a NFBL?	No.
	Is $P5$ just before the start of a NFFL?	No.
	Go to Case *B*.	
	Step 2 is shown on Figure 11.4.18.	
Step 3	$P5(-1)$	
	Is $P5$ on a NFBL?	No.
	Is $P5$ just before the start of a NFFL?	No.
	Go to Case *B*.	
	Step 3 is shown on Figure 11.4.19.	
Step 4	$P4(0)$	
	Is $P4$ on a NFBL?	No.
	Is $P4$ just before the start of a NFFL?	Yes.
	Go to Case *A*.	
	Step 4 is shown on Figure 11.4.20.	

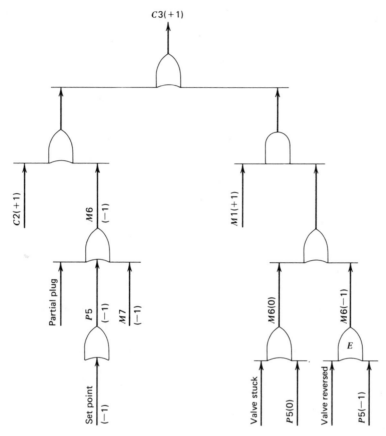

Figure 11.4.17 Construction of fault tree for acid dilution system—Step 1.

Step 5 $P4(-1)$
Is $P4$ on a NFBL? No.
Is $P4$ just before the start of a NFFL? Yes.
Go to Case A.
Step 5 is shown on Figure 11.4.21.

We now combine Figures 11.4.17 through 11.4.21 in Figure 11.4.22 eliminating all gates with no input.

Multiple loops may be encountered in a system. These may be feedback loops, feedforward loops, or combinations of the two. If we have two feedback loops of equal strength and speed, and if either loop is capable of controlling the system when the other loop is inactivated, we proceed using the method shown in Figure 11.4.23. If both loops are necessary to control the system, the method shown in Figure 11.4.24 must be used. Both of these are based on Figure 11.4.6(d). Methods for multiple feedforward loops and combinations of feedforward, feedback, and open loops may

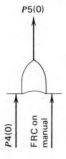

Figure 11.4.18 Construction of fault tree for acid dilution system—Step 2.

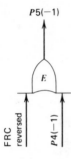

Figure 11.4.19 Construction of fault tree for acid dilution system—Step 3.

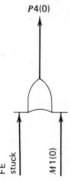

Figure 11.4.20 Construction of fault tree for acid dilution system—Step 4.

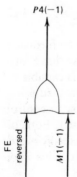

Figure 11.4.21 Construction of fault tree for acid dilution system—Step 5.

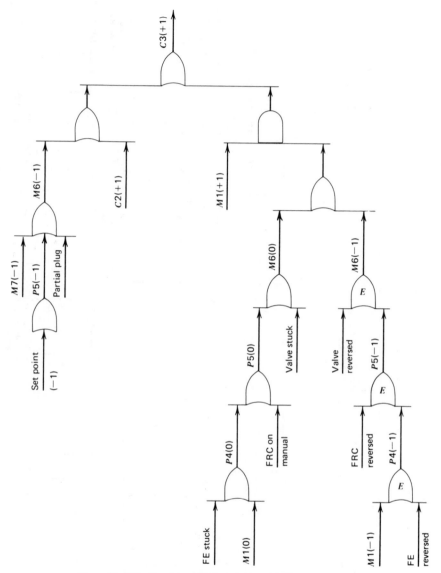

Figure 11.4.22   Combined fault tree for acid dilution system.

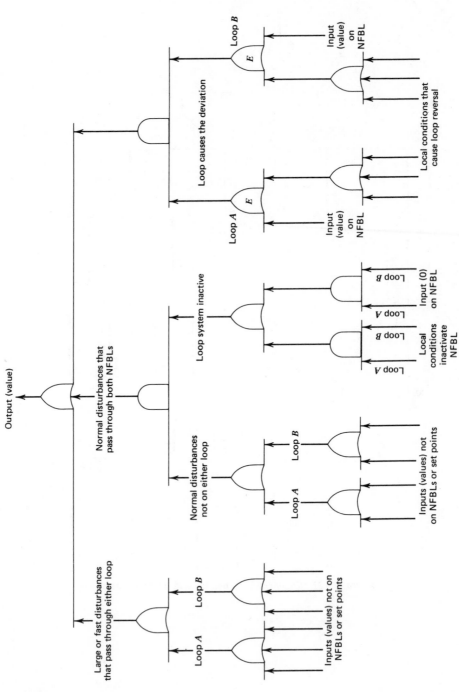

Figure 11.4.23 Method used for two feedback loops when either loop can control the system.

also be developed. It is obvious that the complexity of the system increases greatly as the number of loops increase.

A typical example of a system containing two negative feedback loops is shown in Figure 11.4.25. In this system an increase in the temperature of Stream 3 ($T3(+1)$) will cause a decrease in the outlet air pressure from the *TRC* to $V1$ ($P7(-1)$) and $V2$ ($P6(-1)$). Because $V1$ requires increasing air pressure to open (AO), and $V2$ requires increasing air pressure to close (AC), the flow rate of the hot stream will decrease ($M2(-1)$) and the flow rate of the cooling water will increase ($M9(+1)$).

The digraph for this system is shown in Figure 11.4.26. The fault tree for the case where either loop will control the system is shown in Figure 11.4.27 and that for the case where both loops are required to control is shown in Figure 11.4.28. In this example it is assumed that the loops are of equal strength and speed.

11.5 CUT SETS

The concept of "cut sets" is useful in analyzing a fault tree. A cut set is the set of events along a pathway up the tree which cause the top event to occur. Minimal cut sets are those which contain no other cut sets within them. There may be many cut sets and minimal cut sets in a large tree and they may contain many elements. These cut sets tend to proceed through OR and EOR gates but may also encounter AND gates. In the simple fault tree shown in Figure 11.4.14 there are several pathways and several minimal cut sets. Because of the simplicity of this system most of these sets contain one element only (ignoring $\emptyset$ which is an element of every set but which here indicates the absence of an event). These sets are:

Set number	Elements
1	$\{M1(+10)\}$
2	$\{T1(+10)\}$
3	$\{T4(+10)\}$
4	{Large fire at heat exchanger}
5	{Control valve reversed}
6	$\{M7(-10)\}$
7	$\{IAP(-10)\}$
8	{Set point $(+1)$}
9	{Temperature sensor failed low}
10	{TRC reversed}
11	$\{M1(+1)$, control valve stuck$\}$
12	$\{T1(+1)$, control valve stuck$\}$
13	$\{T4(+1)$, control valve stuck$\}$

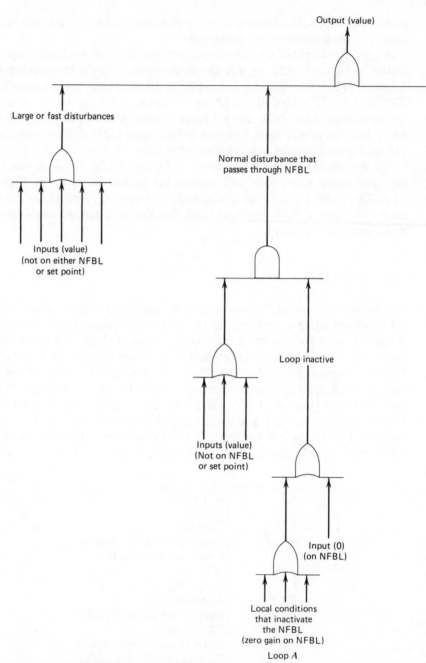

Output (value)

Large or fast disturbances

Normal disturbance that passes through NFBL

Inputs (value)
(not on either NFBL
or set point)

Loop inactive

Inputs (value)
(Not on NFBL
or set point)

Input (0)
(on NFBL)

Local conditions
that inactivate
the NFBL
(zero gain on NFBL)

Loop A

Figure 11.4.24 Method used for two feedback loops when both loops are required to control the system. This is a modification of Case *D* in Figure 11.4.6d.

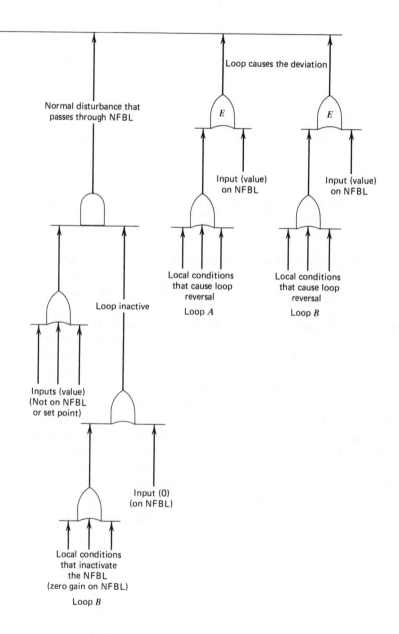

Loop causes the deviation

Normal disturbance that
passes through NFBL

E

E

Input (value)
on NFBL

Input (value)
on NFBL

Loop inactive

Local conditions
that cause loop
reversal

Local conditions
that cause loop
reversal

Loop *A*

Loop *B*

Inputs (value)
(Not on NFBL
or set point)

Input (0)
(on NFBL)

Local conditions
that inactivate
the NFBL
(zero gain on NFBL)

Loop *B*

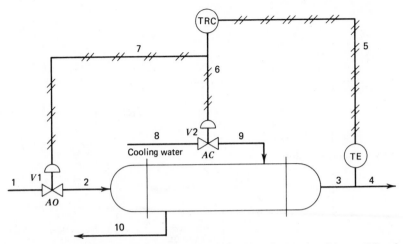

Figure 11.4.25 Shell and tube heat exchanger with two feedback control loops. AO=air to open; AC=air to close. Courtesy of Lapp and Powers.[22]

The first 10 of these are more critical than the last 3 because they depend on 1 event only. Using these 10 only and using the set numbers as event numbers we may reduce the tree in Figure 11.4.14 to the tree in Figure 11.5.1.

The more AND gates we can get into the tree, particularly near the top, the more reliable our system will be—at least theoretically. The control system for the heat exchanger shown in Figure 11.4.4 could be modified as shown in Figure 11.5.2. Here we add a backup system consisting of a second temperature sensor, a pneumatic/electric transducer (I/P), and two solenoid valves. The construction of the digraph and fault tree for the modified system is not included here because of space limitations. Note that there are three feedback loops in this system and that the backup valves fail safe on loss of either air pressure or electric power. If, in a real-life situation, $T8(+1)$ was a critical condition that could cause a hazardous event, something such as this backup system would be justified.

There is, of course, much more to cut sets than is covered here. A more in-depth treatment of the subject is beyond the scope of this work.

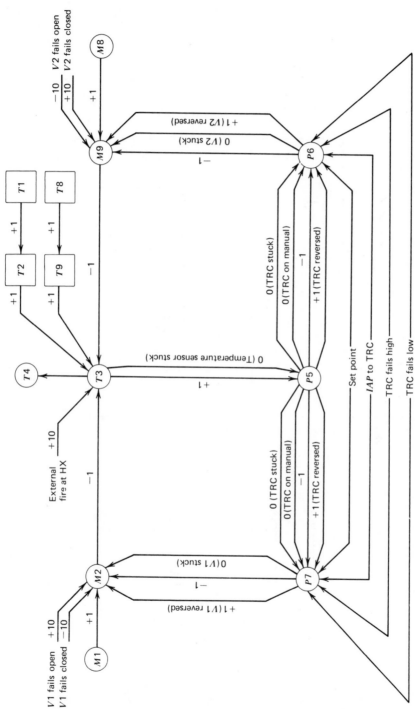

Figure 11.4.26 Digraph for exchanger shown in Figure 11.4.25. Courtesy of Lapp and Powers.

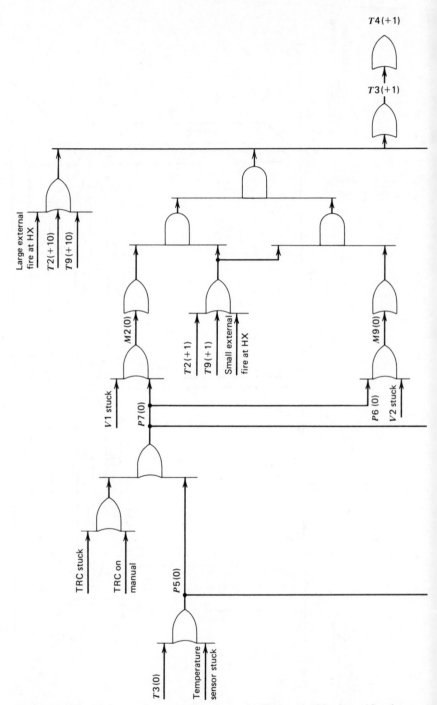

Figure 11.4.27 Fault tree for exchanger shown in Figure 11.4.25 when either loop can control the system.

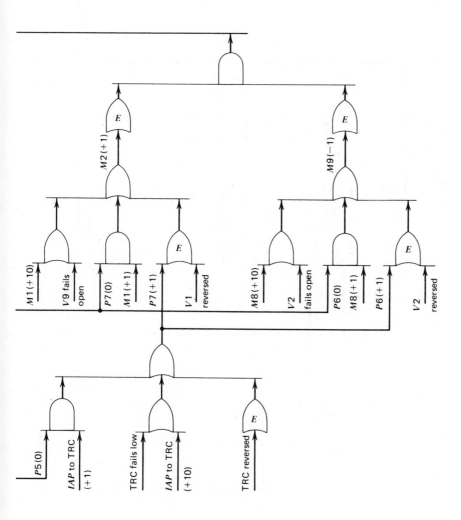

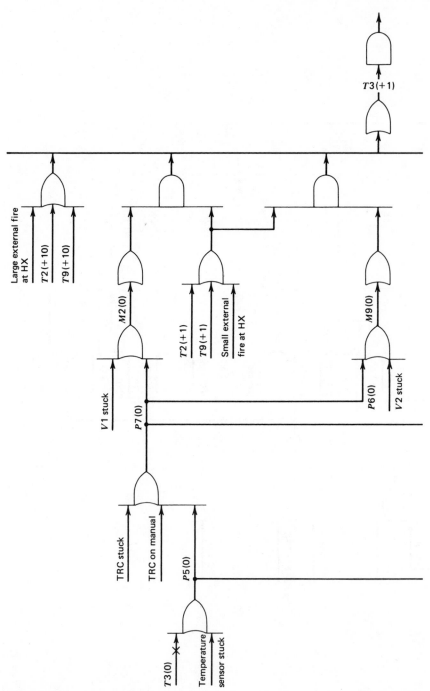

Figure 11.4.28 Fault tree for exchanger shown in Figure 11.4.25 when both loops are required to control the system.

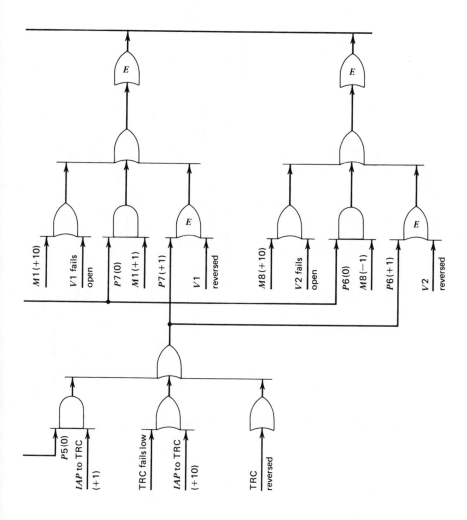

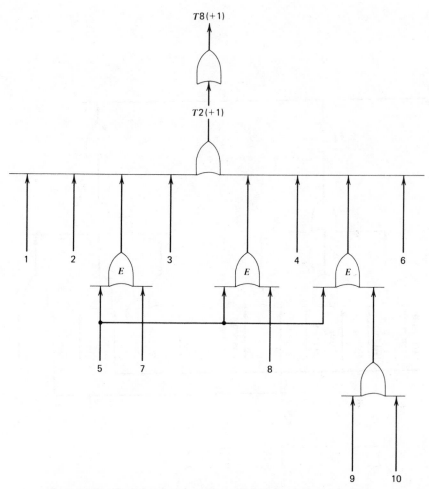

Figure 11.5.1 Fault tree based on Figure 11.4.14 showing cut sets only.

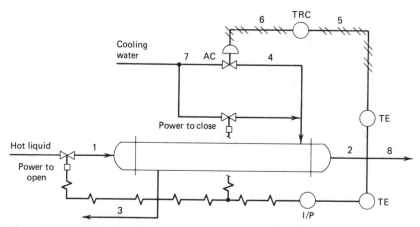

Figure 11.5.2 Shell and tube exchanger with feedback control loop and secondary on–off controls. I/P=electric current to air pressure transducer; AC=air to close.

11.6 FAULT TREE SYNTHESIS—SEQUENTIAL

It is a very common error to assume that the logic encountered in a sequential system is sequential logic. It may or may not be. An example frequently used to illustrate a sequential system is the dual adsorption tower air drying unit with hot air regeneration of the adsorbent. This unit has four distinct modes of operation which are:

Mode	Tower A	Tower B
1	regenerating	in service
2	cooling	in service
3	in service	regenerating
4	in service	cooling

The system operation is sequential in that the modes are established in sequence by a timer. The logic within each mode is, however, combinational and the synthesis of the fault tree is the combination of the subtrees for each mode. Shaewitz, Lapp, and Powers[23] have presented a very thorough analysis of this system. The digraph they show covers all of the modes so some care must be taken in following the loops for each mode.

A system involving sequential logic was described in Chapter 9, Section 3 and the logic diagram for the system was given in Figure 9.3.3. The logic diagram for a simplified version of this system, with only two pumps involved, is shown in Figure 11.6.1. Because this system is completely

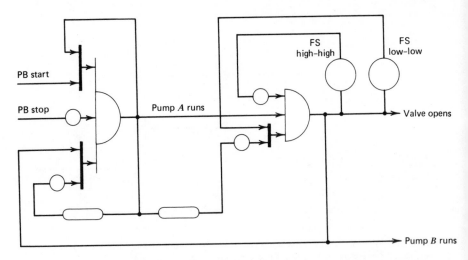

Figure 11.6.1   Logic diagram for a two-pump sequential start system. FS = flow switch.

electrical, a partial* elementary wiring diagram (ladder diagram), constructed from the logic diagram, is shown in Figure 11.6.2. This diagram
indicates relay circuitry, although in actual practice solid-state circuitry
would probably be used. For readers who are not familiar with ladder
diagrams an explanation of the symbols is given in Table 11.6.1. An
excellent explanation of these diagrams may also be found in the November 15, 1971 issue of *Chemical Engineering*. Figure 11.6.3 is the digraph for
this system. In this digraph we use the relay and contact symbols used in
the ladder diagram.

The concept of gain in a relay type electrical system is somewhat
restricted. If a circuit is energized and the corresponding relay, or relays,
are energized, the gain is $+1$. If the circuit is deenergized and the
corresponding relays are deenergized, the gain is -1. If energizing or
deenergizing the circuit has no effect on the relays (relay stuck, burned out,
and so on), the gain is either $+1$ or -1, depending on whether the
contacts are open or closed at the time. Because current is either flowing or
not flowing there is no zero gain. A gain other than these has no meaning
in relay circuitry. This is not true of solid-state circuitry where voltage
surges and such become important. On the fault tree itself, only the circuit
conditions 1 and 0 may appear.

There are four failure modes for this system. They are:

1. Pump A will not start.
2. Pump A starts; Pump B will not start; Pump A shuts down.

*Partial in that thermal overload relays, fuses, and so on are omitted.

Table 11.6.1   Ladder diagram symbols

Symbol	Meaning
Rn	Relay no. n
TDR n	Time delay relay no. n
Sn	Solenoid operator with auxiliary contacts
—‖—	Relay or solenoid contacts, normally open, closed when relay or solenoid is energized
—‖̸—	Relay or solenoid contacts, normally closed, opened when relay or solenoid is energized
	Level switch, open on rising level (LS-low)
	Level switch, closed on rising level (LS-high)
	Flow switch, open on increased flow
	Flow switch, closed on increased flow
	Position switch, closed on movement
	Position switch, open on movement

3. Pump *A* starts; Pump *B* will not start; Pump *A* continues to run.

4. Pump *A* starts; Pump *B* starts; system shuts down after *x* seconds.

The fault tree for this system is found by combining all of the fault trees for the four failure modes. This is shown in Figure 11.6.4. Some of the features of the Lapp–Powers algorithm are found in this fault tree but at present (1979) there is no algorithm available for a system involving truly sequential logic.

A more involved example is the problem of filling four tanks from a common supply tank. This was discussed in Chapter 9, Section 6 and a process logic diagram for the system is shown in Figure 9.6.4. A flow

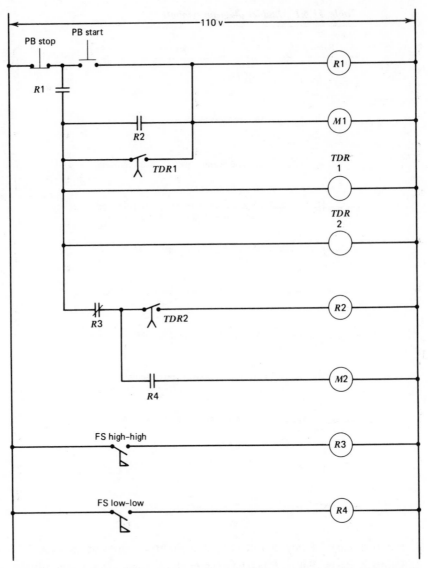

Figure 11.6.2 Partial ladder diagram for the two-pump system. TDR = time delay relay.

diagram and a complete electrical logic diagram for the system are shown in Figures 11.6.5 and 11.6.6. The ladder diagram, Figure 11.6.7, for the system is quite instructive in that it illustrates the use of multiple contact points on a single relay—points that may be either normally open or normally closed. It also illustrates the use of one-shot relays. These, you will recall, are used to trigger a standard binary or the first standard binary in a multiple sequencer. It is essential that the time delay in the one-shot relay is less than the time delays in the standard binary. Otherwise, the standard binary oscillates at a frequency determined by its time delays and a sustained trigger signal results in rapid burnout of the unit.

The logic diagram and ladder diagram are for a four tank system. Space limitations prevent us from showing a four tank system on the digraph and fault tree. These are shown for a two tank system (tanks 1 and 4) and even then it is necessary to code the edge lines of the digraph. This is a cumbersome, but necessary, ploy. The coding used for the digraph is shown in Table 11.6.2, the digraph in Figure 11.6.8, and the fault tree is Figure 11.6.9. There are many possible failure modes for this system but only one of these is shown on the fault tree. This is the failure of Tank 1 to fill after a search cycle has been initiated by a low level in Tank 1. To refresh your memory (which you should have refreshed by referring to Chapter 9), a low level signal from any tank initiates a search routine. When the tank, or tanks, at low level are found, they are filled. The search routine is terminated when Tank 4 is checked and either filled or bypassed. There are, undoubtedly, many smarter ways of doing this but this method involves a delightful amount of sequential logic. This system is elementary but still requires more than casual study. For example, why are relays $7A$, $8A$, $9A$, and $10A$ locked* in as indicated on the ladder diagram? Why is relay 11 locked in? When you have answered these questions you will have a much better understanding of the interplay between logic diagrams and ladder diagrams.

Table 11.6.2 *Condition codes for the digraph shown in Figure 11.6.8*

Code	Condition
A	Contacts fail open
B	Contacts fail closed—sustained signal
C	Contacts fail closed
D	Relay fails to energize
E	Timer fails to time out on one-shot relay—signal sustained
F	Timer on one-shot relay fails to timed-out state
G	Switch stuck closed
H	Switch stuck open
J	Valve stuck closed
K	Supply tank empty
L	Solenoid stuck
M	Instrument air failure
N	Broken air line
P	Sequencer inoperative

*This, again, is commonly used but incorrect terminology. A locking relay incorporates a mechanical device that must be released manually.

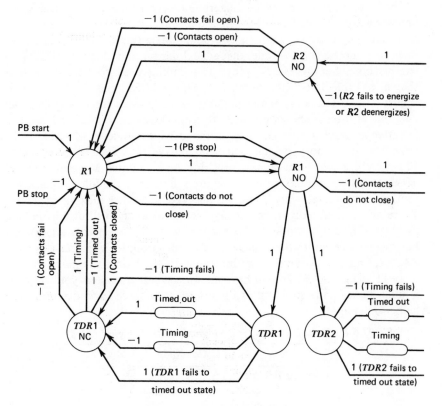

Figure 11.6.3 Digraph for the two-pump system.

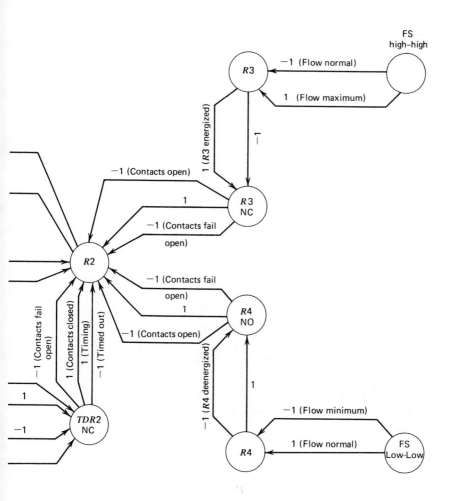

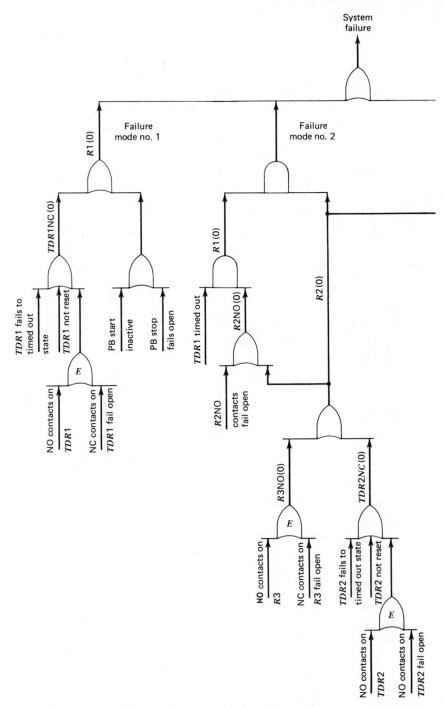

Figure 11.6.4 Fault tree for the two-pump system.

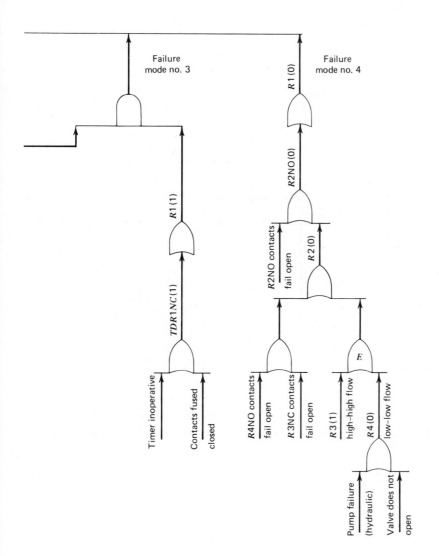

Failure
mode no. 3

Failure
mode no. 4

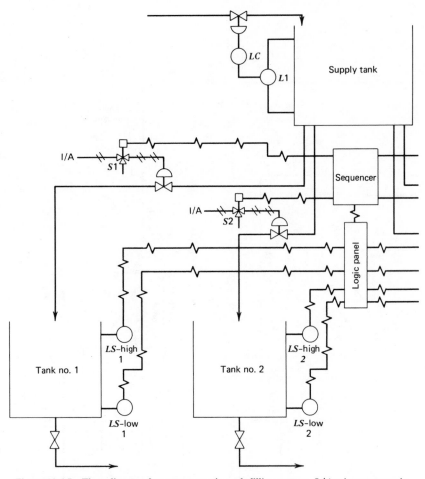

Figure 11.6.5 Flow diagram for an automatic tank filling system. I/A = instrument air.

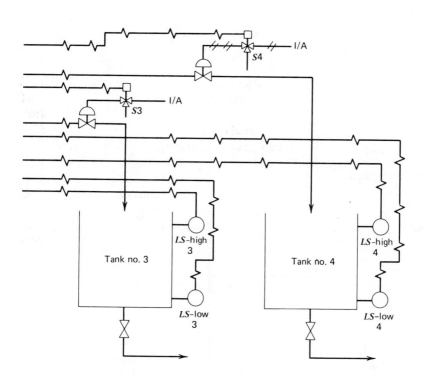

I/A

S4

I/A

S3

Tank no. 3

LS-high
3

LS-low
3

Tank no. 4

LS-high
4

LS-low
4

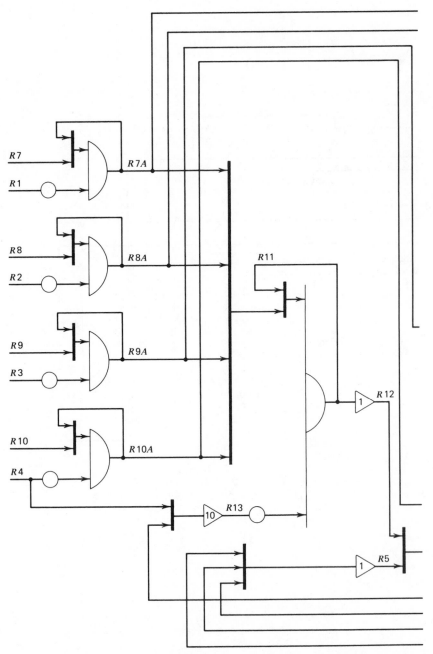

Figure 11.6.6 Electrical logic diagram for the tank filling system.

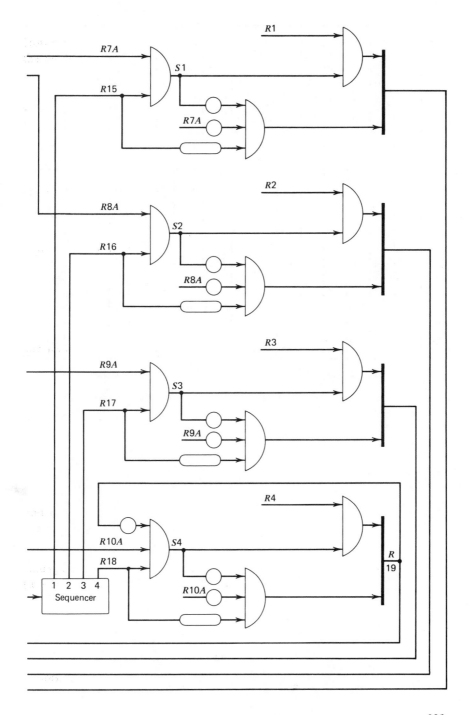

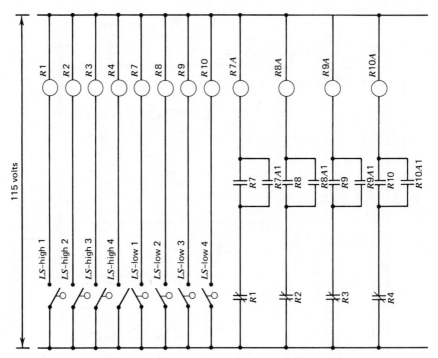

Figure 11.6.7 Partial ladder diagram for the tank filling system.

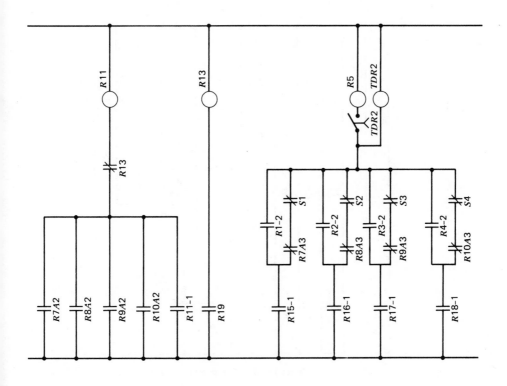

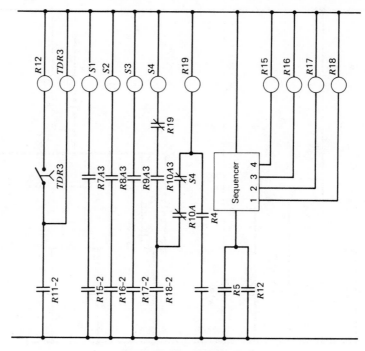

Figure 11.6.7 (*Continued*)

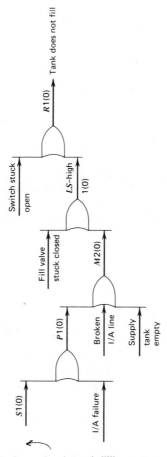

Figure 11.6.9 Fault tree for the tank filling system—two tanks only.

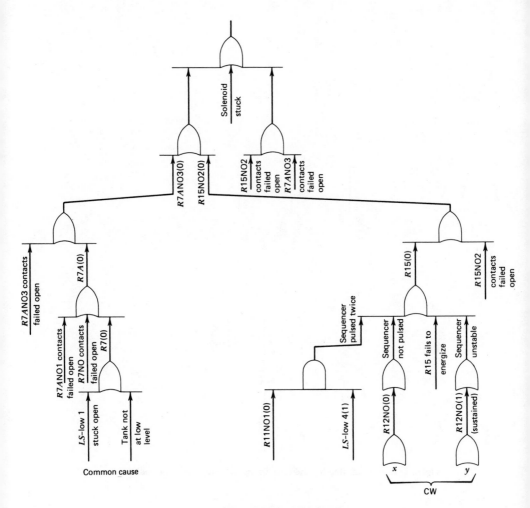

Figure 11.6.9 (*Continued*)

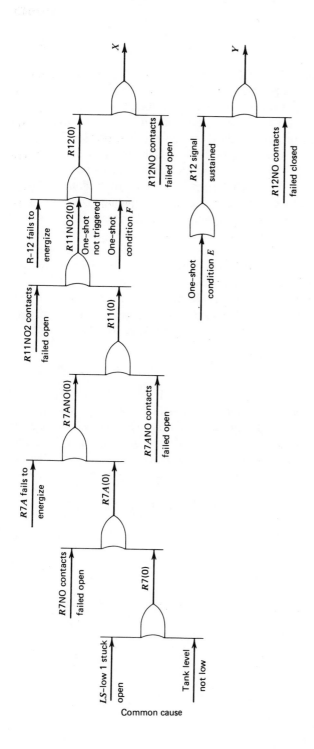

11.7 PROBABILITY

So far we have considered fault tree synthesis only. A fault tree analysis requires assignment of the probability of occurrence to each of the events in the tree and combining these probabilities to obtain the overall probability of the top event occurring. The method of combining the individual probabilities is covered in any standard text on probability. Obtaining the individual probabilities is the problem. Although the body of literature on the subject is growing it is still quite scant and narrow in scope. There is a vast amount of data buried in the maintenance file of all medium to large size companies. Unearthing these data and putting them into useful form would be an extremely expensive and time consuming task. If any of the large companies were willing to undertake such a project they would understandably be unwilling to release the results for general use. If, however, the Federal Government were to fund such a project, the information would be in the public domain and available to everyone.

The most comprehensive listing of reliability data sources is found in the U.S.A.E.C. WASH 1400 Reactor Safety Study. A listing of these sources, as well as some data from this report, is given in Appendix C.

SUMMARY

The fault tree is just one more tool in the engineer's kit bag, but a very powerful tool. The Lapp–Powers methodology has been presented here because it is based on another very powerful tool—symbolic logic. Fault tree synthesis is relatively new and constantly changing and developing. A more extensive use of Boolean algebra in fault tree work could have a very beneficial effect on this development.

REFERENCES

1. E. Kamke, *Theory of Sets*, Dover Publications, Inc., New York (1950).

2. E. V. Huntington, "Sets of Independent Postulates For The Algebra of Logic," *Trans. Am. Math. Soc.*, Vol. 5, pp. 294–309, July 1904.

3. Claude E. Shannon, "A Symbolic Analysis of Relay and Switching Circuits," *Trans A.I.E.E.*, Vol 57, pp. 713–723, December 1938.

4. George P. Roullard, *The Logic of Switching Circuits*, Exposition Press, New York (1967).

5. H. W. Johnstone, Jr., *Elementary Deductive Logic*, Thomas Y. Crowell Co., New York (1954).

6. Susanne K. Langer, *An Introduction to Symbolic Logic*, Dover Publications, Inc., New York (1953).

7. Norman L. Thomas, *Modern Logic*, Barnes and Noble, Inc. New York (1966).

8. R. R. Christian, *Introduction to Logic § Sets*, Ginn § Co., New York (1958).

9. Seymour Lipschutz, *Set Theory and Related Topics*, McGraw-Hill Book Co., New York (1964).

10. Franz E. Hohn, *Applied Boolean Algebra*, MacMillan Co., New York (1960).

11. Elliott Mendelsohn, *Boolean Algebra*, McGraw Hill Book Co., New York (1970).

12. P. J. Brown, *Macroprocessors*, John Wiley § Sons, New York (1974).

13. W. V. Quine, "The Problem of Simplifying Truth Functions," *Am Math Mon.* Vol. 59, No. 8, pp. 521–531, October 1952.

14. E. J. McCluskey, Jr., "Minimization of Boolean Functions," *Bell Syst. Tech. J.*, pp. 1417–1444, November 1956.

15. A. H. Scheinman, "A Method For Simplifying Boolean Functions," *Bell Syst. Tech. J.*, pp. 1337–1346, July 1962.

16. W. E. Vesely, *Analysis of Fault Trees by Kinetic Tree Theory*, Idaho Nuclear Corp., U.S. AEC Research and Development Report, IN 1330, October 1969.

17. W. E. Vesely and R. E. Narum, *Prep and Kitt: Computer Codes for The Automatic Evaluation of a Fault Tree*, Idaho Nuclear Corp., U.S. AEC Scientific and Technical Report, IN 1349, August 1970.

18. H. E. Lambert, "Fault Trees For Location of Sensors In Chemical Processing Systems," presented at the American Institute of Chemical Engineers Annual Meeting, Chicago, Ill., November 28–December 2, 1976.

19. H. E. Lambert, *Fault Trees for Decision Making in Systems Analysis* (Ph. D. Thesis), Lawrence Livermore Laboratory, University of California, Livermore, Calif., UCRL 51829, October 1975.

20. G. J. Powers, and F. C. Tompkins, "Fault Tree Synthesis For Chemical Processes," *AIChE J.*, Vol. 20, No. 2, pp. 376–387, March 1974.

21. R. E. Barlow, J. B. Fussell, and N. D. Singpurwalla, Eds., *Reliability and Fault Tree Analysis: Theoretical and Applied Aspects of System Reliability and Safety Assessment: Papers*, Society for Industrial and Applied Mathematics, Philadelphia, Pa. (1975).

22. S. A. Lapp, and G. J. Powers, "Computer Aided Synthesis of Fault Trees," *IEEE Trans. Reliability*, Vol. R-26, No. 1, pp. 2–15, April 1977.

23. J. A. Shaeiwitz, S. A. Lapp, and G. J. Powers, "Fault Tree Analysis of Sequential Systems," *Ind. Eng. Chem. Process Des. Dev*, Vol. 16, No. 4, pp. 529–549, 1977.

APPENDIX A

SELECTED PROBLEMS

THEORY OF SETS

1. What is the difference between the set of natural numbers and the set of positive integers?
2. What is a power set? Illustrate with an example.
3. What is a truth set? Illustrate with an example.
4. Does the empty set have any subsets? If so, how many?
5. Let K be the set $\{1,4,9,10,11\}$. List the elements of each of the following sets. Use braces.
   a) $\{x \in K | x^2 \neq 16\}$
   e) $\{x \in K | -(x \text{ is even})\}$
   b) $\{x \in K | x+k=9\}$
   f) $\{x \in K | x+5=7\}$
   c) $\{x \in K | x+1 \in K\}$
   g) $\{x \in K | x^2-5x+4=0\}$
   d) $\{x \in K | x \text{ is even}\}$
   h) $\{x \in K | x^2-3x+2=0\}$
6. What is the difference between a proper subset and an improper subset?
7. Draw two Venn diagrams, each showing two nondisjoint sets A and B. On one diagram shade the relative complement. On the other shade the symmetric difference.
8. The definition of implication between conditions is

$$\{x \in \mathcal{U} | p(x)\} \subseteq \{x \in \mathcal{U} | q(x)\}$$

Therefore $p \Rightarrow q$. If $\mathcal{U} = N = \{\text{natural numbers}\}$ indicate for each of the following pairs of conditions whether $p \Rightarrow q$, $q \Rightarrow p$, $p \Leftrightarrow q$, or there is no relation between p and q.
   a) $p(x)$: $2x+3=9$ $q(x)$: $x(x+1)=x^2+x$
   b) $p(x)$: $(x-1)(x-2)=0$ $q(x)$: $x^2+x-2=0$
   c) $p(x)$: $(x-1)(x-2)=0$ $q(x)$: $x^2-2x+1=0$
   d) $p(x)$: $(x^2+1)(x-1)=0$ $q(x)$: $x-1=0$
   e) $p(x)$: $(x+1)(x+2)=0$ $q(x)$: $(x+3)(x+4)=0$
   f) $p(x)$: $(x-1)^{1/2}+(2x)^{1/2}=0$ $q(x)$: $x=2$

9. Given: $\mathcal{U}$ is finite
    $A \subset \mathcal{U}$
    $n(A) =$ number of elements in A
    $n(A') =$ number of elements in A'
    $n(\mathcal{U}) =$ number of elements in $\mathcal{U}$
    find the formula connecting $n(A)$, $n(A')$, and $n(\mathcal{U})$.

10. If p and q are conditions in a universal set $\mathcal{U}$, under what circumstances are the following statements true?
    a) $P \vee q \Leftrightarrow p \wedge q$ c) $p \wedge -q \Leftrightarrow p$
    b) $p \vee -q \Leftrightarrow f$ d) $(p \wedge -q) \vee q \Leftrightarrow p \vee q$

11. Write an expression for each of the numbered portions in this diagram:

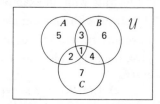

12. For every natural number x, $(x+1)(x-1) = x^2 - 1$. Therefore the truth set for $(x+1)(x-1) = x^2 - 1$ is the set of all natural numbers, N. Write this symbolically using a universal quantifier.

13. Write $(\exists x \in M)q(x)$ in another form.

14. Can either of these statements ever be true? Explain.

$$(\forall x \in \varnothing)p(x)$$
$$(\exists x \in \varnothing)p(x)$$

15. Given the set of integers (Z) from -36 to $+36$. Partition the set, modulo 3, and write the remainder classes.

16. What is Russell's paradox? Explain in set theoretic terms and in layman's terms.

17. Explain the difference, in set theoretic terms, between:
    a) A finite set.
    b) A transfinite set.
    c) An infinite set.
    d) An enumerable set.
    e) An at least enumerable set.

18. Write the dual of each of the following:
    a) $(B \cup C) \cap A = (B \cap A) \cup (C \cap A)$
    b) $A \cup (A' \cap B) = A \cup B$
    c) $(A \cap \mathfrak{U}) \cap (\varnothing \cup A') = \varnothing$
19. Prove that, if $A \cup B = \mathfrak{U}$, then $A' \subset B$.
20. Let $A_n = \{x | x$ is a multiple of $n\} = \{n, 2n, 3n, \ldots\}$ where $n \in N$, the natural numbers. Find:
    a) $A_2 \cap A_7$ d) $A_3 \cap A_{12}$
    b) $A_6 \cap A_8$ e) $A_s \cup A_{st}$
    c) $A_3 \cup A_{12}$ f) $A_s \cap A_{st}$
    $s, t \in N.$

PROPOSITIONAL CALCULUS

1. Under what conditions are two propositions logically equivalent?
2. Under what conditions are two propositions logically true?
3. The conditional $p \rightarrow q$ may be read as "p implies q." There are four other ways in which it may be read. What are they?
4. Determine the truth value of each of the following statements.
    a) If $5 + 2 = 9$, then $3 + 3 = 6$.
    b) It is not true that $3 + 3 = 7$ if and only if $6 + 6 = 9$.
    c) Rome is in Sweden or New York is in Germany.
    d) It is not true that $2 + 2 = 5$ or $3 + 1 = 7$.
    e) It is false that if Rome is in Sweden then New York is in Germany.
5. Generate the truth table for each of these propositions:
    a) $p' \wedge q$ c) $(p \wedge q) \rightarrow (p \vee q)$
    b) $(p \rightarrow q')'$ d) $(p \wedge q)' \vee (q \leftrightarrow p)'$
6. Prove by perfect induction:
    a) $(p \wedge q)' \equiv p' \vee q'$ c) $(p \rightarrow q)' \equiv p \wedge q'$
    b) $(p \vee q)' \equiv p' \wedge q'$ d) $(p \leftrightarrow q)' \equiv p \leftrightarrow q' \equiv p' \leftrightarrow q$
7. Simplify each of these propositions:
    a) $(p \vee q')'$ d) $(p' \wedge q')'$
    b) $(p' \rightarrow q)'$ e) $(p' \leftrightarrow q)'$
    c) $(p \wedge q')'$ f) $(p' \leftrightarrow q')'$
8. Show that
    a) $a \rightarrow t = t$ c) $(a \rightarrow b)' = a \vee b'$
    b) $f \rightarrow a = t$ d) $(a \rightarrow b) \rightarrow (b' \rightarrow a') = t$

9. Prove:
    a) $p'' \to p$
    b) $p \wedge q \to p$
    c) $p \wedge q \to p \vee q$
    What type of implication is this?

10. Which of the following statements have a meaning equivalent to that of the statement "If you go I will go"?
    a) I will go only if you go.
    b) A necessary condition for me to go is that you go.
    c) You will go only if I go.
    d) A necessary condition for you to go is that I go.
    e) A sufficient condition for me to go is that you go.
    f) If you don't go then I won't go.
    g) If I don't go then you won't go.

11. Let x be a natural number whose square is an odd number. Prove that x must also be an odd number.

12. Rewrite the following propositions in Polish notation.
    a) $p' \wedge q$
    b) $p \wedge (p \wedge q)'$
    c) $(p \wedge q)' \wedge (p \wedge q')$
    d) $(p \wedge q)' \wedge (p' \wedge q')$
    e) $(p \wedge (p \wedge q')') \wedge (p \wedge q)'$
    f) $(p' \wedge q' \wedge ((p \wedge q) \wedge (q' \wedge p)))'$

13. Rewrite the following propositions using $\wedge$ and ' instead of A and N:
    a) $NApNq$ d) $ANANqANpqNp$
    b) $ANApqNp$ e) $ANANqANpqNp$
    c) $AApNrAqNp$ f) $ANANpNAqrApNAqNr$

14.* a) No one who is going to a party ever fails to brush his or her hair.
    b) No one looks fascinating, if he or she is untidy.
    c) Opium-eaters have no self-command.
    d) Every one who has brushed his or her hair looks fascinating.
    e) No one wears white kid gloves unless he or she is going to a party.
    f) A man is always untidy, if he has no self-command.
    Find the "best" conclusion using all of the hypotheses. Use this notation:
    a = going to a party e = being an opium-eater
    b = having brushed one's hair h = being tidy
    c = having self-command k = wearing white kid gloves
    d = looking fascinating

*These two exercises are examples of the famous "Lewis Carroll problems." Lewis Carroll (Prof. Charles Dodgson) was a professor of symbolic logic.

15. *a) No shark ever doubts that it is well fitted out.
   b) A fish that cannot dance a minuet is contemptible.
   c) No fish is quite certain that it is well fitted out unless it has three rows of teeth.
   d) All fish, except sharks, are kind to children.
   e) No heavy fish can dance a minuet.
   f) A fish with three rows of teeth is not to be despised.
   Find the "best" conclusion using all of the hypotheses. Use this notation:

   a = able to dance a minuet e = heavy
   b = certain that he is well fitted out h = kind to children
   c = contemptible k = sharks
   d = having three rows of teeth

ON–OFF EVENTS

1. DeMorgan's rules state
   a) $(a+b)' = a'b'$
   b) $(ab)' = a' + b'$
   Prove a) and b). Prove that a) and b) are dual functions.

2. Prove the absorption laws.

3. The "exclusive or" and the "both or neither" are dual functions in two variables. Develop the equivalent of the "both or neither" function for four variables (i.e., the four-position hall light switch circuit). Is the dual of this function equivalent to a four-variable "exclusive or" function? Explain.

4. Given the function $(a(a' + b))' + b = 1$, rewrite this as:
   a) A Scheffer stroke function (NAND).
   b) A double stroke function (NOR).
   Use stroke and double stroke notation in the resulting functions.

5. Rewrite the function given in Exercise 4 in Polish notation.

6. Given the function

$$P1 + P2 + P4 + P5 + P6 + P9 = 1$$

   rewrite this as a cnf (product of sums) function.

7. Given the three-variable function (in dnf)

$$P1 + P2 + P3 + P4 + P5 + P6 + P7 = 1$$

   simplify this algebraically.

8. Given the three-variable function (in dnf)

$$P1 + P3 + P5 + P6 + P7 = 1$$

   simplify this algebraically.

9. Given the function

$$a + bc + ac' + ad + d' = 1$$

   a) Convert this to complete dnf.
   b) Convert this to complete cnf.

10. Given the function

$$ab(c' + d) + (a + c)(b' + d) + d = 1$$

   convert this to complete dnf.

11. Given the three-variable function

$$P3 + P5 + P6 = 1$$

   a) Determine the prime implicants.
   b) Determine the essential prime implicants.

12. Given

$$\beta\langle S, \cdot, +, ', 1, 70 \rangle$$

   where $S = \{1, 2, 5, 7, 10, 14, 35, 70\}$
            $x \in S$
            $y \in S$
            $xy = $ greatest common divisor
            $x + y = $ least common multiple
            $x' = 70/x$
            $1' = 70$
            $y' = 70/y$
            $(70)' = 1$

   Prove that β is a Boolean algebra.

13. Given a three-valued logic with the values 1, 0, and u, where the values 1 and 0 have their usual meanings, the value u is assigned to the transition from 1 to 0 or 0 to 1 and it may have the value of 1 or 0 at any given time, then, using a two-variable system (x and y), generate the truth tables for the operations AND, OR, and NOT.

14. Is the three-valued logic of the preceding exercise a Boolean algebra? Explain.

15. Give an example of a practical use for the three-valued logic of Exercise 13.

APPENDIX B
POLISH NOTATION

This notation was developed by the Polish logician Jan Lukasiewicz for use with the propositional calculus.[7] In essence it consists of placing the operator in front of two variables to be operated upon. Thus, $p \rightarrow q$ becomes $\rightarrow pq$ and $p \lor q$ becomes $\lor pq$. The complex expression $(p \lor q) \rightarrow (q \lor p)$ is $\rightarrow \lor pq \lor qp$.

Certain letters were assigned by Lukasiewicz to replace the symbols normally representing the various operators. A list of these symbols, the operation, and the Polish notation is:

Usual symbol	Operation	Example		Polish notation
		Regular	Polish	symbol
$\rightarrow$	implication	$p \rightarrow q$	$\rightarrow pq$	C
$\supset$		$p \supset q$	$\supset pq$	
		$-p \lor q$	$\lor -pq$	
		$p \rightarrow q$	Cpq	
$\lor$	disjunction (alternation)	$p \lor q$	$\lor pq$	A
$+$		$p + q$	$+pq$	
			Apq	
$\land$	conjunction	$p \land q$	$\land pq$	K
$\cdot$		$p \cdot q$	$\cdot pq$	
		pq	Kpq	
$\Leftrightarrow$	equivalence	$p \Leftrightarrow q$	$\Leftrightarrow pq$	E
			Epq	
$-$	negation	$-p$	Np	N
$'$		p'		
$\sim$		$\sim p$		

Not surprisingly, the first four Polish notation symbols are known as the "cake" letters. Some examples of the use of Polish notation are:

1. Conventional notation:

$$-p \vee (q \rightarrow -r)$$

Polish notation:

$$\text{AN}p\,\text{C}q\text{N}r$$

2. Conventional notation:

$$\{p \rightarrow [-(q \vee -r) \Leftrightarrow (-q \wedge r)]\} \vee (-s \wedge t)$$

Polish notation: we develop this step by step:

Conventional	Polish
$q \vee -r$	$\text{A}q\text{N}r$
$-(q \vee -r)$	$\text{NA}q\text{N}r$
$-q \wedge r$	$\text{KN}qr$
$-(q \vee -r) \Leftrightarrow (-q \wedge r)$	$\text{ENA}q\text{N}r\text{KN}qr$
$p \rightarrow [-(q \vee -r) \Leftrightarrow (-q \wedge r)]$	$\text{C}p(\text{ENA}q\text{N}r\text{KN}qr)$
original function	$\text{AC}p(\text{ENA}q\text{N}r\text{KN}qr)\text{KN}st$

This last function can be written as

$$\text{AC}p\,\text{ENA}q\text{N}r\,\text{KN}qr\,\text{KN}st$$

if you know the rules governing the sequence in which operations are performed in a complex statement. These rules have not been mentioned in this work and quite deliberately so. Elimination of the parentheses, brackets, and braces in a complex statement leads to confusion and errors unless you are extremely adept at reading symbolic logic.

Polish notation is used in conjunction with "stack" type computers. A variation known as reverse Polish notation (where the operator follows the variables) is used in Hewlett-Packard Corporation calculators.

RELIABILITY DATA SOURCES

The tables in this Appendix are from *Reactor Safety Study—An Assessment of Accident Risks in U.S. Commercial Nuclear Power Plants*, WASH-1400 (NUREG-75/014), U.S. Nuclear Regulatory Commission, Washington, D.C., October, 1975.

DATA SOURCES

System Name and Acronym	Address	Type of Data
Air Force Engineering and Logistics Information System (AFELIS)	Headquarters, Air Force Logistics Command, Wright-Patterson Air Force Base, Dayton, Ohio 45433	Information on all types of parts in Air Force inventory
Apollo Parts Reliability Information Center (APIC)	Marshall Space Flight Center, Huntsville, Alabama 35812	Reliability, qualification, and evaluation of electrical, electronic, and associated mechanical parts.
Chemical Propulsion Information Agency (CPIA)	Applied Physics Laboratory, Johns Hopkins University, 8621 Georgia Avenue, Silver Springs, Maryland 20910	Data on liquid propellants, motors, and components; solid fuels, cases, and motor parts
Defense Documentation Center (DDC)	Cameron Station, Building 5, 5010 Duke Street, Arlington, Virginia 22314	All types of data from military contracts; bibliographies issued
Electronic and Mechanical Component Reliability Centers (ECRC and MCRC)	Battelle Memorial Institute, 505 King Avenue, Columbus, Ohio 43201	Summaries of parts tests on electronic and mechanical parts

Failure Rate Data System (FERADA)	U.S. Navy Fleet Missile Systems, Analysis and Evaluation Group (FMSAEG), Corona, California 91720	Compilation of failure rate date and publication of results
Interservice Data Exchange Program (IDEP)	Air Force IDEP Office (SAMSO), Air Force Unit Post Office, Los Angeles, California 90045	Exchange of parts-test data and summaries
	Navy IDEP Office (Code E-6), U.S. Navy FMSAEG, Corona, California 91720	
	Army IDEP Office (AMSMI-RBP), Army Missile Command, Huntsville, Alabama 35809	
Inter-NASA Data Exchange (INDEX)	Headquarters, NASA, 600 Independence Avenue, S.W., Washington, D.C. 20546	Failure and performance data on items used by NASA
Parts Reliability Information Center (PRINCE)	Marshall Space Flight Center, Huntsville, Alabama 35812	Printouts of reliability data from tests on NASA items
Reliability Analysis Center (RADC)	Rome Air Development Center, Griffis AFB, New York 13440	Reliability data on micro-electronic and semiconductor devices

REPORTS

Reference	Contact, Service Office or Originator	Contact, Report or Source Date	Report, Listing Source or Content
Reactor Incident File (1972) (Component Failure Data)	Office of Operations Evaluation (OOE) of Regulatory Operations (RO). Atomic Energy Commission (AEC), Bethesda, Maryland	1/1/72 to 12/31/72	Contains approximately 30% unusual occurrences at nuclear facilities and 90% of reportable abnormal occurrences observed in the year of 1972
Reactor Incident File (1971) (Component Failure Data)	Data control of RSS, Bethesda, Maryland	9/4/73	Contains approximately one quarter of 1971 unusual and abnormal occurrences observed from the files of OOE
EEI Availability Report (Component Failure Data)	Edison Electric Institute (EEI), New York, New York	8/16/73 and 10/12/73	Contains 66 unit years of fossil and nuclear power plants component availability and outage statistics of contributing facilities
Systems Reliability Service, UKAEA	Office of Operations Evaluation (OOE) of Regulatory Operations (RO) are Members of Service	All service publications plus special requests 9/12/73	Contains Failure Rate Assessments derived. UK and other available European sources

Name	Source	Date	Description
FARADA	Converged Failure Rate Data Handbooks, published by Fleet Missile Systems Analysis and Evaluation Group Annex, MWS, Sea Beach, Corona, California	All current issues	Contains Failure Rate Assessments derived from Army, Navy, Air Force, and NASA sources
AVCO	Reliability Engineering Data Services Failure Rates. AVCO Corp.	1962	Contains Failure Rate Assessments for primarily military quality hardware
LMEC	Failure Data Handbook For Nuclear Power Facilities, Liquid Metal Engineering Center	1969	Compilation of failure rates derived from test and research reactor operating experiences
Collins & Pomeroy	Environmental Reports, Directorate of Licensing, Division of Compliance, Regulatory, AEC	11/1/71	Operating experience and related data from literature in support of occurrence rates to be assumed for further interim guidance on accident evaluations
Holmes & Narver	Collection of reliability data at nuclear power plants, Holmes & Narver, Inc.	1968	Contains failure rate data gathered from operating experience, one plant, four months
Chemical Abstracts (Piping Failure Data)	AEC Headquarters Library, Germantown, Maryland	9/24/73	Bibliography listing of metallurgical and piping analysis reports (65) of industrial conduit systems

REPORTS (*Continued*)

Reference	Contact, Service Office or Originator	Contact, Report or Source Date	Report, Listing Source or Content
The Chemical Engineer	The Institution of Chemical Engineers, 16 Redgrave, London S.W.1, England	1971	Contains data on reliability of instruments in the chemical plant environment
NASA Literature Search (Piping Failure Data)	Information Tisco Inc., NASA Scientific and Technical Information Facility, College Park, Maryland	9/12/73	Listing of steam pipe failure reports (393) for normal and limited distribution of industrial steam systems
AEC RECON (Piping Failure Data)	AEC Headquarters Library, Germantown, Maryland	9/10/73	Listing of Nuclear Science Abstracts search on pipe rupture and pressure vessel analysis of primary steam systems
DOT Pipeline Safety (Pipeline Leak Summary)	Office of Pipeline Safety, Department of Transportation (DOT), Office of the Secretary, Washington, D.C.	10/10/73	1971 and 1972 gas pipe line leak and rupture history of transmission and distribution systems throughout the United States
NSIC Literature Search (Piping Failures)	Nuclear Safety Information Center (NSIC) of the AEC, Oak Ridge, Tennessee	9/13/73	Listing of references of piping failures (317) in industrial uses of atomic power
GIDEP "ALERT" (Manufacturing Defects)	National Technical Information Service (NTIS) U. S. Department of Commerce, Springfield, Virginia	9/3/73	Parts, materials, and processes experience summary of NASA and Government-Industry Data Exchange Program (GIDEP) reports

Source	Date	Description
HAVSHIPS Report (Main Steam Piping Data)	Maintenance Support Office, Naval Ship Systems Command, Department of the Navy, Arlington, Virginia	10/3/73	Printouts contain maintenance data covering main steam piping on nuclear submarines and surface ships for a three year period (1970–1972)
DDC Literature Search (Manufacturing Defects)	Defense Documentation Center (DDC), Defense Supply Agency, Alexandria, Virginia	8/23/73	Bibliography on probabilities of manufacturing errors from the standpoint of design evaluations (147 items)
GEAP (Piping Failure Data)	General Electric Company, Atomic Power Department, San Jose, California	1964–1972	Periodic reports (series 10207) of the Reactor Primary Coolant System Pipe Rupture Study summarizing failure mechanisms and probabilities
Nuclear Science Abstracts (Containment Breaches)	Technical Information Center (TIC) of the U.S. Atomic Energy Commission, Oak Ridge, Tennessee	1967–1972	Subject index for nuclear scientific reports over a six year period (a reference book)
NSIC Literature Search (Special Common Mode Failures)	Nuclear Safety Information Center (NSCI) of the U.S. Atomic Energy Commission, Oak Ridge, Tennessee	8/2/72	A ten year literature search for five categories of qualitative reports and bibliographies
Engineering Index (Environmental Factors)	AEC Headquarters Library, Germantown, Maryland	8/17/73	A search for quantitative reports on the earthquakes, electrical fires, and airplane crashes

Reference	Contact, Service Office or Originator	Contact, Report or Source Date	Report, Listing Source or Content
Geologic Literature Search (Disaster Impact Data)	American Geologic Institute, Washington, D.C.	8/17/73	A listing of topics (220) associated with earthquake predictions from the standpoint of geologic effects
DDC Literature Search (Disaster Impact Data)	Defense Documentation Center (DDC), Defense Supply Agency, Alexandria, Virginia	8/21/73	Bibliography on unusual natural occurrences (192)
Insurance Facts (1972) (Disaster Impact Data)	Insurance Information Institute, New York, New York	8/20/73	A yearbook of property and liability insurance facts of losses as reported by U.S. companies
RESPONSA (Seismic Effect Data)	Selected Nuclear Science Abstracts (RESPONSA), AEC Headquarters Library, Germantown, Maryland	8/15/73	Listing of seismic topics (245) for reactor siting and nuclear application: includes docket material
RESPONSA (ECCS Analysis Data)	Selected Nuclear Science Abstracts (RESPONSA), AEC Headquarters Library, Germantown, Maryland	8/1/73	Listing of Emergency Core Cooling System (ECCS) topics (approximately 928) and associated analysis

RESPONSA (Parts and Materials Data)	Selected Nuclear Science Abstracts (RESPONSA), AEC Headquarters Library, Germantown, Maryland	8/24/73	Listing of topics (approximately 936) on fractures of reactor parts and materials with emphasis on steel and alloys
NASA Literature Search (Disaster)	Information Tisco Inc., Scientific and Technical Information Facility, College Park, Maryland	8/17/73	Listing of disaster prediction or forecasting reports (608) on meteorological and climatological measurements
NASA Literature Search (Manufacturing Defects)	Information Tisco Inc., NASA Scientific and Technical Information Facility, College Park, Maryland	8/23/73	Quality control in manufacture of machinery or power generating equipment, a brief survey
Docket 50-289 (Aircraft Impact Data)	Files, Bethesda, Maryland	8/28/73	Three Mile Island Unit 1 (Metropolitan Edison Co. of Pennsylvania) report, Summary of Aircraft Impact Design
FAA (Air Traffic Data)	Federal Aviation Administration (FAA), Department of Transportation. Washington, D.C.	March 1972	En Route IFR Air Traffic Survey Peak-Day FY 1971, authored by the FAA Statistical Division

Task	Average Number of Failures Per 10,000 Occurrences
Read technical instructions	82
Read time (Brush recorder)	79
Read electrical or flow meter	55
Inspect for loose bolts and clamps	45
Position multiple-position electrical switch	43
Mark position of component	42
Install lockwire	39
Inspect for bellows distortion	39
Install Marman clamp	39
Install gasket	38
Inspect for rust and corrosion	37
Install "O" ring	35
Record reading	34
Inspect for dents, cracks, and scratches	33
Read pressure gauge	31
Inspect for frayed shielding	31
Inspect for QC seals	30
Tighten nuts, bolts, and plugs	30
Apply gasket cement	29
Connect electrical cable (threaded)	28
Inspect for air bubbles (leak check)	26
Install reducing adapter	25
Install initiator simulator	25
Connect flexible hose	25
Position "zero in" knob	24
Lubricate bolt or plug	21
Position hand valves	21
Install nuts, plugs, and bolts	21
Install union	21
Lubricate "O" ring	21
Rotate gearbox train	20
Fill sump with oil	19
Disconnect flexible hose	18
Lubricate torque wrench adapter	18
Remove initiator simulator	17
Install protective cover (friction fit)	17
Read time (watch)	17
Verify switch position	17
Inspect for lock wire	17

HUMAN RELIABILITY (*Continued*)

Task	Average Number of Failures Per 10,000 Occurrences
Close hand valves	17
Install drain tube	17
Install torque wrench adapter	16
Open hand valves	15
Position two-position electrical switch	15
Spray leak detector	14
Verify component removed or installed	12
Remove nuts, plugs, and bolts	12
Install pressure cap	12
Remove protective closure (friction fit)	10
Remove torque wrench adapter	9
Remove reducing adapter	9
Remove Marman clamp	9
Remove pressure cap	8
Loosen nuts, bolts, and plugs	8
Remove union	7
Remove lockwire	7
Remove drain tube	7
Verify light illuminated or extinguished	4
Install funnel or hose in can	3
Remove funnel from oil can	3

COMPARISON OF ASSESSMENTS WITH INDUSTRIAL EXPERIENCE

Component/Primary Failure Modes	Lower Bounds		Upper Bounds	
	Assessed	Industrial[a]	Assessed	Industrial[a]
Pumps				
Failure to start	3×10^{-4}/day	5×10^{-5}/day	3×10^{-3}/day	5×10^{-3}/day
Failure to run (normal environments)	3×10^{-6}/hour	1×10^{-7}/hour	3×10^{-4}/hour	1×10^{-4}/hour
Failure to run (extreme environment)	1×10^{-4}/hour	1×10^{-4}/hour	1×10^{-2}/hour	1×10^{-3}/hour
Valves				
Motor operated				
Failure to operate	3×10^{-4}/day	2×10^{-4}/day	3×10^{-3}/day	7×10^{-2}/day[b]
Plugs	3×10^{-5}/day	6×10^{-5}/day[a]	3×10^{-4}/day	3×10^{-4}/day[a]
Solenoid operated				
Failure to operate	3×10^{-4}/day	2×10^{-5}/day	3×10^{-3}/day	6×10^{-3}/day
Air operated				
Failure to operate	1×10^{-4}/day	1×10^{-6}/day	1×10^{-3}/day	2×10^{-2}/day[c]
Check				
Failure to open	3×10^{-5}/day	2×10^{-5}/day	3×10^{-4}/day	3×10^{-4}/day
Reverse leak	1×10^{-7}/hour	1×10^{-7}/hour	1×10^{-6}/hour	1×10^{-6}/hour
Vacuum				
Failure to operate	1×10^{-5}/day	1×10^{-5}/day	1×10^{-4}/day	1×10^{-4}/day
Relief				
Failure to open	3×10^{-6}/day	1.4×10^{-5}/day	3×10^{-5}/day	3.6×10^{-5}/day
Manual				
Plug	3×10^{-5}/day	3×10^{-4}/day[d]	3×10^{-4}/day	3×10^{-4}/day[d]
Pipes, plug/rupture				
≤ 3 inches diameter	3×10^{-11}/hour	2×10^{-9}/hour	3×10^{-8}/hour	5×10^{-6}/hour[e]
> 3 inches diameter	3×10^{-12}/hour	1×10^{-10}/hour	3×10^{-9}/hour	5×10^{-6}/hour
Clutches				
Mechanical				
Failure to engage/disengage	1×10^{-4}/day	1×10^{-4}/day	1×10^{-3}/day	4×10^{-3}/day
Clutches, electrical				
Failure to operate	1×10^{-4}/day	1×10^{-4}/day	1×10^{-3}/day	4×10^{-3}/day
Motors, electric				
Failure to start	1×10^{-4}/day	7×10^{-5}/day	1×10^{-3}/day	3×10^{-3}/day[f]
Failure to run, given start (normal environments)	3×10^{-6}/hour	5×10^{-7}/hour	3×10^{-5}/hour	1×10^{-4}/hour
Failure to run, given start (extreme environments)	1×10^{-4}/hour	1×10^{-4}/hour	1×10^{-2}/hour	3×10^{-2}/hour

Component/Primary Failure Modes	Lower Bounds		Upper Bounds	
	Assessed	Industrial[a]	Assessed	Industrial[a]
Transformers				
Open/shorts	3×10^{-7}/hour	1×10^{-7}/hour	3×10^{-6}/hour	1×10^{-6}/hour
Relays				
Failure to energize	3×10^{-5}/day	4×10^{-5}/day	3×10^{-4}/day	1×10^{-3}/day[g]
Circuit breakers				
Failure to transfer	3×10^{-4}/day	2×10^{-5}/day	3×10^{-3}/day	3×10^{-3}/day
Limit switches				
Failure to operate	1×10^{-4}/day	1×10^{-5}/day	1×10^{-3}/day	7×10^{-4}/day
Torque switches				
Failure to operate	3×10^{-5}/day	2×10^{-5}/day	3×10^{-4}/day	1×10^{-4}/day
Pressure switches				
Failure to operate	3×10^{-5}/day	5×10^{-5}/day	3×10^{-4}/day	1×10^{-3}/day
Manual switches				
Failure to transfer	3×10^{-6}/day	3×10^{-6}/day	3×10^{-5}/day	7×10^{-4}/day[h]
Battery power supplies				
Failure to provide proper output	1×10^{-6}/hour	1×10^{-7}/hour	1×10^{-5}/hour	6×10^{-6}/hour
Solid-state devices Failure to function				
(High power application)	3×10^{-7}/hour	2×10^{-6}/hour	3×10^{-5}/hour	1×10^{-4}/hour[i]
(Low power application)	1×10^{-7}/hour	2×10^{-7}/hour	1×10^{-5}/hour	2×10^{-6}/hour
Diesels				
Failure to start	1×10^{-2}/day	1×10^{-3}/day	1×10^{-1}/day	1×10^{-1}/day
Failure to run (emergency loads)	3×10^{-4}/hour	1×10^{-4}/hour	3×10^{-2}/hour	1×10^{-3}/hour
Instrumentation				
Failure to operate	1×10^{-7}/hour	3×10^{-7}/hour	1×10^{-5}/hour	6×10^{-5}/hour[j]

[a]Some demand values derived from data on continuously operating systems.
[b]Derived for values in high temperature sodium environment.
[c]Includes failures due to improper air supplies.
[d]These values derived from data on continuously operating system; only one industrial source listed this mode.
[e]Due to the varying unit of pipe lengths in the different sources (per foot, per section, per plant, etc.), the failure rates from the industrial sources have extremely wide ranges.
[f]This value obtained from high temperature liquid metal test reactor applications.
[g]Data from average of all modes of relay failures.
[h]Data from average of all modes of switch failures.
[i]This value derived from experimental reactor experience.
[j]Data from chemical industry.

COMPARISON OF ASSESSMENTS WITH NUCLEAR EXPERIENCE

Component/Primary Failure Modes	Assessed Values		Nuclear Experience[a]
	Lower Bound	Upper Bound	
Pumps			
Failure to start	3×10^{-4}/day	3×10^{-3}/day	1×10^{-3}/day
Failure to run			
(normal environments)	3×10^{-6}/hour	3×10^{-4}/hour	3×10^{-6}/hour[b]
Valves			
Motor operated			
Failure to operate	3×10^{-4}/day	3×10^{-3}/day	1×10^{-3}/day
Plug	3×10^{-5}/day	3×10^{-4}/day	3×10^{-5}/day[c]
Solenoid operated			
Failure to operate	3×10^{-4}/day	3×10^{-3}/day	1×10^{-3}/day
Plug	3×10^{-5}/day	3×10^{-4}/day	3×10^{-5}/day[c]
Air operated			
Failure to operate	1×10^{-4}/day	1×10^{-3}/day	1×10^{-4}/day
Plug	3×10^{-5}/day	3×10^{-4}/day	3×10^{-5}/day[c]
Check			
Failure to open	3×10^{-5}/day	3×10^{-4}/day	1×10^{-4}/day
Relief			
Failure to open	3×10^{-6}/day	3×10^{-5}/day	1×10^{-5}/day
Manual			
Plug	3×10^{-5}/day	3×10^{-4}/day	3×10^{-5}/day
Pipes			
Plug/rupture			
< 3 inches diameter	3×10^{-11}/hour	3×10^{-8}/hour	1×10^{-9}/hour
> 3 inches diameter	3×10^{-12}/hour	3×10^{-9}/hour	1×10^{-10}/hour
Clutches, mechanical			
Failure to engage/			
disengage	1×10^{-4}/day	1×10^{-3}/day	3×10^{-4}/day
Clutches, electrical			
Failure to operate	1×10^{-4}/day	1×10^{-3}/day	3×10^{-4}/day
Motors			
Failure to start	1×10^{-4}/day	1×10^{-3}/day	3×10^{-4}/day
Failure to run			
(normal environments)	3×10^{-6}/hour	3×10^{-5}/hour	1×10^{-6}/hour[d]
Transformers			
Open/shorts	3×10^{-7}/hour	3×10^{-6}/hour	1×10^{-6}/hour
Relays			
Failure to energize	3×10^{-5}/day	3×10^{-4}/day	3×10^{-5}/day
Circuit breaker			
Failure to transfer	3×10^{-4}/day	3×10^{-3}/day	1×10^{-3}/day

COMPARISON OF ASSESSMENTS WITH INDUSTRIAL EXPERIENCE

(*Continued*)

Component/Primary Failure Modes	Assessed Values		Nuclear Experience[a]
	Lower Bound	Upper Bound	
Limit switches			
Failure to operate	1×10^{-4}/day	1×10^{-3}/day	1×10^{-4}/day
Torque switches			
Failure to operate	3×10^{-5}/day	3×10^{-4}/day	1×10^{-4}/day
Pressure switches			
Failure to operate	3×10^{-5}/day	3×10^{-4}/day	1×10^{-4}/day
Manual switches			
Failure to operate	3×10^{-6}/day	3×10^{-5}/day	3×10^{-5}/day
Battery power supplies			
Failure to provide proper output	1×10^{-6}/hour	1×10^{-5}/hour	3×10^{-7}/hour[e]
Solid-state devices			
Failure to function	3×10^{-7}/hour	3×10^{-5}/hour	1×10^{-6}/hour
Diesels (*complete plant*)			
Failure to start	1×10^{-2}/day	1×10^{-1}/day	3×10^{-2}/day
Failure to run	3×10^{-4}/hour	3×10^{-2}/hour	1×10^{-3}/hour
Instrumentation			
Failure to operate	1×10^{-7}/hour	1×10^{-5}/hour	1×10^{-6}/hour

[a]All values are rounded to the nearest half order of magnitude on the exponent.

[b]Derived from averaged data on pumps, combining standby and operate time.

[c]Approximated from plugging that was detected.

[d]Derived from combined standby and operate data.

[e]Derived from standby test on batteries, which does not include load.

AUTHOR INDEX

Brown, P. J., 68

Christian, R. R., 54

Fussell, J. B., 179

Hohn, F. E., 51
Huntington, E. V., 4, 27, 57, 62

Johnstone, H. W., Jr., 5

Kamke, E., 4

Lambert, H. E., 179
Langer, S. K., 5
Lapp, S. A., 179, 183
Lipschutz, S., 18

McCluskey, E. J., Jr., 94, 98, 100

Mendelson, E., 68

Narum, R. E., 179

Powers, G. J., 179, 183

Quine, V. W., 92

Roullard, G. P., 5

Scheinman, A. H., 103
Shaeiwitz, J. A., 179
Shannon, C. E., 4

Thomas, N. L., 5
Tompkins, F. C., 179

Vesely, W. E., 179

SUBJECT INDEX

Algebra, Boolean, *see* Boolean algebra
Algorithm, Lapp-Powers, 183-197
Analysis, fault tree, 176, 179-228
AND, 65, 116
Antecedent, 36
Argument, chain, 35, 37, 38
  logical, 34-39
  truth or falsity of, 36, 37

Biconditional, 38, 39
Binary, standard, 139, 140
Bistable devices, 59, 60, 61
Bistable signals, 60
Boolean algebra,
  basic functions of, 76-79
  of conditions of sets, 24, 25
  of logic, 50-57
  multivariable, 68
  of on-off events, intuitive derivation,
      63-67
    rigorous derivation, 61-63
  of propositions, 50-54
  of sets, 25-28
  symbols, for on-off events, 72
  of sets, 25-28
    graphic, 116
    for propositions, 35, 39, 40
    for sets, 12
Boolean functions, in graphic form, 115-120
  simlification of, 92-112
    hybrid method, 110-112
    McCluskey's method, 100-103
    Quine-McCluskey method, 93-100
    Quine's method, 92, 93
    Scheinman's method, 103-110

Calculus, propositional, 50
Canoical forms, 81-91

conjunctive normal, 87-89
disjunctive normal, 81-86
Carroll, Lewis, problems, 38, 234, 235
Categorical syllogism 5, 33-35
Chain argument, 35, 37, 38
Circuit matrix, specific, 85, 86, 88
Circuits, switching, 120-126
  logic of 63-67
Classes, definition of, 5
  logic of, 5
  residue, 21, 104, 105
Code, reflected binary (Gray), 74, 86
  standard binary, 73, 86
Conclusion, 34, 36
Conditional, 35, 36
Conditions of sets, algebra of, 24, 25
  logic of, 9-11, 23, 24
Conjunction, of conditions of sets, 24
  of propositions, 39
Consequent, 36
Contradiction, 49
Contradictory, 36
Contrapositive, 36
Converse, 36
Cut sets, 199, 202, 208

Definition, of classes, 15
  of logic, 29, 30, 33
  of propositions, 29, 30
  of sets, 5
Diagrams, fault tree, 180-227
  ladder, 149-151, 212, 222
  logic, electrical, 116, 120-126
    process, 116, 128-136, 140-147
  Venn, 12-15
Digraph, 180-227
Discourse, universe of, 8
Disjoint sets, 13, 14

Disjunction, of conditions of sets, 24
  of propositions, 40
Disturbances, 182, 183
"Don't Care" variables, 89-91, 162
Double stroke symbol, 80
Dualities, 70, 71
Duality, principle of, 70

Edge, 182
Electrical logic diagrams, 116, 120-126
Empty set, 8, 61
"English" logic, 43
Enumerability of sets, 7
Equivalence of propositions, 11, 38, 39,
    46, 47
Equivalence relations and partitions, 18-21
Essential prime implicants, 97-100, 111,
    170, 171
Exclusive OR, 40-56, 57
  symbol for, 79
Existential quantifier, 12
Expansion theorem, 103

Failure, classification, 177
  prediction and analysis, 178
  prevention, 177, 178
Failure modes and effects analysis, 176
Fault tree, analysis, 176
  diagrams, 180-227
  synthesis, combinational, 179-209
    sequential, 209-227
Feedback control, 179
  loop, negative, 180-190
Feed forward loop, 190-195
Flipflop, 137-140
Functions, basic Boolean, 76-79
  gating, 155-157
  graphical Boolean, *see* Graphical Boolean
    functions

Gain
Gating functions, 155-157
Graphical Boolean Functions, 115-120
  symbols, 116

Huntington postulates, *see* Postulates
Hypothetical syllogism, 35, 37, 38

Identities, 70, 71

Implication, 23, 24, 34, 35
  and basic operations, 42, 43
Improper subsets, 8
Inclusion, tacit, 41
Indexed sets, 16, 17
Induction, perfect, 46, 75
Inference, 30, 34
  inductive, 30
Interlocking, 152-155
Intersection, 12

Ladder diagrams, 149-151, 212, 222
  Symbols for, 211
Lapp-Powers algorithm, 183-187
Laws, algebra of conditions of sets, 25
  algebra of on-off events, 62
  algebra of propositions, 53, 54
  algebra of sets, 27
  algebra of truth-value functions, 53
Logic, algebra of, 50-57
  of conditions of sets, 9-11, 23, 24, 61
  definition of, 29, 30, 33
  diagrams electrical, 116, 120-126
    process, 116, 128-136, 140-147
  "English," 43
  NAND, 42
  NOR, 42, 147-149
  of on-off events, 59-61
  of propositions, 29-48
  of sets, 25-27
  of switching circuits, 63-67
  of truth-value functions, 39-43
  symol cross-reference chart, fig. 9.1.2
Logical argument, 34-39
  product, 81
  propositions, 30-32
    structure of, 32-34
  sum, 81

Matrix, Boolean, 71
  circuit, 71
    specific, 85, 86, 88
  reduced, 95-99, 165-168
  segregated, 94-99, 165-168
Modulo relation, 21, 104, 105
Multiple sequencing, 136-147
Multivalued algebras, 68
Multivariable Boolean algebra,
    68

NAND logic, 42
Negative feedback loop, 180-190
Node, 182
Non-exclusive OR, 40
NOR logic, 42, 147-149
Number tree, 6

On-off events, basic operations with, 60, 61
  Boolean algebra of, 59, 69
    intuitive derivation, 63, 67
    rigorous derivation, 61, 63
Operations, basic, with on-off events, 60, 61
  with propositions, 39-43
  with sets, 12-15
OR, exclusive, 40, 56, 57, 79
  non-exclusive, 40
Ordered pair, 19

Partition of sets, 17, 18, 20, 21, 104, 105
Perfect induction, 46, 75
Polish notation, 237, 238
Postulates, algebra of on-off events, 62
  algebra of sets, 27, 28
  algebra of truth-value functions, 57
Power set, 9
Premise, 34, 36
Prime implicants, 92, 93
  essential, 97-100, 111, 170, 171
Process logic diagrams, 116, 128-136,
  140-147
Product, logical, 81
Product set, 19
Proper subset, 8
Proposition, conditional, 35, 36
  contradictory, 36
  contrapositive, 36
  converse, 36
  definition of, 29
Propositional calculus, 39, 50
  function, 19, 24, 25
Propositions, basic operations with, 39-43
  Boolean algebra of, 50, 54
  equivalence of, 38
  factual, 30, 31
  logic of, 29, 48
  logical, 31-34
  truth value of, 39, 54, 55

Quantifier, existential, 12

universal, 11

Reflected binary (Gray) code, 74, 86
Relation, modulo, 21, 104, 105
Residue classes, 21, 104, 105

Scheffer stroke symbol, 80
Sequencing, multiple, 136-147
Set builder, 9-11
  empty, 8
  power, 9
  product, 19
  truth, 9
  universal, 8
Sets, algebra of, 25-28
  basic operations with, 12-15
  conditions of, 23, 24
  cut, 199, 202, 208
  definition of, 5
  enumerability of, 7
  indexed, 16, 17
  partition of, 17, 18, 20, 21, 104, 105
  structure of, 6-9
Signals, bistable, 60
Simplification methods, hybrid, 110-112
  McCluskey's, 100-103
  Quine-McCluskey, 93-100
  Quine's, 92, 93
  Scheinman's, 103-110
Specific circuit matrix, 85, 86, 88
Standard binary, 139, 140
Structure of sets, 6-9
Subset, improper, 8
  proper, 8
Sum, logical, 81
Supersets, 8
Switching circuits, 120-126
  logic of, 63-67
Syllogism, categorical, 5, 33-35
  hypothetical, 35, 37, 38
Symbols, algebra of propositions, 35, 39, 40
  algebra of sets, 12
  Boolean algebra of on-off events, 72
    graphic, 116
  double stroke, 80
  exclusive OR, 79
  ladder diagram, 211
  logic, cross-reference chart, fig. 9.1.2
  Scheffer stroke, 80

Synthesis, fault tree, combinational, 179-
    209
  sequential, 209-225
Systems, biconditional case, 164-166
  conditional case, 167-174
  diagnostic, 158-172
  mixed case, 166, 167

Tacit inclusion, 41
Tautology, 47-49
Time delays, 126-128
Tree, fault, 175-227
  number, 6
Truth or falsity of arguments, 36, 37

Truth set, 9
Truth tables, 43-46
Truth-value functions, 39
  algebra of, 54-57
  logic of, 39-43

Union, 12
Universal quantifier, 11
Universal set, 8
Universe of discourse, 8

Variables, "don't care," 89-91,
    162
Venn diagrams, 12-15